CAREER DEVELOPMENT: THEORY AND PRACTICE

CAREER DEVELOPMENT:
Theory and Practice

Edited by

DAVID H. MONTROSS, ED.D.

Human Resource Planning and Development Consultant
Digital Equipment Corporation
Maynard, Massachusetts

and

CHRISTOPHER J. SHINKMAN, PH.D.

Director, MBA Career Management
Georgetown University
Washington, D.C.

With Twenty-Six Contributors

CHARLES C THOMAS • PUBLISHER
Springfield • Illinois • U.S.A.

Published and Distributed Throughout the World by

CHARLES C THOMAS • PUBLISHER
2600 South First Street
Springfield, Illinois 62794-9265

© *1992 by* CHARLES C THOMAS • PUBLISHER

ISBN 0-398-05764-8

Library of Congress Catalog Card Number: 91-30245

Printed in the United States of America
SC-R-3

Library of Congress Cataloging-in-Publication Data

Career development : theory and practice / edited by David H. Montross
and Christopher J. Shinkman.
    p. cm.
    Includes bibliographical references and index.
    ISBN 0-398-05764-8 (cloth)
    1. Career development. I. Montross, David H. II. Shinkman,
Christopher J.
HF5549.5.C35C364   1991
658.3′124 — dc20   91-30245
                                             CIP

CONTRIBUTORS

CAROLE W. MINOR, PH.D.
Associate Professor, Counselor Education
Department of Education, Psychology, Counseling, and Special Education
Northern Illinois University
Dekalb, Illinois

DONALD E. SUPER, PH.D.
The Center For Educational Studies and Development
School of Education
University of North Carolina
Greensboro, North Carolina

MICHAEL B. ARTHUR, PH.D.
Professor, School of Management
Suffolk University
Boston, Massachusetts

DEBORAH L. FLOYD, ED.D.
President
Prestonburg Community College
Prestonburg, Kentucky

MARTHA P. LEAPE, M.A.
Director, Office of Career Services
Faculty of Arts and Sciences
Harvard University
Cambridge, Massachusetts

SALLY J. ASMUNDSON
Director, Career Development Center
California Institute of Technology
Pasadena, California

CHRISTOPHER J. SHINKMAN, PH.D.
Director, MBA Career Management
Georgetown University
Washington, D.C.

ZANDY B. LEIBOWITZ, PH.D.
President, Conceptual Systems Inc.
Silver Spring, Maryland

NANCY K. SCHLOSSBERG, ED.D.
Professor, Counseling and Personnel Services
University of Maryland
College Park, Maryland

JANE E. SHORE, M.A. CANDIDATE
Consultant, Conceptual Systems Inc.
Silver Spring, Maryland

LINDA A. HILL, PH.D.
Associate Professor
Graduate School of Business Administration
Harvard University
Boston, Massachusetts

RANDALL P. WHITE, PH.D.
Director, Specialized Client Applications
Center For Creative Leadership
Greensboro, North Carolina

EDGAR H. SCHEIN, PH.D.
Professor, Sloan School of Management
Massachusetts Institute of Technology
Cambridge, Massachusetts

KATHY E. KRAM, PH.D.
Professor, School of Management
Boston University
Boston, Massachusetts

MADELINE C. BRAGAR, PH.D.
Director, Human Resources
Avery-Dennison Corporation
Framingham, Massachusetts

DOUGLAS T. HALL, PH.D.
Associate Dean for Faculty Development
School of Management
Boston University
Boston, Massachusetts

KENT W. SEIBERT, *Doctoral Candidate*
School of Management
Boston University
Boston, Massachusetts

JANE E. MYERS, PH.D.
Professor, Counselor Education
School of Education
University of North Carolina at Greensboro
Greensboro, North Carolina

MARJORIE SYWAK, PH.D.
President, Resource Options
Oakland, California

ANDREW H. SOUERWINE, PH.D.
Professor Emeritus, School of Business Administration
University of Connecticut
West Hartford, Connecticut

BARBARA H. FELDMAN, M.S.
Manager, Organization Development
Corning Incorporated
Corning, New York

SHERRY H. MOSLEY
Manager, Human Resource Systems Development
Corning Incorporated
Corning, New York

MARK L. SAVICKAS, PH.D.
Professor and Chair
Behavioral Sciences Department
Northeastern Ohio Universities College of Medicine
Rootstown, Ohio

JOANN HARRIS-BOWLSBEY, ED.D.
Executive Director
Educational Technology Center
Hunt Valley, Maryland

LOTTE BAILYN, PH.D.
Professor, Sloan School of Management
Massachusetts Institute of Technology
Cambridge, Massachusetts

JAMES W. WALKER, PH.D.
Partner
The Walker Group
Phoenix, Arizona

To our mothers,
Isabelle Montross
and
Elizabeth Shinkman

PREFACE

Our purpose is to present the latest thinking of career development professionals who are contributing to the theory or practice of the growing field of career development. All of the chapters appear here for the first time.

This book is appropriate for several audiences. It can be used as a textbook for graduate level programs in counseling, especially in those programs with an emphasis on career development and career counseling. It is also ideal for graduate business school programs which offer courses in human resource management. This subject is gaining interest as employers look for new and effective ways to manage an increasingly diverse work force. In addition, this book will be a resource for practitioners in organizations, both in higher education and in the business world who are designing or updating career counseling and career development programs and resources. Practitioners in other settings, including government, social service organizations, or in private practice, will similarly find a wealth of creative ideas and new perspectives in this volume.

Part I of this book is devoted to the latest thinking about career theory. The first chapter, by Dr. Carole Minor, provides us with an excellent overview of the various theories which exist. We are indeed fortunate to have a contribution from Dr. Donald Super, who has added greatly to our understanding of career theory. In his chapter, Dr. Super summarizes his attempt to create a comprehensive theory and provides two models which visually depict his theory and exemplify the career stages his theory suggests. In addition, the chapter by Dr. Michael Arthur introduces many new elements to, and challenges our thinking about, career theory and practice. By looking at changes in both the composition of the work force and in the way organizations are being structured, Arthur suggests a need for rethinking our approach to career theory-making, and for greater clarity and linkage between theory and practice.

Part II of the book is organized around the career stages of exploration, establishment, maintenance, and decline explicated most clearly by Super. Issues, and programs to address them are the focal point of this section.

Part III is devoted to current thinking about the resources and interventions available to individuals in organizational settings, including computer-based systems, innovative approaches to assessment, and the role of the manager in providing career counseling assistance.

Part IV looks to the future, with excellent contributions about the changes occurring in the work force, as well as a look at the ways in which organizations are changing, and the implications of those changes for the way we design and deliver career programs.

We are grateful to all of the outstanding professionals who have contributed original chapters to this book, and for their patience with us as material was edited and revised. We are grateful to Sharon Tredeau for her assistance in the preparation of this manuscript, and to Mary Jane Namian and Karla Stillwell for their dedicated assistance and editorial skills. We are grateful, also, to our employers for providing support and encouragement as the book progressed. And we thank our wives and children for their patience and understanding.

D.H.M.
C.J.S.

INTRODUCTION

DAVID H. MONTROSS

There have been significant advances made in our understanding of both career development theory and practice. In 1989, Arthur, Hall, and Lawrence, in *The Handbook of Career Theory*, found existing attempts at career theory-making incomplete. To those attempts at providing a truly comprehensive and integrated explanation of career behaviors, they identified twelve additional perspectives which were omitted from previous theoretical statements.

On the practitioner side, new and more sophisticated resources and programs have been developed, and refinements and improvements have been made to existing ones. Not only are career resources available to a wider audience, but also the variety and appropriateness of these resources has improved. Based on research from the Center for Creative Leadership and from the longitudinal studies by Bray and Howard, we have a much better understanding of the factors which influence careers from both the individual and organizational perspectives. Similarly, these and other research efforts have increased our understanding of, and therefore, our ability to intervene in, the careers of women and minorities. As the workplace becomes more diverse, we will continuously need to examine our practices, reexamine our assumptions, and revise and revitalize our programs.

The future will bring new challenges to theorists and practitioners alike. Most research on career development, and in turn most theory, has been based on a world of work characterized as stable and predictable, and dominated by white males. Into this picture, beginning in the late 1980s, and as far as we can see into the future, a very different scenario emerges. The demographics of the work force have changed, and will continue to change, with white males eventually being the minority. The old patterns of career progress and stability are becoming a part of history. The ways in which people think about their careers is changing, too. Organizations of all types are becoming less hierarchical, more flexible, and are in a constant state of change and adaptation. Old notions of career paths, and of steady upward mobility, are likewise becoming a thing of the past.

What is replacing them is as yet not well understood. There appears to be less loyalty on both sides, with employers downsizing and "out-placing" at ever increasing rates, and employees responding with more concern for their own welfare, and less allegiance to any one organization. We will need more dynamic and flexible theories and practices to reflect these changes as we enter the next century.

REFERENCES

Arthur, M.D., Hall, D.T. and Lawrence, B.S. (Eds.) 1989, *Handbook of Career Theory*. New York: Cambridge University Press.

Brown, D. and Brooks, L. (Eds.) 1990, *Career Choice and Development*, (2nd Ed.) San Francisco: Jossey-Bass.

Holland, J.L., 1985, *Making Vocational Choices: A Theory of Vocational Personalities, and Work Environments (2nd Ed.)*, Englewood Cliffs, NJ: Prentice-Hall.

Howard, A. and Bray, D., 1988, *Managerial Lives in Transition: Advancing Age and Changing Time*, New York: Guilford Press.

Montross, D. and Shinkman, C., 1981, *Career Development in the 1980's: Theory and Practice*, Springfield, IL: Charles C Thomas.

Osipow, S.H., 1990, *Convergence in Theories of Career Choice and Development*, Journal of Vocational Behavior, 36, 122–131.

CONTENTS

SECTION IV THE FUTURE

CAREER DEVELOPMENT:
THEORY AND PRACTICE

SECTION I
THEORY

INTRODUCTION TO SECTION I—THEORY

DAVID H. MONTROSS

There is not, at present, a single, comprehensive, well-integrated theory of career development. There are, rather, a number of theories which are presented from various disciplines and perspectives, and these are summarized in Chapter 1 by Dr. Carole Minor. These include psychological, social learning, developmental, and sociological theories, to name a few. There are several books which cover each of these approaches in greater detail, including books by Brown and Brooks (1990); Osipow (1984) and Montross and Shinkman (1981). What is presented in this section, however, is the latest thinking of Dr. Donald Super, whose theory comes the closest of existing theories to being comprehensive, and a chapter by Dr. Michael Arthur, an editor of *The Handbook of Career Theory* (Arthur, Hall, and Lawrence, 1989), which enumerates those elements still absent.

In Dr. Super's chapter, we are presented with two models depicting the authors' view of those elements which make up a person's career. In the first model, The Career-Life Rainbow, Super shows us pictorially what his theory describes in words: that we each play various roles in our lives; that these roles evolve over time; and that we may be playing several of these roles simultaneously, with varying degrees of commitment. These roles include student, parent, worker, etc. Career, in Dr. Super's model, is more than simply the jobs one holds. It is a broader, more all-encompassing concept. His second model, that of the Arch, points to the elements, both personal and environmental, which influence one's career. It is the influence of both personal characteristics (such as one's values, skills, and abilities) and external factors (such as the state of the economy) which combine to determine one's career path. These two models, then, serve to provide a broad, multidimensional view of career, and as such represent the most comprehensive extant theoretical statement.

Dr. Arthur, while taking the more traditional view of equating career with the sequence of positions held by individuals over the course of their lives (positions here referring only to jobs, not life roles as defined by Dr. Super), points out several perspectives which are still missing from even the broadest

5

attempts at theory-making. He argues that much research, and therefore much theorizing, is based on a world that essentially no longer exists. Changing demographics, organizational structures, and the rapidity of change itself have made existing theories at best incomplete. He then identifies the key perspectives which need to be incorporated into a truly integrated theory.

And so we have two important points of view. The first, summarizing a lifetime's work, provides a broad, multifaceted statement of the elements of career theory. It remains, by its author's own accounting, incomplete. The second, pointing the way to the future, provides us with fresh thoughts and great challenges.

Chapter 1

CAREER DEVELOPMENT THEORIES AND MODELS

Carole W. Minor

For almost a century theories that explain career behavior and prescribe interventions have been formulated, discussed, and researched. These theories have developed chronologically from a prescriptive model of matching individuals with jobs (Parsons, 1909) through stage models of career choice and career development (Ginzberg, Ginsburg, Axelrad, & Herma, 1951; Super, 1953) to more specific explanations of factors involved in career choices and adjustment (Holland, 1973, 1985; Krumboltz, 1979; Roe, 1956). This discussion is organized around the following assumptions (see Fig. 1-1):

1. Career development is a continuous process over the life span.
2. Career development involves both career choice and career adjustment issues.
3. Both career choice and career adjustment involve content and process variables.
4. Theories tend to focus on either the content or the process of career choice or adjustment.

DEVELOPMENTAL FRAMEWORK

Developmental career theories provide a useful framework from which to view all other theoretical work. Historically, prior to the early 1950s, there was little career theory per se. In the first decade of this century, Frank Parsons (1909) developed a process of vocational guidance—an intervention model—which underlies most practice to this day. He stated that vocational guidance consisted of three steps:

> First, a clear understanding of yourself, aptitudes, abilities, interests, resources, limitations, and other qualities. Second, a knowledge of the requirements and conditions of success, advantages and disadvantages, compensation, opportunities, and prospects in different lines of work. Third, true reasoning on the relations of these two groups of facts (Parsons, 1909, p. 5).

Reprinted with permission of the National Career Development Association.

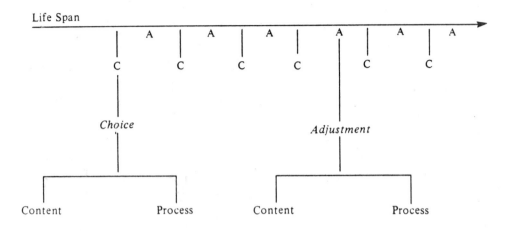

C = Choice
A = Adjustment

Figure 1-1. The process of career development over the life span.

E. G. Williamson (1939) amplified and improved Parsons' intervention model, stating its assumptions. Other forces, including the increasing sophistication of the methods of differential psychology, improved the practice of what was known as vocational guidance. Basically, however, until the early 1950s both the general public and professional practitioners viewed occupational choice as a once-in-a-lifetime event. At some particular point, individuals chose to enter occupations and generally continued in them for their entire productive lifetimes.

In the early 1950s two career theories represented a different view.

Ginzberg

Ginzberg, Ginsburg, Axelrad, and Herma in 1951 described a career theory contending that:

1. Decision making is a process that occurs from prepuberty to the late teens or early twenties.
2. Many decisions are irreversible.
3. The resolution of the choice process is a compromise.

In 1972 Ginzberg revised his model to focus on the continuation of the career choice process throughout the life span. He revised his ideas as follows:

1. Occupational choice is a process that remains open as long as we make decisions about work and career.

2. Early decisions have a shaping influence on career but so do continuing changes of work and life.

3. People make decisions with the aim of optimizing satisfaction by finding the best possible fit between their needs and desires and the opportunities and constraints in the world of work (p. 173).

His recent writings (Ginzberg, 1984) support this reformulation with the addition of one point, "Occupational choice is a lifelong process of decision making for those who seek major satisfactions from their work. This leads them to reassess repeatedly how they can improve the fit between their changing career goals and the realities of the World of Work" (p. 180).

These changes that Ginzberg has made in his ideas over the past 35 years exemplify the changing view of occupation and career in our society. This view probably has resulted from the increase in both our knowledge of the adult work experience and the actual changes in our society in terms of stability of occupations and career patterns. For example, the idea of person/environment fit is important in each of Ginzberg's statements. However, it progresses from the idea that the resolution of the choice process is a compromise between what one would like and what is available (static choice) to choice being a lifelong process, for those who seek major satisfaction from work, between their own changing goals and the new realities of the work place (dynamic choice).

Super

Super (1953) presented a theory that was much more explicit and extensive. It was based in part on the early work of Charlotte Buehler (1933) in Vienna. Super's original propositions with more recent updates and modifications appear below.

1. People differ in their abilities, interests, and personalities.

2. They are each qualified, by virtue of these characteristics, for a number of occupations.

3. Each of these occupations requires a characteristic pattern of abilities, interests, and personality traits, with tolerance wide enough to allow both some variety of occupations for each individual and some variety in each occupation.

4. Vocational preferences and competencies, the situations in which people live and work, and hence their self-concepts change with time and experience, although self-concepts, as products of social learning, are increasingly stable from late adolescence until late maturity, providing some continuity in choice and adjustment.

5. This process of change may be summed up in a series of life stages (a maxicycle), characterized as a sequence of growth, exploration, establishment, maintenance, and decline, and these stages may in turn be subdivided into (a) the fantasy, tentative, and realistic phase of the exploratory stage and (b) the trial and stable phases of the establishment stage. A small (mini) cycle takes place in the transition from one stage to the next or each time an individual is destabilized by a reduction in force, changes in type of manpower (sic) needs, illness or injury, or other socioeconomic or personal events. Such unstable or multiple-trial careers involve new growth, reexploration, and reestablishment (recycling).

6. The nature of the career pattern—that is, the occupational level attained and the sequence, frequency, and duration of trial and stable jobs—is determined by the individual's parental socioeconomic level, mental ability, education, skills, personality characteristics (needs, values, interests, traits, and self-concepts), and career maturity and by the opportunities to which he or she is exposed.

7. Success in coping with the demands of the environment and of the organism in that context at any given life-career stage depends on the readiness of the individual to cope with these demands (that is, on his or her career maturity). *Career maturity* is a constellation of physical, psychological, and social characteristics; psychologically, it is both cognitive and affective. It includes the degree of success in coping with the demands of earlier stages and substages of career development, and especially with most recent.

8. Career maturity is a hypothetical concept. Its operational definition is perhaps as difficult to formulate as is that of intelligence, but its history is much briefer and its achievements even less definitive. Contrary to the impressions created by some writers, it does not increase monotonically, and it is not a unitary trait.

9. Development through the life stages can be guided, partly by facili—ting the maturing of abilities and interests and partly by aiding in reality testing and in the development of self-concepts.

10. The process of career development is essentially that of developing and implementing occupational self-concepts. It is a synthesizing and compromising process in which the self-concept is a product of the interaction of inherited aptitudes, physical makeup, opportunity to observe and play various roles, and evaluations of the extent to which the results of role playing meet with the approval of superiors and fellows (interactive learning).

11. The process of synthesis of or compromise between individual and social factors, between self-concepts and reality, is one of role playing

and of learning from feedback whether the role is played in fantasy, in the counseling interview, or in real life activities such as classes, clubs, part-time work, and entry jobs.

12. Work satisfactions and life satisfactions depend upon the extent to which the individual finds adequate outlets for abilities, needs, values, interests, personality traits, and self-concepts. They depend upon the establishment in a type of work, a work situation, and a way of life in which one can play the kind of role that growth and exploratory experiences have led one to consider congenial and appropriate.

13. The degree of satisfaction people attain from work is proportional to the degree to which they have been able to implement selfconcepts.

14. Work and occupation provide a focus for personality organization for most men and many women, although for some persons this focus is peripheral, incidental, or even nonexistent. Then other foci such as leisure activities and homemaking may be central. (Social traditions, such as sex-role stereotyping and modeling, racial and ethnic biases, and the opportunity structure, as well as individual differences, are important determinants of preferences for such roles as worker, student, leisurite, homemaker, and citizen.) (Super, 1990, pp. 206–208)

More recently, Super (1976, 1990) has discussed the roles people play at different times in their lives and the theaters in which these roles are played.

A significant contribution of Super and Ginzberg and their colleagues was the idea that career development and even career choices were the result of a process rather than being a point-in-time event. They also presented the idea that career choices and career development could be described by means of stages. These developmental stages are considered to be hierarchical, sequential, and qualitatively different.

The reader will note similarities in Super's and Ginzberg's stages and in their more recent formulations, particularly Super's proposition 11 and Ginzberg's proposition 3 (revised).

Gene Dalton, Paul Thompson, and Raymond Price (1977) developed a model that describes the career stages of professionals in organizations. Although limited in the population it describes, the model does make a significant contribution to the understanding of successful careers in organizations. Basically, four stages illustrating the progression of successful professional careers in organizations are described.

Stage I. In stage I the individual is newly hired in the organization. The central activities of this stage are learning about the work of the organization, doing routine work under the close supervision of someone more experienced, helping, following directions, and so forth. The others in the organization view this individual as a learner or "apprentice." The major psychological issue to be dealt with in this stage is dependence—following orders and being successful at routine work. The major task of this stage is accepting the routine work and doing it well, while demonstrating the ability and initiative to progress to the stage of independent contributor.

Stage II. The primary activity in this stage is being responsible for projects from conception to completion—doing all the work oneself. In this stage one is viewed as a colleague, an independent contributor. The major psychological issue to be dealt with is independence. The task of this stage is to develop an area of expertise and become skilled and respected in it. Some individuals tend to want to move through this stage too quickly, without fully laying the groundwork for the next stage by developing a high level of expertise in the work of the organization.

Stage III. This stage involves taking responsibility for the work of others. It may be in the form of line management, informal group leadership or mentoring, or the offering of expertise in ideas and suggestions. An individual in this stage is involved in training, supervising, and interacting with other parts of the organization or with other organizations. He or she is seen by others as an expert, a leader in the field, and sometimes a mentor to individuals in stage I. Many individuals remain productive in this stage for the remainder of their careers.

Stage IV. The final stage is one that few reach. Tasks of this stage involve policymaking and shaping the direction of the organization. The close mentoring relationships are no longer possible as this person moves to delegate responsibility for the day-to-day work of the organization. This person "sponsors" individuals by creating experiences in which they can learn what is necessary to move up to the organization. The two major psychological issues of this stage are giving up the control of the day-to-day operations—delegating that responsibility—and exercising power. One of the major responsibilities of individuals in this stage is to exercise power for the benefit of the organization and the individuals in it.

Thus Dalton and associates take up where Ginzberg and others left off in describing what happens to an individual after an initial occupational choice is made. They amplify the tasks and experience of Super's establishment and maintenance stages. Although they do not discuss this directly, the assumption is that individuals changing occupations—the midlife career changers—would have to begin again in stage I, although they may progress through the stages much more rapidly than before.

Similarly, the latest work of Super (1990) suggests that although indeed he still believes there is a "maxicycle" over the life span, there can also be a number of "minicycles" during which the individual recycles through the stages.

This cyclical approach seems to be the most applicable to present-day career stages. The work of all the stage theorists may be viewed as presenting a maxicycle over the life span but also describing the minicycles of career change as it occurs in our society today. Figure 1-2 can be seen as describing this maxicycle. It should not be considered restrictive, but as possibly including several minicycles.

A significant limitation of all developmental career theories as well as of almost all other career theories is that the supporting research has been done exclusively on men. Super (1957), Zytowski (1969), and others have done research on career patterns of women as differentiated from those of men. The differences they found, however, have not been attended to in theory building. Gilligan (1982, 1988) found that moral development of women was different from that of men. It is reasonable to assume that career stages, as well as patterns, may also be different for women. It is inappropriate to use models developed on men to categorize the development of women. Inevitably, under those models women may be found lacking, when actually they are only different. Recently developed models of influences of women's career decisions are presented in the section describing career choice content and process theories.

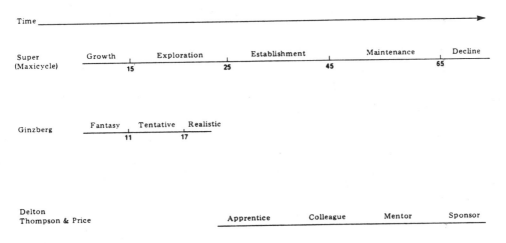

Figure 1-2. Developmental stage models.

John Crites (1981) added to the developmental view of career the idea that career choice can be viewed in terms of process and content. That idea provides the last level of organization for the model of understanding career theory (Fig. 1-1).

In summary, this section has discussed the assumptions, propositions, and evolution of the developmental view. The following sections will provide some details as to how that developmental process operates. They will address what theory and research tell us of career choice and adjustment in terms of content and process.

CAREER CHOICE CONTENT THEORY

Career choice content theories predict career choices from individual characteristics. For example, Ann Roe (1956, 1990) postulated that the type of parental environment in which an individual is reared predicts occupational choice. John Holland (1985) predicted occupation from personality type using a six-category typology. Some sociologists have predicted occupational choice from demographic variables such as age, sex, and socioeconomic status. Trait-factor interventions are based in part on career choice content theories.

Holland

John Holland (1973, 1985) has developed the most heavily researched and widely used career choice content theory. The ideas that led to the development of the theory grew out of his experience as a military interviewer during World War II. After interviewing hundreds of young inductees who needed to be assigned a military occupational specialty (a job), he began to see patterns in what these individuals were saying about themselves, their interests, and their skills. These patterns were the beginnings of his personality typology.

The four primary assumptions of Holland's theory are:

1. In our culture, most persons can be categorized as one of six types: realistic, investigative, artistic, social, enterprising, and conventional.

> The *Realistic* type likes realistic jobs such as automobile mechanic, aircraft controller, surveyor, farmer, electrician. Has mechanical abilities but may lack social skills. Is described as conforming, materialistic, modest, frank, natural, shy, honest, persistent, stable, humble, practical, and thrifty.
> The *Investigative* type likes investigative jobs such as biologist, chemist, physicist, anthropologist, geologist, medical technologist. Has mathematical and scientific ability but often lacks leadership ability. Is described as analytical, independent, modest, cautious, intellectual, precise, critical, introverted, rational, curious, methodical, and reserved.
> The *Artistic* type likes artistic jobs such as composer, musician,

stage director, writer, interior decorator, actor/actress. Has artistic abilities: writing, musical, or artistic, but often lacks clerical skills. Is described as complicated, idealistic, independent, disorderly, imaginative, intuitive, emotional, impractical, nonconforming, expressive, impulsive, and original.

The *Social* type likes social jobs such as teacher, religious worker, counselor, clinical psychologist, psychologist, psychiatric case worker, speech therapist. Has social skills and talents, but often lacks mechanical and scientific ability. Is described as convincing, helpful, responsible, cooperative, idealistic, sociable, friendly, insightful, tactful, generous, kind, and understanding.

The *Enterprising* type likes enterprising jobs such as salesperson, manager, business executive, television producer, sports promoter, buyer. Has leadership and speaking abilities but often lacks scientific ability. Is described as adventurous, energetic, self-confident, ambitious, impulsive, sociable, attention-getting, optimistic, popular, domineering, and pleasure-seeking.

The *Conventional* type likes conventional jobs such as bookkeeper/stenographer, financial analyst, banker, cost estimator, tax expert. Has clerical and arithmetic ability, but often lacks artistic abilities. Is described as conforming, inhibited, practical, conscientious, obedient, self-controlled (calm), careful, orderly, unimaginative, conservative, persistent, and efficient.

2. There are six model environments: realistic, investigative, artistic, social, enterprising, and conventional.
3. People search for environments that will let them exercise their skills and abilities, express their attitudes and values, and take on agreeable problems and roles.
4. Behavior is determined by the interaction between personality and environment (Adapted from Holland, 1985b, p. 2–4).

Several elaborations need to be made on these points. First, the instrument that Holland developed to measure his personality types is called the Self-Directed Search (SDS) (Holland, 1985a). Upon completion of this instrument, an individual has devised a three-letter code composed of the first letters of his or her three most important personality types. This is called the individual's "Holland code."

Holland has assessed individuals who have entered or plan to enter many occupations and has defined the occupational environment by the predominant three-letter code in that environment. In this way an individual may look into an Occupations Finder and find listed occupations that are related to his or her Holland code. This correspondence is a most useful tool for career counselors. It has now been extended to relating Holland codes to each occupation listed in the *Dictionary of Occupational Titles* in the *Dictionary of Holland Occupational Codes* (Gottfredson & Holland, 1989).

Holland states that people search for environments in which they can express their personalities. He does not state that individuals will be more successful or satisfied in congruent environments, although that is the assumption from which most counselors operate when using Holland's theory.

Several other important concepts Holland uses are calculus, congruence, consistency, differentiation, and identity. He states that the relationships within and between types or environments can be ordered according to a hexagonal model (see Fig. 3). He calls this concept *calculus*. Using the hexagonal model, *congruence* is defined as close correspondence between the individual's personality type and the environment. The degree of congruence is determined by the closeness of the individual and occupational types on the hexagon. For example, a social person in a social environment represents a high level of congruence; a social person in an enterprising or artistic environment represents a lower level of congruence; a social person in a conventional or investigative environment even less; and a social person in a realistic environment represents the lowest level of congruence.

Consistency is also defined by distance apart on the hexagon: the closer the codes, the more consistent they are. For example, SEA is composed of types adjacent on the hexagon and has a high degree of consistency. ACR is composed of types that are opposite or nonadjacent and are in the most inconsistent category. Individuals with inconsistent codes tend to have difficulty in finding occupations in which to express all facets of their personalities.

Differentiation refers to the degree to which a person or an environment is well defined—that is different from the other types or models. Individuals who are young and/or inexperienced tend to have low differentiation. This concept is related to that of identity. *Personal identity* is defined as having a clear and stable picture of one's goals, interests and talents.

One of the reasons for the widespread use of Holland's theory is that he has developed two instruments, the Vocational Preference Inventory and The Self-Directed Search, to measure personality types and to relate them to specific occupations. The Self-Directed Search, in particular, has been attractive to practitioners as well as easy to use in research. Other instruments, including the highly respected Strong Interest Inventory and, most recently, the Armed Services Vocational Aptitude Battery, have used Holland's typology as an organizing tool.

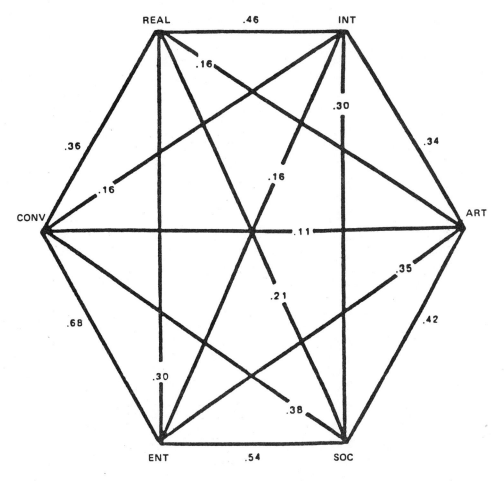

Figure 1-3. A hexagonal model for defining the psychological resemblances among types and environments and their interactions. From An Empirical Occupational Classification Derived from a Theory of Personality and Intended for Practice and Research (p.4). *ACT Research Report No. 29, 1969, Iowa City: The American College Testing Program. Copyright 1969 by ACT.* Reprinted by permission.

Another reason, it is hoped, for the widespread use of Holland's typology is that the overwhelming body of research it has stimulated generally supports the theory (Holland, Magoon, & Spokane, 1981). In general, individuals do seek environments similar to their personality types, and there is some evidence that adults changing occupations do seek more congruent environments.

Roe

Anne Roe developed a theory that predicts occupational choice from the type of childhood relationships with parents. Her goal was to explain the origin of interests and needs. Her ideas were based on Maslow's (1954) concept of basic needs arranged in a hierarchy of prepotency. That hierarchy arranged in order from most to least potent is: (a) the physiological needs, (b) the safety needs, (c) the need for belongingness and love, (d) the need for importance, respect, self-esteem, and independence, (e) the need for information, (f) the need for understanding, (g) the need for beauty, and (h) the need for self-actualization.

Roe stated that: "In our society there is no single situation that is potentially so capable of giving some satisfaction at all levels of basic needs as the occupation" (1990, p. 69).

In order to study occupations, Roe first developed a classification scheme based on the primary activities of occupations. She developed a continuum based on the nature and intensity of interpersonal relationships required in the occupation. The resulting eight occupational groups are: (1) service, (2) business contact, (3) organization (managerial), (4) technology, (5) outdoor, (6) science, (7) general culture (preservation and transmission of the culture), and (8) arts and entertainment. She also classified the levels of responsibility of occupations. The levels are: (a) professional and managerial (independent responsibility), (b) professional and managerial (lower levels), (c) semiprofessional and small business, (d) skilled, (e) semiskilled, and (f) unskilled.

Roe hypothesized three categories of parental behavior toward children: (1) emotional concentration on the child (overprotective or overbearing), (2) avoidance (emotional rejection on neglect), and (3) acceptance (casual or loving). These types of childhood environments were then related in a predictive way to occupations categorized as either oriented toward persons or not toward persons. Later she expanded her dimension of classification of occupations to a two-dimensional system (Roe & Klos, 1972). One axis is orientation to interpersonal relationships-orientation to natural phenomena, and the other is orientation to purposeful communication-orientation to resourceful utilization. Her picture of occupational classification is symbolized as a truncated cone with the eight occupational groups spaced around the circle with wider divisions at the highest levels and narrowing spacing as the levels progress downward.

Although Roe's propositions are intuitively sensible and her classification system useful, there is little empirical support for her propositions. Roe herself stated that in the attempts to find a direct link between parent-child relations and occupational choice, "The results have been consistently negative" (1990, p. 86). The only support comes from a few studies of specializations within occupations or occupational fields.

Roe's contribution may be seen in part as an expansion of the earlier developmental work (Ginzberg et al., 1951; Super, 1957) in describing the process of career choice. She described the limitations of heredity and parental expectations do influence both educational and occupational choices (Conklin & Dailey, 1981; Lavine, 1982).

More recent and more applicable propositions (Holland, 1973, 1985) are similar to Roe's classification of occupations and levels. Thus, although her specific propositions have, in general, not been supported, her general ideas have stimulated research and thinking that have advanced the formulation of career theory.

Psychodynamic Theory

Bordin (1990) presented a psychodynamic model of career choice as a synthesis of previous applications of psychodynamic theory to career choice. The basis of this model is that " . . . the participation of personality in work and career is rooted in the role of play in human life" (p. 104).

Bordin's propositions are:

1. This sense of wholeness, this experience of joy is sought by all persons, preferably in all aspects of life, including work.
2. The degree of fusion of work and play is a function of an individual's developmental history regarding compulsion and effort.
3. A person's life can be seen as a string of career decisions reflecting the individual groping for an ideal fit between self and work.
4. The most useful system of mapping occupations for intrinsic motives will be one that captures life-styles or character styles and stimulates or is receptive to developmental conceptions.
5. The roots of the personal aspects of career development are to be found throughout the early development of the individual, sometimes in the earliest years.
6. Each individual seeks to build a personal identity that incorporates aspects of father and mother, yet retains elements unique to the self.
7. One source of perplexity and paralysis at career decision points will be found in doubts and dissatisfactions with current resolutions of self. (p. 105)

The predictive aspects of this theory include the emphasis on needs and satisfactions that are developed at an early age. These are shaped by early experiences, identifications with mother and father, and sex role socialization (all of these being overlapping factors). Knowledge of these needs and satisfactions predicts how they will be acted out in the work place. For example, individuals whose needs are satisfied by the role of nurturer will go into nurturing occupations.

This theory also incorporates the idea of development, but it is primarily predictive. Its usefulness is in developing the notion that the part of our lives called work can satisfy some (but not all) of our psychological needs. It also does a good job of describing career choices in the context of a larger theory of personality and development.

As far as practical applications go, there are no instruments that effectively make these predictions for an individual. In usual practice based on psychodynamic theory, those relationships are specified directly by the individual therapist and depend on the skill and knowledge of that particular person.

Sociological Theory

Sociological research into occupational choice uses basically demographic variables to predict types of occupations entered. Its emphasis is on factors that are beyond the control of the individual, such as parent's (father's) occupation and education and labor market conditions. The categories of occupations studied are defined by occupational status.

There are several major foci of the sociological study of individuals and occupations. One is the area of status attainment. This line of research relates father's education and occupation to son's educational and occupational attainment. Blau and Duncan (1967) developed a model that indicates that father's education and occupation predicts son's education and that all three of those predict the son's occupational status. Other research by Sewell, Haller, and Portes (1969); Sewell, Haller, and Ohlendorf (1970); and Clarridge, Sheehy, and Hauser (1977) followed a population of Wisconsin residents from youth to middle age. They found that both family status and mental ability predicted occupational achievement through influence on significant others, career plans, and educational level.

Status attainment research has been done on differences among the majority group (white men), and minority groups. Differences in income are larger between men and women than between whites and other races (Bridges, 1982; Corcoran & Duncan, 1979; Hartman, 1976; Mincer & Polacheck, 1974; Treiman & Hartman, 1981). Bielby and Baron (1986) found that within some firms job segregation by sex is nearly complete, with corresponding differences in pay grades. Being of a racial minority or a woman, then, would predict lower educational level and occupational status than for a comparable white man.

Another area of sociological research in occupations has to do with the social and economic systems. Blau, Gystad, Jessor, Parnes, and Wilcock (1956) developed a model that incorporates social structure (values, stratification, demography, technology, and type of economy), physical conditions, historical change, socioeconomic organizations, and immediate job requirements and characteristics as predictors of occupational entry. They described parallel determinants of biological attributes and personal qualifications and information about particular occupations that also influence occupational entry. Others have studied occupational aspirations and entry as a function of local labor market conditions, availability of information, and role models related to specific occupations and cultural restraints that narrow the consideration of potential occupations (Asbury, 1968; LoCascio, 1967; Schmeiding & Jensen, 1968).

Accident theory, or the effects of chance on vocational choices, has been discussed by Bandura (1982), Caplow (1954), Miller and Form (1951), and others. Basically, this is the idea of "being in the right place at the right time," of meeting an individual who has an important influence on one's career, of being born at a certain demographic time when there are few or many jobs or into a family with certain socioeconomic values and geographical location. Although "chance," thus described, certainly plays a part in everyone's life, other theories incorporate these and other variables related to occupational choice (Krumboltz, 1979). Thus chance cannot be looked at as an explanation of career behavior on its own.

Although there is not just one sociological theory of career choice or development, sociological research predicts occupational choice primarily in terms of status, using such variables as father's education and occupation, educational level, race, sex, and influence of significant others. Accident theory also falls into this category.

CAREER CHOICE CONTENT AND PROCESS THEORY

Krumboltz

John Krumboltz (1979) developed a theory of career decision making that is an application of social learning theory. This theory incorporates both the content and process aspects of career choice. It also explains some concepts discussed more generally in other theories. Two examples are accident theory from the sociological perspective and the development of the personality types from Holland's typology. This theory attempts to specify all of the "accidents"—they are described as genetic endowments and special abilities, environmental conditions and events, and learning experiences. John Holland (1983) said that this theory "...fills in the cracks in my typology." It explains how interest and personality patterns develop, an issue not addressed by Holland.

Krumboltz (1979) specified influences on career decision making, outcomes of interactions among influences, a set of theoretical propositions, and a description of the process of career planning and development.

Influences on Career Decision Making. Four influences on career decision making are described. First are genetic endowments, such as race, sex, physical appearance and characteristics, and special abilities, including intelligence, musical and artistic abilities, and muscular coordination.

Environmental conditions and events also influence career decision making. They include such factors as job and training opportunities available; labor laws and union rules; amount of rewards for various occupations; catastrophic events such as earthquakes and floods; natural resources; technological developments; social organization and government policy; and family, educational, and community influences.

Learning experiences are the third category of influences. Krumboltz divides them into instrumental and associative learning experiences. Instrumental, or direct, learning experiences occur when an individual acts on the environment to produce consequences (operate conditioning model). That is, one or more of the events or conditions previously described interacts with a particular problem or stimulus presented to an individual. The individual responds and receives consequences (feedback, praise, reward, punishment, etc.) from the environment. The skills necessary for career planning and educational and job performance are learned through these direct experiences.

Associative learning experiences are basically the development of attitudes, feelings, and positive or negative occupational stereotypes through observation of the behavior or responses of others. This is done via a classical conditioning model—a previously neutral stimulus is paired with a positive or negative response and the neutral stimulus (e.g., occupational title) stimulates that positive or negative response.

The fourth influence on career decision making is task approach skills. These skills are developed as a result of the previous three influences. They are a set of skills and attitudes that influence career planning behavior as well as occupational performance. They include specific occupational and other skills, values, and work habits.

Outcomes of Interactions Among Influences. As a result of interactions among the preceding four factors, three outcomes can be described. The first is the development of self-observation generalizations. These are a set of generalizations (such as, "I am good at telling funny stories") individuals make about themselves as a result of past learning experiences. They may not remember the actual experiences but do remember and generalize the feedback they received in those types of experiences. Self-observation generalizations may or may not be accurate. They can be collected and organized by means of interest inventories.

The second outcome is the development of task approach skills. They are developed as a result of learning experiences. One of the more significant of these is the person's view of whether or not individuals can influence their own environments. If individuals have a number of experiences in which they attempt unsuccessfully to influence their environments, they develop the idea that "fate," not their own actions, is controlling their lives.

The final outcome of these interactions is action. This theory focuses primarily on entry behavior, that is, entering into an occupation or a training program for an occupation.

Theoretical Propositions. Krumboltz's propositions state that:

1. An individual is more likely to enter an occupation if he or she (a) has been positively reinforced for activities related to that occupation, (b) has seen a valued model be positively reinforced for activities related to that occupation, (c) has been positively reinforced by a valued person who advocates that he or she engage in that occupation, or (d) has been exposed to positive words or images relating to that occupation.
2. A person is less likely to engage in an occupation or its related training and activities if he or she (a) has been punished or not reinforced for engaging in related activities, (b) has observed a valued model being punished or not reinforced for those activities, or (c) has been reinforced by a valued model who expresses negative words or images related to the occupation.
3. An individual is more likely to learn appropriate career decision making skills if he or she (a) has been reinforced for those activities, (b) has observed a model be reinforced for those activities, and (c) has access to people and other resources with the necessary information.
4. An individual is less likely to learn the skills necessary for career decision making if he or she (a) has been punished or not reinforced for such behaviors, (b) has observed a model be punished or not reinforced for those behaviors, or (c) has little or no access to people or other resources with the necessary information.
5. An individual is more likely to enter an occupation if that individual (a) has recently expressed a preference for that occupation, (b) has been exposed to learning and employment opportunities in

that filed, and (c) has learned skills that match the requirements of the occupation.

6. An individual is less likely to enter an occupation if the individual (a) finds the cost of preparation to be greater than the eventual return or (b) is denied access to the minimum resources necessary for entering the occupation.

Krumboltz views the career planning and development process as an interdependent sequence of learning experiences that follows the above stated rules. Although he describes this as a lifelong process of each experience building on the last, he stops short of describing "development" as a process that could be composed of discrete, hierarchical, sequential stages.

This theory provides an explanation of the mechanism of all the career choice content and process theories. The addition of some of the developmental concepts and some propositions regarding work adjustment could make it a more comprehensive career theory.

Models Including Variables Important to the Career Choices of Women

Several models have been developed more recently which incorporate variables that have been shown to influence women's career decisions (Astin, 1984; Farmer, 1985; Gottfredson, 1981; Hackett and Betz, 1981). Each explains the process of the development of career choice content and makes predictions using that content.

Hackett & Betz. Hackett and Betz (1981) developed a model which explained factors in the development of self efficacy expectations in women—that is, how women view their ability to perform certain tasks and be successful in certain activities. They discussed three ways in which women are socialized to feel successful in different tasks than men. Young girls are encouraged to have more involvement in domestic and nurturing activities and less involvement in sports, mechanical activities, and other traditionally male activities. This leads them to feel more successful and comfortable at domestic and nurturing activities and less comfortable in most other activities. Young women still have a predominance of role models in traditional roles and occupations. They tend to have a lack of exposure to female role models representing the full range of career options. Thus, they develop stronger feelings of self-efficacy, again, regarding traditional roles and occupations. Women of all ages tend to have a lack of encouragement, sometimes an active discouragement, to engage in nontraditional roles and pursuits. This gives them a lower sense of self-efficacy toward nontraditional roles and occupations. This explanation of socialization mechanisms enables the prediction that women will predominately choose traditional roles and occupations.

Gottfredson, also in 1981, described the mechanism by which women determine a range of acceptable occupational alternatives. She stated that self-concept (having the components of gender, social class, intelligence, interests and values) interacts with occupational images (sex type, prestige level and field) to determine occupational preferences. These preferences, together with perceptions of job accessibility (opportunities and barriers), determine a range of acceptable occupational alternatives. This model highlights the significance of the sex-role socialization of the individual, the perceived sex type (appropriateness for one sex or the other) of the occupation, and the perceptions of opportunities or barriers to women or women's career choices. It also specifies the role of feedback from the environment in the development of women's perception of themselves, of occupations, and of barriers or opportunities in the environment. She also notes that many of these perceptions are developed at a very early age.

Astin (1984) proposed a model of career choice and work behavior that includes the influence of work motivation, sex role socialization and the structure of opportunity. She indicates that sex role socialization takes place at play, in the family, at school and at work. It interacts with the structure of opportunity, including the distribution of jobs, sex typing of jobs, discrimination, job requirements, the economy, family structure and reproductive technology. This interaction is influenced by the three basic motivators for work (survival, enjoyment of the work, and a sense of contribution) to influence individual expectations, which also influence career choice and work behavior.

Farmer (1985) presented a model of career and achievement motivation. She described three aspects of career motivation—aspiration, level of occupation chosen; mastery, motivation to accomplish challenging in the short-term tasks; and career, the degree of commitment to the long-range prospects of the career. She suggested that three groups of factors influenced this motivation: personal variables (academic self esteem, success attributions, intrinsic values and homemaking orientation), background variables (sex, social status, school location, race, age, math and verbal abilities), and environmental variables (parent support, teacher support and support in the environment "for women working").

The contribution of these models is that they take into account variables, heretofore unspecified, that are important influences of the career choices of women. The gender and socialization issues important to women are generally important to men also. Therefore these models can be applied to men as well as women.

CHOICE AND ADJUSTMENT PROCESS THEORY

The work of David Tiedeman and his associates over the years describes the processes of both career choice and adjustment. Originally, Tiedeman and O'Hara (1963) described a model that was directional (though not irreversible), developmental (based on the ideas of Erik Erikson), and somewhat similar to that of Super (1953) in that it specified a series of stages individuals progress through over the life span. They formulated a model that described an individual's progress of career choice and implementation (see Fig. 1-4).

The first phase, anticipation, consists of four stages prior to entry into an

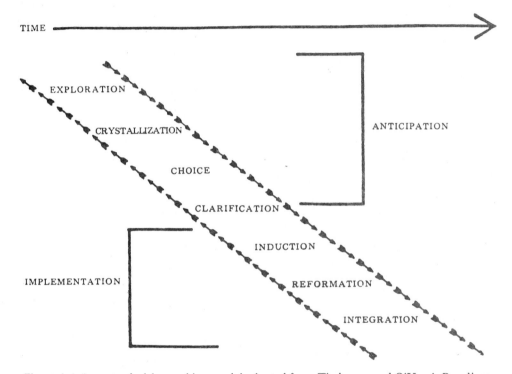

Figure 1-4. A career decision making model adapted from Tiedeman and O'Hara's Paradigm of the Processes of Differentiation and Integration in Problem Solving. From *Career Development: Choice and Adjustment* (p. 40) by D.V. Tiedeman and R.P. O'Hara, 1963; New York: College Entrance Examination Board. Copyright 1963 by CEEB. Adapted by permission.

occupation. Exploration is a period of somewhat random behavior in which the individual interacts with the environment and receives feedback. It is a period of collecting observations about that interaction (differentiation) and incorporating that information into the ego identity (integration). Crystallization begins as these observations begin to form patterns (e.g., "I like to work with my hands" or "I am good at influencing other people"). Choice is the process of using those observations to make a tentative choice and to begin to act upon it. Clarification is the period of preparation for entry into the occupation, during which the choice is reconsidered and specializations are considered.

The second phase is called implementation. First, there is induction. This is the first entry into a job in the field. It is a period when the individual is primarily conforming to the organization and learning how to be successful. The second stage is reformation. This happens after the individual gains credibility in the organization. The individual is then able to act on the organization to make changes deemed necessary. Finally, there develops a balance, integration, between the organization acting on the individual and the individual acting on the organization. This is a period of relative satisfaction that lasts until something happens to change the balance. At that time the individual may begin the cycle again or return to any of the other stages, as indicated by the two-way arrows in the model. Tiedeman and O'Hara also described the process by which an individual progresses through the stages. The core of their formulation was that an individual developed an ego identity through the processes of differentiation and integration.

Differentiation is the process of differentiating oneself from the environment, that is, observing different outcomes of one's own behavior and that of others. This process goes on continuously as individuals interact with the environment and observe the consequences. This information is then integrated into the ego identity. That is, new information is then integrated into the ego identity. That is, new information that results from interaction of the person and the environment is constantly being incorporated into and changing the ego identity.

More recently Tiedeman and Miller-Tiedeman (1990) defined a two-dimensional model that further amplifies the anticipation phase of the original model. This model is based on the idea that how an individual views decision making is a function of how far the individual has advanced in his or her career. An important way of measuring this advancement in the career process is the language individuals use to describe their careers.

They defined two perspectives from which individuals describe their careers—personal reality and common reality. Common reality is a notion similar to societal, parental, or other external expectations: "They" expect me (all men) to be able to support a family. Personal reality is what feels "right" or good to the individual, irrespective of outside expectations. It is similar to the notion of internal locus of control. Recognizing and acting on one's personal reality is the goal of interventions based on the Tiedemans' model.

Another idea important to the recent work of David and Anna Tiedeman is "life as career" (1983). That is, the notion that each individual's life is his or her career; that individuals make choices about how they will create or "construct" their careers (or spend their lives); and that the goal for the individual is to integrate all aspects of life by becoming empowered to act on his or her personal reality (Miller-Tiedeman, 1988, 1989).

CAREER ADJUSTMENT CONTENT THEORY

Much work that is not usually noticed by counselors has been done in the area of work adjustment and job satisfaction. Work adjustment has been defined as success (or "satisfactoriness") and satisfaction on the job. Success is typically operationally defined by longevity on the job and by supervisory ratings. Satisfaction is typically measured by asking the individual whether he or she is satisfied on the job.

A key factor in work adjustment is the match between the expectations of the organization and the expectations of the employee. Davis, England, and Lofquist (1964) developed a number of propositions in their theory of work adjustment. Their basic points are:

1. Work adjustment is composed of satisfactoriness and satisfaction.
2. Satisfactoriness is determined by the relationship of the individual's abilities and the requirements of the work place, assuming the individual's needs are being met by the organization's reward system.
3. Satisfaction is determined by how well the reward system of the organization meets the individual's needs, assuming the individual's skills meet the organization's requirements.
4. Satisfaction and satisfactoriness have moderating effects on each other.
5. Tenure is a function of satisfactoriness and satisfaction.
6. The fit between the individual (needs and skills) and the environment (requirements and rewards) increases as a function of tenure.

More recently, the fit between organizational and individual expectations has been specified as important in the process of the individual joining the organization. This is sometimes called the "psychological contract" (Argyris, 1960; Levenson, 1962).

Berlew and Hall (1966) and later Kotter (1980) developed two sets of dimensions on which individuals and organizations have expectations. The first dimension is composed of areas in which individuals have expectations of receiving and organizations have expectations of giving. These areas are:

1. a sense of meaning or purpose in the job;
2. personal development opportunities;
3. the amount of interesting work that stimulates curiosity and induces excitement;
4. the challenge in the work;
5. the power and responsibility in the job;

6. recognition and approval for good work;
7. the status and prestige in the job;
8. the friendliness of the people, the congeniality of the work group;
9. salary;
10. the amount of structure in the environment (general practices, discipline, regimentation);
11. the amount of security in the job;
12. advancement opportunities; and
13. the amount and frequency of feedback and evaluation. (Morgan, 1980, p. 65)

Areas in which organizations have expectations of receiving and individuals of giving are:

1. performing nonsocial job-related tasks requiring some degree of technical knowledge and skill;
2. learning the various aspects of a position while on the job;
3. discovering new methods of performing tasks; solving novel problems;
4. presenting a point of view effectively and convincingly;
5. working productively with groups of people;
6. making well-organized, clear presentations both orally and in writing;
7. supervising and directing the work of others;
8. making responsible decisions well without assistance from others;
9. planning and organizing work efforts for oneself or others;
10. utilizing time and energy for the benefit of the company;
11. accepting company demands that conflict with personal prerogatives;
12. maintaining social relationships with other members of the company outside of work;
13. conforming to the folkways of the organization or work group on the job in areas not directly related to job performance;
14. pursuing further education on personal time;
15. maintaining a good public image of the company;
16. taking on company values and goals as one's own; and
17. seeing what should or must be done and initiating appropriate activity. (Morgan, 1980, p. 65)

The clearer both parties are about expectations in each of these areas the easier it is to make appropriate judgments about individuals joining organizations. Unclear expectations or a change from either the individual or the organization without a comparable change in the other can upset the balance and cause dissatisfaction and unsatisfactoriness. A check on the expectations on these dimensions can be of great assistance in problem identification when counseling dissatisfied workers.

INTEGRATION AND IMPLICATIONS

By combining elements of all these theories, a number of statements can be made that are useful to counselors who seek to develop interventions for adults.

1. Individuals regard their careers differently and emit different career-related behaviors at difference times in their lives.
2. Choices of occupational field and specific jobs at specific times are influenced by and can be predicted from certain individual characteristics. These characteristics include sex, race or ethnic group, intelligence and achievement; special skills and talents; ability to relate to people; individual needs, values, and goals, and personality type.
3. Choices of occupational field and specific jobs are also influenced by factors external to the individual. These factors include the reinforcement received from parental and career-related activities, community influence, family requirements and values, the economic and social condition of the society, opportunities for learning, availability of information, and historical events.
4. The process of making choices about occupational fields or specific jobs follows the general pattern of exploration, crystallization, choice, and clarification.
5. The process of making adjustments to those choices follows the general pattern of induction, reformation, and integration—or balance between the needs of the individual and the needs of the organization.
6. Adjustment of the consequences of occupational or specific job choices depends on factors in the work environment and on characteristics of the individual. The most powerful of these factors is the magnitude of the discrepancy between with the individual expects to find in terms of requirements and rewards and what the environment provides in those areas.
7. Satisfaction and success in an occupational field or in a specific job depends on the person/environment fit. That is, individuals must be able to express their values and interests and play roles and perform activities that they deem appropriate for themselves.
8. Satisfaction in a specific job comes from receiving feedback on successful performance of tasks or activities the individual considers important.
9. The individual's occupational career is very much a part of the individual's life career. The interactions of occupational and family life cycles, life style, leisure, and other issues cannot be separated. They must be considered together in career planning.
10. Individuals can be assisted in making choices and planning their careers by helping them understand their own characteristics as

described in item 2 above, by helping them understand the work environment and other external forces described in item 3 above, by providing access to information and appropriate training, and by assisting in the consideration of the impact of occupational and job choices on other aspects of their lives.

11. The goals of career counseling are:
    - to enable clients to have sufficient information about their own characteristics; about training, assistance, and other resources available; about occupations and their characteristics; about potential barriers and how to deal with them; and about how to use that information in decision making; and
    - to enable them to view themselves as having the ability to make their own choices and to act on their "personal reality."

CONCLUSION

This discussion has described career theories in light of their contribution to the current state of knowledge of career development and behavior. An attempt has been made to identify areas of overlap and areas in which each theory makes unique contributions. A model for organizing current knowledge was presented and explained. A summary of current knowledge and its implications was described.

It is hoped that this model will be useful in applying these theories to facilitate the career development of adults.

REFERENCES

Argyris, E. (1960). *Understanding organizational behavior.* Homewood, IL: Dorsey Press.

Asbury, F.A. (1968). Vocational development of rural disadvantaged eighth grade boys *Vocational Guidance Quarterly,* 17, 109–113.

Astin, H. S. (1984). The meaning of work in women's lives: A socio-psychological model of career choice and work behavior. *The Counseling Psychologist, 12,* 17–126.

Bandura, A. (1982). The psychology of chance encounters and life paths. *The American Psychologist, 37*(7), 747–755.

Berlew, D.E., & Hall, D.T. (1966). The socialization of managers: Effects of expectations on performance. *An Administrative Science Quarterly, 10,* 207–223.

Bielby, T. & Baron, N. (1986). Men and women at work: Sex segregation and statistical discrimination. *American Journal of Sociology, 91,* 759–799.

Blau, P.M., & Duncan, O.D. (1967). *The American occupational structure.* New York: Wiley.

Blau, P.M., Gustad, J.W., Jessor, R., Parnes, H., S., & Wilcock, R.C. (1956). Occupational choice: A conceptual framework. *Industrial Labor Relations* (rev. ed.), *9,* 531–543.

Bordin, E.S. (1990). Psychodynamic model of career choice and satisfaction. In D. Brown and L. Brooks (Eds.), *Career choice and development* (2nd ed., pp. 102–144). San Francisco: Jossey-Bass.

Bridges, W.P. (1982). The sexual segregation of occupations: Theories of labor stratification in industry. *American Journal of Sociology, 88,* 270–295.

Buehler, C. (1933). *Der menschliche Lebenslauf als psychologisches Problem.* Leipzig: Hirzel.

Caplow, T. (1954). *The sociology of work.* Minneapolis: University of Minnesota Press.

Clarridge, B.R., Sheehy, L.L., & Hauser, T.S. (1978). Tracing members of a panel: A seventeen-year follow-up. In K.F. Schussler (Ed.), *Sociological methodology* (pp. 185–203). San Francisco: Jossey-Bass.

Conklin, M.E., & Dailey, A.R. (1981). Does consistency of parental educational encouragement matter for secondary school students. *Sociology of Educations, 54,* 254–262.

Corocran, M.E., & Duncan, G.J. (1979). Work history, labor force attachment, and earnings differences between the races and sexes. *Journal of Human Resources, 14,* 3–20.

Crites, J.O. (1981). *Career counseling:* Models, methods and materials. New York: McGraw-Hill.

Dalton, G., Thompson, P., & Price, R. (1977). Career stages: A model of professional careers in organizations. *Organizational Dynamics, 6,* 19–42.

Dawis, R.V., England, G.W., & Lofquist, L.H. (1964). A theory of work adjustment. *Minnesota Studies in Vocational Rehabilitation,* no. 15. Minneapolis: University of Minnesota Industrial Relations Center.

Farmer, H. S. (1985). Model of career and achievement motivation for women and men. *Journal of Counseling Psychology, 32,* 363–390.

Gilligan, C. (1982). *In a different voice.* Cambridge, MA: Harvard University Press.

Gilligan, C. & Attanucci, J. (1988). Two moral orientations: Gender differences and similarities. Merrill-Palmer Quarterly, *34,* 223–237.

Ginzberg, E. (1972). Restatement of the theory of occupational choice. *Vocational Guidance Quarterly, 20*(3), 169–176.

Ginzberg, E. (1984). Career development. In D. Brown and L. Brooks (Eds.), *Career choice and development* (pp. 169–191). San Francisco: Jossey-Bass.

Ginzberg, E., Ginsburg, S.W., Axelrad, S., & Herma, J. (1951). *Occupational choice: An approach to a general theory.* New York: Columbia University Press.

Gottfredson, G. D. & Holland, J.L. (1989). *Dictionary of Holland occupational codes.* (2nd ed.) Odessa, FL: Psychological Assessment Resources, Inc.

Gottfredson, L. S. (1981). Circumscription and compromise: A development theory of occupational aspirations. *Journal of Counseling Psychology Monograph, 28,* 545–579.

Hackett, G., & Betz, N. E. (1981). A self-efficacy approach to the approach to the career development of women. *Journal of Vocational Behavior, 18,* 326–339.

Hartman, H.I. (1976). Capitalism, patriarchy, and job segregation by sex. *Signs, 1,* 137–169.

Holland, J.L. (1973). *Making vocational choices: A theory of careers.* Englewood Cliffs, NJ: Prentice-Hall.

Holland, J.L. (1983). In C. Minor & Burtnett (Producers). *Career development: Linking theory with practice* (Videotape) Arlington, VA: American Association for Counseling and Development.

Holland, J.L. (1985). *Making vocational choices: A theory of vocational personalities and work environments* (2nd ed.). Englewood Cliffs, NJ: Prentice-Hall.

Holland, J.L. (1985). *The self-directed search professional manual.* Odessa, FL: Psychological Assessment Resources, Inc.

Holland, J.L., Magoon, T.M., & Spokane, A.R. (1981). Counseling psychology: Career interventions, research and theory. *Annual Review of Psychology, 32,* 279–305.

Kotter, J.P. (1980). The psychological contract: Managing the joining up process. In M.A. Morgan (Ed.), *Managing career development* (pp. 63–72). New York: Van Nostrand Reinhold.

Krumboltz, J.D. (1979). A social learning theory of career decision making. In A.M. Mitchell, G.B. Jones, & J.D. Krumboltz (eds.), *Social learning and career decision making* (pp. 19–49). Cranston, RI: Carroll Press.

Lavine, L.O. (1982). Parental power as a potential influence on girls' career choice. *Child Development, 53,* 658–663.

Levenson, H. (1962). *Men, management, and mental health.* Cambridge, MA: Harvard University Press.

LoCascio, R. (1967). Continuity and discontinuity in vocational development theory. *Personnel and Guidance Journal, 46,* 32–36.

Maslow, A.H. (1954). *Motivation and personality.* New York: Harper & Row.

Miller, D.C., & Form, W.H. (1951). *Industrial sociology.* New York: Harper & Row.

Miller-Tiedeman, A. (1988). *Lifecareer: The quantum leap into a process theory of career.* Vista, CA: Lifecareer Foundation.

Miller-Tiedeman, A. (1989). *How not to make it . . . and succeed: Life on your own terms.* Vista, CA: Lifecareer Foundation.

Mincer, J., & Polacheck, S.W. (1974). Family investment in human capital: Earnings of women. *Journal of Political Economy, 82* S74–S108.

Morgan, M.A. (1980). *Managing career development.* New York: Van Nostrand Reinhold.

Parsons, F. (1909). *Choosing a vocation.* Boston: Houghton Mifflin.

Roe, A. (1956). *The psychology of occupations.* New York: Wiley.

Roe, A., & Lunneborg, P. (1990). Personality development and career choice. In D. Brown and L. Brooks (Eds.), *Career choice and development* (2nd ed., pp. 68–101). San Francisco: Jossey-Bass.

Roe, A., & Klos, D., (1972). Classification of occupations. In J.M. Whitely and A. Resnikoff (Eds.), *Perspectives on vocational development.* Washington, DC: American Personnel and Guidance Association.

Schmeiding, O.A., & Jensen, S. (1968). American Indian students: Vocational development and vocational tenacity. *Vocational Guidance Quarterly, 17,* 120–123.

Sewell, W.H., Haller, A.O., & Ohlendorf, G. (1970). The educational and early occupational attainment process: Replications and revisions. *American Sociological Review, 45,* pp. 1014–1027.

Sewell, W.H., Haller, A.O., & Portes, A. (1969). The educational and early occupational attainment process. *American Sociological Review, 34,* 89–92.

Super, D.E. (1953). A Theory of vocational development. *American Psychologist, 8,* 185–190.

Super, D.E. (1957). *The psychology of careers.* New York: Harper & Row.

Super, D.E. (1976). *Career education and the meanings of work.* Washington, DC: U.S. Government Printing Office.

Super, D.E. (1990). Career and life development. In D. Brown and L. Brooks (Eds.). *Career choice and development* (2nd ed., pp. 197–261). San Francisco: Jossey-Bass.

Tiedeman,m D.V. (1983). In C. Minor & F. Burtnett (Producers). *Career development: Linking theory with practice* (Videotape) Arlington, VA: American Association for Counseling and Development.

Tiedeman, D.V., & Miller-Tiedeman, A. (1984). Career decision-making: An individualistic perspective. In D. Brown and L. Brooks (Eds.), *Career choice and development* (pp. 281–310). San Francisco: Jossey-Bass.

Tiedeman, D.V., & O'Hara, R.P. (1963). *Career development: Choice and adjustment.* New York: College Entrance Examination Board.

Treiman, D.J., & Hartman, H.I. (Eds.) (1981). *Women, work, and wages: Equal pay for jobs of equal value.* Washington, DC: National Research Council, National Academy of Sciences.

Williamson, E.G. (1939). *How to counsel students.* New York: McGraw-Hill.

Zytowski, D.G. (1969). Toward a theory of career development for women. *Personnel and Guidance Journal, 47,* 660–664.

Chapter 2

TOWARD A COMPREHENSIVE THEORY
OF CAREER DEVELOPMENT

Donald E. Super

We see the future but "through a glass, darkly," even the futurists (Ch. 3, 20, 21), whether they spell that term with an initial capital or with lower case. The present is seen more clearly: The glass through which we look may be smudged or grimy, or freshly cleaned and sparkling, but through it we do see more clearly than we do when we look into the future.

The three chapters referred to above look into the future, some further into it than others, but all beyond the present. This chapter is designed to help see where we are, for if we don't know where we start, we are likely to get lost when moving into the future. Knowing where we started and how we got here can also be helpful, but this does not attempt to be a history: for that, and for a closer look at the present, we can refer to Brown & Brooks (1990) and to Dunnette & Hough (1991). In writing what follows, however, an attempt is made to draw on the understanding of one who has been on the scene since before the term and the concept of career development (as contrasted with matching people and occupations or jobs) were formulated. It will be clear from this chapter that the writer is attached to the present; it should also be clear, however, that he looks forward to the future, believing that societies, like careers, develop. What else can one do but accept, adapt, and contribute to change in the hope of making the future better?

It has been made amply clear in current books on career development that there is no such thing as *a theory* of career development, but that there are, instead, *a number of theories* of career development. There are theories propounded by Bordin, Holland, Krumbolz, Roe, and this writer, all played up as theories in leading textbooks written or edited by authorities such as Osipow (1983) and Brown and Brooks (1990). To some extent this is the fault of the "theorists" themselves, who proclaim their work as that of theory building and testing. But to some extent the fault is not intentional, as in the case of this writer who, in proposing a number of propositions concerning career development (Super, 1953), deliberately refrained from using the title "Toward a Theory..." which was his intent, but shortened it "A

Theory . . . " This saved space, and in his judgment avoided the posturing that seemed to him to be implicit in the longer title. It was a mistake, for critics and supporters alike also called it a theory. This, despite the fact that several times (e.g., Super in Whitely & Resnikoff, 1972, pp. 29–30) it was stated that this was not a comprehensive, cohesive theory, but rather a "segmental theory" which might one day be worthy of being called a true theory.

This chapter seeks both to pave the way for the chapters that follow and to try once again to set the record straight, not in self-justification, but in justice to the topic and to the field of career development. This kind of attempt should now seek to go beyond the "classical" or pioneer theorists, and to draw on the current and the nontraditional theorists, writers such as Arthur et al. (1989), Betz & Fitzgerald (1987), Fiske & Chiriboga (1990), Harmon (1970), Howard & Bray (1988), Krumboltz et al. (1976), Nevill (1984), Sekaran (1986), and Vetter (1973). To do that adequately is beyond the scope of any one chapter, but some other chapters will help to strike the needed balance.

This chapter will

1. Present a global, life span developmental, multirole concept of emerging careers;
2. Add to this an up-to-date picture of the determinants of careers.

A Life Span, Life Space Concept of a Career

If one picture can be worth a thousand words the Life-Career Rainbow may be one such picture, for it depicts nine major life roles, showing in Figure 2-1 when each of them began, peaked, and ended in the life of one person. The arcs of the Rainbow, with the amount of space that is shaded and the depth of the shading, depict the peaking and diminishing or ending of each role. At the same time, the legend and arrows above remind the reader that a number of important social determinants are at work and to some extent shape the career, while the comparable data below the Rainbow list some of the personal determinants. Just what the specifics are, and how they operate, is not one of the messages that this model carries. It focuses on the major life roles, their beginnings and endings, their growth, peaking and decline, including the facts that some peak early and decline early, some peak late and end late, while others, such as that of worker, have what are here portrayed (to simplify the graphics) as having abrupt ups, downs, and interruptions.

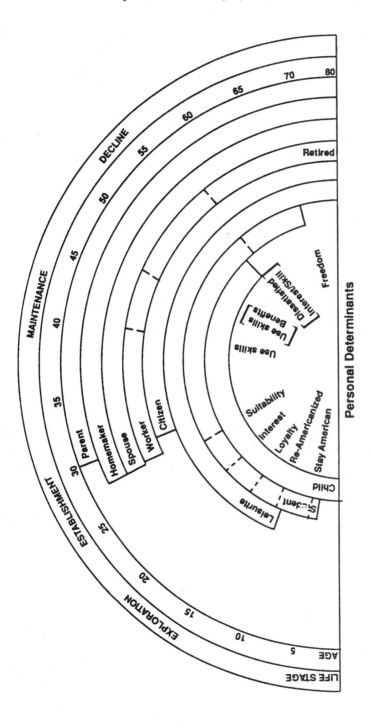

Figure 2-1. The life-career rainbow.

An Architectonic Concept of a Career

In seeking to depict the determinants of careers, an unexpected term and an unexpected structure have proved useful. The term is *architectonic,* which in one use refers to the system of forces which constitute a structure and which, in their interaction, maintain that structure while giving it shape and form (it is "unexpected" because it is arcane, rarely used, and not generally thus understood). The *structure* is inspired by the Norman door of the village church at Hauxton near Cambridge, England, elaborated in ways that are true to the style to show the complexity of the interacting determinants of a career, in this case the elements of a door in which each element (stone) is a determinant. Here some of the psychological and socioeconomic variables which shape a career are shown in more detail than in the Rainbow, and perhaps more importantly, they are shown in schematic position and sequence, as segments which constitute a whole. The stones of the arch are the determinants, and their positions in the arch show something of their interaction in producing the whole which is the arch, the career.

The basic determinants are both biological (personal to the individual and to his or her family and antecedents), and environmental (geographic in the comprehensive sense of that term). The old controversies as to the relative importance of "nature and nurture" now seem archaic and even ridiculous, given the importance of both from the beginning of life in the individual, and given the complexity of their interaction as the individual and his or her environment evolve and develop.

Figure 2-2 is a second attempt at this model, deliberately kept simple and therefore an oversimplification of what it seeks to represent. It makes some assumptions which may in due course be proved not only oversimplified, but even unwarranted. One example is the widely made postulate that needs have a physiological basis, as in the work of Maslow (1954) and Murray (1938). Another is that put forward by this writer several times (Super, 1949: 1973: Super and Bohn, 1971) and only recently made the subject of research (Claes & Coetsier, 1990; Dagley, Super & Lautenschlager, 1990 and in press; Tetreau, 1990). Often referred to as "the Onion Model," it proposes that just as the *biological basis* of personality may be viewed as a core surrounded by *needs* which are the internal result of interaction with the environment, *values* may be viewed as another, surrounding layer, with *interests* an outer layer of personality (the outer layer of the onion). Being more a product of interaction with society than are the inner layers, interests are the best predictors of what a person will study, what occupations he or she will enter, and how stable and satisfied he or she will be in the pursuit of a career in that occupation. And here, it should be noted, we have left the realm of speculative theory and preliminary research to deal with amply *tested* theory,

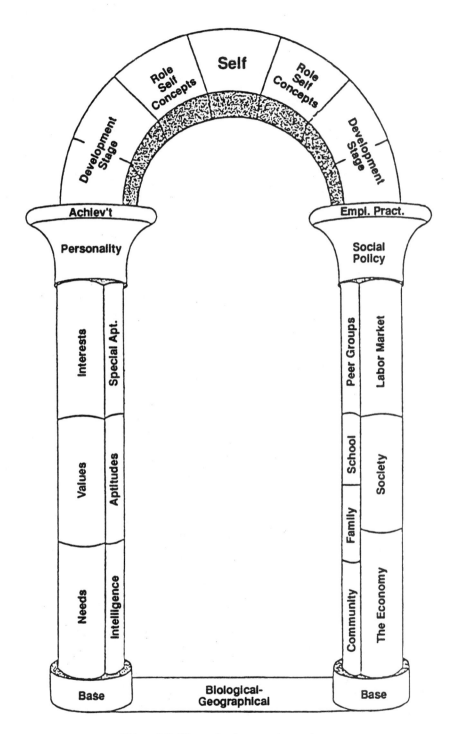

Figure 2-2. The arch of career determinants.

for interest inventories have consistently proved better occupational career predictors than have values (Anastasi, 1989; Super, 1949; Super and Crites, 1962).

The Arch shows the various types of *aptitudes* only schematically; like the personality columnar segments it does not make finer distinctions which we have long been able to make. The fact that some segments (stones) are narrower than others in the model is not meant to imply that they are less important: it is a function of the fact that some segmental flutes of the columns are partly hidden by others in the drawing. In the capital, to continue toward the top of the column, we see the term *personality* used in its more comprehensive sense, to include all that makes up a person psychologically. *Personality traits* and *attitudes*, however, have been deliberately omitted. Bloom's (1964) landmark review of stability and change showed that these are less stable than other human characteristics, and furthermore, it has generally been shown (Super and Crites, 1962) that while they influence *how* roles are played (style, manner, etc.) they are not important determinants of *what* roles are played. A complete model would include them, but this is a *schematic model* and hence simplified.

The other column and its fluted segments show some of the aspects of the environment that play parts in determining careers. Their sequence from base to capital is not intended to be definitive: for example, the family should surely be portrayed as a primary socializing agent, the school as secondary. But where to place the community is a graphic problem, at least, for while the family has a primary impact on the child (more so than the community), the community is more fundamental and helps to form both the family and the child (and although these last two do help to form the community, their individual impact is generally slight and not very evident). The capital on this side has as some of its major components social policy (e.g., protectionism, public health services) and employment practices (e.g., fair employment, training requirements).

In some versions of this Arch the interaction of person and society is shown by lines drawn with arrowheads at each end, from one column to the other: for example from values to family, from peer group to interests, etc. But again, the graphic representation of the model becomes cluttered by so many crisscrossing lines. Words and text are used here, to fill out the schema and to make it interactive.

The arch at the top of the model is conceptually, as it is architecturally, the final product of the two columns. In it, the (unportrayed) interactions of the person and the environment help to shape the arch, first in the Developmental Stages (childhood and adolescence unlabelled at the left, adulthood and old age at the right, to suggest progression through the life span—"span" is indeed an appropriate term here). The *Self* (the Person) and his or her Role Self-Concepts are the culminating products of the interaction of the person and of the environment: these are concepts of self as family member, as pupil and student, as athlete, as friend, as worker, etc. To write of "the self-concept" is in many ways erroneous and always confusing, for a person may see some personal qualities as highly relevant to some roles, irrelevant to others, and may esteem him/herself "self-efficacy" in some roles (e.g., athlete) but not in others (e.g., scholar).

Does One Theory Really Require Two Models?

It may, at first thought, appear to be the inadequacy or superfluity of a theory that proposes two models for the conceptualization of a career. But it can be argued that models that combine both the life-span/life-space constructs and the determinant/choice constructs are too complex adequately to convey the theories. House plans thus require three "models": floor plans, elevations, and sketches, leading in some instances to three-dimensional cardboard models. The model proposed by Vondracek and associates (1986, p. 79), although serving them in their own research, seems in its complexity to discourage rather than to stimulate research—the passage of five or ten more years will tell. Holland's hexagon (1985, p. 29; Weinrach and Srebalus, 1990, p. 43), at the other extreme, is a simple matching model easily used to generate hypotheses that are easily tested.

Simplicity in the exposition of a theory may thus be facilitated by the use of two or more, rather than just one, models, each focusing on different aspects. In this instance the *life-span/life-space model* (*the Rainbow*) and the *determinant/ choice model* (*the Arch*) may suffice, but one must still draw on existing decision-making models to supplement them . . . a deliberate omission here.

One may still ask, which of the two (or three) models is central to a theory of career development? It is the Rainbow Model, for it portrays development. Both professionals and the laity are accustomed to thinking in terms of choices: at the beginning of the century that is now about to end, Frank Parsons (1909) laid the foundations for such thinking in his book, *Choosing a Vocation*. The writer's volume, *The Psychology of Careers*, introduced the life-span perspective, drawing on developmental psychology, and spelled out what he then considered to be the main characteristics of each life stage (Super, 1957, Ch. 5–11).

Career decision making has now established its place, as evidenced by the book by that title edited by Walsh and Osipow (1988). In a monograph prepared as the basis for a longitudinal study of career development (Super, Crites, Hummel, Moser, Overstreet, and Warnath, 1957) career stages were described in tabular format; they have been slightly modified from time to time, as new data and new insights have been developed. These stages appear here in a current, updated version.

The Stages of an Occupational Career

1. **Growth** (Birth until pubescence at about age 12–14)

   Occupations, vocations, are not a central or even conscious issue during most of childhood. But curiosity, now generally seen as an instinct thanks to studies of infants and animals (Berlyne, 1960), leads children to explore the world around them in-so-far as they have access to it, physically and psy hologically. In exploration they acquire information in encounters with their environments, and especially through contacts with key adult figures who may become role models. In this experiential learning theory they develop concepts of themselves in adult roles, concepts of autonomy and its limits, self-esteem or self-denigration, perspective on the future or lack of such, feelings of being able to plan or of helplessness in a world dominated by others. With a sense of autonomy, self-esteem, and of the future, supplemented by interests developed through satisfying experiences, they become forward planners. Lacking these, they tend to become conformists, drifters, flounderers, psychological and social aliens. Fantasy helps in the development of interests, while experience and feedback bring awareness of capacities; this helps, along with the opportunity structure, of which awareness tends to come later, to temper interests and to make them more realistic.

2. **Exploration** (Adolescence, age about 14–25)

   During this stage exploration continues, not always consciously or systematically: in fact, systematic exploration is generally lacking except as provided by the school, scouts, or other organization. Social exploration is more spontaneous and parent or peer-stimulated, and occupational career exploration sometimes rides on that. Part-time and summer work help out. At first career or occupational exploration is likely to be very open and tentative, later becoming more focused. But sometimes exploration is so highly focused that it precludes consideration of alternatives, as when a son or daughter pursues from childhood or early youth an occupational objective inspired or set by a parent or other adult. Such early foreclosure sometimes leads to later dissatisfaction, with frustration or change of occupation (generally called "career crisis" and "career change," a misuse when "occupation" or even "job" is intended, for each person has just one "career," one life, and not every change-evoking event is a crisis: "change of career direction," or of "career role," would be correct usage rather than making words that have different specific meanings all have the same multiple meanings). Exploration sometimes ceases before the mid-twenties, but when it does it is likely to be followed by further exploring at greater depth or even greater breadth, as when the historian who starts out as a Medievalist becomes interested in the Renaissance, or a physiologist finds special challenge in nutrition and disease. And exploration sometimes continues beyond the mid-twenties, as when flounderers become interested in a field into which they have opportunistically moved and at age 29 decide to look into the possibility of so equipping themselves (by planned sequential work experience, further education, or savings and the acquisition of capital) that they can stabilize, consolidate, and advance in that field.

3. **Establishment** (Early adulthood, about 25 to 45)

    Not everyone stabilizes, for some people pursue (especially the disadvantaged but also the numerous "reasonable adventurers" and flounderers), often without consciously doing so, lives of changing jobs and occupations, changes of both field and level of employment. American sociologists documented this more than 50 years ago (Davidson and Anderson, 1937), and again a few years later (Miller and Form, 1949). There is, however, some consistency in even this seemingly random movement when it is viewed in terms of socioeconomic status, for the children of the better-educated parents, employed at higher occupational levels, tend to get more education and to pursue (even if erratically) occupations at higher levels than do those of less well-educated parents. These last tend to find employment largely at the lower occupational levels (Miller and Form, 741 ff). These classical studies have since been confirmed by many studies such as those by Sewell and associates (e.g., 1975). But the classical notion of process, with a sequence of trial in the late 1920s and of stabilization in the 1930s and early 1940s, seems still to be supported despite the current focus on transitions as in Fiske and associates (1975, 1990) and Levinson and associates (1978). This focus on transitions has been strengthened by the attention given to women's careers during the past score of years, in which the prior neglect of that group (Super, 1957, pp. 76–79) has been replaced by numerous studies and popular writings. If attempts to stabilize are successful, a period of consolidation and perhaps advancement is likely to follow; if not, frustration may lead to stagnation or to change. Many of the least economically-favored "stabilize" in careers of frequent job changes at the lowest skill levels or even of unemployment. Economic depressions, wars, periods of expansion, technological change, and changes in social policy have real impact on the efforts of the individual, as portrayed in the Arch (Fig. 2-2), and as discussed in many works over the last half century (McDaniels, 1989; Miller and Form, 1949; Peters, 1987; Sewell and Hauser, 1975; Stern and Eichorn, 1989; Super, 1942, 1957). The recession/depression of the 1990s is already having a familiar, but magnified, effect on the occupational stability and careers even of the better-educated and seemingly better-established segments of the population. Stage theory is being modified, some say radically changed or even replaced (Arthur in Ch. 3) by the rapid pace of economic, social, and technological change. On a positive note, for those who value and achieve stability and for those who thrive on change, these are still the "best years of our lives."

4. **Maintenance** (Middle age, about 45 to 65)
   For those who stabilize in early adulthood, the focus now is generally on preserving the place one has made in the world of work, on holding one's own despite its changes and despite the competition of younger men and women whose training may be better attuned to emergent needs and whose eagerness to establish themselves may constitute a threat to those who would like to rest on their oars as they get older. Some, disillusioned by failure to advance in a world in which "getting ahead" is generally confused with material success, stagnate and become embittered. They "mark time," go through the routines of their paperwork, operate their machines, but avoid learning opportunities. This is merely "occupying a chair" to put it in academic terms, but occupying it passively rather than actively developing new knowledge or putting new knowledge and methods to work. Thus a recent revision of a 1972 text on the social psychology of work is described by a reviewer as "looking backwards in its research in a more stable era, not forward . . . " (Rouseau, 1991). But many in this career state make a point of keeping up to date, greatly helped by the current emphasis on continuing education. And some, not content with merely keeping up, handle their careers as though they were still in the establishment stage, breaking new ground. These are the innovators, as contrasted with the updaters and the stagnaters. The futurists put the emphasis on innovative, "chaotic" careers (e.g., Arthur, Ch. 3; Peters, 1987).

5. **Decline** (Old age, from sometime in the mid 1960s on)
   It is a commonplace that as people get older their physical and mental powers decline, but as this happens many come to dislike this term and its negative implications for themselves. Less negative terms such as "disengagement" are sought. But decline actually starts by age 25, when athletes no longer run the 100 meters as fast as they did at 19, and continues as tennis players lose speed and power, changing to planning and placing, in their thirties. Sensing their decline, older people **decelerate**, then perhaps begin to selectively to **disengage**. Just how and when depends upon their occupations and circumstances: the professor may request a lighter load, the physician take fewer patients or start referring those who provide less satisfaction as patients to other practitioners, the business executive may become a free-lance consultant, and the garage mechanic may set up a small shop in his own garage to serve only a few friends and neighbors. Some who have a choice specialize more, profes-

sors teaching only the advanced seminars that they love, physicians giving up obstetrics but keeping a gynecology practice, executives who are not ready to move perhaps finding ways to limit travel or obtaining assistants to break-in for relief, mechanics becoming shop supervisors rather than working on the repair line. At some point, if the worker lives long enough, he or she may actually retire at age 70, 75, 80, 85, or even 90. Some say, "if you like the work, and people are willing to have you do it, why stop just because of the calendar?" Death may well come before retirement. It observes no general calendar, but the average age of death keeps advancing. A generation ago most counselors and psychologists shrank from the idea of death. They were not interested in working with the dying or bereaved, leaving that to the clergy as they left planning for retirement to insurance agents. But the helping professions have matured, they are better staffed, and the needs and the profitability of retirement counseling are now recognized. When the writer's *Adult Career Concerns Inventory* (Super et al., 1986), a "first," was announced by its publisher, there were many eager enquiries and users. Retirement can be sad indeed, and so it is for many; but for many others it is most comparable to graduating from college or completing an advanced degree, for it can mean facing a world of new opportunity, the gratification of being wanted in more than one place, and the excitement of exploring, choosing, and getting established again.

This, then, is occupational career development theory as conceived by this writer and accepted by many (e.g., Hackett, Lent & Greenhaus, 1991). It is important, now, (1) to see what current critics and synthesizers of career development research and theory think of it, and (2) to examine some of the major current studies that bear on the subject, whether directly or tangentially . . .

How the Critics and Synthesizers See this Approach

Two books have stood out for some time as covering the fields of career choice and development. The first is authored by Osipow (1988), and the latter is edited by Brown and Brooks (1990) with chapters by major contributors to theory and practice. It is upon these two that this section relies.

After reviewing the various theories nearly ten years ago Osipow (1983, p. 307–310) concludes that this writer's ("Super's") theory has stood the tests of research, criticism and the marketplace. Holland's methods are more widely used, but his are methods of "Making Vocational Choices" (Holland, 1985) and a theory supporting them, not a theory or methods of career development over the life span or any major segment thereof. The theory expounded in this chapter is in Osipow's words, "As a conceptual model . . . the most highly developed and advanced ... in its explicitness, its fairly high degree of empirical support, and its number of applications to human affairs."

Brown & Brooks, after thoughtful reviews and critiques, and with cautions and *caveats,* arrive at the following conclusions (1990, pp. 356 and 362): "The current status of Super's theory of career development is obvious: it occupies stage center, along with Holland's thinking. There seems to be no reasonable doubt that it will continue to be of considerable importance ... However, the lack of integration of the various aspects of the theory is worrisome for those who wish to see parsimonious models ... However, of all available theories, Super's holds the greatest promise of providing an explanation of the birth to death processes involved in career development." Brown continues (p. 362): "Super's ideas stand alone as the developmental influence on career development practice and research ... For Super's theory to continue to be viable, he must integrate his segments, which means selecting some central construct and using that as a focal point for reformulating his ideas. Since his idea of a self-concept seems to be the most basic of his constructs, it would appear to be the logical point of departure."

In the *Journal of Vocational Behavior's* "Advances in Vocational Theory and Research: A 20-Year Retrospective" (Hackett, Lent & Greenhaus, 1991), the following evaluation of the writer's work on career development appears (p. 6):

> of the career theories prominent in 1971, Super's theory was viewed as the most technically adequate, comprehensive, and advanced (Osipow, 1963, 1973), and Super was regarded as the single most influential person in the field (Holland, 1969) ... In particular, the theory sparked research on vocational maturity, career exploration, and self concept implementation, and the findings were generally supportive of Super's theory (Osipow, 1973) ... The major weaknesses of the theory ... were its lack of attention to economic and social factors.

The review and evaluation later turns its attention to subsequent developments, from 1971 to 1991. It states (p. 8):

> Developmental models, particularly Super's theory, have profoundly influenced vocational terminology (e.g., career maturity) and thinking about career behavior. Despite the continuing tendency of career researchers to study career choices as static events, on a conceptual level there is a general acknowledgement of career development as a dynamic process. This shift in thinking began to take hold prior to 1971, and seems to have been firmly established by that time.
>
> Super's concepts of career stages, vocational identity, career maturity, developmental tasks, and career patterns have stimulated a wide range of research during the past two decades. Unfortunately, however, empirical study of these

developmentally related concepts has often been conducted outside the framework of Super's theory per se . . .

A major expansion of Super's theory involved elaboration of the "Life Career Rainbow" (Super, 1980), a model representing the overlap of roles the individual adopts, the importance of those roles, at different points in the life cycle. The concept of role salience, represented an important addition to Super's theory (Brown, 1990) and assessment instruments were constructed to measure role salience and values (Nevil & Super, 1986, 1988), enhancing the theory's accessibility to counselors.

And, the writer would add, to researchers.

This writer agrees that self-concepts are still, as in 1955 (Super, 1955 & 1990) and in a more elaborated statement (Super et al., 1963), fundamental and central. As the Arch of Determinants and Choice (Fig. 2-2) shows, they are highlighted again and more clearly in current writings. Career development theory certainly developed very slowly, in this writer's work, from 1942, to 1951 and 1957, to 1963, to 1980. The life span does not lend itself to brevity and its research is time consuming. In this writer's opinion, although "parsimony" may be an important criterion for judging the adequacy of theories in some domains, it can hardly apply in the standard way to a phenomenon that evolves over the years and that has many personal and social determinants. It is more important, in theorizing, to attend to that about which the theorizing is being done than it is to attend to extraneous criteria that have been developed for other theoretical domains.

What Recent Development Theory and Research Contribute

One of the landmark researches bearing on career development in the 1980s is the AT&T study of managers seen in assessment centers from the 1950s to about 1977, a span of 20 years (Howard & Bray, 1988). This sample was all male, a mix of college graduates and nongraduates. A later sample was studied, also repeatedly and longitudinally, from the late 1970s until 1982: reflecting the changing times, it included both men and women and had a higher average level of education.

Despite the fact that the early sample was studied periodically in the assessment centers, and thus constituted a longitudinal study, this was not a traditional developmental study. The focus was on advancement in a structured setting that has now changed, and the criterion was step-on-the-managerial-ladder, a six-point scale in which steps 4, 5, and 6 were combined in most analyses (there were of course fewer subjects near the top of the pyramidal ladder). The analyses consist of relationships between potential determinants (predictor variables) and management level (the criterion). Some of these data are discussed in the next major section, on determinants of choice and success. But some light is thrown, indirectly, on stage theory and is reflected here. The men who, in the 20-year period, advanced furthest, tended not to have moved up on one single career ladder. Movement between departments was common, as was geographic change: cross-training was being recognized (belatedly, after years of advancement up a single specialty line) as desirable in managers. Lateral movement was closely related with vertical movement, as a number of brief case histories illustrate. It is noteworthy that the noncollege men, although tending not to have advanced as far or as fast as the college men, showed better decision making, leadership skills, and tolerance of uncertainty; they were also less dependent on the approval of superiors and peers. They were better satisfied with their work and careers. It seems that the noncollege men may have been held back despite their greater practical abilities, by the lack of a college degree and perhaps by their lower rated and tested mental ability. Over the years, the emerging differences in experience magnified the differences between the more and the less "successful": "the rich got richer and the poor got poorer."

Perhaps it is just as well that Howard and Bray did not attempt to analyze their data in terms of stage theory, for their subjects were employed in *one* corporation, in *one* general type of work: utilities management. Careers were thus highly structured in advance by the immediate environment, as are those of men and women in a mining or in a mill town. The only real questions are how far and how fast they run the course! The focus was thus appropriately on career *determinants, not on choice,* certainly *not on stages.* The nearest thing to stages were length-of-time on a rung of the ladder or of an adjacent ladder (a better simile would be pyramidal lattices, a set of adjacent truncated-cone shaped ladders).

A second study is that of Fiske and Chiriboga (1990). Its setting structure creates a stage-theory project, even though it is not construed in such terms. The subjects were chosen as belonging to one of four categories: high-school seniors about to graduate and enter the labor force, newlyweds who might be expected soon to start a young family, parents of high school seniors who might be expected to face empty nests in the near future, and couples facing retirement. All were residents of one West Coast, blue-collar community, interviewed first in 1968–69, again in 1970–71, a third time in 1974, a fourth in 1977, a fifth and final time in 1980. Starting with a sample of 216 men and women, the number had shrunk to 168 (78%) by the end of the study—a remarkable retention rate given the mobility of the 1970s and the socioeconomic level of the subjects. In some ways the sample thus resembles that of the writer's Career Pattern Study, conducted in a predominantly blue-collar city, but longitudinally with one junior high school class followed with about the same retention rate until they were about 25 years old in the middle 1960s (Jordaan & Heyde, 1979; Super & Overstreet, 1960) and again at age 36 (not yet reported).

The characterizations of each of the four "stage" (developmental task) groups are worth summarizing here. *The high school seniors* tended to be timid, restless, dissatisfied, unhappier than the older cohorts. The boys' goals were primarily to get good jobs and have plenty of freedom to do other things, but they were quite unsure of attaining them. The girls were not interested in occupations, but sought fulfillment in a way of life that would be uniquely their own. Like the boys, they were quite vague as to how to go about it.

The *newlyweds* were selected to provide first-marrieds, as-yet-childless. They ranged in age from 20 to 38 at first contact. These men and women had much more in common than did the high school seniors and they shared a complex life style with many activities, "as though to make the most of the preparenthood phase." Some of the men were still community college students, working part-time. Most men and women worked, some of the women paying part of their husband's college expenses. Both sexes were emotionally involved with each other, responsive, understanding, and "enjoying each other." They still saw the husband as the rightful head of the family, but the authors note that this view soon changed. The newlyweds had more friends and saw more of them than did any other sample in the study. The picture is very much that of young marrieds developing common interests while establishing their new homes and new life styles.

The empty-nesters were seen by the researchers as quite the opposites of the newlyweds, with the men concerned primarily with money and with security for retirement, the women feeling housebound, but yet more concerned than their men with the society around them. The marriages were not generally happy, although there was a good deal of "making allowances."

The preretirees averaged about ten years older than the middle-aged empty-nesters. They tended to worry about retirement: full-time homemakers without children at home thought they might have to give up their well-established social life with women friends, or feared that retired husbands would become stay-at-homes and interfere with their household ways. Many were afraid of increasing interpersonal conflict in the confines of the home. The men tended to view their marriages as more egalitarian than did the males of any other group, but the women tended to see them as either male- or female-dominated. This older group was closer to their parents than were others, and they had more and richer friendships. They were as future-oriented as younger people and less concerned with the past. They tended to be more humanitarian and less materialistic. The researchers note that "the glow dims" as the group gets older, very much so for a few, moderately for most. This seems altogether to be expected, given increasing infirmities, the loss of friends and family through death or moving away, and, often, declining income with retirement and higher living costs.

Although stage theory has often been criticized as being middle and upper-middle-class-oriented, the data from this carefully conducted blue-collar study do tend to support a theory of life stages, at least in life-in-general and in the home and family, if not in work. But these different roles or aspects of life, we know, are interactive, and despite the lack of occupational career data in this study, its findings may be taken as relevant to occupational careers. It is a loss to the field, however, that no note seems to have been taken of the importance of occupation: and paid work, or of life-stage theorist-researchers who did, such as Buehler (1933), Erikson (1959), Levinson (1978), or Super (1942, 1957, 1980, 1990). It is worth noting, in this connection, that Brooks (in Brown & Brooks, 1990), writing about life span/life role approaches, refers to "a frequent complaint about career development theory . . . that it neglects adult development and the interaction of one's career with one's other important life roles." Brooks responds to these criticisms briefly but cogently, as follows:

"Sonnenfeld and Kotter (1982) note in their critique of career development theory that a recent emerging perspective is that of the life as a cycle. According to these authors, the life-cycle approach, sparked by the life-stage approach of Gould (1972), Levinson (1978), Sheehy (1974), and Vaillant (1977) includes factors associated with work, family and the individual." Brooks goes on to describe their "two-dimensional model (that) includes time, on the horizontal axis (from birth on), and life space, on the vertical axis (non-work/family space, individual personal space, and work occupational space)."

This is, of course, what this writer did in proposing his "Rainbow Model" of the life span and life space (Super, 1980), using it again here and in several other publications. The same comprehensive approach characterized some earlier work (Buehler, 1933; Super, 1942, 1957), but without the graphic model. The more recent writers deserve special credit for making life span, life space, theory more widely known outside of career counseling circles.

Two more relevant sources need citation in this context. One of these focuses on women's careers (Betz & Fitgerald, 1987), the other deals with both men and women in the province of Quebec (Riverin-Simard, 1988 English edition).

Betz and Fitzgerald (1987), like many writers, focus more on the determinants of career than on life stages, no doubt because this is what counselors and personnel workers need to be concerned with: the determinants help understand immediate aspects of the unfolding of the career and how to guide it. But they do refer, briefly, to work on career patterns, a topic closely related to that of stages. Here they cite this writer's (Super, 1957) early hypothesizing about women's career patterns, at a time when little attention had been paid to them. The patterns outlined were therefore frankly based on data on men, modified by observation in counseling and in everyday life. Since then others have carried out empirical studies testing this model. Not cited is a supporting study by Mulvey (1963); one which Betz and Fitzgerald do cite is by Vetter (1973), using a national cross-sectional sample. Vetter found 22 percent in Super's stable homemaking (no employment) category, 27 percent conventional (employment until marriage) homemaking, 3 percent stable working, 14 percent double-track (homemaking and working during the same period of time). 16 percent interrupted (homemaking, working, etc.), 18 percent unstable (unstable job history). Harmon (1967) did a classification of her own in a 25-year follow-up of University of Minnesota students, using five categories of career patterns, and Zytowski (1969) also pioneered, rather differently, finding a "mild" occupational pattern (early or late entry with brief, low-degree participation, with an "unusual" career pattern of early-entry, lengthy or uninterrupted work span with a high degree of participation (it must be noted here that these samples were all from before 1975). Betz and Fitzgerald (pp. 21–24) cite more studies: one by Ellen Betz is up-to-date and thus of most importance. Nancy Betz and Fitzgerald (1987, p. 24) summarize its findings thus:

" . . . (the) study makes it clear that the pattern of high commitment of a pioneer occupation is no longer unusual (in women college graduates), since it was followed by 23.5% of the sample. More unusual, rather, was the never-worked pattern, followed by only 1.4% of the sample. Betz' addition of the low-commitment-pioneer and moderate-commitment pioneer categories proved useful, accounting for a 5% share of the sample, who would have been unclassifiable under previous schemes." To round out the picture, it should be added that 12.4 percent were classified as low-commitment to a traditional occupation, 21.7 percent moderate-commitment traditionals, and 35.9 percent high-commitment traditionals. Current data of the same type would be most useful.

And what do these patterns suggest about life stage, career stage, theory in women and in men? In women there is clearly a stage-structure caused, if by nothing else, by childbearing and childrearing, as shown by Vetter's 65 percent or 79 percent whose patterns strongly imply periods devoted at least in part to childrearing. However, the focus on traditional vs. pioneering and or degree of commitment in the more recent studies makes it impossible to draw any stage-theory conclusions from them, valuable though they are for other purposes.

The remaining independent study of careers is that of Riverin-Simard (1988), an empirical study of 786 employed adults in Quebec Province in 1981–82, a group drawn randomly from lists provided by (1) private companies such as banks, clinics, architects, soft-drink distributors, ship-yards, insurance companies, and a yacht club; (2) public agencies such as the ministries of social affairs, agriculture, education and energy; (3) the para-public sector including the universities, council of universities, the several hospitals, and the industrial development society of Quebec.

Riverin-Simard's data are organized according to both age, career concerns, and developmental tasks. Her stages are named in poetic rather than in scientific terms, as follows:

Age 23–27:   Landing on the Planet Work, characterized by self-questioning resulting from the cultural shock transition from education and youth to work and adulthood.

Age 28–32:   Seeking a Promising Path, giving more emphasis to abilities and learning the roles and mores of the world of work. Further education comes to be viewed as the means of attaining career goals.

Age 33–37:   Running the Occupational Race, in which men and women of all social levels discover that there is an obligation to move ahead at an accelerated pace and to overcome obstacles without delay (this appears to be a social class/occupational level concern, noticed in the Career Pattern Study's blue-collar group at about age 25). The focus in Quebec was found to be more on the present than on the future, with a feeling that success comes now or never.

Age 38–42:   Testing New Guidelines, in which age is viewed as a negative, in some, for whom there is a tendency to expect to decline while others react more adaptively and rethink their roles. Still others are more optimistic and become proactive, taking even more control over their careers and refusing to stagnate. The researcher calls them "exceptional explorers," or "reasonable adventurers."

Age 43–47:   Searching for the Guiding Thread in One's Life History, a period of career stock-taking, examining old goals, actions and progress made, and reviewing future objectives. Much importance is attached to the past; age and circumstances are seen as barriers to goal-attainment; but some expect new bursts of energy and new progress towards their goals.

Age 48–52:   Considering Modifying Trajectories, a phenomenon observed in people with histories of job change and in others afraid of decadence or eager to keep on growing. This is a period when people are aware of both their youth and of their maturity and wish to capitalize on both.

Age 53–57:   Seeking a Promising Exit, a period of wanting to be able to leave work in a dignified, self-respecting and other-respected way, and to prepare for and assure a good retirement. It is for many a period of existential thinking. Some seek to perpetuate themselves by developing teams who will carry on themselves. But some feel desperate in their negative self-evaluations. About 15 percent in this study are called "Exceptional Finalists" in that they make plans for later work or leisure-work (serious avocations), thus assuring self-fulfillment and public esteem by continuing to have a visible, valued role.

Age 58–62:   Moving into a New Gravitational Field is a period of reflections on one's career and of desire to share them with others. There is a recognition of the limit imposed on oneself by the biological changes that come with age, and a need to cope with one's own feelings about the attitudes of others towards older people. At the same time the anticipation of a major drop in income at the time of retirement is often a cause of concern. Both men and women are aware that this is a time of questioning and reorganization. The world of work begins to recede in the mind of the prospective retiree as he or she looks forward to living in another world, even if in full view of the world of work. Some people feel worn out, others feel more self-actualized and more secure. There are some special people in this stage, people whom Riverin-Simard calls "Exceptional Astronauts" because of the way in which they handle their movement from one world to another.

Age 63–67:   Grappling with the Vocational Attraction of Retirement, involves finding time to reflect, coping with changing physical capacities, planning for retirement, and in some, coping with what may be less suitable job assignments. Some people resist or even deny the coming of retirement, causing greater transition problems when the time comes. Others, a small majority, feel that they are about to achieve a new type of independence, one which will give them even more opportunity than they have had in the past. For some, retirement is simply an occasion, an opportunity, to change activities. This writer liked, and still (some years later) likes to compare retirement with getting one's highest degree and facing a number of challenging occupational choices on entering or reentering the world of work.

Riverin-Simard devotes two pages to the following generalizations:

1. Adults of all ages tend to alternate between periods of exploring and of establishment. Such periods are essential to career development.
2. Vocational development is multidirectional and multirhythmic, the rhythms being irregular.
3. Each period of life lasts about five years, and each has some specific vocational experiences.
4. Age plays a preponderant though not itself causal role in vocational development: the passage of time is not the same as age, and it too is important.
5. The content of each life stage or substage is linked both to the passing of time and to the context in which the individual lives and works.
6. Depending on the life stage, people tend to focus on either the goals of their working lives or on the means of attaining them.

In leaving this challenging and stylistically unorthodox work, it seems necessary to elaborate on the "multidirectional character of development," which "implies above all that no period of the working life is superior or inferior to another" (p. 163). This is stated despite elsewhere identifying one period as the "golden years"; it further "signifies that the sequences of periods of working life are not hierarchical" (meaning that the later periods do not necessarily depend upon what happens in the earlier). "This differs from what has been previously indicated by Kohlberg (1973) and Piaget (1972)." And, one might add, Havighurst (1953). "Contrary to the majority of developmental theories conceived in terms of stages, the results of the three-year research study indicate that it is not necessary to have succeeded sufficiently in one vocational phase to move on to the next" (pp. 163–64). This writer questions whether the type of data analysis carried out warrants such a conclusion: furthermore, it was not a specific research question.

One further source of evidence on life stages is to be found in research carried on by a number of psychologists, sociologists, and management specialists with the writer's Adult Career Concerns Inventory (Super, Thompson & Lindeman, 1986, Manual 1988).

The Adult Career Concerns Inventory (ACCI) was developed as part of the longitudinal Career Pattern Study (Super et al., 1957) for use with the CPS subjects when they were about 36 years old. A doctoral dissertation (Zelkowitz, 1974) planned as part of the CPS developed the first form of the ACCI, which underwent several revisions in the thesis and later work by the authors. Based on career stage theory and made up of developmental task items, data on it may be considered to throw light on the validity of the theory.

A series of studies of the concurrent and predictive validity of the ACCI have been done by Slocum, Cron, and colleagues at the School of Business of Southern Methodist University, throwing light on life-stage theory. In one study Slocum and Cron (1985) had data from 636 salespersons in seven companies, using an early form of the inventory. Subjects whose age placed them in the Trial substage of Exploration had been employed for a shorter period, were more willing to move and less involved in their jobs than were those whose age placed them in the Maintenance Stage, but were as involved as those chronologically in the Establishment Stage. The chronologically Early Exploration (Trial) Stage group showed more concern with the ACCI tasks of Crystallization, Specification, and Implementation (substages of Exploration) and with Establishment than did others. Those whose age placed them in the Maintenance Stage were most concerned with holding their own, updating, and innovating, three ways in which stage theory postulates that people cope with maintaining their places in the world of work. While these findings may be viewed (as in the ACCI Manual) as evidence of instrument validity, they are at the same time evidence of the validity of stage theory which the ACCI seeks to embody or implement.

In an intensive study of small samples (25 and 30) of adult evening-class students, Cross (1981) found that his 25 "explorers" (identified by that ACCI scale) were in fact engaged in recycling, in contrast with his 30 nonexplorers who were more concerned with establishment.

A study by Costello (1981) of a sample of 1095 evening students in a large urban university, mostly employed, found that many were recycling through the Exploration Stage during the ages of 40–49 and 55–64, while in the 20–24 year-old group both Exploration and Establishment were appropriately major concerns. But, contrary to theory, many in the 25–44 year old group were more concerned with Maintenance than with Establishment tasks— "prematurely" according to theory. Many in the 45–64 group were more concerned with retirement ("Disengagement," etc.) than with Maintenance. Are night-class university students perhaps a special segment of their age group, more inclined to look ahead and thus to be more concerned with the next stage than with the present?

Sex differences have been looked at in at least two studies (Herr et al.,

1983) and Phillips (1982). The former had data from a follow-up study of 980 high-school students from six to eight years after graduation, the latter from 133 professionals; taking continuing education courses. Neither study found any sex differences. It is interesting that this conceptualization of career life-stage theory thus appears to apply equally well to both men and women, but this may, again, be due to the nature of the samples, which do not include women who are temporarily out of the labor market for childrearing or related health problems.

The nature of the career path being followed appears also to affect life stage when viewed chronologically, for Herr et al. (1983) found that young adults (aged about 24–28) who had pursued academic as contrasted with vocational courses were more concerned with Exploration than with Establishment, whereas there was no such difference in the former vocational students. It thus appears that those who are less immediately occupationally-oriented, who have longer time perspectives, who are more willing to postpone the gratification of immediate income, and who aspire to late-entry, less visible, occupations, take, perhaps need, longer periods of exploration. What is not very visible in high school may take longer to find than does that which is highly visible!

Using data collected at AT&T's New York headquarters by Peter Cairo of Teachers College, Columbia University, the current ACCI form was used by Mahoney (1986) with 393 employees of whom 64 percent were women and 36 percent men. They ranged in age from 18 to 65, largely in the 25–44 year-old group; 64 percent were managerial, 7 percent technical, and 32 percent clerical (this group largely female).

Stage concerns were examined in terms of both substage (developmental tasks) and of stage (coarser groupings of tasks). Half of the subjects were "accurately" placed, somewhat better than chance or one in three. As theory postulates, the developmental tasks that people face *are* thus somewhat related to age, but they *are not* limited to any one age group: people mature at different rates, and they recycle, facing earlier types of tasks as their interests, their jobs, their environments, and their health change and they again explore and seek to establish themselves in other fields or locations. Exploration is part of coping with transitions.

Other evidence from the ACCI, a career-stage, developmental task instrument, could be cited. The Cron & Slocum (1986) Southern Methodist University group, Ralph (1986 and since) at the University of South Alabama's School of Nursing, and others have produced other studies, and new research by others continues to appear. But one may now conclude that the evidence in support of career stage (developmental task) theory described here is clear and convincing. The theory will no doubt be refined and modified in the light of accruing knowledge, but as it stands it has been proved usable.

However, current rapid changes in the world of work, described elsewhere in this book, may modify the theory. Time will tell.

The Determinants of Occupational Choice and Success

There have, as elsewhere, been "fads, fashions, and folderol" in personnel psychology and career development. A focus on aptitudes resulted from the early wartime successes in measuring verbal, numerical, spatial, and mechanical aptitudes: a familiar World War I story. Attention then moved to interests, attitudes, personality, with great progress especially in interest measurement (e.g., Strong 1943). Freudian and neo-Freudian theory also had an impact in instrument-development based on the work of Murray (1983) and of others who turned projective into inventory methods (Edwards, 1954).

The Second Fall from Favor and Second Rise

But then came the new reaction, as it was realized that matching was not enough; useful in the short run even though imperfect, its imperfections became clearer as time passed. People change with time and experience, so do economic conditions, industry, and occupations: careers emerge. Rogerian nondirectivism and new-Freudian "dynamic" psychology also were gnawing at the foundations of testing. And so, in the 1950s, the time became ripe for what is now beginning, in some circles to be called "career psychology," one aspect of life-span developmental psychology, as described at the beginning of this chapter.

This approach to vocational guidance and to employee development (Super, 1983) is used in many college and university counseling centers. Holland (1985) modified his static matching approach based on interests to make it one of successive approximations as individuals seek more suitable work, thus helping to merge his theory and methods with those of the developmentalists. With a focus limited to advancement in one corporation, developmental matching has been widely applied and much heralded in business and industry (e.g., Howard & Bray, 1988). The corporate focus has been largely on men and women in the higher-level occupations, in people in whom the company makes a substantial investment over a period of time. In educational institutions it is found largely in colleges and universities, in which students make a great investment in themselves and the institution responds with more time-consuming and elaborate assessment and counseling methods. Some scholars (e.g., Fiske & Chiriboga, 1990) have, independently of corporate interest, begun to study blue-collar workers and their labor-force-bound children.

In these studies of personal and social determinants, it should be noted, the focus has *not* been on *life stages,* even when it is on careers over the working life span: it has been, rather, on the *determinants* themselves. This has been true even when, as in the work of Fiske and Chiriboga (1990), subjects have been studied in relation to their life stage.

The AT&T study (Howard & Bray, 1988) is a mine of information, one that should be carefully read by personnel and career development specialists working in or with business and industrial organizations of any size. Having data accumulated over a period of 20 years on one sample studied from the 1950s on, and from another sample studied from 1977 on, Howard, with ample AT&T support, carried out a detailed and inspired analysis of a gargantuan mass of data.

Success was defined as the level of management attained over the years; it was therefore in one sense a behavioral measure, although the objective fact of climbing the ladder is, of course, to a considerable extent, dependent on the opinions of higher-level managers: it is thus partly subjective.

Table 2-1. Success† Correlations of Dimension Factors c. 1955 and c. 1975.

Dimension Factor	n = 137	n = 129	n = 266
Administrative Skills	.15	.39**	.19**
Interpersonal Skills	.13	.33**	.22**
Intellectual Ability	.14	.22**	.25**
Advancement Motivation	.22**	.30**	.28**
Work Involvement	.19*	.21*	.15*
Stability of Performance	.13	.13	.12
Independence	.18*	.05	.00
Md.	.15	.22**	.19**

*p .05   **p .005
†"Success" is measured by managerial level attained.

The predictors were converted into dimension factors, condensing the data even further on the basis of their intercorrelations (Table 2-1). Here the correlations in the college sample ranged from .13 to .22 in the non-college from .05 to .39; the medians were respectively .14 and .22, not bad for long-term predictions which perforce do not include intervening variables. In the college sample, the motivational and personality factors had rather more validity than did the cognitive, natural enough given the intellectually selective function of college; in the noncollege group, they appear to be about equally important, as shown in Table 2-1 (Howard & Bray, 1988, Table 3.10, p. 76).

From this landmark study of managerial personnel in a large corporation there is ample evidence that abilities and personality have both short-term and long-term bearing on success and satisfaction in work. But these are, one may object, all higher-level personnel and one may well ask, what of the lower levels on the occupational scale? Two classical studies, the work of Paterson and associates (Paterson and Darley, 1936) and the massive Air Force projects (Flanagan, 1947) have amply demonstrated that what holds for middle and high level personnel is true also of those at lower levels.

Conclusions

One point that should emerge clearly in the material which constitutes the bulk of this chapter is that the question of "which is better, Career Development Theory or Trait-and-Factor (Matching) Theory?" is not a meaningful or a valid question. Neither theory is sufficient without the other. Thus the AT&T study (Howard & Bray, 1988) acquires more meaning if one considers both its longitudinal aspects (advancement) and its cross-sectional aspects (what determines advancement). And we have seen that even these are not enough for a full understanding of either development or determinants: the opportunity structure, the freedom to move and pressures to move in a context such as that of AT&T need to be taken into account, just as the social class structure in Sewell's (1969, 1975) Wisconsin studies has to be taken into account as a basic determinant of careers; it is within the opportunity structure of AT&T, of Wisconsin, or of England (Cherry, Ch. 5 in Watts, Super & Kidd, 1981) that other social and personal determinants shape the career pattern.

The objects of this chapter have been fourfold: (1) To describe life-span development, with the focus on emerging occupational careers and on their determinants; (2) To focus on occupational choice and success over the life span; (3) To identify and to put some of the major changing determinants in perspective; and (4) to give this theory and data meaning, in terms of the Life-Career Rainbow.

The studies cited, both the "classics" and those that are current, tend to stress career and occupational determinants. Holland's familiar work, Howard and Bray's new and novel work, and the writer's Arch of Career Determinants do this developmentally. Even the stage-organized recent study of Fiske and Chiriboga focuses on the characteristic concerns and their determinants at each life stage. The work of Riverin-Simard, and the Career Pattern Study, with two volumes still due to be completed, are rare in their focus on career development, asking how one substage or stage develops out of those preceding it in the larger American society.

Another issue that has arisen is that of whether two theories, two models, are needed for complete understanding. The answer to that question has been, "Not two, but three: a theory and model of development, a theory and a model of matching, and (not treated directly here) a theory and model of career decision making." *Matching theories* will soon be a century old. *Career development* models have been proposed only during the last half-century, but only very recently have they commanded widespread attention from theorists and practitioners in this field. *Career decision making,* some may contend, is a distinct topic and field for research and theory while others say that it needs to be seen in the context of developmental as well as of matching theory. This writer agrees with the latter position.

New insights, or highlighted old understandings, include the stressing of the fact that "stages" and "substages" are but convenient groupings of similar developmental concerns and tasks, that they have no rigid boundaries of age or of concern, and that people recycle through some of them throughout the life course. True, exploration at age 18, age 33, age 45, and age 65 or 70 has different content and is done somewhat differently, but it is basically the same psychological process and social phenomenon at any age. This is a researchable question. And not everyone who should explore does, and not everyone recycles later in life.

Individual differences have proved their importance even in situations as highly structured as that of a great, monolithic, corporation. The ladders, the lattices, are there and they are or become visible, but there are individual differences in the speed, direction and distance of movement, both lateral and vertical.

The developmental study of Riverin-Simard seems to confirm Levinson's findings and theory of five-year cycles. But she reports many variants. Therefore, one cannot but wonder, given the focus on the nature of the tasks rather than on their relative frequencies, whether her evident agreement with Levinson may be contaminated by advance acceptance of his theory. The insights yielded by anecdotal data are informative but they need appropriate quantification.

A sizable amount of data has been accumulated by the Adult Career Concerns Inventory and has fit a flexible life-stage theory. The ACCI was developed to assess substage and stage concerns, and structures data that way. But as both the authors and an independent researcher (Phillips, 1982) found that randomized items yield the same results, the basic theory appears to be supported. Are these results clearer because the studies, rather exceptionally, focused on four stages, as did Levinson? As usual, more research is needed.

In an attempt at a current theory of career development, it is important to come back to the view "through the glass, darkly," to views of the future, and to the argument of the futurists that today's theories are already obsolescent or even obsolete.

The disagreement may not be as great as it seems to be unless one simplistically views career development as the finding of a path and following it or as the finding of a ladder and climbing it. The term "career development" denotes development, not just climbing, not just following a path. Careers evolve, they emerge: that is what development means when applied to lives. There is no built-in biological mechanism that governs *career* development. To "biologize" human behavior after the manner of Piaget and Levinson is a major error. Although it does seem important to borrow some of the terms of the natural sciences, e.g., growth, maturity, decline, and decay, when we do so as behavioral scientists we need to redefine them for our purposes and keep these more specific definitions clearly in mind. The term "career maturity," for example, has been defined as readiness to make career decisions, and that has been operationalized as attitudes and knowledge that can be behaviorally defined and objectively measured. These attitudes, bits of knowledge, and wisdom come with experience which is culturally as well as biologically associated with age.

Given a truly interactive view of career development, the valid point of our futurists is that economic, industrial, and occupational change is happening with increasing rapidity, and that attitudes, information, and behavior must change with it. This means that flexibility in dealing with the present and alertness for impending changes are essential in contemporary career planning. We are evidently entering an age of *emerging* rather than of *preset* goals.

REFERENCES

Anatasi, A. (1988) *Psychological testing* (6th ed.) New York: Macmillan.

Anderson, V.V. (1929) *Psychiatry in industry.* New York: Harper & Row.

Arthur, M.B., Hall, D.T. & Lawrence, B.S. (Eds.) (1989) *Handbook of career theory.* New York: Cambridge University Press.

Betz, N.E. & Fitzgerald, L.F. (1987) *The career psychology of women.* Orlando, FL: Academic Press.

Bloom, B.S. (1964) *Stability and change in human characteristics.* New York: Wiley.

Brown, D. (1990) Issues and trends in career development. In Brown, D. & Brooks,L. (Eds.) *Career choice and development.* San Francisco: Jossey-Bass.

Buehler, C. (1933) *Der menschliche Lebenslauf als pychologisches Problem.* Leipzig: Hirzel.

Costello, D.K. (1981) *Vocational maturity of career-oriented adults.* Unpublished doctoral dissertation, University of San Francisco, San Francisco.

Cron, W.L. & Slocum, J.W. (1986) The influence of career stages on salespeoples' job attitudes, work perceptions, and performance. *Journal of Marketing Research, 23,* 119–129.

Cross, S. (1981) *The vocational coping strategies of adult males.* Unpublished doctoral dissertation. University of California at Los Angeles, Los Angeles.

Dagley, J.C., Super, D.E. & Lautenschlager, G.J. (1990) *Needs, values and interests:*

empirical relationships. Paper presented at a Symposium on that topic at the International Congress of Applied Psychology, Kyoto. Submitted for journal publication.

Davidson, P.E. & Anderson, H.D. (1937) *Occupational mobility in an American community.* Stanford, CA: Stanford University Press.

Dunnette, M.D. et al. (1991) *Handbook of industrial and organizational psychology,* Vol. I. Palo Alto, CA: Consulting Psychologists Press.

Edwards, A.L. (1954) *The Edwards Personal Preference Schedule.* San Antonio, TX: The Psychological Corporation.

Erikson, E.H. (1959) Identity and the life cycle. *Psychological Issues,* 1, the entire number.

Fiske, M., Thurnher, M. & Chiriboga, D.A. (1975) *Four stages of life.* San Francisco: Jossey-Bass.

Fiske, M. & Chiriboga, D.A. (1990) *Change and continuity in adult life.* San Francisco: Jossey-Bass.

Flanagan, J.C. (1947) *The Aviation Psychology Program in the Army Air Force.* Washington: Government Printing Office.

Gould, R. (1972) The phases of adult life. *American Journal of Psychiatry,* 129, 521–531.

Hackett, G., Lent, R.W. & Greenhaus, J.H. (1991) Advance in vocational theory and research: a 20-year retrospective. *Journal of Vocational Behavior, 38,* 3–38.

Harmon, L.W. (1967) Women's working patterns related to their SVIB housewife and "own" occupational scores. *Journal of Counseling Psychology, 14,* 299–301.

Harmon, L.W. (1970) Anatomy of career commitment in women. *Journal of Counseling Psychology, 17,* 77–80.

Havighurst, R.J. (1953) *Human development and education.* New York: Longman.

Herr, E.L. et al. (1982) Secondary school curriculum and career behavior of young adults. *Journal of Vocational Behavior, 21,* 243–258.

Holland, J.L. (1959) A theory of vocational choice. *Journal of Counseling Psychology, 6,* 35–45.

Holland, J.L. (1969) A critical analysis (of Super's theory). *The Counseling Psychologist, 1,* 15–16.

Holland, J.L. (1985) *Making vocational choices: a theory of vocational personalities and work environments.* (2nd ed.) Englewood Cliffs, NJ: Prentice-Hall.

Howard, A. & Bray, D. (1988) *Managerial lives in transition: advancing age and changing times.* New York: Guilford Press.

Jordaan, J.P. & Heyde, M.B. (1979) *Vocational maturity during the high-school years.* New York: Teachers College Press.

Kohlberg, L. (1976) Continuities in childhood and adult moral development. In Baltes, P.B & Schaie, K.W. *Life-span developmental psychology: personality and socialization.* Orlando, FL: Academic Press.

Krumboltz, J.D. et al. (1976) A social learning theory of career development. *The Counseling Psychologist, 6,* 71–81.

Levinson, D. (1978) *The seasons of a man's life.* New York: Ballantine.

Mahoney, D.J. (1986) *An exploration of the construct validity of a measure of adult vocational maturity.* Unpublished doctoral dissertation, Teachers College, Columbia University.

Maslow, A.H. (1954) *Motivation and Personality.* New York: Harper & Row.

Miller, D.C. & Form, W.H. (1951) *Industrial sociology.* New York: Harper & Row.

Mulvey, M.C. (1963) Psychological and sociological factors in the prediction of the career patterns of women. *Genetic Psychology Monographs, 68,* 309–386.

Murray, H.A. (1938) *Explorations in personality.* New York: Oxford University Press.

McDaniels, C. (1989) *The changing workplace.* San Francisco: Jossey-Bass.

Nevill, D.D. (1984) The meaning of work in women's lives: role conflict, preparation, and change. *The Counseling Psychologist, 12,* 131–134.

Nevill, D.D. & Super, D.E. (1986) *Manual for the Salience Inventory.* Palo Alto, CA: Consulting Psychologists Press.

Nevill, D.D. & Super, D.E. (1988) Career maturity and commitment to work in university students. *Journal of Vocational Behavior, 32,* 139–151.

Osipow, S.H. (1969) Some revised questions for vocational psychology. *The Counseling Psychologist, 1,* 17–19.

Osipow, S.H. (1973) *Theories of career development.* (2nd edition); (1983, 3rd edition). Englewood Cliffs, NJ: Prentice-Hall.

Osipow, S.H. (1990) Convergence in theories of career choice and development: review and projections. *Journal of Vocational Behavior, 36,* 122–131.

Parsons, F. (1909) *Choosing a vocation.* Boston: Houghton-Mifflin. (Reissued in 1988, Alexandria, VA: National Career Development Association).

Paterson, D.G. & Darley, J.G. (1936) *Men, women and jobs.* Minneapolis: University of Minnesota Press.

Peters, T. (1987) *Thriving on chaos.* New York: Harper & Row.

Phillips, R. (1982) *The relationship between the professional career development and the adult life cycle for men and women.* Unpublished doctoral dissertation, University of New Mexico.

Piaget, J. (1972) Intellectual evolution from adolescence to adulthood. *Human Development, 15,* 1–12.

Riverin-Simard, D. (1988) *Phases of the working life.* Montreal: Meridian Press.

Rousseau, D.M. (1991) Review of Argyle's Social Psychology of Work. *Contemporary Psychology, 36,* p. 132.

Sekaran, U. (1986) *Dual career families.* San Francisco: Jossey-Bass.

Sewell, W.H. & Hauser, R.M. (1975) *Education, occupation and earnings: achievement in the early career.* Orlando, FL: Academic Press.

Slocum, J.W. & Cron, W.L. (1985) *Job attitudes and performance during three career stages,* Unpublished manuscript, Southern Methodist University, Dallas, TX.

Sonnenfeld, J. & Kotter, J.P. (1982) The maturation of career theory. *Human Relations, 35,* 19–46.

Stern, D. & Eichorn, D. (1989) *Adolescence and work.* Hillsdale, NJ: Erlbaum.

Strong, E.K. (1943) *The vocational interests of men and women.* Stanford, CA: Stanford University Press.

Super, D.E. (1942) *The dynamics of vocational adjustment.* New York: Harper & Row.

Super, D.E. (1949; rev. with J.O. Crites, 1962) *Appraising vocational fitness.* New York: Harper & Row.

Super, D.E. (1953) A theory of vocational development. *American Psychologist, 8,* 185–190.

Super, D.E. (1955) Vocational adjustment: implementing a self-concept. *Occupations* (now *Journal of Counseling and Development*), 30, 88–92.

Super, D.E. (1957) *The psychology of careers.* New York: Harper & Row.

Super, D.E. (1972) Vocational development theory: persons, positions and processes, and, Vocational development theory in 20 years: How will it come about? In Whitely, J.M. & Resnikoff, A. (ed's) *Perspectives on vocational guidance.* Alexandria, VA: National Career Development Association.

Super, D.E. (1973) The Work Values Inventory. In Zytowski, D.G. (ed) *Contemporary approaches to interest measurement.* Minneapolis: University of Minnesota Press.

Super, D.E. (1980) A life-span, life-space approach to career development. *Journal of Vocational Behavior, 16,* 282–298.

Super, D.E. (1983) Assessment in career guidance: toward truly developmental counseling. *Personnel & Guidance Journal* (now *Journal of Counseling and Development*), *61,* 555–562.

Super, D.E. (1990) A life-span, life-space approach to career development. In Brown, D. & Brooks, L. (ed's) *Career choice and development.* San Francisco: Jossey-Bass.

Super, D.E. & Bohn, M. (1971) *Occupational psychology.* Pacific Grove, CA: Brooks/Cole.

Super, D.E., Crites, J.O., Hummel, R.C., Moser, H.P., Overstreet, P.L. & Warnath, C.F. (1957) *Vocational development: a framework for research.* New York: Teachers College Press.

Super, D.E., Starishevsky, R., Matlin, N., & Jordaan, J.P. (1963) *Career development: Self-concept theory.* New York: College Entrance Examination Board.

Super, D.E., Thompson, A.S. & Lindeman, R. H. (1986 & 1988) *The Adult Career Concerns Inventory.* Palo Alto, CA: Consulting Psychologists Press.

Vetter, L. (1973) Career counseling for women. *The Counseling Psychologist, 4,* 54–67.

Vondracek, F.W., Lerner, R.M. & Schulenberg, J.E. (1986) *Career development: a life-span developmental approach.* Hillsdale, NJ: Erlbaum.

Walsh, A.G., Super, D.E. & Kidd, J.M. (ed's) (1981) *Career development in Britain.* Cambridge, UK: Hobson's Press.

Weinrach, S.G. & Srebalus, D.J. (1990) Holland's theory of careers. In Brown, D. & Brooks, L. (ed's) *Career choice and development.* San Francisco: Jossey-Bass.

Yerkes, R.M. (ed) (1921) Psychological examining in the U.S. Army. *Memoirs of The National Academy of Sciences,* Vol. *15.*

Zelkowitz, R.S. (1974) *The construction and validation of a measure of vocational maturity for adults.* (Doctoral dissertation, Teachers College, Columbia University) Ann Arbor, MI: University Microfilm, 75-18, 456.

Chapter 3

CAREER THEORY IN A DYNAMIC CONTEXT

Michael B. Arthur

The wealth of nations, after all, rests on how the efforts of people are channelled into jobs. And *careers* as well as jobs matter at the societal level because behavior in *today's* work—and thus the choices made—is often a function of the expectations for *tomorrow's* work.

Rosabeth Moss Kanter (1989a)

Careers matter, and therefore career theory—representing the way careers are presently understood—also matters. However, most existing career theory is drawn from observations about people and organizations quite different from what will be seen in the future. How urgent is the need to respond to the changes taking place? How can the base of existing career theory be used to best advantage? What do projections about the future workforce and work opportunities mean for the further development of career theory? How can theoretical and applied perspectives about careers be brought together for the future benefit of both people and organizations? These are the kind of questions that this chapter will address.*

Much of established career theory was developed before recent changes in both the work force and the organization of work began to set in. Yet, by the year 2000, women, minorities, and immigrants in the U.S. work force will far exceed the number of white males, and the average worker's age will increase markedly. Many workers will have limited formal education; many more will have education made redundant by the pace of technological evolution. Meanwhile, the work environment ahead will involve more automation, an even greater emphasis on services, more flexible forms of organization, and increased interorganizational networking and alliance formation. There will be greater competition at both national and international levels, and—let us hope—a "peace economy" driven by interdependencies among nations in a market-driven global arena. All of this imagery is far removed from the relatively stable views of people and organizations, or of their development, from which much existing career theory is drawn.

This chapter highlights challenges to career theory—and inseparable challenges to career development activity—through successive explorations

---

*I am deeply indebted to Lotte Bailyn for her support throughout the writing of this chapter. Tim Hall, David Montross and Chris Shinkman also gave helpful feedback.

of the "supply side" and the "demand side" of new theory generation. The supply side is defined as the flow of ideas and concepts stemming from career theory itself, and is examined by reference to a recent attempt to build new career theory from its present base (Arthur, Hall and Lawrence, 1989a). The demand side is defined as the need for fresh theory stemming from applied activity—in our case career development activity—and is examined by reference to projections about both the work force and work organizations for the year 2000. This chapter also explores the opportunity to bring the supply and demand sides together. As an example, recent supply side theory about "careers in self-designing organizations" is reconsidered for its applicability to the future workforce. The emphasis throughout the chapter is on the pace of environmental change to which interdependent career theory and career development efforts must respond.

The Supply Side of Career Theory

To promote shared understanding, let us begin by defining various terms associated with the concept career and suggesting a simple model to connect them. The discussion will then explore that part of the model concerned with career theory, and inputs and outputs associated with it. This will anticipate a subsequent shift to the remainder of the model, concerned with career development activity and its effectiveness.

The Links Among Career Theory, Career Development, and the Work Environment

What is career theory? Career development? The work environment? A simple definition of *career* is *the evolving sequence of a person's work experiences over time.* Central to this definition is the idea of a "moving picture" of a person's unfolding life (Hughes, 1958). Central, also, is the claim that from both theoretical and applied perspectives, further refinement of the career concept is unhelpful. Notions of "public conspicuousness" or of "social progress" (cf. Oxford English Dictionary, 1961, Vol. II, p. 117) prejudge and can rigidify status differences. Distinguishing between careers, for some, and jobs, for others, denies the relevance of studying time effects across the workforce at large. All who work have a career, and all work involves careers (Arthur, Hall and Lawrence, 1989b).

Career theory is the body of all generalizable attempts to explain career phenomena. Through its focus on work, career theory is simultaneously concerned with both the *person* doing the work and the *institution* (prominently, but not exclusively, an employing organization) that gives definition to the work. And work, in addition to providing the essential experiences that evolve into careers over *time*, also locates a person relative to others in *social space*. Thus, the essence of career theory is that it obliges us to look at individuals and institutions, through time and social space, all at once (Arthur, Hall and Lawrence, 1989b).

What is not career theory? Organizational behavior approaches looking at less than the whole person, or psychological theories absent any focus on work organization, are not career theory. Nor are trait-based views on leadership that neglect organizational position, or organization structure models insensitive to changing employee needs over time. Such views, albeit useful in various social science arenas, lack the inherent simultaneity of treatment career theory demands for both job performer and provider, and for present and future perspectives.

Career development distinguishes itself from career theory by its applied focus. The focus may be on present or future workers, or on organizational or educational systems, but one way or another career development deals directly with career issues in the work environment. The *work environment* can be viewed, in the same language as the definition of career, as the milieu of individuals and institutions that give rise to the unfolding of careers over time. Linking the three constructs of career theory, career development and the work environment, also introduces concerns about career theory *relevance* (for career development), career development *effectiveness* (in the work environment) and career theory *openness* (to new signals from the work environment) as outlined in Figure 3-1.

As depicted in Figure 3-1, the supply side of career theory emphasizes the link between the work environment and career theory, and in turn the possibility of introducing fresh ideas into career development efforts. The demand side of career theory emphasizes the link between the work environment and career development, and in turn the possibility of introducing fresh questions for career theory to interpret. The present section, focused on the supply side of career theory, emphasizes three elements in Figure 3-1: transformation occurring within career theory itself; openness of career theory to the work environment; and relevance of career theory to career development.

Career Theory Transformation

Delectable food is of little use to a person who can't digest it. Similarly, a work environment rich in signals about the interaction of people and organizations over time is of little help to a body of career theory that cannot transform itself in response. How then does transformation of career theory take place? There are two general possibilities: one, of transformation within a particular career theory or set of theories (called a line of inquiry in the discussion below), and two, of transformation across the body of career theory as a whole.

Transformation *within* a line of inquiry can be looked at through any of several cyclical models of theory development (e.g., Quinn, 1988). The

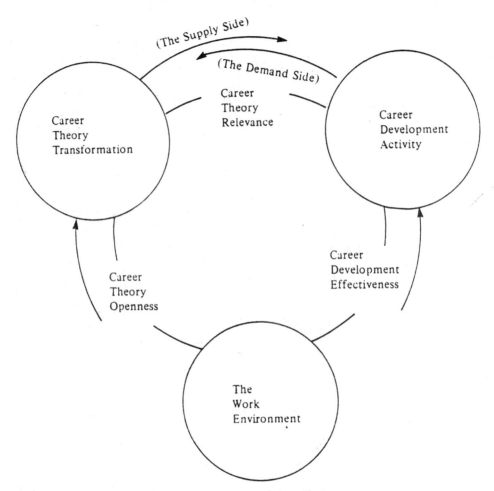

Figure 3-1. The links among career theory, career development, and the work environment.

recent *Handbook of Career Theory* (Arthur, Hall and Lawrence, 1989a) describes nine established lines of inquiry about careers, whose foci and theoretical origins are:

- vocational choice, derived from trait-factor theories of work adjustment;
- social roles, derived from sociological inquiry into person-situation interaction over time;
- career adjustment, derived from accumulated adult development theory;
- organizational careers, derived from studies of career processes in organizational settings;
- women's careers, derived from the study of gender-distinct patterns of work;
- minority careers, derived from the study of racial differences;

- dual-careers, derived from concern over the intersection of work and family spheres;
- transitions, derived from the study of key pauses and turning points in working lives;
- organizational career systems, derived from the study of internal labor markets and human resource management.

Authors representing each of the above lines of inquiry express optimism about the prospects for further theoretical transformation as exemplified by the reports below:

- Trait-factor theory development has been limited by the static nature of most research, insufficient attention to structural factors such as race, sex, and socioeconomic status and an overall reluctance to expand the range of variables studied beyond the individual. Further transformation is dependent on fuller integration of individual and organizational variables, attending to the process of individual-organization career negotiations, and accommodating time-dependent effects of both individuals and organizations upon one another (Betz, Fitzgerald and Hill, 1989).

- Much of the potential of the early Chicago sociologists' treatment of careers has been lost in subsequent adaptations of their work. In particular, widespread emphasis on the objective properties of organizations and occupations has meant neglect of parallel subjective forces whereby people grant definition to the institutions through which careers occur. Fresh attention to the latter, especially in a time of rapid occupational change, can greatly increase knowledge of how career behavior and the social structure are bound together (Barley, 1989).

- A limitation of the research on two career couples has been its highly descriptive character. In particular, a developmental perspective has been lacking that incorporates both the family life cycle and the career stages of the partners. Attention to the phenomenon of *asynchronism* between a partner's career and organizational norms, between the two partners' careers, or between family development and societal expectations, can help build more gender-free and more accommodating career models. The prospect of greater choice for dual career partners can also lead to more effective use of their work potential. (Sekeran and Hall, 1989).

- The separate strands of adult development and career development theory invoke persistent dilemmas about generalizability between male and female models, the relative contributions of individual and social system parameters, and the integration of both theoretical strands into future theoretical models. More work is needed along the lines of Vrondacek et al. (1986) who acknowledge the relatively primitive state of career theory and promote the notion of "developmental contextualism" emphasizing both an active organism and an active world. New studies that help illustrate how individual development processes contribute to career development, and how career dynamics can influence the individual's passage through adult life stages, need to be encouraged (Cytrynbaum and Crites, 1989).

All of the above, along with reports about other lines of inquiry, call for an expansion of theory-building across different levels of analysis. Such expansion in turn suggests a need for fresh debate to handle the greater overlap among approaches that would result.

Transformation *across* the body of career theory calls for explicit comparison of different theories, including the nine lines of inquiry already noted. However, other perspectives from outside established career theory have the potential to add to understanding of how work unfolds over time. A number of *Handbook of Career Theory* authors, accepting a challenge to make the career implications of their ideas explicit, offer twelve "new perspectives" on career theory, as follows:

- personal control versus situation-dependency as an explanation of career outcomes;
- the significance of job stress to the management of careers and organizational health;
- "re-visioning" career concepts from an explicitly feminist perspective;
- individual-organization reciprocity as a basis for interpreting career development implications;
- "self-designing" organizations as forums for career improvisation;
- organizational career "tournaments" and their shaping of employee perceptions;
- blue-collar careers and the derivation of meaning within constrained work opportunities;
- the political interpretation of career behavior and career systems;
- rites of passage as stabilizing influences on career forms;
- the economic and labor market determinants of individual career strategies;
- rhetoric and the management of meaning in organizational career contexts;
- the internal and external career dimensions of cross-cultural (including international) career systems.

Examples of how these new perspectives can add to established career theory include the following:

- The individualistic model of careers, implying that individuals are the main agents of their own job progress, neglects the structural constraints facing managers who must infer ability and make investments in employees. A "tournament" model of organizational career attainment through progressively selective competitions, with winners at each stage signalling higher ability and earning fresh organizational investments, offers a way to recognize structural effects. Exposing the rules of the organizational career tournament would provide a basis for interpreting and in turn enhancing the tournament's effectiveness (Rosenbaum, 1989).

• Career theory has traditionally neglected a *political* perspective, yet insights about the politics of hiring, job classification, job succession and wage distribution suggest that building a political theory of careers is a critical task. Such a theory would recognize the primacy of people's *interests*, reflected in organizational subunit, class, demographic (including sex) and multiple extraorganizational affiliations. A greater appreciation of interests and of the interactions among interests, networks and relative power, could provide more realistic—and in turn more useful—models of how careers come about (Pfeffer, 1989).

• The notion of individual-organization reciprocity fundamental to early views of organizational behavior has been neglected in subsequent studies of careers. Exploring reciprocity in the light of current knowledge about both individual and organizational stages of development raises new questions about the nature of organizational careers and their consequences. A stage-based analysis suggests a range of reciprocal effects of individuals and organizations on one another, with associated developmental, political and strategic consequences for both parties (Arthur and Kram, 1989).

• Modern microeconomic theory, and especially the work on imperfect labor markets, suggests a new way of thinking about people's career strategy in organizations. Economic views on human capital, market signaling, implicit contracts and related topics suggest employees make career investments based on two dimensions: the organizationally perceived value of an investment and the number of others making the same investment. Interpreting individual career strategies according to these dimensions in turn suggests a different way to think about organizational strategy, and its degree of match with the career rewards offered (Barney and Lawrence, 1989).

These positions both broaden and strengthen the call for debate about career theory. They also suggest new ways of viewing the host environment for careers, to which this chapter now turns.

Career Theory Openness

Being receptive to other theories, especially those from outside the traditional boundaries of career theory, is in itself a form of openness to new work environment interpretations. However, more direct examples of openness can be drawn from both established and new approaches in career theory that highlight the changing nature of the work environment. Examples of such openness in the *Handbook of Career Theory* include the following:

• The complex and shifting picture of the population of organizations means that any assumptions we make about organizational career rewards can be dangerous. Competitive forces now spurring the redesign of office and factory worker roles, and a shift towards smaller firms for provision of jobs, make accommodation of the individual life span within a single organization unrealistic. Organizations seeking to exploit high commitment from employees will need to find new ways of earning it that avoid the false promises of "career pathing" traditionally made (Dalton, 1989).

• To more fully involve women in the workforce calls for an explicitly feminist *re-vision* of the contents, structure and methods of career theory. For example, from a feminist perspective the contents of career theory should integrate cyclical and sequential views of career phases; the structure of career theory should accommodate notions of heterarchy alongside those of hierarchy; and the methods of career theory should emphasize personal, internal assessment of career outcomes alongside external assessment. A basic test of the adequacy of any new contribution to career theory would be whether it grants equal value to female and male principles (Marshall, 1989).

• Several tensions in career research — including reluctance to study occupational groups where the proportion of minorities is higher, resistance to within-group research that could provide new descriptive data, and lack of focus on minorities as supervisors — have interfered with theory-building on race and career dynamics. Moreover, the career research community still boasts few minority members and harbors theory and method developed by white males. If race is to enter the mainstream of career theory, the internal dynamics of the research community need to change to reflect more openness to controversy, more use of cross-race teams, and greater commitment to self-scrutiny (Thomas and Alderfer, 1989).

• The possibilities inherent in "self-designing organizations" — organizations intentionally designed to be able to adapt to a changing environment — can be realized only through nontraditional career adjustments. To support design principles such as organizational impermanence, learning, and removal of informational filters calls for career behavior that celebrates rather than condemns the instability of an organization's career structure. For example, a "spiral" view of one's own career, involving regular reassessment and redirection of career goals (Driver, 1979), appears distinctly suited to self-designing principles. Successful self-designing organizations will be those that can both nurture and accommodate these nontraditional career views (Weick and Berlinger, 1989).

At least in certain situations, then, career theory is clearly open to new messages stemming directly from the changing work environment. This intermediate conclusion invites a preliminary visit to the question of relevance.

The Supply Side of Career Theory Relevance

The supply side of career theory described above emphasizes the need for career theory to be open to the work environment. This need spans both established and fresh theoretical perspectives, and can lead to transformation through efforts both within and across the diverse lines of inquiry being explored. The discussion has offered multiple examples of transformational efforts and the prospect of more relevant career theory in the future. However, two cautions should be noted.

First, while the authors cited promote new theory-building, the broader picture in career studies is less encouraging. Much work still takes place in relatively cloistered academic disciplines, and among scholars reluctant to internalize fresh perspectives (Collin and Young, 1986; Sonnenfeld and Kotter, 1982). Neither Dewey's (1933) old dictum that the problems of social science should define the way they get studied, nor Bailyn's (1989) new characterization of the career as an interstitial—and therefore interdisciplinary—concept, have yet found great favor. Yet, to press for more relevant career theory calls for the very best each academic discipline can offer, and for continuing transdisciplinary inquiry and debate. We should be circumspect about career scholars not open to the range of social science disciplines, or unprepared to make connections among them.

The second caution is that while the supply side of career theory incorporates openness to the work environment it fails to calibrate the pace of environmental change. What to social scientists might appear useful transformation could still involve a net loss in relevance, if the environment is changing faster, or simultaneously moving in a different direction. It is therefore necessary to consider the call for new career theory the work environment itself makes.

The Demand Side of Career Theory

In contrast to the supply side, the "demand side" of career theory can be seen to stem from direct experiences in career development efforts. These experiences precipitate the demand for new theory, which can be expected to increase in proportion to the pace of change in the work environment. So what can be predicted about the future work environment? The stance that career theory maintain parallel interests in both individuals and institutions, calls for predictions about both parties. Let us turn to sketch two separate pictures for the coming decade, one of "Individuals 2000," the other of "Institutions 2000."

Individuals 2000

The Hudson Institute (1987) *Workforce 2000* report has been widely read for its projections about career actors of the future. For example, Figure 3-2 shows net new entrants to the U.S. work force from the year 1985 to the year 2000 by various demographic categories. The emphasis on net new entrants should be noted, since the proportions shown are derived by adding new work force entrants and subtracting predicted leavers (largely white males) over the interim period. However, the figure does highlight the pace of change in the work force. Focusing on this pace of change calls attention to certain concerns about career theory and the new realities it must accommodate.

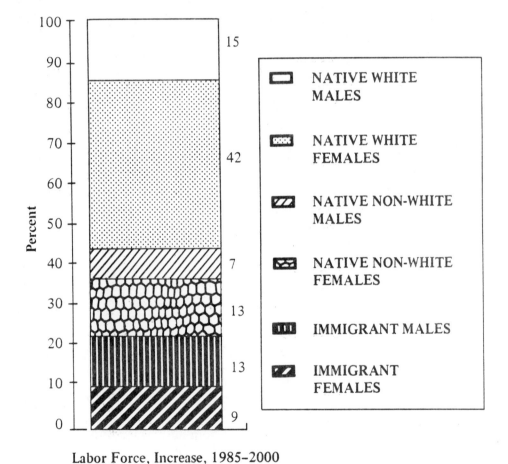

Labor Force, Increase, 1985–2000

Figure 3-2. New work forces entrants, from 1985–2000 (source: Hudson Institute. 1987).

- If there is white male bias in established career theory as many would contend, then how suited is this theory to new work force entrants? The stark answer is that it will serve a mere 15 percent of net new entrants, and even if the qualifier "white" is dropped the match only rises to 35 percent. Moreover, arguments that sex-role behavior should change for both sexes challenge the utility of applying traditional career models even among males.

• If there is a lack of adequate theory about dual career couples, how ready is society to accommodate the rapid rise in such couples that the new demography portends? The past tendency to view dual career activity as a component of women's studies seems clearly inadequate, and discriminatory toward couples wishing to find creative solutions that address both parties' career concerns in parallel with family issues.

• The striking image of *diversity* — along gender, race, and ethnic dimensions — raises further questions about the state of career theory. How helpful are universal views of careers in the face of such diversity? How can diversity be reconciled with the generalizability career theory seeks to provide? How much is known about the processes within employing organizations through which the diverse population's careers unfold?

• A further challenge regarding the workforce of tomorrow involves assumptions about education. How much does career theory still rely on its traditional assumptions that vocational education precedes the career? How well will this assumption serve new immigrants, or meet the realities of public high school experiences, or provide industry with the workforce and technical retraining that it seeks? How ready are observers to see education as an inherent component of people's careers, rather than an antecedent to them?

The questions raised above are not new, but they are *urgent*, and career development must respond. However, if the response is based only on awareness of the listed questions it will be inadequate on two counts. First, efforts grounded in new ideas about individuals, but old ideas about the institutions that frame careers, may not work. Second, the same efforts will miss a new *opportunity* manifest in the different forms of organization now springing up, and to which this chapter now turns.

Institutions 2000

The Hudson Institute (1987) report offers general economic forecasts about work in the year 2000, and a spirited follow up prepared for the U.S. Department of Labor (Hudson Institute, 1988) urges how "employers as problem solvers" should respond. Recommendations include providing more support for families, making more productive use of minorities, the disabled and the economically disadvantaged, and capitalizing more on older workers. Such initiatives must be emphasized in career development in the years ahead. Yet, as proposed they lack sensitivity to a new challenge to career theory stemming from changes in the nature of employing organizations themselves. Employers as problem solvers must attend not only to the changing workforce, but also to the following realities emerging from among their own ranks:

False Assumptions. Assumptions about the effectiveness of large firms, drawn from the post World War II era, have been misplaced. The stability, dominance, and orderly growth of those firms is now recognized as a function of the economic circumstances of the day (Furino, 1988). Vertical integration is no longer seen as so necessary for organizational efficiency (Williamson, 1985), and the layers of supervisory and staff positions (and therefore career ladders) once deemed necessary for such integration are being cut drastically.

New Models of Competitiveness. Radically different yet more competitive forms of organization have now become visible. Examples from Japan and Europe point to much greater use of horizontal rather than vertical communication, emphasis on strategic alliances among firms, and flexibility rather than stability as a key organizing principle (Piore and Sabel, 1984; Pucik, 1988). Drastic acts of downsizing, restructuring, and spinoff activity reflect the urgency with which traditional organizations are trying to adopt these new competitive principles (Halal, 1986).

A Dominance of Small to- Medium-Sized Business Units. The economic significance of the small-to-medium business unit (SMBU) is becoming clearer. In Japan, for example, more than 80 percent of all employment occurs in firms with fewer than 300 people (Koike, 1988). In European countries, the increasingly dominant form of employment is the independent firm with less than 500 employees (Storey, 1988). In the U.S., a count of separate geographical establishments suggests the infrastructure for an SMBU-driven economy is already in place (Granovetter, 1984), and being further promoted by urgings for "loose coupling" across the parts of a commonly owned whole (Miles and Snow, 1986).

New Possibilities from Technology. Technological changes have added to the impetus for new forms of organizing, notably by allowing greater flexibility in manufacturing (Piore and Sabel, 1984), and establishing new possibilities for information processing (Child, 1987). These changes emphasize "small batch" over "large batch" production runs, the associated use of flexible manufacturing equipment, and greater ease of horizontal coordination through computerized information systems.

An Emphasis on Services. Technological progress means that manufacturing, like agriculture before it, continues to produce more with fewer employees. Services are already estimated to account for 75 percent of all employment (Peters, 1987), yet our thinking about jobs (and therefore careers) remains grounded in ideas from manufacturing. In particular, services involve the employee directly in delivery of the "product" received by the customer, and therefore expose most careers directly to shifting patterns of consumer preference and the changing marketplace (Bowen and Schneider, 1988).

The Emerging "Dynamic Network." The result of the interplay of the above and other factors is an emerging new pattern of organization, based on a "dynamic network" of many specialist firms instead of a stable body of dominant employers (Miles, 1989). The smaller, more focused, form of organization that is becoming the norm is driven directly by market forces, rather than by fiat from above. What were traditionally viewed as "organizational careers" (and therefore the models that career development programs were designed to support) now take place across multiple organizational boundaries, emphasizing skill and reputation over seniority and loyalty as the anchors of people's careers (Kanter, 1989b).

The Demand Side of Career Theory Relevance

The first section of this chapter depicted the transformation of career theory preceding its application in career development. We have now suggested the reverse: career development activity preceding the call for fresh career theory. Also, while the first section suggested a forum for debate about career theory, this last section suggests a need for parallel debate about career development, so that the full effects of "Individuals 2000" and "Institutions 2000" can be brought into view (and this more urgently so, since the overall effects of the forthcoming changes may be less visible to the single, smaller, organization). Also, the risk of failing to calibrate the pace of environmental change can be applied to both career theory and career development efforts.

Taken together, of course, the two completed sections raise the common question of how theory and practice can each help the other. How can the supply and demand sides of career theory contribute to one another, and serve the shared goal of greater relevance in the years ahead?

CONNECTING SUPPLY AND DEMAND: THE EXAMPLE OF SELF-DESIGNING ORGANIZATIONS

It was suggested earlier that career theory has so far been slow to appreciate the changing nature of organizations. It was also suggested that emerging new forms of organization might provide fresh opportunities for career theory. The example below explores the latter suggestion by taking an exceptional case of a contribution to career theory that does address "Institutions 2000", namely the account of careers in self-designing organizations (Weick and Berlinger, 1989) referenced earlier. Does this supply side contribution, aimed at "Institutions 2000," have further relevance when matched against predictable demand side concerns about "Individuals 2000"?

Careers in Self-Designing Organizations

A theory of "self-designing organizations" was sketched out in the mid-1970s in response to growing awareness that organizations needed to become more adaptive to their external environments (Hedberg, Nystrom and Starbuck, 1976; Weick, 1977). The central idea is to assume a continually challenging, fast-changing environment instead of the relatively benevolent, stable environment found in traditional organizational forms. Thus, a self-designing organization's primary purpose is to read, interpret, and learn from signals available in the host environment, and to respond accordingly, as "yesterday surges in and tomorrow gushes out" (Hedberg, Nystrom, and Starbuck, 1976). As a result, a self-designing organization focuses on the internal processes through which self-design occurs, deplores inertia, celebrates experiments, and values impermanence.

The self-designing organization view has influenced later ideas on organizational learning (Hedberg, 1981), and on "loosely coupled" or "network" arrangements of firms (Miles and Snow, 1986; Orton and Weick, 1990). There is also clear overlap with recent ideas about managing innovation (Van de Ven and Angle, 1989) and "riding the waves of change" precipitated by the modern marketplace (Morgan, 1988). The self-designing organization is therefore representative of a broad group of recent ideas about organizations, all concerned with rapid adjustment to shifting environmental opportunities.

Despite the currency of self-designing organization ideas in thinking about organizations, attempts to incorporate these ideas into career theory have been rare. Yet, the self-designing form of organization calls for career behavior radically different from that implied by traditional organizational forms. As Weick and Berlinger (1989) have recently pointed out, "career improvisation" in self-designing organizations calls for employees to cultivate spiral career concepts, decouple identity from jobs, preserve discretion, identify distinctive competence, and synthesize complex information as summarized below.

Cultivate Spiral Career Concepts: A person with a "spiral" career orientation develops a complex career plan that changes often, incorporates multiple visions of self, is responsive to work and nonwork stimulants, uses trial and error as important sources of information, and makes deliberate and substantial career movements every five to seven years. To develop a spiral career concept is the most straightforward answer to how to survive in a company that is always changing.

Decouple Identity from Jobs: Relying on jobs for identity means that people will be reluctant to change jobs because of new questions about who they are. However, jobs viewed as temporary are less likely to become benchmarks of identity. Emphasizing professional identity that transcends a particular job (or rank) and "playing" with new career identities both can help a person thrive in a self-designing organization environment.

Preserve Discretion: Discretion at work is a precondition for continuous learning, but can be impeded by a lack of perceived job alternatives or by high commitment situations that screen out fresh ideas. People preserving discretion can maintain the kind of career insight that continually recognizes new choices and therefore contributes to the self-designing nature of cluster companies, e.g., in Silicon Valley, since they feel less obliged to accept any one company's ideas and more willing to take risks.

Identify Distinctive Competence: People with diverse competencies, abilities, and expertise have the potential to bring their skills together to contribute to a primary self-designing organization goal, namely its redesign. However, assertiveness in promoting one's distinctive competencies, and trust in intuition to transform fragmented information into richer meanings, are also critical qualities if effective interaction among a self-designing organization's members is to be achieved.

Synthesize Complex Information: Once an organization has the capacity for self-design it must also be able to move from idea generation to effective synthesis and implementation of proposals. It therefore needs people who are able to integrate the patterns of awareness in the organization into larger visions, and to articulate how individual contributions fit together. Such people will be more valuable to, and exercise more influence in, the organizations that they serve.

Self-designing organizations and "Individuals 2000"

To exhibit the above career improvisation calls for a shift from objective to subjective career thinking; that is, to cease interpreting careers according to organizational position and status, and instead to rely on personal interpretation of one's shifting and cumulative work experiences (Van Maanen and Schein, 1977). As Weick and Berlinger (1989) note, in the self-designing organization the objective career dissolves, and gets replaced by the subjective career as a framework for career growth. In this course of events, subjective careers not only provide career definition for each person, they play back as expressions of career preferences both to immediate employers and to society's institutions generally (Barley, 1989). One can therefore ask the following: if self-designing organizations are successfully established, and if their members exhibit the five career qualities noted above, what are the prospects for accommodating the future work force within those organizations? Let us revisit the Weick and Berlinger recommendations with this question in mind.

Spiral career concepts could serve most directly to offset expectations about traditional "linear" careers grounded in assumptions of organizational hierarchy and stability. They could also allow careers to be acted out in "chunks" so necessary to effective accommodation of work and family (Bailyn, 1984). The spiral concept promises less debilitating effects from parental leave, since missing a step on the career ladder is less significant the less ladder-like the career paths. Also, the career spiral, in contrast to the masculine career arrow, offers greater potential for accommodating feminist perspectives about careers (cf. Marshall, 1989).

Decoupling identity from jobs could lead to people being less protective about the way jobs are presently assigned. Thoughts about work sharing, reallocation of work to better use the available work force, or redesign of work for greater productivity (e.g. Kravetz, 1988) could be more acceptable to people keeping the specifics of their jobs (but not necessarily their overall commitment to work) at a safe psychological distance. Supervisors' need for control, often seen as a barrier to new work arrangements (Lawler, 1986) may also be more open to change if the recommended decoupling occurs.

Preserving discretion can be viewed as a preventative or an antidote to identification with a job, and therefore as reinforcing the possibilities of decoupling noted above. At an aggregate level, discretion could also serve to provide a more open marketplace for talent and ideas based on near-term benefits to both individuals and organizations (Bailyn, in press). This could in turn open up opportunities for new or returning work force members to compete for vacated positions.

Emphasizing *distinctive competence* suggests a more dynamic view of the organization again less dependent on the specifics of existing jobs or roles, and less assumptive about sex, race or age linked biases. It opens up the prospect of recruiting supplementary competence, by use of specialists or part-time workers, whose contributions do not neatly fit old arrangements (e.g., Millner, 1989). An emphasis on competence can also make the prospect of working from home more attractive, as people become better valued for the contributions they make, rather than for the time they spend at the office (Perin, in press).

Finally, *synthesizing complex information* could lead to new interpretations of how to utilize the available workforce, and the nurturing of on-the-job learning in a way that benefits both individual and organizational purposes (e.g., Hedberg, 1984). One challenge in this synthesis would be to reinterpret established models of education, vocational training, and work according to present-day realties (cf. Auerbach, 1988). Another challenge would be to more fully appreciate the entanglement of cross-cultural and diversity issues that can interfere with the way people work together (Thomas & Alderfer, 1989).

The above exploration suggests that theoretical ideas serving the cause of "Institutions 2000," hold out fresh possibilities for accommodating "Individuals 2000." If the supply and demand sides of career theory can be brought together, and driven by future visions of *both* the individual and the institution, we may be able to offer a more adequate, and more helpful, theoretical response. Meanwhile, the dangers of applying new models of the work force to old models of organization, or vice-versa, may be clearer.

SUMMARY AND CONCLUSION

The supply and demand perspectives on career theory covered in this chapter offer separate lessons. On the supply side, career theory holds much potential for further transformation. This can be pursued through intensive cross-disciplinary debate spanning both established lines of inquiry and new perspectives. The challenge for contributors to career theory is to both welcome and promote this new debate.

The demand side of career theory can work in tandem with the supply side to promote more relevant theory, and more effective career development. The urgency on the demand side is that the assumptions on which much career theory is based are inconsistent with the predictions for "Individuals 2000" and "Institutions 2000." Moreover, these predictions have rarely been faced simultaneously. The example of careers in self-designing organizations has shown how fresh ideas about future organizations can open up new possibilities for the future work force.

To paraphrase this chapter's opening quotation, the wealth of nations will indeed rest on expectations for tomorrow's work. The thought not only applies to career actors in the abstract, but also to people directly involved with career theory and career development activity. The expectations of those who specialize in careers will critically affect the services provided, and in turn the wealth of "Individuals 2000" and "Institutions 2000." May both parties prosper.

REFERENCES

Arthur, M.B., Hall, D.T. & Lawrence, B.S. (Eds.) *Handbook of Career Theory*, New York: Cambridge University Press, 1989a.

Arthur, M.B., Hall, D.T. & Lawrence, B.S. Generating new directions in career theory: the case for a transdisciplinary approach. In M.B. Arthur, D.T. Hall and B.S. Lawrence (Eds.), *Handbook of Career Theory*. New York: Cambridge University Press, 1989b, pp. 7–25.

Arthur, M.B. & Kram, K.E. Reciprocity at work: the separate, yet inseparable possibilities for individual and organizational development. In M.B. Arthur, D.T. Hall and B.S. Lawrence (Eds.), *Handbook of Career Theory*. New York: Cambridge University Press, 1989, pp. 292–312.

Auerback, J.D. *In The Business of Child Care: Employer Institutions and Working Women*. New York: Praeger, 1988.

Bailyn, L. Issues of work and family in organizations: responding to social diversity. In M.B. Arthur, L. Bailyn, D.J. Levinson & H.A. Shepard, *Working With Careers*. New York, Center for Research in Career Development, Columbia University, 1984, pp. 75–98.

Bailyn, L. Understanding individual experience at work: Comments on the theory and practice of careers. In M.B. Arthur, D.T. Hall & B.S. Lawrence (Eds.) *Handbook of Career Theory*, New York: Cambridge University Press, 1989, pp. 477–489.

Bailyn, L. Changing the conditions of work: responding to increasing workforce diversity and new family patterns. In T. Kochan and M. Useem (Eds.) *Transforming Organizations*, Oxford University Press, in press.

Barley, S.R. Careers, identities and institutions: the legacy of the Chicago School of Sociology. In M.B. Arthur, D.T. Hall and B.S. Lawrence (Eds.), *Handbook of Career Theory*. New York: Cambridge University Press, 1989, pp. 41–65.

Barney, J.B. & Lawrence, B.S. Pin strips, power ties, and personal relationships: the economics of career strategy. In M.B. Arthur, D.T. Hall & B.S. Lawrence (Eds.) *Handbook of Career Theory*. New York: Cambridge University Press, 1989, pp. 417–436.

Betz, N.E., Fitzgerald, L.F., & Hill, R.E. Trait-factor theories: traditional cornerstone of career theory. In M.B. Arthur, D.T. Hall and B.S. Lawrence (Eds.), *Handbook of Career Theory*. New York: Cambridge University Press, 1989, pp. 26–40.

Bowen, D.E. & Schneider, B. Services marketing and management: implications for organizational behavior. In B.M. Staw & L.L. Cummings (Eds.) *Research in Organizational Behavior, Volume 10*, 1988, pp. 43–80.

Child, J. Information technology, organization and response to strategic challenges. *California Management Review*, 1987, Fall, 33–50.

Collin, A. & Young, R.A. New directions for theories of Career. *Human Relations*, 1986, 39, 837–853.

Cytrynbaum, S. & Crites, J. The utility of adult development theory in understanding career adjustment process. In M.B. Arthur, D.T. Hall & B.S. Lawrence (Eds.), *Handbook of Career Theory*. New York: Cambridge University Press, 1989, pp. 66–88.

Dalton, G.W. Developmental views of careers in organizations. In M.B. Arthur, D.T. Hall and B.S. Lawrence (Eds.), *Handbook of Career Theory*. New York: Cambridge University Press, 1989, pp. 89–109.

Dewey, J. *How People Think*. Boston: Heath, 1933.

Furino, A. (Ed.) *Cooperation and Competition in the Global Economy: Issues and Strategies*. Cambridge, MA: Ballinger, 1988.

Granovetter, M. Small is bountiful: Labor markets and establishment size. *American Sociological Review*, 1984, 49, 323–334.

Halal, W.E. *The New Capitalism.* New York: Wiley, 1986.

Hedberg, B. How organizations learn and unlearn. In P.C. Nystrom and W.H. Starbuck (Eds.) *Handbook of Organizational Design* (Volume 1). New York: Oxford University Press, 1981, pp. 1–27.

Hedberg, B. Career dynamics in a steelworks of the future. *Journal of Occupational Behaviour*, 1984, 5, 53–69.

Hedberg, B.L.T., Nystrom, P.C. & Starbuck, W.H. Camping on seesaws: prescriptions for a self-designing organization. *Administrative Science Quarterly*, 1976, 21, 41–65.

Hudson Institute. *Workforce 2000.* Indianapolis: The Hudson Institute, 1987.

Hudson Institute. *Opportunity 2000.* Washington, DC: U.S. Department of Labor, 1988.

Hughes, E.C. *Men and their Work.* Glencoe, IL: Free Press, 1958.

Kanter, R.M. Careers and the wealth of nations: a macro-perspective on the structure and implications of career forms. In M.B. Arthur, D.T. Hall & B.S. Lawrence (Eds.) *Handbook of Career Theory,* New York: Cambridge University Press, 1989a, pp. 506–521.

Kanter, R.M. *When Giants Learn to Dance:* New York: Simon and Schuster, 1989b.

Koike, K. *Understanding Industrial Relations in Modern Japan.* New York: St. Martin's Press, 1988.

Kravetz, D.J. *The Human Resources Revolution — Implementing Progressive Management Practices for Bottom-Line Success.* San Francisco: Jossey-Bass, 1988.

Lawler, E.E. *High Involvement Management.* San Francisco, Jossey-Bass, 1986.

Marshall, J. Re-visioning career concepts: a feminist invitation. In M.B. Arthur, D.T. Hall and B.S. Lawrence (Eds.), *Handbook of Career Theory.* New York: Cambridge University Press, 1989, pp. 275–291.

Miles, R.E. Adapting to technology and competition: A new industrial relations system for the 21st century. *California Management Review*, 1989, 31, 2, 9–28.

Miles, R.E. & Snow, C. Organizations: New concepts for new forms. *California Management Review*, 1986, 28, 3, 62–72.

Millner, G.W. Professional "temps" in today's workforce. *Personnel*, 1989.

Morgan, G. *Riding the Waves of Change: Developing Managerial Competencies for a Turbulent World.* San Francisco: Jossey-Bass, 1988.

Orton, J.D. & Weick, K.E. Loosely coupled systems: a reconceptualization. *Academy of Management Review*, 1990, 15, 203–223.

Oxford English Dictionary. Oxford: Oxford University Press, 1961.

Perin, C. The moral fabric of the office: panopticon discourse and schedule flexibilities. In S. Bacharach, S.R. Barley and P.S. Tolbert (Eds.), *Research in the Sociology of Organizations.* Greenwich, CT: JAI Press, in press.

Peters, T. *Thriving on Chaos.* New York: Knopf, 1987.

Pfeffer, J. A political perspective on careers: interests, networks, and environments. In M.B. Arthur, D.T. Hall and B.S. Lawrence (Eds.), *Handbook of Career Theory.* New York: Cambridge University Press, 1989, pp. 380–396.

Poire, M. & Sabel, C. *The Second Industrial Divide.* New York: Basic Books, 1984.

Pucik, V. Strategic alliances, organizational learning, and competitive advantage: The HRM agenda. *Human Resource Management,* 1988, 27, 1, 77–93.

Quinn, R.E. *Beyond Rational Management: Mastering the Paradoxes and Competing Demands of High Performance.* San Francisco: Jossey-Bass, 1988.

Rosenbaum, J.E. Organizational career systems and employee misperceptions. In M.B. Arthur, D.T. Hall & B.S. Lawrence (Eds.) *Handbook of Career Theory.* New York: Cambridge University Press, 1989, pp. 329–353.

Sekaran, U. & Hall, D.T. Asynchronism in dual-career and family linkages. In M.B. Arthur, D.T. Hall and B.S. Lawrence (Eds.), *Handbook of Career Theory.* New York: Cambridge University Press, 1989, pp. 159–180.

Sonnenfeld, J.A. & Kotter, J.P. The maturation of career theory. *Human Relations,* 1982, 35, 19–46.

Storey, D.J. The role of small and medium-sized enterprises in European job creation: key issues for policy and research. In M. Giaoutzi, P. Nijkamp & D.J. Storey (Eds.) *Small and Medium Size Enterprises and Regional Development.* London: Routledge.

Thomas, D.A. & Alderfer, C.P. The influence of race on career dynamics: theory and research on minority career experiences. In M.B. Arthur, D.T. Hall and B.S. Lawrence (Eds.), *Handbook of Career Theory.* New York: Cambridge University Press, 1989, pp. 133–158.

Van de Ven, A.H. & Angle, H.L. (Eds.) *Research on the Management of Innovation.* Cambridge, MA: Ballinger, 1989.

Van Maanen, J. & Schein, E.H. Career development. In J.R. Hackman and J.L. Suttle (Eds.) *Improving Life at Work.* Santa Monica, CA: Goodyear, 1977, pp. 30–95.

Vrondracek, F.W., Lerner, R.M. & Schulenberg, J.E. *Career Development: A Life-span Development Approach.* Hillsdale, NJ: Erlbaum, 1986.

Weick, K.E. Organization design: organizations as self-designing systems. *Organizational Dynamics,* 1977, 6, 2, 30–46.

Weick, K.E. & Berlinger, L.R. Career improvisation in self-designing organizations. In M.B. Arthur, D.T. Hall and B.S. Lawrence (Eds.), *Handbook of Career Theory.* New York: Cambridge University Press, 1989, pp. 313–328.

Williamson, O.E. *The Economic Institutions of Capitalism.* New York: Free Press, 1985.

SECTION II
PRACTICE

INTRODUCTION TO SECTION II—PRACTICE

DAVID H. MONTROSS

Despite the many changes occurring in the work place, the general pattern of an individual's career, as described by Super, Hall, and others, still seems to have relevance. That is, people still go through a period of exploration, during which they identify, examine, and ultimately select (at least initially), a career. Subsequently, they spend time in the establishment stage, gaining experience and further credentials as needed, before moving into a maintenance stage in which they acquire additional skills, become fully established in their field, and either continue to move up or settle in at some level of an organization. Finally, individuals move into a period of preretirement, and finally, retirement, during which other nonwork interests may dominate. There are now, and will be in the future, more people for whom this pattern will not apply. There will be others who, given the turmoil in the world of work, and varying commitments to work and family, will have minicycles of the stages throughout their career. Others, of course, will fit no discernible pattern.

In Part A, chapters by Floyd, Leape, Asmundson, Shinkman, Leibowitz et al. deal with the issues faced by, and the resources and assistance available to, individuals in the exploratory stage of their career. Beginning in the 1970s, greater attention was paid to providing comprehensive career counseling and placement services to college-age students. Increasingly, college age can mean almost any age, as continuing education and lifelong learning become commonplace. New entrants to the workplace will continue to need assistance in "managing the joining-up process" and as people change career direction more frequently, for all the reasons cited in this book, it will be increasingly important to provide a broad range of services and programs.

In Part B, the issues faced by those moving into the establishment stage are examined. Hill discussed the difficulties of making the transition from individual contributor to first-line manager, and provides excellent advice on how career development professionals can assist with that transition. White addresses the critical importance of job experience in relation to the acquisition of management and leadership competencies. His research, and that of his colleagues at the Center for Creative Leadership, points the way to a new way of thinking about how organizations might more effectively develop their management talent. Finally, Schein describes how "career anchors" can be used by both individuals and organizations to help insure that people are placed in, or choose to pursue, positions that are consistent with their unique pattern of interests, values, and abilities.

In Part C, on the maintenance stage, Kram and Bragar offer an innovative way to tie mentoring programs to the strategic direction of the organization. From the point of view of the individual in this stage, mentoring younger colleagues provides a developmental opportunity at a point in the career that might otherwise be characterized by a declining commitment to the organization and personal growth. Hall and Siebert then offer a model of development, and an innovative approach to succession planning which promises to assist both individuals and organizations keep the flow of talent current and strategically focused. In the concluding section, Myers outlines the issues faced by individuals as they move into the disengagement stage of their career.

Thus, the chapters in this section of the book provide a comprehensive view of the range of resources and assistance available to individuals as they move into and through the major stages of their career, from the time they first come to terms with the need to decide the direction their career will take, through the time when the focus of their lives shifts to retirement, and for most people, to nonwork activities.

Part A
The Exploration Stage

Chapter 4

CAREER SERVICES IN COMMUNITY AND JUNIOR COLLEGES

Deborah L. Floyd

"Colleges that make dreams come true" is an ambitious and lofty goal for any type of institution, especially one that serves a diverse group of students. Community college student affairs practitioners play a key role in working with their teaching and nonteaching colleagues to ensure that the best efforts are implemented to help students' dreams come true.

Dislocated workers, homemakers returning to college, non-English speaking immigrants, recent high school graduates who cannot afford to attend the university, and employed professionals who are seeking job upgrading skills all deserve quality services and programs to help them reach their dreams and fulfill their aspirations. Quality classroom instruction is an obvious and important means to help them achieve their dreams. But without student affairs professionals working with faculty colleagues to assist students in setting goals, developing plans, implementing their plans, and making the transition to further study or work, the community college is merely another type of learning environment that falls short of truly helping students with holistic approaches to achieve their dreams and aspirations.

Imagine a college whose mission is primarily to help students set career goals and plans, and to train for the world of work, or for further study to enter the world of work. Fantasize, if you will, a college that is supported through state and federal resources, and often local tax dollars, so that tuition rates are very low in efforts to provide educational opportunities for all. This is a college that is deeply grounded in the community in which it is located and as the community changes, through plant closings or new companies entering the area, the institution is ready and willing to provide educational and training opportunities. This is a comprehensive community college—the fastest growing and most criticized higher education institution in the United States.

Community, junior, and technical colleges enroll and serve more students than any other institution that comprises the higher education system. More

91

than 50 percent of America's college freshmen are community college students. Enrollment at two-year colleges accounts for approximately 43 percent of this nation's total undergraduate population (Atwell and Parnell, 1988) with more than 5.7 million students enrolled in credit classes and another five million in noncredit classes (Rowan and Mazie, 1990). Thus, the 1,222 community, junior, and technical colleges in the United States annually enroll more than 10.7 million people.

Despite these impressive numbers, the average American still tends to define college as either a baccalaureate or research institution.

Prior to 1900, only a few "junior colleges" existed anywhere in the world. Today, community, junior, and technical colleges comprise the largest and fastest growing segment of American higher education. Most community colleges have open-door admission policies and serve a diverse student population through credit and noncredit classes and community service programs. Comprehensive community colleges offer certificate and associate degree programs, some of which are designed to prepare students to enter the employment market immediately, while others are for the purpose of senior college transfer.

Community colleges have been praised for making "dreams come true" (Rowan and Mazie, 1990) and criticized for "diverting dreams" (Brint and Karabel, 1989). Rowan and Mazie (1990) praise community colleges for their open-door programs which serve a diverse segment of society, involving single parents on welfare, recent high school graduates, homemakers, working students, and dislocated workers.

Critics contend, however, that many educational and career dreams are diverted by attending a community college. According to sociologists Brint and Karabel (1989), community colleges have higher attrition rates than other institutions. Their research is disturbing since it paints a picture that challenges the quality and overall fulfillment of the promises of community colleges.

These criticisms of American community colleges are not new. In fact, in 1960 Burton Clark coined the term "cooling out" to describe the process of toning down the career and academic aspirations of underprepared community college students. The "cooling out" function actually encourages students toward more realistic aspirations and plans than they had when they originally enrolled in the institution. In 1976, Steven Zwerling criticized community colleges and called them "second best" institutions because they tended to preserve the social status quo. Thus, some critics contend that community colleges are overemphasizing vocational education and are in fact increasing social inequities by creating a two-track higher education system (Rowan and Mazie, 1990). Nevertheless, vocational and career education remains an important and unique role in community college as this sets community colleges apart from universities.

Who are community college students? Representing the largest single student group attending any type of American higher education institution, community college students represent a broad spectrum of ages, ethnic backgrounds, and gender. More than 50 percent of community college students are 22 or older, 56 percent are women and 37 percent are enrolled part-time. The most popular major fields for associate degree studies include business (26.6%), liberal and general studies (23.4%), health (15.1%), and engineering technologies (13.2%) (El-Khawas, 1988). Many adults attending community colleges are facing self-concept and role conflict issues. They are either juggling jobs, trying to attend classes, transition of returning to college, retiring, changing careers, or facing some other crisis that affects adults in various stages of development (Haskel and Wiener, 1986).

Why do these students enroll in community colleges? Most students enroll to gain credit for freshman and sophomore level courses which will transfer to a four-year college for a baccalaureate degree, to upgrade skills, or to obtain a certificate or a degree so that they may immediately enter the world of work. They may simply seek career exploration and development. In addition to the 5 million-plus students served through noncredit courses and programs, millions of other citizens utilize local community college facilities such as libraries, museums, and other educational and cultural programs. According to Floyd and Weihe (1986), student affairs professionals are, for the most part, neglecting the counseling and support needs of the noncredit learners.

Why is the noncredit and continuing education enrollment so large in community colleges? Most community colleges pride themselves in offering noncredit and continuing education programs that are easily accessible and affordable. Job upgrading skills are frequently taught through noncredit and continuing education courses and often these courses and programs are offered in off-campus locations convenient for working students. Easy access, flexibility, and affordability are keys to successful noncredit programming.

In short, community colleges strive to reflect the communities they serve. They are challenged to meet the needs of adult learners, youth, citizens entering and reentering the job market, as well as those needing life planning, job placement, and senior college transfer. Comprehensive community colleges aspire to serve transfer learners, occupational and technical learners, noncredit and continuing education learners, and learners who are exploring career and life options.

Imagine a college whose mission is career development. This is the community college.

Issues and Challenges for the 1990's

It is quite clear from predictions and opinions of Dale Parnell (1990) in his book *Dateline 2000: The New Agenda for Higher Education* that the 1990s will be known for rapid change in population growth, economics, technology, and other aspects of American society, forecasts that are grounded in sound empirical data. Angel and DeVault (1991) have emphasized the importance of embracing these predictions by conceptualizing the challenges and by approaching the future with proactive plans.

Community college student affairs practitioners would be wise to become well-versed in these global issues affecting American society, higher education, and specifically community colleges. To be successful and effective in providing quality career services and programs requires an in depth understanding of the breadth and depth of our rapidly changing society.

At the very heart of the mission of the community college is the fulfillment of the challenge of student success. That success is often tied to career exploration and training for job skills or for transfer to higher levels of study. Most community colleges have some sort of career laboratory or center in a centralized location to provide career exploration and job placement needs of students. The strong vocational component of community colleges coupled with the challenges of the open door are clear reasons for the need for career services.

As we face the challenges ahead, which include serving an even more diverse student clientele and a more complex and evolving community college mission, the need to articulate issues and challenges which will help improve career services and student success becomes paramount. To that end the following challenges for action are suggested:

I. *Community colleges must make a commitment to career services and must develop written plans for career development services that are grounded in appropriate theories, research, and models.*

Although most community colleges have career resource centers and other formalized career programs (Haskell and Wiener, 1986), few colleges actually have developed written plans, including a written model, for their particular institution. The Metropolitan Community Colleges in Kansas City, Missouri, have created and implemented such a career development model designed to serve the diversity of their students career planning needs. Their model is not a linear process, rather it recognizes that students have changing needs during the various stages of their education. These needs may include assessment, self-exploration, career resource investigation, career planning, job search, job placement, and networking. The Metropolitan Community College Career Center focuses heavily on intake and referral. The benefits of this model to the student body are many:

A. Improved student retention—students who have ill-defined career plans do not persist to the same degree as those who have career plans.

B. Increased enrollment in vocational courses—these career services have increased the retention of students who may only enroll for one or two semesters.

C. Support for the college recruitment efforts—the center has provided a positive, professional image that has assisted in attracting students.

Fullerton College professionals in Orange County, California, have also recognized the importance of developing a career plan. The Fullerton College plan focuses on integrating both life plans and career services, and includes a career laboratory grounded in theory and research about the adult life span. Staff has developed an adult reentry handbook designed to assist adult reentry students in addressing various needs and in offering services to assist them in being successful.

Another example of a successful career model is the one developed by the Collin County Community College District (Floyd and Money, 1989). In 1988 this College District in Texas conducted a project to develop, implement, and evaluate a model career laboratory called a Future Shop. The model laboratory had three components: (1) career assessment and exploration—including a career resource library for career interest assessments, mentor programs, job fair, and employee education; (2) job transition and grooming—including interview coaching, seminars and résumé writing, senior college transfer, and video interviewing; (3) placement and transition support—including computerized job referral system, college-related job listings, job library, assistance with résumés, and senior college transfer articulation resources. The Future Shop was initially funded through Carl D. Perkins Vocational Education Act monies. The model was piloted at 10 community colleges and served over 15,000 students during its first year. Evaluations of the model are most supportive of the concepts and the program.

II. *Community colleges should ensure that career services and programs reflect the comprehensive mission of the institution especially the commitment to student success.*

Community colleges are accustomed to serving diverse populations. The dislocated worker, part-time evening student, non-English speaking immigrant, and recent high school graduate are typical examples of the student diversity found on community college campuses. Therefore, to ensure student success, career services, and programs must be designed to reflect that diversity. Most student matriculation and student success models describe a "student flow" from the period preceding enrollment through testing, assessment, advising, course placement, matriculation, and transition into the world of work or on to senior college. Effective and successful career services and programs should be an integral component of these plans in efforts to enhance the total institutional student success model.

Seminole Community College in Sanford, Florida, has recognized the importance of supporting student success by integrating the process of orientation into their comprehensive career services and programs. During their orientation for all new students, a survey is conducted to assist staff in learning about the career counseling concerns and other issues of new students. The results are used by career planning and placement staff to develop targeted workshops and to allocate resources for the year.

At Normandale Community College in Bloomington, Minnesota, a successful career clinic project was designed for adults who want to change careers, reenter the job market, or to further their educational careers and goals. Through the clinic, numerous programs are offered including career assessment, workshops, a career resource and job hunting skills library, seminars and programs, and out-placement counseling for companies. The clinic is staffed by both counselors and continuing education personnel thus encouraging collaboration in serving the noncredit learners. Credit student retention has been increased through the development and implementation of this career development program which includes a component of individualized career planning.

Midlands Technical College in Columbia, South Carolina, has aggressively embraced the student success model by implementing a "success made easier" orientation program that links many aspects of orientation with career planning. Midlands is also a participant in a student outcomes research project, Project Cooperation, which studies student success variables on community college campuses.

An important key to effective career services and programs in community colleges is integrating these services in a manner that is understandable and easily available to students. While centralized career laboratories are effective and useful with certain students, career services should be broadened to reach the diverse students enrolled in programs during day and evenings, for credit and noncredit, and in multiple locations throughout the service area.

III. *Community colleges must establish effective academic advising programs and services that integrate the resources of faculty and student affairs staff and focus on student success.*

Most community colleges have centralized career counseling services and laboratories. However, very few colleges have effective academic advising programs that utilize the expertise of faculty and student affairs staff toward the implementation of worthy student goals.

An important part of the career exploration process is the enhancement of the quality and quantity of contact between students and faculty. A student contemplating a career in psychology, teaching, or child development may learn a great deal from working with a career counselor in a career resource library, but the value of contact with faculty in those disciplines is much more greater.

Unfortunately, few community colleges have been able to implement effective "shared" academic advising programs. Although most professionals recognize the value of an effective faculty advising program most community colleges are still implementing traditional approaches to advising through centralized counseling and advising personnel.

However, as mandates for advising increase (often without additional resources), community colleges are finding it necessary to creatively develop academic advising programs. For instance, in direct response to a state mandated program called TASP (Texas Academic Skills Program), Richland College of the Dallas County Community College System implemented a mandatory assessment and advising program for over 13,000 credit students. In response to this mandate for academic advising of all students, the Richland College staff developed a plan to handle the increased load without adding additional counseling staff (Darin, 1990). According to Darin, the College saved approximately $98,000 by utilizing faculty and staff in the advising and registration process. Thus, the use of faculty in academic advising and career planning is not only beneficial to students, but also resulted in significant savings to the College.

Where feasible, community college, student affairs, and instructional faculty should collaborate to make career services and programs a part of the curriculum through workshops, seminars, and cocurricular activities. Sheridan College in Sheridan, Wyoming, defines their career services offering as a "college success curriculum." The curriculum is designed to prepare students in basic skills, GED, job upgrade, and self-improvement. Sheridan College staff pride themselves on collaborative efforts between counseling and advising staff, learning center personnel, and other professional colleagues.

Brookhaven College of the Dallas County Community College District has effectively integrated their career planning program into the curriculum by developing a series of in-house manuals on career decision-making highlighting the services, programs, and processes. These career planning guides describe the planning process in a cyclical manner that includes: (1) taking control of your future and clarifying your future life planning; (2) completing self-assessment exercises and increasing the awareness of your unique self; (3) identifying career options; (4) getting the details of research and making those options real; (5) evaluating, weighing, and choosing options; and (6) setting goals and planning action. These guides are supplemented by courses and programs available through the credit and noncredit curriculum.

The St. Charles Community College District in St. Charles, Missouri, a fairly new college district, demonstrated their commitment to career development early on by the establishing a career planning and placement center. In addition, the College has recognized the importance of providing credit and noncredit courses and programs.

Piedmont Technical College in Greenwood, South Carolina, offers a series of programs and services through their career counseling service, including a program called Program for Adult Learners (PALS). This program is designed to facilitate the successful transition of the returning student to college life and includes a series of workshops and activities offered on a quarterly basis designed to assist the learner in overcoming fears about returning to school. Faculty and staff work together to assist prospective students with decision making, self-esteem building, career and curriculum exploration, test anxiety, academic survival skills, financial aid, support services, and other aspects of interest to the adult reentering learner. Piedmont Technical College's career counseling center also provides services to thousands of local high school students each year through various programs designed to increase the students' exposure to occupations and careers. Counselors offer career planning workshops, administer interest inventories, and offer a number of programs designed to assist high school counselors and students in the career decision-making process.

IV. *Community colleges must provide the noncredit learner should be afforded effective career services and programs.*

Almost half of all community college students today are enrolled in non-credit continuing education courses and programs. As Floyd and Weihe (1986) noted, community college student affairs professionals are, for the most part, ignoring this important population. Often noncredit learners are enrolled for the purpose of learning job skills and student affairs professionals should be providing more support to these learners and faculty. Economic development is playing an emerging role in community college education. Student affairs practitioners must meet, with their colleagues, the diverse challenges associated with training, retraining, and economic development missions.

Collin County Community College District with its model Future Shop program has experienced difficulty in keeping programs available to noncredit learners without charging fees for various services. The Future Shop was originally implemented in 1988 as an open laboratory for students (credit and noncredit) and for community residents. Services initially were free of charge but this policy was changed in 1991 when a fee for services was instituted for those not enrolled in credit classes. This is an unfortunate trend, limiting these important services to the credit learner, especially since most community colleges are funded, in part, through local tax dollars.

It is refreshing, however, to see a reversing of that trend in some institutions which have taken a stand to make a commitment to serve the community learner through career services and programs. Cabrillo College in Aptos, California, has made this commitment and is providing specific career and job placement services to community residents, credit students, and noncredit learners. According to the Cabrillo College staff they serve as a transfer feeder institution to the University of California-Santa Cruz and the majority of their students find the burden of initial career decision making falling on their shoulders while enrolled for credit or noncredit programs at Cabrillo.

Triton College in River Grove, Illinois, has creatively addressed the challenge of providing comprehensive services for the career development needs of credit and noncredit learners by offering career planning and placement services and professional assessment services to businesses on a fee basis. In addition, Triton College staff sponsors retraining assistance programs and free job training and placement services in various locations in response to layoff, plant closings, or changes in technology. *The Triton Connection: A Guide for Success in the Job Market* (Triton College, 1989) was published by Triton College and the College Placement Council, Inc. to provide career planning and placement guidelines at two- and four-year colleges as well as to employers who hired the graduates of the institutions. This publication is an excellent example of Triton College's efforts to help students with the processes of career decision making and the complex and often discouraging aspects of the job search. Triton College also sold advertising for the publication, thus limiting the financial burden in offering these materials for students.

As community college practitioners strive to become more community-based, and to reach out to noncredit and credit learners alike, the sheer numbers of part-time and evening students can often be overwhelming. A recent survey of California community colleges revealed that most community colleges offer job placement services as a part of their comprehensive career services programs (Hood, 1990). However, these services are limited and are not consistently available for evening students. Nor are the offices open for a full 40 hours a week. But there is some evidence to support the fact that younger students are generally in greater need of career services than older students and perhaps California community colleges are simply channeling their resources to the students most in need (Healey and Reilly, 1989).

As community colleges become more community-based in their work, the need for them to increase their partnerships with the business community is becoming more apparent. The career center at Johnson County Community College in Overland Park, Kansas, encourages students to participate in various internships with businesses and other area organizations to learn practical, hands-on skills and to experience first-hand the career decision-making process. The Collin County Community College District in Texas includes a mentor program as part of its Future Shop that is intended to connect students with volunteer mentors in the business community to enhance and enrich the students' resources in the career decision-making process. Both of these college districts have successful cooperative education programs. Student affairs professionals should collaborate with instructional colleagues to utilize internships and cooperative education programs to enhance career services opportunities for students.

V. *Community colleges should use technology career services and programs.*

The days of the career laboratory with shelves of books including the *Dictionary of Occupational Titles*, files that include transfer guides, career interest inventories, and other paper resources are history on most community college campuses. While these resources are important and most colleges have a career resource library that includes these materials, colleges must recognize the value of technology in this arena. Many institutions and various state groups are recognizing the importance of utilizing technology in career decision making, in the development of job placement databases, and in the senior college transfer articulation processes.

The Florida State Department of Education, for instance, has developed and maintains an information database called MicroChoices.

MicroChoices contains both a career file and an education file that includes information about over 1,200 Florida careers. The computerized education file contains information about programs of study, degrees, admissions requirements, costs, and suggested areas of study based on a student's interest. Many Florida community colleges utilize MicroChoices in addition to other computerized programs such as DISCOVER. Through the Seminole Community College (Florida) career resource library students may access a program called SOLAR (Student On Line Advisement and Articulation) which is a computerized program added to the DISCOVER database.

Triton College in Illinois routinely provides out-placement counseling and other career services such as CHIPS (Computerized Help and Planning System) which is a work-style assessment for prospective employees. The CHIPS program has been effective in providing information about personality traits that link to various job titles and the individual.

In the State of Virginia, many public school districts, four-year colleges, universities, and community colleges have joined together to form a consortium to implement DISCOVER. This type of shared use of technology was also implemented by the 10 Texas community colleges when they developed the Future Shop Laboratory and various other computerized programs (Floyd and Money, 1989).

VII. *Community college student affairs staff members need to aggressively tell their story about their efforts to meet the career development needs of students in order to ensure student success.*

As fiscal resources become more competitive and critics of the community college continue to sing about failures, community college practitioners would be wise to aggressively accept the challenge of telling about their successes. In cases in which dreams have come true for students, student affairs practitioners must celebrate and publicize those stories. Success stories will undoubtedly become increasingly important for career development staff who are often seen as "frills" and "nonessentials."

Most community colleges have at least one or more "shining stars" — glowing examples of successful efforts with students in the area of career services and programs. Unfortunately, too few practitioners write for publication, speak at professional conferences or catalog practical documents with the ERIC Clearinghouse on Junior Colleges at the University of California—Los Angeles. Community college practitioners often give the excuse that they are too busy "doing" great things to write about and share information about their successes. While writing an article may not be a high priority for practitioners, sending reports and research to ERIC is relatively painless and helps tell the story of successes.

It is imperative that community college practitioners form multiple networks and ways to share information, ideas and resources in efforts to meet the needs of an everchanging and diverse student clientele. Since the future will guarantee challenges and change, sharing information and success stories will be beneficial to all.

For the most part, classical career development theories and research have not addressed the needs of English-as-a-second-language students, ethnic minorities, the first generation college-bound student or the diverse population of adult learners. Deep in the files and minds of community college practitioners is valuable information that could provide useful insights to serving this diverse student clientele.

SUMMARY

For student affairs practitioners to meet the challenges of working with their colleagues in efforts to help students' dreams come true, practitioners must be well-versed in the global issues facing community colleges. Rapid enrollment increases, growing diversity among students broadening of the missions in more community-based ways to include economic development, and increasing dialogue among critics of community colleges are important issues for all community college educators.

Community colleges hold a unique place in the higher education arena in that they serve the most diverse student body through the most diverse mission of any segment of higher education. The press of diversity presents many challenges and rewards as practitioners strive to help instructional colleagues fill the academic cups of students who are often so thirsty for knowledge and training.

The opportunities for practitioners during the next decade are as diverse as the students served by community colleges. Leading the list, are these basic challenges:

1. Community colleges must make a commitment to the career services function and to the development of career plans that are grounded in appropriate theories, research, and models.
2. A commitment to student success should be a driving and penetrating force throughout all career services and programs.
3. Comprehensive academic advising programs that integrate student affairs and instructional efforts are a must for effective career development services for students.
4. During the coming years practitioners should develop creative and

effective ways to serve noncredit learners, a group of students largely ignored by career services.

5. This decade will likely be known as a decade of much change due to technology—career services should embrace the challenges of effectively using technology to enhance and deliver programs.

6. Too often, the best programs and stories go untold. Practitioners should increase efforts to tell stories of their successes in career services and programs—these stories will be useful for community college practitioners and university colleagues alike as all segments of higher education seek ways to effectively serve an increasingly diverse student body.

By the year 2,000 community colleges will likely hold the strongest and most effective position in higher education, especially in serving diverse students through a variety of programs and services. Since 1900 these colleges have grown from a handful of "junior colleges" that served a very small number of students to "community colleges" that serve the largest number of students in higher education today. We've come along way in 100 years toward "making dreams come true!"

REFERENCES

Angel, Dan and Mike DeVault (Eds.). (1991) *Conceptualizing 2000: Proactive Planning.* American Association of Community and Junior Colleges: The Community College Press.

Archer-Hetland, B. and Sandra Aase (Eds.). (No date) *Adult Re-entry Handbook.* Handbook published by Fullerton College, Fullerton, California.

Atwell, Robert H. and Dale Parnell. (1988) "Forward." In El-Ehawas, Elaine, Deborah Carter and Cecilia A. Ottinger, *Community College Fact Book.* AACJC and ACE/MacMillian.

Brint, Steven and Jerome Karabel. (1989) *The Diverted Dream: Community Colleges and the Promise of Educational Opportunity in American, 1900–1985.* New York, 1989.

Brookhaven College Counseling Center. (No date) *Career Planning Guide.* Guide published by Brookhaven College, Farmers Branch, Texas.

Clark, Burton. (1960) *The Open Door College: A Case Study,* New York: McGraw Hill.

Darin, Mary. (1990) "Mandatory Advising for Students (Without Increasing the Budget). *The Student Development Network.* Winter/Spring 1990, pg. 6.

El-Khawas, Elaine, Deborah J. Carter and Cecillia A. Ottinger. (1988) *Community College Fact Book.* AACJC and ACE/MacMillian Series on Higher Education.

Floyd, Deborah and Barbara Money (Eds.). (1989) *Future Shop: A Career Planning Adventure.* Cataloged in ERIC Clearinghouse on Junior Colleges, UCLA, ED308899, JC890330.

Floyd, Deborah and Lois E. Weihe. (1985) "Commitments to non-credit students:

Issues for Community College Student Development Educators. *Journal of Staff Program and Organization Development.* Vol. 3, No. 4, pp. 128–132.

Haskell, Patricia and Nancy Wiener. (1986) Career Counseling Adults in a Community College Setting. In Zandy B. Leibowitz and H. Daniel Lea (Eds.). *Adult Career Development: Concepts, Issues, and Practices.* National Career Development Association.

Healy, Charles C. and Kathryn C. Reilly. (1989) "Career Needs of Community College Students: Implications for Services and Theory. *Journal of College Student Development.* Vol. 30, No. 6, Nov. 1989, pp. 541–45.

Hood, Lyn. (1990) California Community College Job Placement Services Survey. Unpublished research available from the author. Cabrillo College, Aptos, California.

Parnell, Dale. (1990) *Dateline 2000: The New Higher Education Agenda.* American Association of Community Junior Colleges: The Community College Press.

Rowen, Carl T., and David M. Mazie. (1990) "Schools that Make Dreams Come True." *Reader's Digest.* Nov. 90, Vol. 137, pp. 37–40.

Schueler, Judy and Terry Fuller. (1990) "Triton College Transfer Articulation System." *Student Development Network.* Winter/Spring 1990. pp. 2 and 7.

Triton College and the College Placement Council, Inc. (1989) *The Triton Connection: A Guide for Success in the Job Market.* River Grove, Illinois: Triton College.

Vaughan, George and Associates. (1983) *Issues for Community Colleges in a New Era.* San Francisco: Jossey-Bass.

Zwerling, Steven. (1976) *Second Best: The Crisis of the Community College.* New York: McGraw Hill.

Chapter 5

CAREER DEVELOPMENT AND THE LIBERAL ARTS STUDENT

Martha P. Leape

The students of the late 1990s will be developing their careers in a world characterized by change: change in the volume and accessibility of information, change in the economic and political interdependence of nations, and changes in the structure and types of work opportunities. Liberal education, with its emphasis on the development of intellectual skill, is a strong foundation for survival in a rapidly evolving environment.

I. LIBERAL EDUCATION AND CAREERS

Liberal education is excellent preparation for participation in the information age. It helps to develop facility in gathering, organizing, and utilizing information; it provides experience in various modes of analyzing and synthesizing information, and it enhances appreciation of the value of information and ideas. These are important attributes for functioning effectively in an age in which access to information is central to productivity.

To prepare young people for a more interdependent world, liberal education programs are not only promoting the study of foreign language and cultures, but are also encouraging students to take time to study or work abroad. The ability to understand the global nature of political, economic, and environmental issues and events will be essential for an effective contribution to human welfare in the future.

During their lifetime, today's undergraduates will need to adapt to change in types of work opportunities, in the structure of institutions and in career patterns. Corporate mergers, entrepreneurial start-ups, and structural transformations in the professions of medicine, law, and education will affect job opportunities, avenues for advancement, and reward systems. Liberal arts graduates will be prepared to cope with these changes because they will have been educated to think creatively, to view situations from several perspectives, to utilize qualitative and quantitative data, to communicate effectively in speech and in writing, and to appreciate cultural and individual differences.

The academic program in liberal education is not designed to prepare the student for specific vocations. There is often little direct relationship between a student's major and future vocation. It is not usually a part of the academic program to help liberal arts students learn how to apply their intellectual skills to career decision making and job hunting. Therefore, career planning professionals in the liberal arts college have special challenges.

II. SPECIAL CHALLENGES FOR CAREER PLANNING PROFESSIONALS IN THE LIBERAL ARTS COLLEGE

Most liberal arts students have little knowledge of the world of work. Many young people do not know what their parents do at work. In times past, children had daily interaction with the adult world of work. As boys and girls walked home from school, they could stop by to visit their father or mother at his or her office or store. They were often expected to work in the family business after school. Now that most parents commute to work, the lives of young people have become increasingly separated from the adult world of work.

Most liberal arts students have broad interests and diverse talents. Usually the students who choose a liberal arts program are intellectually curious and enjoy learning. When evaluating career opportunities, they give high priority to opportunities in which they can continue to grow intellectually.

Liberal arts education does not require that students make career decisions when they are choosing a major. Alumni records show that there is little direct relationship between undergraduate majors and eventual careers of liberal arts graduates. Students should make sure, however, that their academic program includes courses that require utilization of quantitative data and the writing of research papers.

Liberal arts students are often vocationally undecided during college and for some years after graduation. The decision to pursue a liberal arts education does not require making a career decision and, therefore, students can postpone commitment to a specific goal until they are more knowledgeable about the working world and about themselves. They can explore career opportunities during their college years by experimenting with new and different occupations during the summers or term-time and in the first years after graduation.

Liberal arts students who have a career goal as freshmen often question their goal as their intellectual and vocational horizons expand. The exposure to new ideas, people, and worlds, and the development of new personal insights may lead to a reassessment of career goals developed prior to college. Some students explore different careers; others reaffirm their initial career goals.

Liberal arts graduates usually do not have the exact job skills that the employer requests and therefore must learn to translate their experiences and skills into language that persuades the employer that they can do the job. Many employers are interested in liberal arts graduates because they respect the breadth of knowledge and skills developed in a liberal education. However, from any pool of applicants, employers usually hire the candidate who has learned about their business through work experience, activities, and researching the literature.

Many liberal arts faculty members do not interact with the nonacademic world in their professional research. Faculty advisers help students to develop intellectual and communication skills and to grow in self-understanding, but assisting students in researching and evaluating careers is usually outside their sphere of interest.

III. EDUCATIONAL MISSION OF THE CAREER PLANNING OFFICE

The educational mission of the career planning office is to prepare students to take charge of their own career development. To participate productively in this complex and changing world, liberal arts graduates need to learn how to apply their research, analytical, and communication skills to the development of their careers. They need experience in learning about different fields, making career decisions, identifying interesting employers, and competing for jobs. They need to be able to adapt to, and become effective in, new and changing work environments. And they need guidance and support, not only while they are undergraduates, but also during their first few years after graduation.

Students who graduate from college without having conducted at least one job search for a summer or full-time job have not had a complete education. They have not learned the job search skills that will enable them to flourish in today's changing world of work. They are much more likely to become prisoners of their first employment. If they have never initiated a job hunt, they may not have the courage to make a job change when they are unhappy in their work. If their job is phased out or if they are passed over for promotion or partnership, they may experience far greater distress than those who have confidence in their job search skills.

The major share of the resources of the career planning office should be committed to educating students in the skills and strategies of career development. The mission of a career planning office in a liberal arts college or university should include the following:

1. To teach students how to begin to identify career preferences by thinking evaluatively about educational and work experiences;
2. To assist students in gathering information about careers and about themselves as workers;
3. To encourage students to engage in new experiences through college activities, public service, and international experience;
4. To help students develop an understanding of career development and career decision making;
5. To instruct students in researching employers and presenting themselves as job applicants;
6. To teach students how to research graduate schools and fellowships and how to be competitive applicants;
7. To facilitate and support students' transitions from college to work.

1. To Teach Students How to Begin to Identify Their Career Preferences by Thinking Evaluatively About School and Work Experience

Most college students need to be introduced to the importance of thinking evaluatively about their work experience and their school life. Most have had part-time jobs or summer jobs, but usually in environments in which their coworkers were also students and their sole purpose was to earn money. Their primary work experience has been that of a student fulfilling academic requirements and participating in extracurricular activities. They tend to discount these student activities and jobs as not real work, and to believe that they have learned nothing from these experiences that is helpful in thinking about their future career.

This perception should be challenged. There is much that students can learn by identifying what is fulfilling and what is not that is relevant information for career decision making. There are aspects of any job that most people like or dislike, but there are other aspects that individuals respond to differently. Some people find satisfying the very activities that other people experience as frustrating, stressful or boring. Beginning to see oneself as an individual who finds different challenges and rewards in particular activities from one's friends is an important step towards self-awareness. From an analysis of past jobs and activities, the student can identify some of the characteristics of a job or activity that are important and that contribute to making the activity rewarding.

There are several ways that students can be introduced to this process. In individual counseling, the professional can lead the student through an evaluation of past experiences, identifying positive and negative aspects. In this discussion, the counselor demonstrates the process of learning from one's past experiences and reinforces for the student the value of life experience as a source of information about career preferences.

Vocational interest instruments can also be helpful tools in learning to think analytically about career options. The correlation of the individual's interest profile with populations in an array of occupations often helps identify careers to be explored. In the interpretation session, the student should be encouraged to think about the characteristics that closely matched occupations have in common with his or her past experiences. Integration of past experience data and interest inventory data often adds clarity to the emerging identification of career preferences.

The counselor can also use autobiographical exercises to help students think evaluatively about their past experiences. In these exercises, the student is asked to describe experiences and evaluate them while looking for common themes. Examples of commonly used exercises include: asking the student: (1) to describe three significant experiences and list the rewarding and frustrating aspects of each; (2) to focus on three important decisions and to list the considerations that led to each one; (3) to list three accomplishments and describe why they were important. These exercises can be given as homework to be completed between interviews or between meetings of a seminar group.

Whichever methods are used, the objective of evaluating life experiences is to help students learn to value their own perceptions and reactions, to learn how to be analytical about experiences, and to begin to develop a list of characteristics that make an activity or a job rewarding.

2. To Assist Students in Gathering Information About Careers and About Themselves as Workers

Having learned how to learn from past experiences, students will approach career information and career-related experiences more purposefully. A variety of resources and programs can be developed to help students learn about careers.

Career panels at which visiting professionals talk about careers are an excellent way to provide students firsthand career information. Advanced preparation of the speakers is essential so that they are ready to discuss the rewards and satisfactions that they experience in their careers, to give advice on how students might arrange jobs or internships in that field, and if possible, to serve as career advisers for interested students. A handout which lists the names, titles, and addresses of each panelist enables students to make follow-up contact with the speakers whose careers they found to be especially interesting.

Career fairs which bring together a large number of employers in one location, preferably on campus, make career information easily accessible to all students. During the fair, employer representatives are available to talk with students and distribute literature about career opportunities in their organizations. The atmosphere is friendly and informal. All types of questions are welcome: do you have summer jobs, what do financial analysts do, do you have a training program, how many college graduates will you be hiring?

Summer jobs and internships provide the opportunity to be a participant/observer in the actual work setting of an occupation that a student is exploring. While fulfilling responsibilities as an employee, the student has the opportunity to interact with professionals and managers. If the student expresses interest in learning about the career field, the professionals on the job are usually willing to discuss what they find most and least rewarding in the work. For some students, career-related summer jobs are the best way to begin exploring careers. As full-time members of the work force, students often develop the confidence to initiate interviews with people in responsible positions.

Another way to experience a career field is through short-term internships. During term-time, internships involve the opportunity to spend a few hours each week with the sponsor. During college vacation periods, the intern might spend one to ten working days with the sponsor. Alumni are recruited to act as sponsors and most take the time to give college students a valuable "inside" look at the rewards and frustrations of their work. Internship programs should be administered by a career planning office because sponsors are seldom willing to take the time to review applications and make selections.

Alumni career advisers who volunteer to be available to meet with students at their place of work are an invaluable resource. Information about each adviser's current position and career history should be kept in files or databases accessible to students. Students can select advisers in careers they want to explore and make appointments by telephone or by letter. In order to make the best use of the career adviser's time, students are advised to prepare for each visit by reading about the career field and the organization. To introduce themselves, students should hand a resume to the adviser and then proceed to focus the conversation on the adviser's career experience and what he/she finds rewarding in his/her work. This generates a discussion that is interesting to the adviser as well as the student because it requires that the adviser reflect evaluatively on his or her career experience rather than just describe work performed. If after one career adviser interview, a student becomes interested in the field, visits to other advisers in the same field will help to further inform and verify that interest.

Reading career literature which describes job functions and responsibilities, organizational structure, and work environment is important preparation for career exploration experiences. Familiarity with the vocabulary, job titles, major functions, and goals and objectives of a career field make it possible for the student to engage in a more informative interview, whether it is with a career adviser or a potential employer. In addition, reading newspapers, magazines, and journals which are read by people in a field introduces the student to current problems and issues in that field. Students need to learn that just as every academic field has its journals, so every profession and industry has its own literature.

Both literature research and experiential research are important in career exploration. Career literature is valuable as an introduction to a field and also as a resource for more detailed information as the students' career search becomes more focused. Experiencing the work environment and meeting with professionals to discuss career decisions gives the student insights into how individuals experience their work. This can help the student make a personal assessment of whether or not the work is rewarding.

3. To Encourage Students to Engage in New Experiences Through College Activities, Public Service, and International Experience

The academic program is only part of the college experience; extracurricular activities also provide important opportunities to learn. Participation in the theatre, athletics, music groups, publications, and student government offers opportunities to explore what might be rewarding and to develop talents and skills which will enrich one's career.

The functions of a student organization are similar to those of any organization: developing goals and objectives, securing funding or generating revenues, budgeting, developing policies and procedures, advertising, and producing an event or publication, playing a game, or providing services. Students who take on responsibilities in extracurricular activities learn what roles they enjoy and develop useful, transferable skills. Employers are interested in students' ability to function effectively in organizations, especially as team members.

Students sometimes fail to realize that producing a play, for example, provides real experience in recruiting and supervising a team, delegating responsibility, managing a budget, planning and producing a publicity campaign, and taking care of administrative details in a timely fashion. Writing for a college newspaper provides experience in researching stories, conducting interviews, and meeting deadlines. Student publications also require a business staff which sells advertising space, supervises distribution, and designs marketing campaigns to improve circulation.

Founding a new organization with a particular objective (developing an AIDS education program, for example) is a creative and entrepreneurial project and takes initiative, persistence, careful planning, and commitment. If successful, the founder can take great satisfaction in the achievement because it has made a worthwhile contribution to the community.

Jobs or volunteer service outside the college community, in which students take on responsibilities in new situations with new people, can broaden their world view and build self-confidence. Students should be encouraged to become involved in volunteer service. They can benefit immeasurably from experiences which expand their knowledge of work, people, and cultures.

In recent years, many liberal arts colleges have increased their efforts to promote public service activities. Growing numbers of college students are involved in services to children, the elderly, the homeless, the illiterate, and the disadvantaged. Through volunteer service in the college community or in far-away cities and villages, students gain increased understanding of the range of human experience and of the possibilities and limitations of one person's efforts to make a difference.

International experience introduces students to foreign cultures and to different world views. They learn to adapt to living in a different culture and to consider issues from multinational perspectives. They gain an appreciation of the difficulties of cross-cultural communication. Experience in living abroad is important preparation for developing a career in an increasingly global society. By offering programs which make it possible for students to study, work, or serve as volunteers overseas, the career planning office facilitates the exploration of experiences abroad as well as in the United States.

4. To Help Students Develop an Understanding of Career Development and Career Decision Making

Many college students believe that one career decision will determine their lifework. The question, "What are you going to be when you grow up?" as asked by concerned parents and relatives, tends to reinforce this limited view. To help students realize that career development is a lifelong process, the career planning office should make available career panelists and career advisers whose careers have evolved through different stages. These professionals can share with students the experience of researching alternatives, developing new options, and making decisions that launched a new career.

Students who have begun their career exploration by analyzing what they have learned from past experiences are better prepared to carry out ongoing evaluation of work experiences. As they develop a list of characteristics that are important, they are able to research careers more efficiently because they know what they need to know. They can interview career advisers more productively because they know what questions they want answered. And they can recognize more readily whether a specific career is interesting or not.

There is no right style of career decision making—different individuals make their career decisions differently. The balance between rational, step-by-step processing of facts, meditative reflection, and intuitive leaps varies from one person to another. It may also change for an individual from one decision to the next. In most cases, the quality of a decision is related to the quality of relevant information available to the individual. However, because it is not possible to know all the facts relevant to a career decision, the role of intuition is important.

Learning to make career decisions takes practice. When students develop a plan for exploring careers, when they choose a summer job or an internship, they are learning to make career-related decisions. Therefore, career exploration programs should be structured so that students gain practice in making choices. These decisions help them take responsibility for their own career development.

5. To Instruct Students in Researching Employers and Presenting Themselves as Job Applicants

Students are motivated to learn how to job hunt when they want a job. A career planning office should design its resources so that, in the process of arranging a job or internship, a student will gain experience in all aspects of job hunting. Students prefer to be presented with a list of available summer jobs from which they can select the one they want; unfortunately, programs which match students with jobs or internships (usually by computer) rob students of the opportunity to learn and to practice job hunting skills.

Workshops on researching employers, preparing resumes, writing cover letters, and interviewing for jobs are effective ways to instruct students in the elements of job hunting. These functions are not sequential steps, but interdependent, ongoing activities.

Researching employers is a process that continues throughout the job hunt. As the job search progresses, the applicant needs specific information about the job, the employer, and the industry. This information is usually available from company literature, trade publications, company representatives at career fairs, and alumni career advisers. Being knowledgeable about a job opportunity makes it possible to tailor one's written presentation and prepare for interviews. It also communicates to the employer that the candidate is interested in the organization.

Preparing a resume is particularly challenging for the liberal arts student. A résumé is not a life history. It is a presentation in outline form of education, jobs, and activities which communicates one's qualifications for employment. Because liberal arts students often do not appear to employers to emerge from their academic programs with readily identifiable skills, it is important that they describe accomplishments that indicate that they will be able to fulfill the responsibilities of the job. Employers look for applicants who can learn quickly, who are energetic, reliable, and enthusiastic workers, who can function effectively in an organization, who are adaptable and cooperative, and who set high standards for their work. These attributes can be communicated on the résumé.

Writing is supposed to be a special strength of liberal arts students. As samples of the student's writing, cover letters are an opportunity to demonstrate the ability to write clear, concise, informative statements in a creative and memorable style. If the cover letter attracts the employer's interest and curiosity, the resume is likely to be read more attentively. In workshops, students can be instructed in the objectives, forms, style, and process of preparing resumes and cover letters, and can be provided with samples to critique and use as models. As follow-up to group instruction, individual advising on these documents in the context of a career counseling session can be very productive.

Interview training in seminars with role playing, and in individual sessions or small groups with videotaping, can be very educational. When students learn to interview effectively and confidently, they have learned a skill that will be useful throughout their lives. Feeling confident about one's interviewing skill is not a substitute, however, for being well prepared for an interview. The student needs to research the job and the employer and to know the qualifications the employer is seeking. The student must communicate to the employer how skills learned in past experiences have served as preparation for that particular job. Researching the organization and the industry prepares the student to participate intelligently in the conversation, to make appropriate responses, and to ask informed questions.

6. To Teach Students How to Research Graduate Schools and Fellowships and How to Be Competitive Applicants.

For those students who are interested in graduate study, resources should be available to assist in identifying the information they need; the information available from directories, periodicals, and special references; and the information available only from knowledgeable individuals such as faculty members, graduate students, and career advisers.

Learning to research fellowships is a similar process. There are directories that describe fellowships available for specific purposes and/or for special populations. Directories list grants for students who want to go abroad to study, do research, or serve as a volunteer; who want to go to graduate school in this country; and who have a special project that they would like to carry out in the arts or public service. Career advisers and other experts in the field can also be a source of information about grants.

Advice on competing for admission to graduate school or for a fellowship may improve the candidate's chances for success. Learning how to prepare application essays and grant proposals is a skill which liberal arts graduates will use many times in any/all careers in the arts, academe, museums, and public service. Advice on the content and format of interviews for each type of competition helps guide the student's preparation. Interview training with videotaping can improve a student's ability to present research objectives, special projects, career interests, or long-range plans more articulately.

Most graduating seniors choose to work first before considering graduate study. Being employed gives them the opportunity to be self-supporting, to experience life as a full-time working adult, to learn about a specific career field, and to evaluate the relevance of graduate study as a factor in career advancement. Many of these young alumni return to the career planning office for advice on graduate school plans if the college opens its services to alumni.

7. To Facilitate and Support Students' Transitions from College to Work

The transition from college to work is a major life change and graduating seniors need to prepare for it. Their years of returning to college each fall have ended and they need to make decisions about what they are going to do next. Most seniors seek employment in order to be financially self-supporting. Some, however, enter graduate school and a few win fellowships to support study or travel.

The readiness of individual seniors for this next step ranges from the student with a clear vision of his/her career goals and first job, to the student who has enjoyed every job and activity that he has experienced and therefore does not know in which direction to turn, to the student who wonders why any employer would hire him. Programs and services need to be available to assist each of these students and their classmates with individual concerns and uncertainties about postgraduate plans.

For those seniors who have not made progress in identifying a long-range career goal, the immediate need is to decide on one or two types of employment that will be interesting and will make them self-supporting. They need to be prepared to make a short-term commitment to an employer; they do not need to make a lifelong commitment. If they have not engaged in any career exploration activities as underclassmen, it would be wise for them to do so in a concentrated fashion during the senior year. Career fairs, internships, part-time jobs, and interviews with career advisers are ways for the senior to gather information and experience that will assist him in focusing on postgraduate employment.

On-campus recruiting brings to the college employers who are interested in hiring liberal arts graduates. Students should research these employment opportunities carefully to assess interest and to learn the qualifications each employer is seeking. Unfortunately, a limited range of industries recruits on college campuses and employers often select the colleges they will visit on the basis of their success in hiring graduates in previous years. Career planning officers should make an effort to increase the diversity of types of employers represented in on-campus recruiting.

Most types of employers do not recruit on campus. The majority of liberal arts graduates will have to initiate a job search beyond on-campus recruiting in order to find employment. Graduating seniors are usually most eager to learn how to research employers and conduct a job hunt. Staff resources should be allocated so that students interested in employers who do not recruit on campus (such as museums, newspapers, government agencies, research institutes, social service and public interest organizations), will have instruction and support in finding employment.

IV. CAREER PLANNING SERVICES FOR LIBERAL ARTS STUDENTS

Structure

In order to respond to the diverse needs and interests of liberal arts students, the career planning office must offer a broad array of services. There should be resources and programs to assist students in making plans for time away during college as well as postgraduate plans.

The career planning office should encourage participation in new experiences and stimulate expansion of career horizons by making available information about a broad range of options, by providing an environment that supports experimentation, and by advising students to develop opportunities for themselves.

Career development programs and resources should be designed in an open matrix that can be accessed by students at any point in the college experience. Students in liberal arts colleges differ greatly in all aspects of their career development: their interest in careers, their readiness to make career decisions, their sense of themselves as workers, their breadth of experience, their urgency to develop a career goal. In planning the resources, programs, and services of the career planning office, the guiding principle should be to design every resource and program so that it is available and useful to students at any stage of career development.

Resources

Career Counseling. Because the liberal arts population is so diverse in its developmental stage, its interests, and its needs, individual counseling is an essential part of the career services. Career counseling in the developmental context takes into consideration readiness of the student to take responsibility for making plans for his/her future. Counselors use their knowledge about career opportunities, career exploration and decision making to help the student progress in his/her career development. In individual sessions, counselors assist students in thinking evaluatively about past experiences, identifying career preferences, clarifying short- and long-range goals, and designing plans of action to achieve those goals. As counselors learn about students' dreams, aspirations, anxieties, and concerns, they are able to design group meetings and resources that respond to students' ever-changing needs.

Career Library. A career library should include a collection of career planning literature, career descriptive literature, graduate school information, professional and trade journals, and both national and international directories. Special directories such as the **Encyclopedia of Associations, Public Interest Profiles, Foundation Directory, Gale Directory of Publications, Washington Information Directory, Congressional Staff Directory, Reference Book of Corporate Managements** and **International Directory of Research Centers,** are particularly useful for identifying potential career advisers or employers. Professional and trade journals and newspapers are also important in demonstrating to students that occupational fields have their own literature just as academic fields do. Researching a company or an employer in a target industry is similar to doing a research project for a course. The librarian and counselors collaborate to develop a collection of references that meets the students' needs.

Internship Listings. Paid and unpaid internships make students aware of the opportunities in different career fields. There are good published directories of internships, but initiating correspondence with employers, especially in the media, the arts, government, and the nonprofit sector, can elicit information about internship opportunities not listed in any published source.

Job Listings. Although students should not limit their job search to applying for listed jobs, they should certainly apply for any that interest them. Job listings are also an educational resource. Students exploring careers find that reviewing job listings is a helpful way to begin learning what people do in a particular field. For the job hunter, listings provide specific information about the titles and descriptions of jobs for college graduates thus when approaching employers, the job seeker knows how to discuss the kind of work he/she might be able to do in that organization.

Alumni Career Advisers. Alumni who volunteer to serve as career advisers are a valuable resource for students. Alumni should be asked to meet with students at work so that the student has the opportunity to observe the work environment. The information that the student seeks will vary, depending on whether that person is exploring careers, or researching opportunities and evaluating prospective employers within a particular career field.

Publications. There are many excellent career planning books on the market, but there are two important reasons for developing guidebooks and handbooks for one's own students. Specially prepared books can be tailored to meet idiosyncratic needs of the students of a particular college. In addition, the process of preparing materials is excellent in-service training for the staff.

Newsletter. A weekly newsletter that announces group meetings, gives samplings of job and internship listings, provides advice, and lists deadlines relevant to graduate school and fellowship applications is valuable for communicating with students and serves as a reminder that there is a world of opportunities beyond the walls of the college.

Programs

Career Panels and Seminars. Group meetings at which invited guests speak about their careers can be very informative. In their presentations, these guests should discuss what they find rewarding in their work, what they do in a typical work day, how they became qualified for their present position, what kind of graduate study they recommend, etc. When the subject of the panel is internships, work or study abroad, or fellowships, the speakers can be students or recent graduates who have returned from internships or time abroad. A clear advantage of group meetings is that students usually learn from each other's questions and gain information and advice that they had not anticipated.

Workshops. Members of the staff lead workshops at which they offer information and advice and provide a forum for students to ask questions. Workshops are especially suitable for communicating introductory information and for providing instruction in job hunting skills, application procedures for graduate school and fellowships, and preparation of application essays and project proposals. If a student attends a workshop before meeting with a counselor, the counseling session can be used to discuss issues of special interest to the individual student.

Video Interview Training. Videotaping is a powerful tool for improving interviewing behavior. In individual or small group sessions, a counselor conducts brief interviews asking questions appropriate to the type of interview for which the students are preparing and videotapes the student(s) as they respond. The videotape is then reviewed by the counselor and the student(s) to critique it and discuss possible improvements.

Internships. The opportunity to spend time with a person at work either as an observer or working on a special project can be helpful to the novice career explorer or to the person who wants to learn more about opportunities in a chosen career. Internships may be scheduled during term-time or college vacations. Sponsors are usually alumni or parents of students. People with no personal connection with the college often provide internships as well.

Career Days. Held in a large hall with booths or tables for employers, career days are a multipurpose educational event for students. No question is too naive or too sophisticated. The employer representatives are there to inform students about their organization and to discuss summer and full-time job opportunities for liberal arts students. Career days may be held on campus or in urban centers and are sponsored by individual colleges or by consortia. Holding separate career days for government and public service agencies (employers who typically do not recruit on campus) is especially helpful to students seeking career in the nonprofit sector.

On-Campus Recruiting. Employers in certain industries recruit new employees by interviewing graduating students on campus. Competition for interviews with these employers is usually very keen because they allow students to be interviewed with a minimal investment of time and effort. The students who are successful in these interviews are the ones who have researched the organization and the field and are well prepared for the interview.

Increasing the number and/or diversity of employers represented in on-campus recruiting is a worthwhile project, if it can be done without taking time away from advising students on how to initiate their own job search. The on-campus interviews provide important experience for students interested in the organizations represented, but most will get their job through a self-initiated job search.

International Experience. The educational importance of living and working or studying abroad as an integral part of a college experience is becoming increasingly clear. Integrating the resources and advising for international experience into the career planning office enables the career planning staff to help students incorporate plans for time overseas with overall career planning.

Increasing numbers of students are interested in spending time abroad. Those who want to study abroad need information about requirements for receiving credit and assistance in evaluating study programs. If students are allowed to choose from the many programs sponsored by U.S. institutions and from courses of study offered at foreign universities, the career library should have the directories and catalogs necessary for this research. Consultation with faculty members is important in evaluating programs, universities, and faculty.

Working abroad provides a special opportunity for all students and particularly for liberal arts students to become involved in the life of a community in a foreign country. While published directories of overseas jobs and internships, paid and unpaid, are helpful, perhaps the best resource is alumni. Overseas alumni may be interested in providing students with opportunities to learn about a country. They can sometimes help students find jobs or internships and reasonable living accommodations.

V. SUMMARY

To assist students in learning how to apply the research, problem-solving and communication skills learned in their academic program to the development of their careers, the liberal arts college and university needs to provide a comprehensive array of services through the career planning office. With individual career counseling as the basic service and the career library as the basic resource, the career planning office can respond to the individual needs of each student.

BIBLIOGRAPHY

Brown, Duane and Linda Brooks, editors. *Career Choice and Development.* San Francisco: Jossey-Bass, 1985.

Clawson, James G., John P. Kotter, Victor A. Faux, and Charles C. McArthur. *Self-Assessment and Career Development,* 2d ed. Englewood Cliffs, N.J. Prentice-Hall, 1985.

Journal of Career Planning and Employment. Bethlehem, Pa: College Placement Council, Inc. quarterly.

Knefelkamp, L. Lee and Ron Slepitza. "A Cognitive Developmental Model of Career Development—An Adaptation of the Perry Scheme," *The Counseling Psychologist.* 6, no. 3 (1976): 53–58.

Leape, Martha P. and Susan M. Vacca. *The Harvard Guide to Careers,* new ed. Cambridge: Office of Career Services, Faculty of Arts and Sciences, Harvard University, Harvard University Press, dist., 1991.

Powell, C. Randall. *Career Planning Today,* 2d ed. Dubuque: Kendall/Hunt, 1990.

Chapter 6

CAREER COUNSELING WITH COLLEGE STUDENTS IN SCIENCE AND ENGINEERING

SALLY J. ASMUNDSON

College students today are an extremely diverse group, representing a broad spectrum of age, economic status, culture, ethnicity, and academic preparation. Science and engineering students are a much more well defined and focused group in many ways, although they also have career development issues which are related to age, ethnicity, gender, or cultural background. But, the career counseling issues of all college freshmen may be more dependent on their developmental stage than whether their major is English or Electrical Engineering. This chapter focuses primarily on the career development issues of traditional age students whose choice of college major is science or engineering. It also, where relevant, discusses other factors in addition to academic specialization.

Contrary to popular myth, students in the natural sciences and engineering, (NSE) are not all mature, well-focused individuals who do well academically and have a guaranteed job waiting which they will find both challenging and satisfying. This chapter reviews some of the determinants of career and academic choice for technical students, how these are refined and modified during the college years and how counseling issues vary for subgroups of technical students such as women, underrepresented minorities, and international students. Finally strategies and issues for career counseling practice are reviewed with consideration given to both the ideal counseling goals and the realities of many college environments.

The various theories of career development described in Montross and Shinkman (1981), Brown and Brooks (1984), and Bell, Super, and Dunn (1988) each provide a valid perspective and collectively an important academic framework. However, career counselors and other student development professionals in the college environment frequently interact with students in situations which do not allow full exploration of all the factors which can influence a student's choice of major and career/life goals. In many colleges and universities there is little opportunity for one-to-one career counseling and in some career counseling courses may not be required or even offered. Students who enter college with the intent to major in such disciplines as physics, biology, computer science, chemistry, or engineering have first had to successfully pass through some very specific academic filters in mathematics and basic science while in high school. Yet, there may still be great variability in preparation as it relates to the demands of the first-year college mathematics and science classes. Many of these students have also been exposed to an influential role model or been strongly pushed by parents or teachers to pursue a career in science or engineering. This encouragement can be very helpful for students who have both interest and aptitude in NSE but often creates conflict for young people whose interests lie in other areas or whose academic preparation is weak. Because professionals in these areas are not frequently portrayed in the popular media many young people do not have an accurate or realistic picture of science and engineering careers. These factors plus the individual's ability, interest in the subject matter, personality style, and maturity level will all impact both academic success in a technical major and the range of career counseling issues presented. Some of these factors also influence whether or not technical students will seek individual career counseling or participate in career development classes in colleges where they are offered.

While most science and engineering students begin college with a definite idea of their intended major, some other students become interested after experiencing success in introductory mathematics and science courses. A much more common occurrence is for students to abandon NSE career aspirations if they have academic difficulties during their freshman year. While theories of career development are relevant to students regardless of choice of major and the career development process is similar, there are practical differences between technical and nontechnical students which have implications for career counseling. The stereotype of the narrowly focused and predominantly asocial engineering student has some truth to it and college may be the first time these students have been exposed to other academic areas. New interests, both academic and social, can contribute to career indecision and stress for these students.

Much has been written recently about the science and engineering "pipeline." A 1987 NSF study, *The Science and Engineering Pipeline*, predicted that of four million high school sophomores in 1977, 1.5 percent will obtain a B.S. degree in NSE, 1 percent an M.S., and 0.2 percent a Ph.D; and the overwhelming number of these continue to be white males. A 1988 study prepared by the U.S. Congress, Office of Technology Assessment, *Educating Scientists and Engineers: Grade School to Grad School*, lists factors which are associated with students majoring in science and engineering. The most important of these are:

Being in the academic track

Taking the most demanding science and mathematics courses

Race and ethnicity—being white or Asian rather than Black or Hispanic

Sex—male rather than female

Family socioeconomic status—being able to afford college

Parents—having a parent who is a scientist or engineer

Having a good, enthusiastic science teacher and/or guidance counselor

Participation in an intervention program

Being in a science-intensive school

These are important factors for college career counselors to keep in mind when working with NSE students. Another report, *Nurturing Science and Engineering Talent, 1987,* states that the singular most important factor that separates the scientist from the nonscientist is mathematics knowledge. This has implications for career development because students may unnecessarily abandon or never even consider NSE careers if they have not taken advanced mathematics courses in high school or if they lack confidence in their ability to handle technical subjects. If career counselors are to effectively transfer career development theory to practice then they must be constantly aware of their own career stereotyping, especially related to women and underrepresented minorities. It should not be assumed that these groups are not interested or do not have the intelligence for NSE careers, nor should it be assumed that white and Asian male students have always chosen NSE career paths as a result of their real interests and abilities.

A recent booklet by Sheila Tobias, *They're Not Dumb, They're Different: Stalking the Second Tier,* provides some evidence that many students who are fully capable of success in the NSE curriculum are neither interested in nor challenged by the subject matter as it is frequently taught. She offers some provocative thoughts on what she terms the "hemorrhaging" of science talent throughout the college years and some ideas for attracting talented students to science.

College students are already a select group and are basically qualified for 85 percent of the occupations listed in the *Dictionary of Occupational Titles.* They, because of ability, prior academic preparation, and adult encouragement have the potential for both professional success and personal satisfaction in any number of specific occupations. Some students in NSE may in fact have prematurely narrowed their academic focus without adequate information or exploration, and others who have potential in these areas have eliminated themselves solely because of lack of information, inadequate high school preparation in mathematics, or a poor experience in a science class.

Primary academic issues for all beginning students are initial class selection and choice of major. An important consideration for counselors is the fact that NSE students frequently have to commit to a specific major earlier than other students and may have little choice in class selection during the first year or two. In addition, most science and engineering courses build directly upon the skills and concepts learned in a required core of classes which are usually completed during the freshman and sophomore years. Students may not be able to take classes in their major or directly related to their career goals until their junior year. This may require a high level of goal directedness and the ability to delay gratification. Any nontraditional NSE student may be at risk of dropping out of the NSE curriculum for reasons not related to interests and abilities. For these students, positive support of their goals and the opportunity to actively explore and test their career plans in a work environment may be critical to their persistence in NSE.

Students who have chosen NSE specializations, perhaps even more than other students, tend to view their choice of academic major and their occupational goal as irreversible. Those who have personal contact with role models in their chosen field exhibit a better understanding of the multiple career paths available and the realities of on-the-job learning once employed. An important goal of career counselors is to support students in realistic career exploration beginning as early as possible in their college career.

Looking at the twelve propositions in Super's career development theory, college students in NSE, while a small and select group compared to the general student population, are diverse within their cohort. Another important point is that these students, even more than other college students, have experienced academic success at the high school level. A large portion of their self-esteem may derive from the external praise they have received for their academic prowess. Since the academic requirements in NSE are very demanding and there is intense competition at many schools, the development of a self-concept based on a broader range of factors is particularly important for these students. An important goal of universities is to provide a learning and social environment where students will not be artificially limited in their academic growth and career exploration by factors unrelated to abilities and interests.

For NSE students the integration of academic advising, career counseling, career exploration, and academic support are especially important. The prime reason for this is that academic success in the freshman year is critical to persistence in a technical major. Students who are not able to pass freshman courses in mathematics and science are at best behind and are frequently sufficiently discouraged that they abandon an NSE major even when their interest in a career requiring an NSE major is still high. Some common reasons for first year academic difficulties are insufficient math and science background, inadequate study skills, lack of support systems, and lack of information on how introductory courses will relate to major and career goals. Couple this with the general career indecision common among traditional age college students, and the special risk factors of women and minority students, and there is a good argument that NSE students need more rather than less help and support than students in general. These issues need to be acknowledged and addressed by all areas of student services as well as instructors in introductory classes and faculty advisors. It is important that beginning students choose classes for which they are adequately prepared and that academic help be easily available. Specific programs will be dependent on the particular school and the resources available, but wherever possible career development concepts and information need to be integrated into the very fabric of the college experience.

Panel discussions including upperclass students, faculty, and alumni on the various NSE majors can provide first-year students with important information to help in choosing a major and positive reinforcement of their goals. Use of upperclass students as peer advisors is effective. Women and underrepresented minority students especially, can benefit from mentoring programs and all students must have available tutoring. Another valuable resource offered by many career counseling centers is alumni career consultants who have volunteered to talk with students about careers.

International students and recent immigrants frequently have career issues related to their command of spoken English. While it is possible to succeed in an NSE curriculum with minimal English skills, success in landing appropriate employment is much more difficult for students who are not able to communicate easily in English. Speech or technical communications classes are available at many universities and some career centers offer individual help and practice in polishing interviewing skills. This is an issue that needs to be addressed early in the student's education and these students need to be encouraged to practice in a supportive environment.

While exposure to upper-class students, graduate students, and faculty can be helpful to beginning NSE students, the opportunity to test their career choice as early as possible in the "real world" is extremely important. There can be opportunities to do this both on and off campus and NSE students are frequently able to obtain career-related summer or part-time employment fairly early in their academic career. Other opportunities include co-op programs, internships, undergraduate research, independent studies, and senior thesis projects. It is most useful to students when information about the various programs and opportunities is presented in an integrated manner.

As students progress to the junior and senior year it becomes even more important that they gain relevant work experience or direct exposure to professionals in the field. Many students are unsure of both their interest in graduate education or the need for an advanced degree in their field. Participating in research projects on campus or working in industry is an excellent way to gain accurate information on the desirability of graduate education.

It is not just academic success, developing laboratory, computer, and analytical skills and the opportunity to gain relevant work experience which are important career development issues for NSE students. As with all students, more fundamental issues of career maturity, personality, and values come into play. For career counselors it is important to explore values and decision-making skills and how students initially decided on their present career goals. The reasons given may range from genuine delight in science and engineering subjects, to parental pressure, to believing that an engineering degree is a guarantee of a high paying job upon graduation.

As with all students, the counseling goals with NSE students are to help the student gain the self-confidence, the knowledge, and the skills in order to make informed career choices and to effectively pursue goals. In practice, perhaps the only real difference between counseling science and engineering students and liberal arts students is the importance of helping these students broaden rather than narrow their career horizons.

REFERENCES

Brown, D., Brooks, L. and Associates. *Career Choice and Development.* San Francisco: Jossey-Bass, 1984.

Bell, A. P., Super, D.E. and Dunn, L.B. "Understanding and Implementing Career Theory: A Case Study Approach." *Counseling and Human Development,* 1988, 20(8): 1–19.

Montross, David H., and Shinkman, Christopher J. *Career Development in the 1980s.* Springfield, IL: Charles C Thomas, 1981.

Tobias, Sheila. *They're Not Dumb, They're Different: Stalking the Second Tier.* Tucson, AZ: Research Corporation, 1990.

Government-University-Industry Roundtable, *Nurturing Science and Engineering Talent.* Washington, DC: National Academy Press, 1987.

Saanders, J. and Lubetkin, R. "Elitism in Math and Science Hurts Women." *Feminists in Science and Technology.* 1989, 3(1): 1, 8–9.

Pyle, K.R., Ed. "Guiding the Development of Foreign Students." *New Directions for Student Services,* San Francisco: Jossey-Bass, No. 26, 1986.

Wright, D.J., Ed. "Responding to the Needs of Today's Minority Students." *New Directions for Student Services,* San Francisco: Jossey-Bass, No. 38, 1987.

Campbell, P.B. and Metz, S.S. *An Investigation of Women in Engineering Education.* Hobokin, N.J.: Stevens Institute of Technology, 1986.

Dix, L.S., Ed. *Women: Their Underrepresentation and Career Differentials in Science and Engineering.* Washington, DC: National Academy Press, 1987.

Dix, L.S., Ed. *Minorities: Their Underrepresentation and Career Differentials in Science and Engineering.* Washington, DC: National Academy Press, 1987.

U.S. Congress, Office of Technology Assessment. *Educating Scientists and Engineers: Grade School to Grad School.* OTA–SET-377 (Washington, DC: U.S. Government Printing Office, June, 1988).

National Science Foundation. *The Science and Engineering Pipeline,* PRA Report 87-2, April, 1987.

Chapter 7

CAREER MANAGEMENT FOR MBA'S

Christopher J. Shinkman

Introduction

G raduate study in Business Administration is becoming increasingly popular. The number of takers of the Graduate Management Admission Test (GMAT) has risen from 197,793 in 1985–86 to 237,552 in 1989–90 (GMAC, 1991). Also, the number of member programs of the American Association of Collegiate Schools of Business has grown from 796 in 1985 to 864 in 1990. The job market for MBA's has fluctuated widely in recent years and thus the need for effective Career Management for MBA's is getting more attention.

Most graduate programs in Business Administration offer career counseling and placement services that are separate and distinct from those offered to the other students at the institution. In part, the provision of services solely for MBA students is based on the fact that they are a population with special backgrounds needing counseling from a person who knows management and who is dedicated to them exclusively. It is also the case that increasingly competitive Deans and Presidents see MBA placement results as quantifiable and as having a major impact on the quality of the applicant pool and on rankings in the media. Admissions and Career Management Officers are dependent on each other to a certain degree. The work of the Admissions Director plays a great part in determining what happens to the graduates (gold in = gold out). At the same time, the success of each graduating class—measured by number of job offers, types of employers from which those offers come, starting salaries, and number and type of recruiters who interview on campus—has a direct bearing on who applies for admission and how *Business Week, U.S. News and World Report* et al. rank the program.

The Role of Career Management

The Harvard University Graduate School of Business offers an extremely popular course on self-assessment for MBA's. "More than half the 340 students in Stanford Business School's first-year class took occupational choice and personality tests this year, twice as many as the year before" (*Wall*

Street Journal, May 20, 1991). Although the need for *career counseling* is clear and apparent, too often the annual appraisal of the person who provides that assistance is based primarily, if not entirely, on *placement* statistics. Both functions are essential and it is unfortunate when the process of determining what one can and should do with one's life is given less attention than the process of getting a job. While providing career counseling and placement services, professionals in Career Management must make it perfectly clear to students that they must take responsibility for their own lives and careers.

Who Studies for an MBA and Why?

A number of factors motivate people to seek the MBA degree. For some it's the notion that an MBA (particularly one from a highly-ranked institution) is a credential which will open doors otherwise closed, both at the entry level and throughout the career. While other students seek to acquire technical and professional management skills, most national MBA programs now recognize that the objective of the program is, or should be, to train and prepare general managers for a rapidly changing world. These managers will need to be what Charles Handy calls "Portfolio People," with a range of skills to offer (*Lear Magazine,* January 1991). The wave of the future, says Handy, may be for independent managers to apply this varied set of skills to several employers simultaneously. As in virtually all graduate and professional schools (and even on the undergraduate level), the debate continues between the merits of applied vs. theoretical study in MBA programs.

Increases in the number of applicants for MBA study may also result from a poor job market. Junior and midlevel managers choose to use periods of no advancement to acquire an additional degree.

Virtually all of the better known, national MBA programs now require three or more years of full-time employment experience beyond the Bachelors degree as a condition of admission. That's the good news for MBA Placement Directors, since prior experience usually makes students more attractive to potential employers. The bad news is that those three-plus years typically have not been spent in a Fortune 500 company. College graduates who go directly to big companies usually receive one or two promotions or raises in their first three years and are reluctant to interrupt that progress for MBA study. Big companies, too, often pay employees' costs in night MBA programs. So the three years of experience is often "soft" in terms of management (i.e., it has involved work on a political campaign, helping run a family enterprise, service in the military, work in the arts, etc). The acquisition of an MBA is seen as a transition or bridge into the business world. From a career planning and placement standpoint some students are adults who can and have taken full responsibility for their lives and careers.

Others are still very uncertain about employment goals and options and are not much more vocationally sophisticated than bewildered college seniors.

In either case, all the individuals who come to study for an MBA are both paying big tuition bills and sacrificing salary/title for two years. Understandably, they can be a demanding group of clients for the Career Management Director.

Strategies and Techniques for Assisting MBA's

Assuming that the MBA program is full-time, and two years in length, the Career Management Office has two major placement responsibilities — *internships* and *regular jobs.* Both terms deserve some explanation.

"Internship" is in many ways a misnomer. There is no credit being given for this work experience which takes place during the summer between Year I and Year II. It is not a part-time activity, nor is it provided on a volunteer/unpaid basis. In fact, it is a summer job that can pay as much as one-fourth of a starting salary for a graduating MBA although typically does not offer benefits. Much like the Law School model, where the "internship" between Year II and Year III is of critical importance, MBA students need to realize the significance of their one internship and pursue it vigorously. The search for an internship is similar to the regular job search and students learn a great deal from the process of obtaining it, as well as from the internship itself. Internships are frequently a form of trial marriage. No obligation exists on either side but there is a clear expectation/ hope on the part of both parties that the summer experience will result in a regular job offer. Employers need to screen, interview, and select interns with the same care and thought that they use in the regular job hiring process. Many employers correctly view the internship as a valuable recruiting device which allows them to establish an early relationship with the most promising students and, in effect, lock them up before they enter their final year of study. In some cases local employers further strengthen the ties by continuing to employ the student on a part-time basis during Year II. Internships which are most successful are those which require the student to work on a special project of some significance or to serve in a staff role offering substantial responsibility and providing good insight into the organization. It is only by challenging and stimulating the student that the two parties can effectively evaluate one another.

The second major placement responsibility, help in the pursuit of a regular job, is far more important in support of MBA's than it is for undergraduates. MBA's may be married, may have geographical limitations, and probably have made an initial step down some industry-specific path. Help in the job search is critical. The word "regular," rather than "permanent," job is now being used by employers who are worried about even implying a long-term relationship.

Other Resources

MBA Career Management Directors can offer students direction in a variety of ways including one-to-one counseling, seminars, workshops, courses, panel discussions, etc. But they should also be quick to point out ways in which students can help themselves.

MBA students can and should learn from fellow students. As mature adults with some practical experience under their belts they are not bound to accept faculty views as gospel in the way that most undergraduate students do. Study groups provide fresh insight into the mastery of information and help develop problem-solving skills, and the appraisal rating system at the Digital Equipment Corporation, for example, carefully measures teamwork.

Similarly, work as a member of a club can be extremely beneficial. In addition to an added line on the résumé, participation in a Finance/Investment, Marketing, Entrepreneurial, Women-in-Management or other club can result in information and introductions that are invaluable in career planning and placement.

Résumé books have been used for many years as a means of helping to place MBA students. Recently a new version of that marketing tool, a glossy brochure with photographs and autobiographical sketches of students, has been developed by the Owen Graduate School of Management at Vanderbilt University. An inherent weakness in both publications is the fact that students are forced to submit a generic, one-size-fits-all résumé without knowing into whose hands the book will be placed. Career Counselors and Placement Officers must make it clear to students that this shot-in-the-dark approach, one over which they have no control, doesn't often yield positive results. In today's competitive market, job seekers at all levels can best generate the interest of prospective employers by submitting targeted, focused, tailored résumés and other application materials. The availability of computers and word processing equipment has certainly made it easier to individualize written material for each job. And many MBA students will quite rightly find themselves applying simultaneously for two or three totally different types of positions, whether internships or regular jobs.

Salaries

One of the key issues facing Career Management Directors and students alike is that of starting salaries. Students, faculty, and staff all take a keen interest in the average starting salary of graduates knowing that to some degree the ranking of their program will be based on that one number. In the worst case this can result in Career Management Directors attempting to steer students away from more appropriate jobs and toward higher paying ones. In the early 1980s, as Director of the Career Planning and Placement Center at Stanford University, the author had football star John Elway as a member of one of his graduating classes. He still jokes about the temptation to use Elway's multimillion dollar signing agreement with the Denver Broncos to "fudge" that year's placement statistics. The inclusion of Elway's package would have single-handedly driven the average starting salary for that year's graduating class well into six figures!

In the second half of the 1980s, management consulting firms and investment banks had a profound impact on MBA hiring by offering huge starting salaries. Signing bonuses became a common part of compensation packages, and some firms even instituted a shrinking bonus plan in which earlier signees received larger bonuses. This plan to force the most promising students to commit themselves to an employer in November or December prior to a June graduation was widely met with disapproval on the part of Career Management Officers and was soon discontinued.

Among the problems that have resulted from these large salary offers are:

1. Other businesses and industries have stopped coming to recruit MBA's.
2. Students who (at a relatively young age) accept huge starting salaries with consulting firms have subsequently found themselves priced out of the market when they wish to move to a corporate job.
3. The starting salary gap has widened between the private sector and public sector/non-profit organizations.

Another important tool for MBA job seekers is the alumni of the institution. As people with experience in the world of work, MBA students and alumni should be more aware of the value of networking and the development of contacts. The Career Management Officer's role is to foster and facilitate those relationships to the benefit of both parties as well as to the program.

A strategy which Career Counselors for both undergraduate and graduate students must employ in the decade ahead is to emphasize job prospects in small to medium-sized organizations. Virtually all job seekers at all levels and at all times have been victims of the "Fortune 500 Syndrome." Whether it is a desire for status and prestige, the convenience of on-campus recruiting, or simply lack of imagination, MBA students have not been good at seeking opportunities outside the big organization. In 1986, while 215,400 jobs were lost in America's top ten businesses, 700,000 new companies were being formed (McDaniels, 1989). Alumni contacts are extremely helpful here and it is the task of the Career Management staff to promote the sector which offers the largest number of jobs—small and medium-sized employers.

New Directions in MBA Career Management

A number of opportunities and challenges face those practitioners whose responsibility it is to assist MBA students. Among them, the following five stand out as the most pressing:

1. **International Placement.** All MBA programs now proclaim that they are preparing managers for a global economy. The curriculum is being revised and in many cases strenuous efforts are being made to inject an international flavor into all aspects of the program. Regardless of the level and rate of "internationalization," Career Management Officers must inform students in a realistic way about employment options and possibilities and how to pursue them. Foreign nationals face different barriers than U.S. citizens yet also have significant advantages over them. Jobs in this country with multinational companies are obviously different from work abroad. Possibilities early in one's career are certainly different from positions and situations available to more senior people. The only thing that is clear is that "international work" is rapidly becoming a bigger part of the MBA employment picture.

Visa, work permit, travel, and currency issues will require specialized knowledge on the part of MBA Career Management. Relations with the INS and its counterpart overseas, and help with internships connected with study abroad will become a standard part of Career Management activities.

2. **Interest in Nonprofits.** At various times since the John F. Kennedy administration there have been periods of interest, sometimes intense, in public sector and nonprofit employment. The Yale School of Organization and Management has made a strong (though largely unsuccessful) attempt to train a group of talented individuals for high level management positions in government, associations, education, agencies, and other types of non-profit organizations. The presumption is that the same set of management skills and talents can be applied equally effectively to both the public and private sectors. Whether or not that is the case, Career Management Officers face the practical problems of: (a) little or no on-campus recruiting by nonprofits, (b) fewer positions being available, (c) lower salaries being offered, (d) interviews and job offers coming later in the year from the typically smaller nonprofits, requiring MBA's to observe and resist the earlier, more lucrative offers made to their classmates.

The admission into the MBA program of applicants with public sector and nonprofit backgrounds doesn't necessarily mean that those people will want to go back into those arenas. In fact, MBA study for them may be intentionally chosen as a bridge into the private sector.

3. **Considering Broader Functional Areas.** Changes in the economy have had the hidden yet important benefit of forcing MBA students to look at more occupational areas. In addition to, or in some cases in place of, the traditional interest in finance, marketing, consulting, and investment banking students are now looking toward manufacturing, operations, human resources (see Chart I), management information systems, and entrepreneurial opportunities. Entrepreneurs, both those working independently and those within organizations, will become more common.

4. **Mobility and Flexibility.** The new managers will have to be geographically mobile, both in accepting their first post-MBA job and henceforth in their career. They will continue to face dual career couple issues and they will undoubtedly need the flexibility to lead a multicultural work force in technologies and techniques not now known to us. Career Management Officers will have to advise students of this trend and help them to analyze choices with a long-term as well as short-term perspective. It is likely that all MBA programs, whether large or small, regional or national, will soon find it necessary to serve MBA alumni. This is both an exciting and an overwhelming prospect for an already hard-pressed Career Management staff. Progressive Career Management professionals will not simply tell students and alumni that life is hard, but will collaborate with employers to design new ways of working.

5. **Consortia.** In order to provide one-stop-shopping for employers MBA programs across the country are joining together in small groups for a single event. This event brings students and employers face-to-face and may be in the form of an informational career fair, or may be one-to-one employment interviews. One such consortium involves graduating MBA students from Rollins, Vanderbilt, Emory, Georgetown, Rice, Wake Forest, Southern Methodist, Georgia Institute of Technology, Tulane, Florida State, and William and Mary. This event, coordinated by the Career Management Officers of the eleven institutions, takes place in late January each year and brings together 75–100 employers and 600–700 students. All of the individual interviews which take place on that day are based on employer preselection from résumé books. Other MBA consortia take place in Chicago, San Francisco, Washington, and New York, and both universities and employers are finding this to be an effective supplement to their other recruiting activity. It is unlikely that consortia will replace on-campus interviewing, but they definitely get MBA students and employers together for interviews which would not otherwise be available.

CHART I

HUMAN RESOURCES JOBS FOR MBA'S

- College Relations (Recruiting, Corporate Contributions, Research)

- Employee Relations (Grievances, Quality-of-Life, Corporate Culture)

- Labor Relations (Arbitration, Contract Negotiations, Collective Bargaining)

- Staffing--Professional Hourly (Executive Search, Handicapped)

- Compensation & Benefits

- Wage & Salary Administration

- Training (Management Development Programs)

- Career Development (Career Pathing, Job Postings, Career Ladders)

- Succession Planning (Long-Range Human Resources Projections - Forecasting)

- Health & Safety

- Job Analysis & Classification Systems

- Outplacement

- Minority Affairs

- Assessment Centers (Testing, Productivity Measures)

- Quality Circles

- Human Resource Information Systems (Application Tracking, EDP)

- Performance Appraisal/Evaluation

SUMMARY

MBA students are a special population requiring specialized services. Although they are older and are enrolled in a graduate, professional program of study these students need career counseling as well as job search assistance. They bring practical work experience with them when they begin MBA study but the purpose in obtaining the degree is usually to allow a move into a more senior level of corporate management or to facilitate a functional or industry switch.

Placement Officers will need to use new strategies and resources to capitalize on trends in employment and changing hiring needs.

BIBLIOGRAPHY

1. *Admissions Office Profile of Candidates,* Graduate Management Admission Council, 1991.
2. Bronstein, Eugene and Hisrich, Robert D. *The M.B.A. Career—Moving on the Fast Track to Success,* Woodbury, NY, Barron's Educational Series, 1983.
3. Clawson, James G. and Ward, David D. *An M.B.A.'s Guide to Self Assessment and Career Development,* Englewood, Cliffs, NJ, Prentice-Hall, 1986.
4. Fowler, Elizabeth M. "M.B.A.'s Told to Look into 'Green Jobs'," *New York Times,* May 7, 1991.
5. Fuchsburg, Gilbert. "First-Year M.B.A. Students Discover Summer Jobs Are a Scarce Commodity," *Wall Street Journal,* March 20, 1991.
6. Handy, Charles. "The Coming Work Culture," *Lear's,* January 1991, 54–63.
7. Holland, John L. *Making Vocational Choices: A Theory of Careers,* Englewood Cliffs, NJ, Prentice-Hall, 1973.
8. Holton, Ed. *The M.B.A.'s Guide to Career Planning,* Princeton, NJ, Peterson's Guides, 1989.
9. Kotter, John P., Faux, Victor A., and McArthur, Charles C. *Self-Assessment and Career Development,* Englewood Cliffs, NJ, Prentice-Hall, 1978.
10. McDaniels, Carl, *The Changing Workplace: Career Counseling Strategies For The 1990's And Beyond,* San Francisco, CA, Jossey-Bass, 1989.
11. Montross, David H. and Shinkman, Christopher J., *Career Development in the 1980's—Theory and Practice,* Springfield, IL, Charles C Thomas, 1981.
12. Ranno, Gigi. *Careers and the M.B.A.,* Fall 1989, Holbrook, MA, Bob Adams.
13. Roffwarg, Steven M. *M.B.A. Employment Guide,* New York, NY, Association of M.B.A. Executives, 1986.
14. Steele, John E. and Morgan, Marilyn S. *Career Planning and Development for College Students and Recent Graduates,* Lincolnwood, IL, VGM Career Horizons, 1991.
15. Stuart, Bruce S. and Stuart, Kim D., *Top Business Schools—The Ultimate Guide,* NY, Prentice Hall, 1990.
16. Walz, Garry R., Smith, Robert and Benjamin, Libby, *A Comprehensive View of Career Development,* Washington, DC, American Personnel and Guidance Association, 1974.
17. Whitely, John M. and Resnikoff, Arthur, Career Counseling, Monterey, CA, Brooks/Cole, 1978.

Chapter 8

NEW EMPLOYEES: A CAREER
DEVELOPMENT CHALLENGE

Zandy B. Leibowitz, Nancy K. Schlossberg, and Jane E. Shore

Of the various challenges faced by human resources practitioners as the twenty-first century approaches, new employee career development and retention is emerging as one of the most pressing. Turnover among new hires places an inescapable pressure on companies to manage the "joining-up process" (Kotter, 1973) in ways that actively promote employee retention. As most managers will readily attest, turnover among any segment of the work force is expensive, time-consuming, and often demoralizing. Yet with as many as 60 percent of new hires leaving their jobs within seven months (Wanous, 1980, in Stevens-Long, 1988), it has become evident that turnover among new employees is a problem of considerable scope and urgency.

In recent years some HR professionals have begun focusing on issues related to the integration and socialization of new employees. Concerned with minimizing and managing newcomers' job disappointment, discontent, and turnover, a growing number of career development specialists are looking closely at the joining-up process—a time when employees' fundamental career concerns appear to be raised and keenly experienced. How these concerns are addressed and resolved has interesting and important implications for employees' subsequent tenure and their organizations' smooth functioning.

This chapter is aimed at HR practitioners who want to learn more about and address new employee issues. A look at the context in which new employees have become a major organizational concern is followed by a description of how this concern links to the practice of career development. Next, newcomers' crucial adaptation needs are examined along with several promising programs that deal with those needs. Finally, strategies for integrating new employees, and roles that managers and organizations can play in directing and managing that integration, are proposed.

NEWCOMERS IN CONTEXT:
THE WORKFORCE OF THE FUTURE

The increased attention to new employees' needs relates directly to demographic changes that are dramatically altering the workplace. The emerging picture reveals a large and growing need for skilled, educated workers precisely when the supply of such workers is dwindling rapidly. If current trends continue, the United States will face an unprecedented shortage of skilled workers by the year 2000 and will rank seventh in global productivity by 2003 (American Society for Training and Development, 1989). The U.S. population's percentage of 18-year-olds dropped roughly 8 percent in 1990, and demographers expect it to continue dropping until 2003. Government projections indicate that by 1995 there will be 27 percent fewer 16- to 19-year-olds available for work than were available in 1978 (Shulman, 1988).

Coupled with the shortages of skilled, educated workers and potential employees of traditional entry-level age is the frequency and cost of new employee turnover. An estimated one of every five employees starts a new job each work day—that is, roughly 80,000 people (Cadwell, 1988). This phenomenon has become a major drain on corporate resources. One study (Kotter, 1973) noted that for organizations hiring 25 college graduates a year, the financial difference between a well-managed and poorly managed joining-up process represents at least $200,000 per year; a more recent publication cited a study that found the average cost of hiring to be over $6,000 per employee (*Recruitment Today*, 1989).

All these factors have sparked a growing concern with how new employees are brought into organizations. In the 1960s and 1970s, recruiters could be assured of a seemingly endless supply of new workers to replace those who left—but clearly the situation has changed. Therefore, organizations have a strong incentive to examine ways in which the joining-up process can be better managed in order to foster employee retention and development.

CAREER DEVELOPMENT AND
THE CHANGING WORK FORCE:
NEW EMPLOYEE CONCERNS

Interest in new employee issues arose initially in an era of heightened organizational awareness of and attention to the career development concerns of all employees. The 1980s saw rapid expansion of services and programs provided by organizations to enhance their employees' skills, motivation, and (it was hoped) long-term growth within the organization. This mushrooming of different types of career development programming as well as career-related research also stimulated awareness of the career issues of new employees.

What are some of the key findings with respect to these issues? Six have particular significance:

- *The importance of life-span approach.* Because the typical worker is now expected to change jobs at least three to five times in the course of a career, new employees can no longer be viewed organizationally in the context of the school-to-work transition. Other transitions occur frequently. New employees may well be seasoned workers in mid-career, women entering the workforce after raising families, or "un-retirees" starting part-time work. Taking a career "life-span" approach has obvious merits for organizations because new employees enter the work force at all ages, and individuals may be new employees many times in their lives.

- *The rise of the new-value worker.* Not only do people change jobs frequently, but the expectations that they bring to the workplace stem from new values. A paycheck is no longer enough; many employees look to their jobs to provide challenge, fulfillment, personal growth, social contact, and benefits ranging from health care to elder care. As these "new-value workers" change jobs throughout their careers, they will enter organizations with the anticipation that their needs will be met during the transition process. Many will be what Maccoby (1988) calls self-developers, and they will expect organizations to demonstrate concern for their developmental needs early in their tenure. Organizations that do not meet these workers' needs soon will be scrambling to recruit again from an ever-shrinking labor supply.

- *The major influence of the first job-first boss.* More and more organizations recognize that a person's first job has a far-reaching effect on his or her subsequent career success and, moreover, that the first boss is particularly influential. The relationship with the first boss has long been cited as a key factor determining whether a new employee will stay in an organization and/or the quality of the employee's time there. Chao (1988, p. 39) cites the research of Berlow and Hall (1966), which indicated that newcomers whose bosses "assigned [them] challenging work were found to perform at higher levels than did new employees who were assigned more mundane tasks." One study of young managers in their first job showed that "the more challenging a person's job was in his first year with the organization, the more effective and successful he was even five or seven years later" (Hall, 1976, p. 67). Schein (1978, p. 104) noted "growing evidence from studies of the early career that the first boss is critical."

- *Organizational entry and the consequences of disappointment.* Beyond looking at first jobs, recent research has examined the ramifications of employees' overall experiences with organizational entry. Baum (1990, pp. 15, 30) has studied the tacit negotiations that occur as individuals enter a workplace and the consequences of disappointments that they may experience in the process. In discussing workers' needs for such things as authority, recognition, and interpersonal relationships, he states that these "cannot be negotiated in any formal way. Rather, they emerge and may be resolved in interactions over time. Yet matters like these may be the most important ones for workers in their 'psychological contract' with organizations. If they can get the organization to satisfy these demands, they will join and think of themselves as members. If not, they may take home a paycheck but give little thought to the organization. . . . When workers are not satisfied with what an organization can give them, they may give little of themselves in return."

- *Reasons why employees leave.* In light of concerns about new employee retention and turnover, it is not surprising that several studies have examined the reasons why employees leave their jobs. Unrealistic expectations created during the recruitment process and the resulting "reality shock" are cited by Wanous (1980) and Stevens-Long (1988). Cadwell (1988, p. iii) states that "one reason people change jobs is that they never feel welcome or a part of the organization they join." Rosenberg and McCullough (1981, p. 163) refer to this dimension as "mattering" or "inferred significance" and state that "mattering represents . . . a powerful source of social integration." In other words, people need to believe that they are noticed, appreciated, and depended upon; they need to feel that their efforts are of importance. Another study found that commitment to the organization is a more important determinant of a person's remaining in a job than is satisfaction with wages or other job conditions (Porter, Steers, Mowday, and Boulian, 1974; in Baum, 1990, p. 15). Moreover, Kennedy (1986, in Chao, 1988) interviewed executives and found that that the strongest reason for turnover is newcomers' "failure to fit into the organization's culture."

- *The need for a systems approach.* Addressing the career needs of new employees requires a collaborative, system-building approach that encompasses the different roles of employees, managers, and the organization. To be effective, the best orientation process that a human resources department can devise still requires a system of supports and accountability mechanisms and the endorsement of organizational leaders. Plainly, new employees' needs are directly connected to an organization's overall career development planning and programming.

NEW EMPLOYEE NEEDS: THE TRANSITION PROCESS

What happens to a new employee? How can an organization help new employees make the transition to integration into the organization? Are there identifiable issues that arise or stages that employees experience as they go through the entry process? What does a person need when he or she is "in a strange environment, unfamiliar with policy and procedures and what is expected . . . [feeling] a high degree of anxiety, wanting and needing to gain control of [t]his new environment and yet still trying to make a good impression . . . [while] inundated with reams of new information" (Loraine, 1988, p. 3)?

Some of the answers to these questions lie in the wealth of literature on new employee adaptation (how the individual adjusts to a new environment) and socialization (how the organizational environment facilitates that adjustment). Other answers lie in empirical data. Only a small portion of the literature is mentioned here, with emphasis on work validated by findings from interviews conducted in 1989 and 1990 to explore the organizational entry experiences of a sample of employees in the aerospace and financial industries. (Readers interested in a more in-depth review of the literature in this area may wish to survey the references and selected resources cited at the end of this chapter.)

Interview Background and Findings

A telephone interview instrument (see chapter appendix) was designed by the authors to assess interviewees' needs as they began working in their current organization and to discover how they and their organization addressed those needs. The instrument is patterned after a transition model developed by Schlossberg (1989). In this model self, situation, supports, and strategies are the potential resources (variables) of individuals as they approach a new transition (such as a first job). This model provides a useful framework for conceptualizing the individual's transition into an organization.

Schlossberg recommends that for any transition, an individual needs first to approach the transition as a process of moving in, through, and out of a change. Next, the person needs to take stock of potential resources by asking questions related to the model's four variables. For example:

- **Self:** Am I usually challenged or overwhelmed by transitions? Do I usually feel a sense of control or mastery as I face transitions? Am I usually an optimist or a pessimist? Am I resilient?
- **Situation:** Does this situation change my roles, relationships, routines, or assumptions? Can I plan for this transition in such a way as to control it or to benefit from previous experience? Does this change

come at a good time in my life? What are the stresses in my life? Do I evaluate the transition situation as positive, negative, or "ok"?

- **Supports:** Am I getting what I need for this transition in terms of affirmation and aid? Do I have support from a spouse or partner, other close family or friends, coworkers and colleagues, neighbors, and organizations or institutions? Have my normal sources of support been disrupted by this transition?

- **Strategies:** Am I flexible and able to choose from a range of strategies depending on the situation? Do I sometimes take action—negotiate, seek advice, brainstorm a new plan, and so on—to change a situation? Do I sometimes try to change the meaning of a transition—by rearranging my priorities, selectively ignoring, using denial, relabeling or reframing, using humor, having faith, and so on? Do I try to manage stress by using relaxation skills, expressing emotions, playing, being physically active, reading, seeking counseling or support groups, and so forth? Do I know when to do nothing?

According to Schlossberg, once the individual has asked and answered those types of questions, he or she is in a good position to take charge of the resources that are subject to his or her influence or control.

The interview instrument's questions guided interviewers, but the interviews were largely open-ended. Schlossberg's model was adapted to the organizational entry transition, and both the interview questions and subsequent analyses of answers also drew on the work of several other researchers.

Self questions concentrated on where interviewees believed they were in their careers. For example, they were asked whether they had any prior work experience and, if so, how it had affected their entry into their current organization. Louis (1989) asserts that a person's level of prior experience in making role transitions is related to the coping strategies he or she uses. Other aspects of the self variable that lend themselves to further study include how people handle new situations, whether or how being an optimist or pessimist affects their strategies, and what motivates them at work, as these would also seem to have an effect on the experience of organizational entry.

Situation questions dealt with new employees' expectations, surprise, and reality. According to Louis, the major features of newcomers' experiences are change, contrast, and surprise. Change may occur in role, status, or basic working conditions or may involve crossing functional, hierarchical, and inclusionary boundaries. Contrast is a person-specific "noticing" of aspects of the new setting versus the settings of past experience. (For example, one newcomer may notice how people dress, while another may notice that nearly all offices have windows.) Contrast also has to do with letting go of old roles while adopting new ones. Surprise is based on "an individual's anticipations and subsequent experiences in the new setting . . . [and] reactions to any differences" (p. 237).

Louis holds that newcomers cope with entry through *sense making*. In this process they attribute meaning to surprise. They do so on the basis of their past experiences, personal characteristics, cultural assumptions or interpretive schemes, and information and interpretations from others in the situation. Problems may arise because newcomers lack sufficient organizational "history" to check their assumptions and have not developed relationships that allow them to test their perceptions. Organizational "insiders" are therefore a rich source of potential help for newcomers.

Pearson (1982) states that as a rule, the gap between desired and actual job features is greater for younger new employees and may inhibit attainment of personal career goals. The gap may take the form of a new employee's internal conflict over clashes between personal values and loyalties (to a profession versus a company, for example). Loss of a former role (such as student status) may also generate internal conflict.

Support questions dealt with the new employee's involvement with other people on the job. Pearson (1982) finds that one of the most essential tasks facing new employees involves learning which relationships one must develop in order to be successful (this may be surprising to recent graduates, who often come to this task unprepared); becoming an accepted member of a work group; and developing a working relationship with a supervisor. The quality of supervisory feedback is key to the accomplishment of this task. Recent graduates acclimated to academic methods of performance feedback (such as grades and honors) may be unprepared for the less clear-cut feedback methods of the workplace.

In studying 60 health care workers during their first three months of employment, Pearson (1982, pp. 288–289) found that developing on-the-job relationships was "the most important single task in predicting outcomes . . . this task was the strongest predictor of the composite outcome, of the amount of influence employees believed they had over how work was done in their department, as well as the supervisor's appraisal of a newcomer's personal adjustment and need for disciplinary action."

Reichers (1987) found that new employee interactions with organizational "insiders" can accelerate the adjustment process. Such acceleration is desirable for newcomers because it reduces their anxiety, and for organizations because it means that these employees can focus more readily on job performance. Accelerated adjustment derives from proactive behaviors "such as asking questions, stopping by other people's offices or work areas to talk, initiating social opportunities . . . asking for feedback, and participating in discretionary social activities" (p. 281). The factors affecting the extent of such behaviors are both individual and situational. For example, proactive people—newcomers or insiders—tend to need affiliation and to possess interpersonal skills that facilitate interaction. Situations that support pro-action include orientation programs, on-the-job training, early performance evaluations, and formal mentoring/coaching programs.

Louis (1989, p. 1) looks at acculturation, "the process by which new members come to appreciate cultures and climates indigenous to work settings and organizations." Her discussion of acculturation is framed in terms of resources, which are the potential contributions of various organizational members to the process; strategies that newcomers use to seek information; and occasions or situations in which newcomers and organizational members interact. She finds that newcomer interaction with veteran peers facilitates acculturation. Although interaction among newcomers provides social support, acculturation is more difficult for newcomers if they interact primarily amongst themselves.

Supervisors may help acculturation if they are good at encouraging newcomers to call on them for help, but generally supervisors are less helpful than veteran peers because they have less of the necessary information and because newcomers do not turn to them as often. Relationships with mentors or advisors also facilitate newcomers' acculturation especially by helping newcomers appreciate the organization's culture and gain a view of themselves within it.

Strategy questions dealt with ways in which employees coped with their new roles. Louis (1989) identifies newcomer information-seeking strategies as follows: overt means or direct questioning of a primary source such as a supervisor; indirect questioning of a primary source; third-party questioning of a secondary source such as a coworker; testing limits; engaging in disguised conversations; observation of interactions; and casual surveillance or monitoring. The more novel the context and the less experience newcomers have with making transitions, the more they will use observational strategies rather than overt questioning. But the higher the newcomers' self-esteem and the more sophisticated they are with regard to integration, the more they will use overt questioning.

The author's interview findings validated four key points in the literature on new employee needs. Each point is related to at least one of the variables in the Schlossberg model:

1. New employees find that some of their major expectations are not met; consequently, they experience surprise or reality shock. (This point relates to the situation variable in the Schlossberg model.)
2. Newcomers have a strong need for information on their specific roles, how their roles fit into the big picture, and formal and informal

organizational realities. (This point relates to both the situation and strategy variables.)

3. Newcomers need to master their job tasks and achieve a feeling of competence. (This point relates to both situation and strategy variables.)
4. Interactions with other people on the job are a crucial element of the adaptation process. (This point relates to the support variable.)

The ways in which each of these points is validated by the interviews are revealed by some representative interviews. The names ascribed to interviewees are fictitious.

1. *New employees find that some of their major expectations are not met; consequently, they experience surprise or reality shock.*

All the interviewees commented on having this kind of experience. For Stan, fresh from college, the experience was a matter of "welcome to the real world." He expected that his technical skills would be valued and heavily used but found himself being called on to do "generalist" work, such as making presentations and doing project administration—activities in which he had little interest. This experience caused him to reexamine his entire career path.

Frank and Bill, also in their first positions out of college, were surprised about the flow and organization of their workloads. One of them remarked, "I never expected such a lack of predictability. The work here comes in peaks and valleys."

The fact that Mike, Jill, and Jonathan had prior professional work experience did not lessen their surprises. Mike was not prepared for the changes involved in moving from the government to the private sector. He had expected to find people working closely in teams. Looking back, he felt that perhaps he was naive not to foresee the individualistic mentality and friction that abounded in his workplace.

Jill's summer internships did not prepare her for the bureaucracy and associated "red tape" she encountered on her job. It was both a surprise and a disappointment for her to find that the drive and enthusiasm for which she was rewarded at school were met in the workplace with skepticism and even resentment. Jonathan, who had been recruited at a high level for his new position, expected a hearty welcome on his first day. "Frankly," he said, "I was expecting them to roll out the red carpet. It was a bit of a shock when the boss didn't even come by to say hello until late in the afternoon." He described his feelings of abandonment and his doubt about whether he should have left his former job.

2. *Newcomers have a strong need for information on their specific roles, how*

their roles fit into the big picture, and formal and informal organizational realities.

The interviewees all spoke of the need for organizational information that includes but exceeds formal policies and procedures. Mike, for example, referred to this as "unwritten" information about office politics, who is important to know, and so on—the knowledge that "gets you into the throes of the company." For Frank, the value of the weekly project meetings that he attended during his first year was in allowing him to learn who the "players" were. This social information, he said, was different from the technical information that he could gather more easily on his own.

Mike and Bill also expressed the desire to understand their jobs and how they fit into the big picture, rather than simply knowing the objectives of individual tasks. Bill stated that he was very disappointed to be rushed through a half-day orientation that failed to cover either the larger corporate environment or where to go for information. When Jonathan finally managed to get an organizational chart, he was told that it had been developed just two weeks earlier and that much of it was a secret.

The importance of role definition was underscored by Stan, who was uncomfortable with the vagueness of procedures for his task area. He experienced a lack of managerial direction and felt that he was left to make decisions that others should be making. This situation made his transition into the organization much harder.

3. *Newcomers need to master their job tasks and achieve a feeling of competence.*

Stan's experience highlights the importance of this issue. Because of vague task definition and lack of documented job procedures, he found that he always had to ask his supervisor questions (rather than, for example, consulting a manual). He said that he prefers to work independently. Besides, he felt that he must be asking obvious questions: "I felt that I should know the answers." Similarly, Bill said that after about six months he was afraid to ask certain things because he supposed that others assumed he already knew those things, and he didn't want to appear incompetent.

Jonathan described how people expected him to offer his opinions right away at meetings, although he is much more comfortable observing for a while until he feels that he knows what he is talking about.

Mike adjusted to the organization by proving his competence. He came in, analyzed problems, and proposed solutions so that "people saw that this is someone who knows what's going on in his area and can make a contribution to the company. They reacted positively to my confidence."

4. *Interactions with other people on the job are a crucial element of the adaptation process.*

The importance of personal interaction was emphasized in several interviews. Bill started with two other newcomers; the three of them helped each other in trying to get questions answered and found that their peers were the most helpful source of information. Stan's most important adaptation strategy was "making friends, introducing myself to people, and getting to know people in my department."

For Jill, seeking her supervisor's advice and getting involved with coworkers proved to be the key methods to adapting to the organization. She believed that the main value of her participation in a six-month rotational training program derived from the network of personal contacts she developed in various areas of the company. "Making those connections has helped me get my own job done better, because my department interacts with theirs very often," she said.

Mike's adjustment was helped most by a mentor. The person who had held his job before him became an informal advisor who showed him around and helped him "learn the ropes."

When it came to interactions with others, Frank and Jonathan described mixed experiences. When Frank started, he said he "was thrown in the job and information was dumped on my desk. I felt very much alone. There was no orientation until three months into the job. Yet I had a coworker who started the same time I did who had experience in this type of work. Being able to talk with him was the most helpful thing." Jonathan noted that some of his coworkers sought him out to introduce themselves and invite him to lunch. Other coworkers he had to approach. He felt that "there was a major difference in these two experiences. . . . It's not nice doing the seeking, but it sure is a nice experience being sought out and accepted."

In light of new employees' needs for information and interaction, the next section of this chapter explores promising programs that offer processes and practices for meeting those needs.

ADAPTATION: MODELS FOR SUCCESS

Despite organizations' growing awareness of the importance of addressing new employee socialization, integration, and development needs, general practice in this area remains impoverished. Currently, most U.S. organizations either have no process for helping new employees adjust, or use a "one-shot" orientation approach that involves giving employees information. This often means overwhelming new employees with facts and procedures on their first day, when their anxiety level probably precludes absorbing much useful information. (Moreover, as Frank recounted, a so-called orientation may not take place until months after an employee enters an organization.)

There are, of course, better ways. Among them are the three innovative programs profiled in this section. These programs treat new employee adaptation as an ongoing empowerment process that equips people with tools for fostering their own skill development and organizational acculturation. From the managerial point of view, the goal of such a process is to build a loyal, committed group of employees who understand the organization's culture and resources and know how to facilitate their own growth and development in collaboration with others.

After presenting the three models separately, the following section synthesizes the features and activities that they have in common in relation to organizational and individual needs.

Model 1: Self-Managed Peer Groups

In the mid-1980s the U.S. Department of Education found an unusual solution to a problem rooted in four years of budget cutbacks and layoffs. The Department devised a way to bring in 62 new professional employees through a Career Internship Program (CIP). The Department's training unit, the Horace Mann Learning Center, developed a process through which the new employees would be directly involved, along with their supervisors, in designing and implementing their own training and development plans. In addition, the CIP was planned so that each year's new employees (or interns—the terms are used interchangeably here) would come in as a group and experience their transition and orientation process collaboratively. The Department launched its new program with the awareness that the interns would be working in a setting in which morale was low.

The major features of the program included the following:

- *Supervisory action planning.* Small groups of supervisors of the new employees used their own organizational entry experience as the foundation for developing written action plans that new employees would use to become oriented to the Department's physical, social, and work environments.
- *Personnel Team and Career Intern Councils.* These groups consisted of human resource staff members and representatives of the organizations in which interns were placed. They helped plan program activities, review progress and goals, and solve problems.
- *Monthly one-day training sessions.* These sessions had several purposes: to teach new employees about the organization, to ensure that they met as a group on a regular basis, and to respond to their concerns. In practice, the sessions proved useful beyond their initial goals. Because of the lack of resources mentioned earlier, new employees were given responsibility for identifying their informational and training needs,

tracking down the information through project teams, and then presenting their findings to the larger group through appropriate means (such as a speaker or film). The Learning Center's CIP coordinator served as a resource to the project teams. The result was a combination of sessions devoted to particular areas within the Department and sessions covering special topics, such as the personnel system, software applications, and how laws become programs (a session that included a trip to Capitol Hill). Several of these efforts developed products that benefited others at the Department, including a catalogue of software applications and a video of new employee orientation sessions.

- *Individual development plans.* New employees, their supervisors, and a career counselor teamed up to develop plans that outlined employees' training needs for their first two years of employment.
- *Adopt-an-Intern.* The first group of interns established this program for the second group. Each new intern was paired with one who had fresh experience as a new intern and who would then serve as the new employee's "sponsor." This arrangement ensured that new employees each had at least one peer to welcome them to the organization and respond to their questions or concerns.

Although the program ran for four years, organizational priorities changed, and the program ceased to be as important a focus of interest within the Department as it had been. Interns are still hired but in far fewer numbers, and they are no longer brought in as a group. However, there continues to be interest within the Department in reviving the program.

The assessments of coordinators, former interns, and intern supervisors with regard to the program's effectiveness were mixed. For the most part, however, there was consensus on what worked, what was missing, and how similar programs should be run.

Significant organizational benefits of the program included decreased turnover among interns, lowered training costs (only $400 a year for all intern training), increased quantity of training, and development of useful products. The interns benefited in many ways. In particular, they cited the value of entering with a group and building a cohesive network of support among newcomers. The monthly meetings alone had numerous positive outcomes: new employees learned about the Department, took responsibility for their own informational needs, built contacts and visibility throughout the organization, developed relationships with peers on project teams, and developed their confidence and presentational skills. These employees were enthusiastic about the "feedback loops" that developed between one group of interns and the next, and which encouraged program fine-tuning.

Supervisors spoke of the value of new employees having "a sponsor who is like a big brother or sister—a positive influence who knows the ropes and can answer important questions without being a person of authority."

Most people who were involved in the program agreed that it lacked top leadership commitment and a system of accountability and support. The CIP had its champions but fell short in terms of ongoing budgetary and programmatic commitment. Some individuals suggested that a staff person and office should have been assigned to deal with new employee affairs.

Moreover, supervisor involvement was somewhat haphazard and arbitrary. One of the program's founders lamented the lack of attention to the importance of the first boss. He recommended, as did some of the supervisors, assigning new employees only to supervisors known to be good coaches and people-developers. Furthermore, several people believed that supervisory training and orientation should have been mandatory rather than simply encouraged. In addition, several others recommended the establishment of an accountability system, with division heads monitoring, evaluating, and supporting ongoing supervisory involvement with new employees' orientation and development.

Other issues raised had to do with the recruitment process and means of integrating the new employees into the organization. Some interns reportedly developed unrealistic expectations during the recruitment and orientation process and then ended up "victims of their own success." They received so much special attention and support that they expected to achieve their major career goals soon without going through a normal "dues-paying" process, and this misapprehension led to some turnover. In certain instances other employees resented the special treatment that interns received. As with supervisors, these employees did not receive adequate advanced notice or briefings about the new employee program.

Despite the problems, however, there was a strong appreciation for the values and goals that the CIP embodied. One supervisor described his approach to socializing new employees: "I mentor or 'babysit' them a lot in the first few weeks. Then I 'wean' them for about two months, during which I observe them and watch how they're doing from a distance. Based on what I see, I assign them to a specific project for which they have ownership. At the end, I have them make a presentation on it. This whole process enables them to build confidence and take risks within a supportive, nurturing environment. I believe this is the way for organizations to really invest in their people."

Model 2: Rolling Out the Red Carpet

Decatur Federal, a savings and loan association based near Atlanta, Georgia, has developed new employee orientation as part of its customer service initiative. One of its orientation's major goals is to convey the organization's service philosophy as well as other corporate objectives. New employees participate in a half-day formal orientation in which they are encouraged to ask as many questions as possible. They are afforded a unique opportunity to meet and talk informally with the association's top executives.

When new employees arrive, they meet as a group. The newcomer group is then split up for two weeks of training. On the last day of training, they reconvene for the orientation, after which they begin working in their specific locations.

In sequence, the half-day orientation includes introductions and net-working, an introductory video on the organization's scope and philosophy, lunch in the Executive Club, a preliminary question-and-answer period, a slide presentation on executive/senior officers, question-and-answer sessions with the CEO and the president in their offices, a presentation on personnel issues, a complete question-and-answer session, a slide show on the organization's history, and a game to review the afternoon's information.

A Human Resource representative and two new employees described and commented on this process in interviews. Both new employees (each with work experience in several other organizations) were impressed by the lengths to which the company went to make them feel welcome. One said, "It gave me a very warm and comfortable feeling; I felt like I already belonged here. At other places I felt like a real outsider, and it was always up to me to make myself fit in."

That Decatur's orientation program differs from many others was echoed by the other new employee, who noted that he "never knew the chain of command" in places where he worked before. "Here it's very clear, and information on every aspect of the company is given out during both the recruiting and orientation process. I was looking for this kind of environment. In my last job, the people I worked with were very nice, but the lack of organization definitely affected my longevity there."

The accessibility of top executives and the encouragement of questioning that occurs during orientation exemplify the organizational culture. During the orientation the president states that his door is always open and that employees should feel free to talk with him if they have problems. One new employee said he was somewhat skeptical when he heard this; however, the sincerity of those remarks was confirmed by his subsequent experience in the organization and his conversations with long-term employees who related instances in which they had gone to the president and received help or guidance.

The other interviewee recalled that she sat in the CEO's chair in the visit to his office; not surprisingly, he remembered her when he saw her later. She said that in the orientation visit, employees asked such frank and direct questions, as how the executives got to be where they were and what the chances were for new employees to reach that level.

Encouragement of questioning is pervasive at Decatur. The chief messages delivered by the orientation are "if you don't know, ask" and "all questions are welcome; if we don't know, we'll find out for you." In their orientation new employees are given specific information about where to go to find things out. According to the two new employees interviewed, this spirit of helpfulness was also much in evidence in their work locations.

The Human Resources representative indicated that Decatur has conducted this type of orientation procedure for more than ten years. The meetings with the president and the CEO have always been very well-received—and not just by new employees; the president apparently "loves" the meetings, according to the representative.

One of the new employees summed up the orientation experience in this way: "I liked the opportunity to know up front just what the company expects of me and how to do my job. All in all, the orientation was a nice way of being welcomed into the Decatur family."

Model 3: Learning the Big Picture

In the early 1980s Corning Glass Works (now Corning Incorporated) became concerned about problems it was having retaining employees, particularly high-potential employees it had actively recruited. When it examined its own processes, Corning learned that the organization was doing a good job of recruiting but came up short in terms of integrating employees once they were brought on board. There was a "sink-or-swim" attitude, and many new employees became overwhelmed and left.

After researching other organizations' experiences in this area, in 1982 Corning initiated a new process, the Corporate Orientation System. This system was designed to facilitate the integration of new employees into the company. The system's process, still in place today, has three major features:

- *Manager Preparation.* Managers who hire are given guidelines and checklists that keep them aware of the key steps they should take, beginning before a new employee's arrival. (For example, a manager is to "keep in touch with the new hire from the time of the hiring agreement through the first day.") The guidelines spell out what should happen on the new hire's first day (such as having breakfast with the manager) and continue with references to actions related to the employee's first 12 to 15 months on the job.

- *Guided Self-Learning.* Managers are encouraged to spend the first week or two orienting a new employee to the job and the local organization instead of just focusing on regular duties. This orientation is accomplished through use of the New Employee Workbook. The workbook takes a guided self-learning approach. An employee is guided by questions or activities to learn about the organization, customers, suppliers, objectives, expectations, and so forth. The manager determines the people whom the employee should interview to find out this information. The process, designed to bring new employees "up to speed" as soon as possible, incorporates accountability. The hiring manager requires the employee to review his or her answers, learnings, and discoveries in a formal review. The two individuals then decide together, on the basis of the employee's newly acquired information, whether or not the employee understands the critical aspects of the organization and how to get the job done. If he or she needs more information, the interviewing period is extended.

  This self-guided learning approach is a direct outgrowth of Corning's highly successful "SmartProcess"™ (Self-Directed, Motivational, Awareness, Responsibility, and Technical Competence), an approach modeled on a U.S. Navy training method. The approach is designed to shorten trainees' "start-up" time and build their operational skills and knowledge by having them answer key questions and go through an oral peer review to certify mastery of sufficient information. At Corning the process is used with new engineers and plant supervisors, among others.

- *Organizational Acculteration.* During their first three months, employees attend eight seminars on Corning's philosophy, culture, and values. Seminar subjects include the Corning community, managing pay and performance, employee benefits, total quality, technology, valuing the individual, and financial and strategic management. The first seminar is on the employee's first day. The company runs this seminar every Monday, and new employees attend it after having breakfast with their manager. The next seminar is at the end of the first month. Other than the weekly "first day" seminar, the series is repeated every three months so that new employees go through the remaining seven seminars as a group. Spouses and other guests are also invited, and those who attend find it very helpful.

The importance of having new hires understand Corning's culture quickly has increased because the company has begun hiring more midcareer managers. They have a special need to "get on board" in a hurry; moreover, they often bring their own developed styles to the job. As a result, Corning is about to initiate a program to address the needs of midcareer new employees.

Corning's Corporate Orientation System has had a significant effect on retention problems. For more than 5 years the company tracked retention of new employees who used the orientation system versus those who had not. Retention rates were between 25 and 35 percent better for those who had used the system. On the strength of these results, the program has continued to receive funding; its return on investment more than compensates for its considerable costs.

Despite the benefits, some managers are not yet convinced that it makes sense for their new hires to take time off the job to go through this orientation process. In theory, managers' participation is mandatory; in fact, they are not held accountable (although this is starting to change in some Corning organizations that use Management By Objectives and are making participation in the program a managerial objective).

The Manager of the Corporate Orientation System has considered what he would do differently if he were starting the program over again today. First, he said, he would hold managers accountable for using the process. Second, he would plan to do "a better job of training managers and communicating the value of the process to them. The importance of how you bring employees into an organization is not intuitively obvious to people; it needs to be illustrated. In those parts of the organization that use the SmartProcess,™ people understand the need and value of this type of orientation." Third, he would streamline administrative procedures to make it easier to manage the many logistical details. Otherwise, it is too easy for managers to avoid conducting the orientation for only one or two employees. He says that some managers "decide to wait until they have a whole group of new hires. . . . But by then it may be too late; the damage of not getting oriented may already be done."

Common Features and Activities of the Model Programs

The three models profiled here demonstrate how innovative management of the joining-up process can boost employee retention and complement an organization's general employee development culture. The models share several similar features and activities. Table 8-1 illustrates how these program features and activities are linked to specific organizational needs and new employee needs.

Organizations need to recruit and retain loyal, skilled, and motivated employees who understand the formal and informal dynamics of the environment. New employees need to fit into an environment where they

Table 8-1. Organizational and Newcomer Needs Linked to Program Features and Activities.

Organizational Need	Newcomer Need	Program Features and Activities
Recruit appropriate workers	Find a good job "fit" Develop realistic expectations	Realistic job previews Exchange of expectations
Build employee loyalty and commitment	Belong and "matter"	Top leadership participation in orientation sessions First boss/new employee pairings Managerial accountability for new employee socialization Mentoring and "buddy" programs Newcomer peer group orientations and follow-up
Foster employee understanding of the organization	Know how job fits into the big picture and understand organizational culture and resources	Orientation sessions on organizational culture and resources Informational interviews and self-guided learning across the organization Self-managed projects and presentations
Facilitate employee skill development	Feel competent and develop mastery of the job	Clear task guidelines Accessible, ongoing supervision Challenging first job assignments Self-guided learning Self-managed projects and presentations
Maintain employee motivation	Be challenged	Encouragement of risk-taking Challenging job assignments Self-managed projects
Retain employees	Build a career	Managerial accountability for people development Provision of ongoing realistic feedback Organizational information on plans, resources, and opportunities Development planning resources and activities

can build competence, discern the resources and culture, cultivate a sense of belonging, and develop a career by staying challenged.

Successful strategies and solutions for meeting these needs include ongoing orientation programs with managerial involvement, accountability mechanisms, mentoring and newcomer support systems, self-guided learning projects and processes, challenging first job assignments, and ongoing coaching and development.

THE CHALLENGE: NEW STRATEGIES AND ROLES

Career development practitioners have recently directed their attention to the important career concerns of employees entering organizations. These practitioners realize that demographic and economic changes mean that far fewer new employees will be available in the decade ahead and that most employees will change jobs a number of times throughout their working lives. Both factors provide strong incentives for organizations to foster retention by meeting new employees' special career development needs. Moreover, fewer skilled employees will be available, and they will expect development from the workplace. In addition, because the typical new employee is not necessarily just out of school, effective management of the joining-up process must adopt a life-span approach.

On the face of it, the situation may seem alarming, but a closer look reveals new opportunities for organizations and employees, especially those charged with building career development systems and programs. New employees experience their greatest fears and hopes during the period of transition into an organization. They know that this period has tremendous implications for the quality of their subsequent careers. On their own side, organizations are aware that the joining-up phase is the point at which employees' loyalty and commitment are secured—or lost. Done well, new employee programming can build a workforce of skilled, motivated, and empowered employees who seek resources and see opportunities for learning and development within their organization.

This chapter has examined the emerging context in which new employees have become a critical focus of career development programming. It has explored new employees' needs in a life-span context and has profiled innovative models for meeting those needs. As Table 8-2 indicates, the task of implementing model approaches to new employee development suggests several strategic roles for organizations, managers, and employees.

Organizations can:

- facilitate new employee programs and networks;
- provide tools, information, and resources; and

Table 8-2: Strategic Roles in Career Development for New Employees.

Organizations	Managers	Employees
Provide programs that facilitate the joining-up process	Be accessible	Let others know informational needs
	Provide honest, ongoing feedback on performance	
Hold managers accountable for orienting and developing new employees		Find a mentor
	Pass on knowledge about the organization's culture	Build networks
		Learn the organization's culture and resources
Link new employees with appropriate bosses and mentors	Offer information and guidance on the organization's resources	
		Use available tools for socialization
Foster newcomer networks	Hold career discussions	
		Take responsibility for learning
Facilitate the learning process	Advise on training and development needs and options	
Provide tools for information gathering		
Provide information on organizational culture and resources		

- demonstrate program support by maintaining accountability.

Managers can:

- be accessible;
- coach and advise their new employees; and
- pass on organizational information to them.

New employees can:

- use available tools, information, and resources and
- take responsibility for their own learning and integration into the organization.

In the early 1980s career development programs grew with the mission of helping organizations meet their human resource needs while assisting employees in achieving greater career fulfillment. In the 1990s, development programming for new employees offers a promising and essential extension of that mission.

APPENDIX

Telephone Interview Guide

A. Critical Incidents
    1. Think back to your first six months in the organization. Identify an incident that you remember as being the most helpful to you as a new employee. Briefly describe:
        a. where and when it occurred,
        b. who was involved (roles or titles), and
        c. what it was about the incident that was so helpful.
    2. Repeat, asking about the least helpful incident and why it was so unhelpful.

B. Self Questions
    1. What is your title?
    2. How long have you been with the organization?
    3. How many years of postcollege work experience do you have?

C. Situation Questions
    1. What were your expectations of your new job? What did you think it would be like?
    2. How was the new job the same as you expected? How was it different?
    3. What was the biggest surprise in your new job?
    4. As a new employee, how clear were you on your roles and responsibilities?
    5. How knowledgeable were you with regard to how your job fit into the larger picture of the organization?
    6. How competent did you feel as a new employee?

D. Supports
    1. In what ways were other newcomers involved with you as a new employee? Repeat the question for:
    2. Peers
    3. Mentors
    4. Human Resource or Personnel staff
    5. Customers
    6. Supervisors

E. Strategies
    1. To adjust to your role as a new employee, did you:
        a. Take action or modify your situation by:
            —seeking information from your supervisor?
            —seeking information from co-workers? (specify roles)
            —observing your surroundings?

      b. Change the meaning of your situation (for example, by using denial, humor, or faith; selectively ignoring; relabeling or reframing; making positive comparisons)

      c. Find ways to manage your stress (for example, through relaxation exercises, expressing emotions, physical exercise, playing)?

      d. Use other means to adjust to your new role? (specify)

  2. How well did the strategies that you used work?

  3. How comfortable did you feel about seeking out information?

F. Outcomes

  1. How long do you predict that you will be with the organization?

  2. How well do you believe you understand how your job fits into the big picture of the organization?

  3. What would you say are some unwritten rules of the organization?

  4. Do you have the sense that you "matter" to the organization? (Aspects of mattering are feeling noticed, appreciated, or important; feeling depended on or feeling that people will be proud of your achievements and disappointed in your failures.)

  5. Has your feeling about mattering changed since your first six months in the organization? If so, how and why?

G. Conclusion

If you were charged with handling new employee programs in your organization, what kinds of things would you do?

REFERENCES AND SELECTED RESOURCES

American Society for Training and Development. *Training America: Learning to Work for the 21st Century* (Alexandria, VA: American Society for Training and Development, 1989).

Ashford, S. J. and Taylor, M. S. "Adaptation to Work Transitions: An Integrative Approach." In *Research in Personnel/Human Resource Management* (Greenwich. CT: JAI Press, forthcoming).

Baum, H. S. *Organizational Membership: Personal Development in the Workplace* (Albany. NY: SUNY Press, 1990).

Cadwell, C. M. *New Employee Orientation: A Practical Guide for Supervisors* (Los Altos. CA: Crisp Publications, Inc., 1988).

Chao, G. T. "The Socialization Process: Building Newcomer Commitment." In London, M. and Mone, E. M. (eds.), *Career Growth and Human Resource Strategies* (New York: Quorum Books, 1988).

Dalton, G. W., Thompson, P. H., and Price, R. L. "The Four Stages of Professional Careers," *Organizational Dynamics,* Summer 1977, 19–42.

Decatur Federal. New Employee Orientation Package (Decatur, GA: Decatur Federal).

Gallese, L. R. "Wooing the New Worker," *Business Month,* July 1989, 48–53.

Hall, D. T. *Careers in Organizations* (Pacific Palisades, CA: Goodyear, 1976).

Kotter, J. P. "The Psychological Contract: Managing the Joining-Up Process." In Jelinek, M. (ed.), *Career Management for the Individual and the Organization* (Chicago: St. Clair Press, 1979).

Leibowitz, Z. B., Farren, C., and Kaye, B. L. *Designing Career Development Systems* (San Francisco: Jossey-Bass, 1986).

London, M. and Stumpf, S. A. *Managing Careers* (Reading, MA: Addison-Wesley, 1982).

Loraine, K. "Strange environment: Taking the Pain Out of Orientation," *Supervision.* May 1988, 3 ff.

Louis, M. R. "Surprise and Sense Making: What Newcomers Experience in Entering Unfamiliar Organizational Settings," *Administrative Science Quarterly,* vol. 25. June 1980, 226–251.

Louis, M. R. "Newcomers as Lay Ethnographers: Acculturation During Organizational Socialization." In Schneider, B. (ed.), *Organizational Climate and Culture* (San Francisco: Jossey-Bass, 1990).

Maccoby, M. *Why Work: Leading the New Generation* (New York: Simon & Schuster. 1988).

160

Newell, T., Redfoot, R., and Dotar, L. "After the Layoffs: Orienting New Employees," *Training and Development Journal,* September 1987, 34–36.

Pearson, J. M. "The Transition into a New Job: Tasks, Problems and Outcomes," *Personnel Journal,* April 1982, 286–290.

Porter, L. W., Steers, R. M., Mowday, R. T., and Boulian, P. V. "Organizational Commitment, Job Satisfaction, and Turnover Among Psychiatric Technicians," *Journal of Applied Psychology,* vol. 59, 603–609.

Reichers, A. E. "An Interactionist Perspective on Newcomer Socialization Rates," *Academy of Management Review,* vol. 12, no. 2, 1987, 278–287.

Rosenberg, M. and McCullough, C. "Mattering: Inferred Significance and Mental Health Among Adolescents," in *Community and Mental Health,* vol. 2 (Greenwich, CT: JAI Press, 1981).

Schein, E. H. *Career Dynamics: Matching Individual and Organizational Needs* (Reading, MA: Addison-Wesley, 1978).

Schlossberg, N. K. *Overwhelmed: Coping with Life's Ups and Downs* (Lexington, MA: Lexington Books, 1989).

Shulman, R. E. "Technology: Decade of the Employee Is at Hand," *Supermarket Business,* vol. 43, no. 11, November 1988, 17–19, 70.

Sharp, A. G. "Retaining the Adolescent Worker," *Management,* vol. 39, no. 3, October 1987, 1, 2, 6–8.

Stevens-Long, J. *Adult Life,* 3rd ed. (Mountain View, CA: Mayfield Publishing, 1988).

Super, D. E., Thompson, A. S., and Lindeman, R. H. *Adult Career Concerns Inventory: Manual for Research and Exploratory Use in Counseling* (Palo Alto, CA: Consulting Psychologists Press, 1988).

Van Maanen, J. "People Processing: Strategies of Organizational Socialization," *Organizational Dynamics,* Summer 1978, 19–36.

Van Maanen, J. (ed.). *Organizational Careers: Some New Perspectives* (New York: John Wiley & Sons, 1977).

Wanous, J. P. *Organizational Entry: Recruitment, Selection, and Socialization of Newcomers* (Reading, MA: Addison-Wesley, 1980).

Part B
The Establishment Stage

Chapter 9

HELP FOR NEW MANAGERS:
CULTIVATING CRITICAL RESOURCES*

LINDA A. HILL

I don't know how much you really can teach a person [about management]. It's like teaching a person to ride a bike. You can go through the motions. You can understand perfectly well what it is you need to do—that you need to get on the bike, hold on to the handle bars, move your feet so you turn the pedals just so, and go down the road to that tree over there. But that still doesn't teach you how to balance. How do you teach somebody that? I'm not sure. You can give them theory, you can give them a good feel for it, and work on the individual skills. But until they get on the bike and start riding it and fall down a couple of times themselves, they just can't know it.[1]

Estimates of the annual investment in management development fall in the tens of billions of dollars (e.g., Sonnenfeld, 1985). Are these funds being put to good use? What form *should* management development programs take? Companies faced with the business realities of the coming years and their attendant demand for superlative managerial talent and prudent financial management are asking these questions. The study described in this chapter provides a rarely considered, but critical, perspective for addressing them.

Most management development programs are devoted to helping managers develop the competencies of management and they focus on classroom training. These emphases are not surprising in light of the conceptual foundation upon which most are built. Of the countless articles and books on the development of management talent, few are based on empirical research, and even fewer look at the phenomenon from the new manager's perspective. Becoming a manager is largely presented as an intellectual exercise, albeit a demanding one. On-the-job developmental experiences are virtually unexplored.[2]

A pointedly different dimension in the development of a new manager emerged from the research on which this chapter is based.[3] In that study, nineteen new managers (ten were individuals making the transition from broker to branch manager in a securities firm and nine were individuals

*This chapter is derived from a book by the author entitled, *Becoming a Manager: Mastery of a New Identity* (working title), Cambridge, MA: Harvard Business School Press, in press.

making the transition from sales representative to sales manager in a computer company) spoke about their first year on the job. Their experiences and impressions unveiled a rich portrait of the process of becoming a manager. Specifically, the new managers' first-year biographies revealed two key themes that are often neglected by those responsible for management development. First, it was clear that the transition from individual contributor (the new managers had been successful salespeople before they chose to become managers) to manager represented a profound psychological adjustment, a *transformation*. The promotion to manager plunged the new managers into a period of considerable change. They were no longer primarily responsible for performing some specific task or function but rather for managing people. Thus, technical competencies were no longer enough; human and conceptual judgment and skill were also demanded. Moreover, becoming a manager involved a fundamental change in identity and point of view. The new managers each had to learn how to think, feel, and value as a manager. It was with the transformation, not the acquisition of competencies, that they struggled most vigorously.

The second theme emerging from the study was that becoming a manager was largely a process of *learning from experience*. Through trial and error, observation and interpretation, and introspection, the new managers learned what it meant to be, and how to be, a manager. Indeed, the new managers conceived of their first year as being primarily a personal sojourn, one they felt forced to travel by themselves.

Although most of the new managers in this study were well on their way to making the requisite transformation, many new managers never adjust successfully to their new identities and responsibilities. In fact, accounts of incompetence, "burnout," and excessive attrition abound in reports about first line managers (e.g., Flamholtz and Randle, 1987). The human and financial costs to the organizations and to those who fail to make the transition are considerable (e.g., McCall et al., 1988). What can be done to help individuals negotiate the transition more effectively? What resources should be provided to help new manager's negotiate their critical first year? These were major considerations in the study, and are the subject of this chapter.

The chapter begins with a description of the resources upon which the new managers relied. Then, based on the new managers' experiences, recommendations are made for refocusing current management development endeavors.

According to the new managers, three resources were especially critical for getting through the first year. These were derived primarily from their past and current work experiences—experiences not deliberately planned for learning purposes. They comprised the lessons they had taken from their careers as well as the work relationships they had established. Each will be considered in turn: career history, network of relationships, and, formal training.[4]

Career History

The new managers' prior work experiences represented not only the knowledge base on which they acted, but also the framework from which they learned about their new circumstances. The specialized knowledge and skills they had gained about the business and the organization were critical assets they called upon to help them meet the many demands of the year. These assets, "judgment and maturity," could only be acquired through experience:

> They [senior management] are thinking about hiring MBAs right out of school to be sales managers. And if they put them through a six-month training program they can learn enough about the business. I don't think so. You need to have an intimate knowledge of the business, because it's about judgment which you *absorb* through experience. Besides you need to feel confident about something. You don't know how to do the people side, so at least you need to know the business side. Without the track record you won't have credibility with your people.

Moreover, those managers with more or varied experiences as individual contributors (for instance, in terms of products, markets, market conditions) argued that they had a "distinct advantage" or "leg up":

> This gray hair lets everybody know that I've had a chance to mature—like a good wine. I know there is some substance here and *they* [his subordinates] know there is some substance here. There is no [technical] problem that is going to come up that I don't know how to grab on to and do something about.

Their years as producers had laid a foundation upon which they were able to build managerial knowledge and skills and a managerial identity. Experience as a producer provided three distinct but related resources: technical expertise (specific to their particular organizational setting) critical for resolving the myriad technical problems that arose during the year; a reserve of self-confidence at a time when they were suffering bouts of self-doubt; and credibility upon which they could build additional sources of power and influence.

The new managers also relied heavily upon past experiences that had provided opportunities to develop human and conceptual skills. These included assignments such as product coordinator, organizer of sales meetings, trainer of inexperienced salespeople, and task force member. The new managers defined these experiences as being opportunities to "play at management." For instance, a new manager who, in his last year as a producer, had been put in charge of training new brokers considered the experience as being a "turning point" in his career. He attributed his decision to pursue a managerial career in large part to this experience. Not only had it allowed him to hone his human and conceptual skills, it afforded him the opportunity to discover the satisfactions derived from such work.

Another manager, who had been given coordinator responsibilities for a large account team, felt that he had found the transition to management less "traumatic" than some of his cohorts because he was "used to dealing with lots of personalities and trying to get them to march to the same drummer." Managers who had been assigned to task forces or project work similarly saw these positions as important to the development of their managerial competencies and identity. These experiences helped them "think like a businessperson" and put decisions into broader contexts.

In addition, the new managers with more extensive experience working with the corporate or regional offices felt they had a richer and broader understanding of the managerial role. They found it easier to "take the organizational point of view." Indeed, they frequently referred to these experiences when "trying to make sense" of corporate policies and directives or in interpreting the requests and complaints of their different constituencies.

In this regard, the new managers in the securities firm, as compared to their counterparts in the computer company, seemed to have more difficulty defining their places in the broader organization and distinguishing between "thinking tactically and thinking strategically." In the computer company, a conscious effort was made to expose potential managerial candidates to the corporate or regional offices and to senior executives. They "got to see how the senior guys think" and hence gained important insights into corporate strategy and culture. But perhaps more importantly, because of the nature of the producer task in the computer company (institutional sales and a team selling approach), the new managers had more first-hand experience working with individuals from different functional areas and hierarchical levels of the company. They had both the forum and the need to develop interpersonal skills (in particular, empathy, influence, and negotiation skills) and conceptual facility (in particular, making sense of ambiguous and conflicting information and priorities, and living with imperfect solutions).

By contrast, the producer role at the securities firm was a more autonomous one. The sales task (primarily retail sales) did not require the producer to interact extensively with peers or superiors in the same or different functional areas. The new managers in the securities firm found the dependency associated with the managerial role to be more unsettling than did the new managers in the computer firm. They were "accustomed to working alone and being [their] own boss." Interestingly, the new managers in the computer company found the position as authority figure "with the final responsibility and accountability" to be more unnerving than did the new managers in the securities firm. The new managers in the securities firm felt they were used to "stepping up to the plate," for they had always seen themselves as "entrepreneurs." In other words, prior work experience had a major impact not only on the knowledge and skills, but also on the basic attitudes toward work, that the new managers brought to their new assignment.

Network of Relationships

The second most important resource for the new managers was their observations of, and interactions with, coworkers: past and current bosses, past and current peers. From these experiences the new managers acquired not only important competencies, but also important values and attitudes, and psychosocial support.

Previous Bosses

The new managers relied heavily upon the vicarious learning gained from their experiences with former bosses. When faced with a decision about a specific circumstance or when choosing a basic managerial style and philosophy, they reflected on these experiences. Exposure to *a variety* of past bosses seemed to be a key resource for the new managers. Former bosses served as both positive and negative role models, and what the new managers had learned depended upon whom they had encountered. As McCall et al. (1988) found in their work, the process was very hit-or-miss. Given the haphazard nature of this learning, it is no wonder that diversity of experience proved so valuable:

> My style is an assimilation of the styles of my past managers, a composite of my experience. Two stand out in my mind. One who got into things with you and helped you think through situations. He was an ally rather than someone who just gave you a raise or dealt with your upset customers. Then the second was the one who talked me into going into management. She helped me when I was going to have to miss an important retreat [at which he would have been exposed to senior management] and visited the customer [in another state] for me. She was sending a key message that she was willing to help people. I still speak to her a lot.

It was the bosses they admired whom the new managers reflected upon the most:

> And when I found somebody who was really good I would try to probe as to why they were so good. I won't ask them directly. Through observation I tried to find out what made them what they were. I tried to get into the mind of the

manager to see the process he went through to make decisions. Occasionally, I asked them directly if it seemed appropriate.

Those new managers who had worked for one of the "company legends" or highly respected managers in the company felt particularly blessed:

> He was a master. One of the brightest and most perceptive people I've ever met. He has a tremendous reputation, one that he had earned. And I had the chance to learn from him. I was smart enough to realize that I didn't know everything so I watched him carefully. And when I could I asked him questions.

Many of the "company legends" were interviewed. Interestingly, very few fully appreciated their profound impact on junior colleagues. And certainly none viewed themselves as mentors to the new managers in this study. Also, in every instance, the "company legends" devoted considerable time and energy to building their work groups into high performance teams. Thus, the new managers who had worked with one of these senior people gained a richer appreciation for the challenges of managing group as opposed to simply individual performance.

The new managers also utilized former bosses in a more active manner, calling on them for advice and support. Mentoring, or long-term apprentice/teacher relationships, were rare. Only two new managers reported that they had a "mentor" upon whom they depended to help them through the year. However, previous bosses who proved to be the best resources had behaved in "mentor-like" ways: they had set high standards, been available, and consciously orchestrated developmental experiences. Because of these qualities, the new managers trusted these individuals for both professional and personal support. These were the people who became their counsellors and confidants. Curiously, the majority had been the new managers' first bosses; they seemed to be people the new managers had a "history with," "bosses who were more like friends in a way than just bosses." They were oriented toward the long-term career development of their subordinates and provided what Hall (1976) has referred to as supportive autonomy. They were also delegators who allowed their subordinates to participate in important decisions and, when appropriate, make such decisions alone:

> He let the power flow away from him. He didn't think he was good. He never got defensive; he was sensitive to you. As you knew more, he loosened up more. You were always learning. Sometimes he'd do these random inspections, to catch you on the details, but you knew it was no big deal, really. He just wanted to keep you on your toes.

In addition, these past bosses held their subordinates accountable for their decisions and actions, giving them timely and candid feedback about their performance. One new manager described this as being given:

just enough rope to hang myself, well not quite enough. . . . He let me feel in control. He built up my status—I felt like I owned my own ten million dollar business. And he talked to me about not just what I did but how I did it when I'd come back from the call. I learned to examine the business a lot closer. He gave me loads of feedback about how other people saw me. Sometimes I'd get mad—I didn't want to always hear what he had to say. But now I can use that information to help me know how to handle myself.

The bosses who had been good teachers also had granted their subordinates the "sacred right to make a mistake." By so doing, they had helped them learn to manage risk, both intellectually (weighing options and their risks) and emotionally (coping with the attendant personal stresses). In short, through their actions, these past bosses had led their subordinates to broaden their perspective beyond that of the producer and to "think like businesspeople" about both the technical and people aspects of doing business. In addition, through role modeling they had demonstrated the value of, and appropriate method for, managing subordinate career development. And finally, they encouraged self-motivation and a "learning attitude" in their subordinates:

He was always stretching me, to stretch just as far as I could without breaking. With him you always wanted to do more and learn more. "What's next?"

Current Bosses

Those new managers who did not have such past boss relationships to "lean on" were at a clear disadvantage, for few *initially* turned to their current bosses for support. Perhaps one of the most consistent and troubling findings in this investigation was that the new managers did not perceive their current bosses to be resources for coping with the challenges of their first year. With few exceptions, most viewed the current boss as more of a threat than an ally:

I know on one level that I should deal more with my branch manager, because that is what he is there for. He's got the experience and I probably owe it to him to go to him and tell him what is up. He would probably have some good advice. But it's not safe to share with him. He's an unknown quantity and he is the last place I'd go for help.

A few of the new managers did turn to their superiors for assistance; their bosses had reputations in the company for being "people developers." This seemed to give the new managers the necessary confidence to approach their bosses as resources. Not surprisingly these superiors exhibited the same characteristics as those past bosses who had offered mentoring experiences.

It was difficult to ascertain why most of the new managers did not rely upon their current boss as a resource. In both organizations, senior management acknowledged that many if not most executives were not "good developers of management talent." In a report in one of the companies, the human resource department concluded that only 10 percent of the executives could be considered "good at coaching and development." Considerable anecdotal evidence indicated that the cultures of both of these organizations embodied a "sink-or-swim mentality." Moreover, there were clear norms against asking for help. As one manager put it, this is a "very macho Wild West kind of place." Another described the predominant managerial style as "autocratic and not having much tolerance for mistakes." Senior management in both organizations was actively engaged in trying to change these aspects of their cultures.

On the other hand the new managers, in some sense, were in "no position to ask for help." They were still struggling with the idea that as the boss *they* were to be the expert, the person in control. Psychologically, many of them were not willing to admit (especially in the early part of the year) that they needed assistance:

> It's difficult to even go back to an old friend and express a lot of frustration. You're afraid, "Oops, I might let something out." As if you have secrets. I'm still tentative about that. It's like leaving home. The first six months you want to be at college. You don't want to talk to mom and dad. Even if they keep soliciting you, "How's it going; do you need help?" You're not going to say yes and start pouring your heart out. You're a grown-up now, out on your own.

Eventually, about half of the new managers turned to their bosses for assistance, and were relieved to find their superiors more tolerant of their questions and mistakes than anticipated. As one manager put it, "he [the boss] recognized that I was still in the learning mode and was more than willing to help in any way he could." Those new managers who did encounter hostile, judgmental, or disinterested reactions from their bosses rarely initiated such interactions again. The new managers' conversations with their bosses were generally very task-oriented and usually focused on a specific problem the new manager was grappling with. These fledglings were reluctant to turn to their bosses for general advice or emotional support. Even at the end of the year, the new managers approached their bosses with some trepidation, all too aware of the risks associated with revealing "any weakness":

> I prepared before I called him so that I would look in more control than I really was. I'd lay out the options and the advantages and disadvantages of each. It's a real bind; you need some help and you know he is the guy that can help you but each time you go for help you invite him to step into your operation.

Previous and Current Peers

In large measure, the new managers failed to take advantage of a potentially valuable resource, their immediate superiors. Instead, they turned most frequently to former peers (individuals who had been salespeople with them at one time but currently held a managerial position) and current peers (individuals in the same positions as the new managers or in managerial positions in other functional areas, with whom the new managers became acquainted during the year). Those with a more extensive and varied network, and who were willing to ask for help, found it easier to cope with the many challenges of the first year:

> At first I didn't know how to utilize different people I'd meet. I'd call and talk pleasure when I should be talking business and wait and see if they'd give me an in to ask a question or two. As I saw what an opportunity for learning it was to talk to as wide a range of people as I could, I got better at calling managers up around the country and getting to the point. I'd admit I was just looking for new ideas. "Here is a situation. What would you do in this situation?" Then, you just sit back and absorb all that wisdom.

As the above quote reveals, unlike the interactions the new managers had with past or current bosses, those with peers were generally very informal, supportive discussions in which the new managers felt free simply to explore ideas and disclose their "real concerns." Many of the new managers had peers they "chatted with" on a weekly or more frequent basis and it was the "people side" of management that dominated these discussions. They needed peers as confidants and "sounding boards" for their ideas, for feedback, and for emotional support about handling the different dilemmas that arose in managing people. They sought advice not only about what to do, but also about how to do it—particularly the latter. They often felt that they could figure out for themselves "the right thing to do," but did not trust their judgment about how to implement their decisions:

> The decision was really cut and dry. I wanted to hear what his thought processes were about how to carry it out. Who would resist? What could I do about it? That kind of thing.

From the peers' comments and questions, the new managers gained feedback on their ideas and performance. This feedback, as informal as it was, played a pivotal role in the new managers' ability to learn from experience. As other researchers have found, learning from experience is not an automatic process (e.g, Bandura and Wood, 1989). Being "successful" or "failing" at handling a particular situation did not tell the new managers much. The new managers often had difficulty ascertaining if their actions "really mattered" and sorting out how much responsibility they should take for various outcomes in their organizations:

> Good sales results can mask the truth. They can hide deficiencies on my part. Maybe I didn't put the best person on the account or maybe I used more of the company resource than I needed to. I don't necessarily know if it worked because of me or in spite of me. I could be pushing people too hard and they could be planning to walk out the door. You never know. So you can't get comfortable just because the dollars are rolling in the door today.

The new managers used feedback from others to help them interpret their experiences and establish cause and effect linkages between their decisions and actions and various organizational outcomes. Many of the discussions focused on *how* to get the job done and the logic involved in making "people decisions." Thus, the new managers gleaned invaluable insights into the managerial process and appropriate criteria for performance evaluation. These discussions helped them develop a fuller appreciation of the variety of expectations people held about the managerial role. As one manager put it, he often learned of "missed opportunities or mistakes of omission [as opposed to commission]" from these conversations, "things [he] just hadn't thought of." Another manager noted that reviewing a situation with a peer often "broadened [his] horizons . . . and made conscious a whole set of assumptions [he] had made [about management] without knowing it." Once the new manager became aware of his assumptions, he realized that some were invalid and others unrealistic.

The new managers also relied upon peers for feedback on how they were perceived and on their performance. They seemed especially receptive to peer evaluations. As many observed, although an individual may be able to appreciate on an intellectual level the need for change, on an emotional level he/she may not be able to. When negative feedback came from a peer whom the new manager perceived to be "in the same boat," the feedback was more likely to be taken as objective and constructive, and the new managers often modified their behavior accordingly. Positive feedback from peers also played a special role in the new managers' development. Many felt it was easier to recognize and learn on their own from their mistakes than it was from their successes. They were much more aware of their shortcomings as managers than their strengths and, hence, suspected that they did not capitalize on the latter to the fullest extent. As one manager said, "you are less likely to bother to do an autopsy of an apparent success than a failure."

Finally, conversations with peers were simply cathartic. They allowed the new managers to release pent up frustration and tension and, therefore, freed them to focus on the substantive problem at hand:

> You know what we [new managers] need most, a suicide hotline and a new-comer club to draw on. If you're lucky, your peers serve the function for you.

It is no wonder that the majority of new managers believed that access to a network of peers was a key ingredient in having a successful year. After the new managers overcame the inhibitory effects of competitive pressures with peers, peer interactions provided a supportive forum in which they could explore how they thought and felt about the challenges they faced. And it was from peers that they received the most candid and timely feedback. Peer, not superior, relationships seemed to be the more important developmental relationships for the new managers.

Formal Training

The new managers all agreed that they learned how to be managers primarily from on-the-job experiences not deliberately planned for learning purposes. Nevertheless, most felt that formal training—mandatory in both companies—played an important although limited role in their development[5]:

> I learned how to do this job 60% from job experience, 25% from relationships and 15% from training.

The new managers reported that formal training fulfilled five critical functions: (1) it acquainted them with corporate policies, procedures, and resources; (2) it provided invaluable insight into corporate culture; (3) it was a forum in which they could receive more systematic and objective feedback; (4) it facilitated developmental relationships with peers and sometimes superiors; and (5) it was a rite of passage.

The new managers described new manager training as a formal orientation to their new position and relevant corporate policies, practices, and resources:

> You get the nuts and bolts. A lot of it seems pretty mundane, but it's nice that they do it. They lay the groundwork.

From the training, they began to get an "understanding of the reality of what [they were] getting into." In this regard, they saw the training programs as being particularly useful in helping them master the administrative aspects of their new positions. In addition, the training gave them an overview of the organizational structure and corporate resources available:

> You understand who the folks are, what their responsibilities are, whom you should be calling, and what are appropriate expectations from them. Actually, you don't really learn the last thing until you're back on the job and you call the person you think should be able to help you and they basically let you

know that "that's not in my job description." But you get a general lay of the land from management training.

The training also provided the "official party line:"

> So it was valuable because it taught you where you could use your discretion and where you absolutely cannot. It establishes the parameters for you. You're taught the tradition; it's sort of like teaching a child that you cannot walk in the street.

They were relieved to discover that the company, in fact, had policies about a wide variety of matters. From formal training, the new managers gained not only specific knowledge about how to do their jobs but much needed confidence as well:

> You see you are not managing in a vacuum. There is somebody out there who has thought about a lot of the different situations that can come up and has thought about ways to handle them. That helps build your confidence level.

Perhaps more importantly, they gained invaluable insight into the corporate culture, often by "reading between the lines":

> They're not just giving you the mechanics. They are imposing a value system on you, especially about how we deal with each other internally. The personnel policies are fundamentally about how we are to execute our jobs. The training inculcates you in the culture. Symbolically it is key because it helps you understand what senior management thinks is most important.

Because formal training conveyed important corporate assumptions, norms, and values, the new managers had a framework for thinking about how to handle common dilemmas. As one new manager put it, it helped her understand what "best practice" was from the company's point of view; therefore, the lessons of training served as "calibration tools" on which she could evaluate her behavior and performance.[6]

The new managers also found that training enabled them to get even more direct feedback on their performance. As part of management training in the computer company site, new managers were required to have their subordinates complete opinion surveys. The results were taken quite seriously and often had a profound impact even on those who received positive overall evaluations. They were all surprised to discover areas of "breakage."

> I was doing an okay job. But my biggest surprise was my biggest weakness. I wasn't listening to people. I didn't let people speak their minds. I had made up my mind before they started talking. My boss had been telling me this, but I didn't believe him until I heard it from my subordinates. When I saw it in black and white I had to face it. When I got back from training I told myself I would change my style. But the next day I went in and said to them, "I

understand you think I don't listen. Well you have to yell louder." I was still being defensive. I talked it over with [a peer manager] and knew I just had to try to be different. Just doing it after a few months, it began to feel easier. But it took months of talking it through with [one of her peers] over and over again and just doing it before it began to feel natural.

Another manager, who got feedback after five months on the job, remarked:

I didn't get religion right afterwards. But there was a greater awareness that they thought I should work for them. Now, I tell them more, explain things and try to be a little looser. I don't just talk the business issue, I talk about what they want to [talk about] sometimes.

From the feedback, the new managers also came to recognize the importance of adapting their style to the particular subordinate. They saw "in black and white" that what seemed like an appropriate amount of delegation to one subordinate was described as "controlling" to another, and a "lack of guidance" to yet another.

The new managers in the securities firm did not get such feedback from subordinates. However, during the selection process they were evaluated on a number of dimensions by more experienced and senior managers. This information was summarized and communicated to them by the human resource department. These new managers also took any criticisms quite seriously:

At first, I felt angry and misunderstood. I dismissed some of it at least consciously, but it was eating at me. And after I got some distance, I saw it as an interesting opportunity for self-analysis and I was able to laugh at myself a little bit. They were entitled to their perception and I damn well better understand why I was being misperceived, if that was all there was to it.

Another function that the formal training served for the new managers was that it facilitated the establishment of developmental relationships, especially with peer managers:

I got a sense that they cared. I lead a sheltered life out in the branch. The only time I see other managers is when we come together in training or seminars. I get to talk to all these people, get their ideas and really learn from them.

I was at one of these programs and [one of the most successful branch managers in the history of the securities firm] was on a panel. I walked up to him afterwards and asked him for a moment of his time and said, "I've heard nothing but good things about you. I've just been appointed resident manager of a very small office and would not mind listening to some of your thoughts." Four hours later I was driving to his house for dinner and we spent the evening just talking. He told me to call him up or better yet come by and visit his office any time. I'm going to take him up on the invitation and go watch him as soon as I can.

Again, the new managers felt that they learned more from the informal than the formal aspects of the training, from socializing with peers, and thereby being socialized into their new role:

> You probably learn more at night going to dinner than during the day. At night the lessons are very practical; people are candid and share failures. It's nice to know you aren't the only one screwing up and it's nice to have new ideas and friends.

Thus, not only did the new managers gain skills and knowledge from formal training, but they also augmented their network of relationships. In fact, the relationships they established during training came to be an important support group for them. If Trice and Morand (1989) are correct, this group will play a key role throughout the new managers' careers.

Finally, training served as a rite of passage. It symbolized for the new managers the company's faith in their ability to master their new role successfully, and its willingness to invest in them. The opportunity to "mingle" with some of the most successful and seasoned executives in the company suggested that they "had arrived" and "entered a new order":

> At first, I didn't quite get it. [The training department] had me here rubbing elbows with these guys to let me know just how much they expected of me, to let me see what my responsibilities as manager really were.
>
> It helped me make the mental adjustment from the old job to the new job. They treat you with a great deal of respect, very valuable. They build you up. Senior management becomes involved socially. They make you part of the team.

As one of the new branch managers remarked, a closing dinner held at one of the finest restaurants in the area "clearly communicated" to the new managers that they were now valued members of the corporate management team. The ritualistic quality of the formal training programs was not lost on the new managers. They appreciated the company's efforts to help them "fit into [their] new status."[7]

Critique of Training

When asked to critique the formal training they had received, the new managers made a number of observations. Although grateful for their management education, in general, the new managers felt it "did not go far enough." The connection between what was taught in the program and what actually occurred on the job was by no means perfect. In this regard, many complained that they gained little insight into the rationale for particular corporate policies and procedures, "why things are done this way." Consequently, they felt ill prepared to handle the many dilemmas they encountered when trying to apply a particular company system or utilize a particular corporate resource. If they had had a general appreciation for the principles underlying a practice or policy, they would have found it easier to apply the practice or policy. Application was by no means "mechanical," but rather required "subtle adaptations to the complexities and realities" of the job. In addition, the new managers contended that the training should have provided them with more insight into the common difficulties they would encounter in trying to apply company policies and practices:

> When I got back on the job and tried to apply what I learned, I found it wasn't mechanical at all. I kept running into brick walls and making mistakes. Many of my buddies [other new managers] did the same thing. Is it really necessary that we have to learn everything by trial by fire? They could have at least warned us of some of the resistance we'd find out there.

The new managers also felt more emphasis should have been placed on real or "very lifelike problems." Over half of them explicitly mentioned the value of the case method, role playing, and simulations. From these methods, they "got to see what it felt like to be a manager and how difficult a job it really was." As one manager put it, he "learned best from taking action." The simulation experiences, in particular, provided him with an important "surrogate for on the job experience." As this manager and others indicated, simulation-like experiences forced them to problem-solve in conditions of uncertainty and ambiguity; hence, they helped new managers learn how to cope with the *emotions* associated with stress and risk-taking. And any opportunity to practice their "people management" skills was especially appreciated.

Finally, the new managers expressed the desire for even more feedback on their behavior and performance, be it formal feedback through videotaping and opinion surveys, or informal feedback from colleagues. When they received explicit feedback on their performance, they found it much easier to learn from their experiences.

Researchers who have studied adult learning in general and management development in particular concur with the new managers' recommendations. Action learning seems to be especially important for the acquisition of interpersonal skills.[8] People usually find it easier to *act* themselves into a new way of *thinking* than they do to *think* themselves into a new way of *acting*. People learn skills best through practice combined with systematic feedback. Mintzberg (1975) made the following observation:

> Management schools will begin the serious training of managers when skill training takes a serious place next to cognitive learning. Cognitive learning is detached and informational, like reading a book or listening to a lecture. No

doubt much important cognitive material must be assimilated by the manager-to-be. But cognitive learning no more makes a manager than it does a swimmer. The latter will drown the first time he jumps into the water if his coach never takes him out of the lecture hall, gets him wet, and gives him feedback on his performance (pg. 58).

This parallel between management training and swimming is strikingly similar to the bike-riding analogy presented at the opening of this chapter. The new managers knew that the key to their success was learning how to learn from experience.

Supporting the New Manager

From this research, it would appear that the goals of management development should be to help new managers not simply acquire competencies, but also learn the lessons of transformation, and to help them capitalize on on-the-job experience. In the remainder of this chapter, recommendations are made in two areas for the achievement of these goals: (1) ways in which corporations can be more proactive and creative in helping new managers establish effective developmental relationships, and (2) suggestions for the refocusing and redesign of formal training.

Establishing Developmental Relationships

The new managers all spoke of relationships, either from premanagerial days or newly established, upon which they relied. Further, having a variety of relationships seemed most useful. Thus fostering connections between new and veteran managers, through both formal and informal channels, is important. New managers can be placed on task forces, for example, where they can meet people from other parts of the organization. Formal working sessions such as regional meetings and training sessions represent other opportunities. Built into these formats should be sufficient time for informal or social activities. On the surface such activities may seem trivial, but they are actually important company-sanctioned events allowing new managers to interact with senior executives whom they might not otherwise meet and to establish camaraderie and trust with their cohort of new managers. During such times, the new managers in this study held rich discussions about what they should be doing and how they should be doing it.

These simple tactics have a second benefit. New managers more clearly see themselves as part of the organization. In working on issues face-to-face with individuals from different parts of the organization, new managers can gain insight into the perspectives of the various constituencies with whom they must interact. Many of the new managers in the study complained about their administrative responsibilities, not understanding their significance. Similarly, at the beginning of their tenure, they were frustrated by the "politics" of their new positions and the need to "network." By getting to know those who request particular administrative tasks and those on whom they are dependent, the new managers' frustration is reduced. Corporate policies become associated with specific individuals and "politics" becomes working effectively with particular people. Procedures, functions, titles and the like become personalized.

Given the provocative finding that the new managers were reluctant to discuss their concerns with their direct superiors, efforts should be made to avoid at least the common pitfalls inherent in new manager-superior relationships. The conflict between evaluation and development goals is an age-old dilemma that will inevitably crop up in the new manager-superior relationship (Souerwine elaborates upon the implications of this dilemma is his chapter on "The Manager's Role in Career Counseling"). The boss need not be the first person to whom the new managers turn when they have a problem nor must they bring most problems to the boss. However, at a minimum, it seems unfortunate that bosses have such limited impact on the new managers' earliest notions of managerial work. These bosses, more than any other constituency with whom the new managers interacted, held the richest appreciation of what the managerial role entailed. Because their bosses had gone through the transition from individual contributor to manager themselves, they were in a unique position to understand and help the new managers with their struggles.

Many senior executives interviewed recognized that they could play an important coaching role, but did not believe they were "effective developers," faced as they were with the unrelenting pressure to meet short-term profit objectives. They lamented that *they* rarely received feedback, much less training, about how to manage effectively and develop subordinates. The "company legends" noted that when they initially instituted practices that would encourage subordinate development they took on considerable personal risk. As one put it, he went "well beyond the call of duty" and it was a "long while" before the company began to reward him financially for his labors.

A critical intervention for an organization is to provide senior executives with training on how to be better developers of new managers. Senior managers can be educated—more accurately, reminded—about the challenges of the transition from producer to manager, its critical lessons, and those resources new managers find most helpful. In particular, they should be given training on how to provide feedback effectively and to respond appropriately to the inevitable mistakes that new managers will make as part of the learning process.[9] One executive said he wished he could find some graceful way to "sit in on" the new manager training on how to do performance appraisals; when he had become a manager some twenty years earlier, the company provided no formal training. He recognized that he had always been ineffectual at providing developmental feedback to subordinates. Finally, if a corporation is serious about new manager development, it must evaluate and reward senior executives in part for their subordinates' development. These latter practices are scarce in organizations.

Another challenge that corporations must address in preparing senior executives for their developmental role is to update or upgrade the senior managers' conceptions of management. Because senior managers rarely received training, they too were often at a loss in dealing with the realities of the new business environment; global competition and a diverse and less loyal workforce which expected a more participative management approach.

Certain corporations, mainly professional service firms, are experimenting with "mentor programs" in which senior and junior people are matched. In some programs, the senior person is instructed to assist a particular junior colleague with his or her career development. In other programs, the junior person is encouraged to select a senior person who can provide performance feedback—someone who is not a direct superior and with whom the subordinate feels comfortable. Such programs have met with mixed success; they seem to work much better in theory than in practice. Reasons commonly cited for their failure include: the senior parties are poor at providing feedback and developing subordinates and are given little incentive to spend time on these activities; the junior parties do not "trust" their mentors and are unwilling to admit their shortcomings and problems. Further, both parties often have unrealistic expectations of what can be accomplished in such relationships.

In everyday language, any developmental relationship across hierarchical lines tends to be characterized as a mentor-protege relationship. However, developmental relationships actually vary greatly and serve a number of functions. Recognizing the range of career-enhancing relationships allows for more flexibility in identifying developmental opportunities for new managers (In their chapter, Kram and Bragar come to a similar conclusion and offer numerous suggestions for how to increase the availability and quality of developmental relationships). Mentors represent the most fully elaborated form of developmental relationship. Mentor-protege relationships serve both career and psychosocial functions and develop from deep levels of mutual identification. They cannot be forced and are difficult to establish and maintain. But as shown by the new managers, there are alternatives to full-blown mentor relationships that can provide mentor-like functions. These alternatives include both superior and more peer-like relationships. Those responsible for management development should help new managers understand the value of having a range of developmental relationships and provide opportunities to facilitate the establishment of such relationships.

Rethinking Formal Training

The new managers in the study described how they utilized formal training and delineated some of its shortcomings. At its best, corporate training provided them with a framework for thinking about the appropriate ways to handle common dilemmas, with knowledge about corporate resources available to help tackle those dilemmas, with much needed feedback, and with a network of relationships. Ideally, formal training should be designed to support new managers' on-the-job training, to help them learn how to learn from experience. From the new managers' observations, it seems that the current emphasis on the acquisition of managerial competencies (especially managerial knowledge as opposed to skill) and on classroom learning may be misplaced.

In terms of the content of formal training, this research revealed some of the critical lessons new managers have to learn.[10] Management training should focus on these. First, new managers should be educated about the intellectual and emotional challenges that lie ahead. It should focus explicitly on the fundamental questions of what it means to be, and what it feels like to be, a manager. Efforts should be made to clarify the differences between the individual contributor and the manager. Such basic orientation is too often ignored.

New managers need an accurate portrait of the nature of managerial work and its inherent tensions and stresses. It is important to alert them to the two kinds of learning, task and personal learning, required to be a manager (e.g., Hall, 1976, 1986). New managers and their corporations too often neglect or underestimate the demands of personal learning. Training programs should legitimize and address explicitly the emotional strain and "soul-searching" associated with becoming a manager for even the most talented individual. Efforts can be made to help new managers realize they are not alone in their anxiety and to provide them with insight into coping with the emotions and undesirable effects of transformation. Training programs should also explicitly consider the manager's place in the larger organization. New managers should be helped to understand the varied perspectives of those upon whom they are dependent to get their jobs done. And they should be given some guidance on how the corporation expects them to balance the various tradeoffs associated with managerial decisions;

for instance, long-term versus short-term interests or the interests of one functional area versus those of another. As one manager put it:

> I am bombarded with variables that will occupy my mind rent-free and cost me a fortune. It takes tremendous discipline to fend off those things that are irrelevant.

Basically, the new manager needs some practical advice on priorities. In addition, the rationale for various corporate policies and practices should be delineated so new managers can better understand the "corporate perspective," anticipate the kind of problems they will encounter when they attempt to implement them, and apply them appropriately on the job. Traditionally, curricula for managers in the lower ranks rarely include much on conceptual skills and on the nature and direction of the corporation's strategy. However, there are clear advantages to introducing new managers to the issues of strategy and to the relationship between the business and environment. If left to their own devices, new managers initially devote little attention to these areas. Instead, training should stretch new managers' point of view, forcing them to incorporate a more complex notion of the managerial role. Besides, organizations are discovering that they need managers at all levels constantly on the lookout for opportunities and threats in the environment, if strategic initiatives are to be realized.

Management training should devote the lion's share of attention and effort to the most pressing needs of the new managers; that is, the particular interpersonal judgment challenges with which they struggle. These were the issues the new managers found most difficult and they embody the essence of the difference between the individual contributor and managerial roles. They developed an understanding of the managerial role and interpersonal judgment, through a heuristic process of continual reframing. They observed a relatively unstructured or ambiguous situation, gathered and synthesized information, made sense of the situation for purposes of problem-solving and decision-making, and finally experimented with possible solutions to address the situation. But new managers can be taught the skills of induction, how to search out information and solve problems in semi-structured situations. They can be taught the skills of observation and diagnosis of interpersonal situations.[11] With such skills under their belt, new managers can avoid much unnecessary and expensive trial and error (In their chapter, Hall and Seibert outline the importance of helping individual managers acquire the "meta-skills" of learning in today's business environment).

Given these training objectives, it would seem that the most effective pedagogies are those that best capture the realities of managerial work (for instance, the ambiguity, risk, overload and dependency associated with management) and that engender the ability to learn from experience. Thus, management training should be based on a practicum approach in which conceptual and skill learning and practice are combined.[12] A practicum learning approach is most appropriate because it requires action by the person and encourages internalization of new attitudes. Certain attitude changes are prerequisites for behavioral ones. For instance, the new managers could not become effective delegators until they understood and accepted the difference between being responsible primarily for people as opposed to task. Receptive methods (for instance, reading and lecturing) are not very effective in improving interpersonal performance skills or changing attitudes and identity. But as many have noted, management development is usually synonymous with formal receptive classroom teaching methods in most corporations.

Instead, case method, role playing, and simulation exercise approaches should be incorporated into management training as much as possible. Corporations are beginning to appreciate the benefits of including business simulation exercises, or better yet, project work on real corporate problems, in training programs. And clearly to reinforce such learning new managers need feedback about their performance, not simply about what they accomplished but also about how they did it. How well did they work with the others participating in the exercise? Did they play a leadership role? Training should ideally include self-assessment exercises as well as feedback from others to help new managers outline a personalized developmental agenda. In addition, time should be built in to allow new managers to reflect on and consolidate their lessons.

Finally, as alluded to earlier, time should be set aside to allow new managers to build strong developmental relationships with their training cohort. This group can play a key role in helping the new managers survive the first year. New manager cohorts might be encouraged to meet periodically to discuss common problems and share ideas. When possible, new managers should also be exposed to, or encouraged to work on issues with, more seasoned and effective managers. For instance, after completing some project in a training program, they might be required to present their work to a senior management committee.[13]

A Prototypical New Management Development Program

Considering the process by which the new managers in the study learned their new roles and identities and the resources upon which they relied, the ideal management development program would be designed as an apprenticeship. Like other artisans, new managers acquire their craft principally through actual and vicarious experiences and through the coaching of other craftspeople. First, the new manager should be assigned a coach to assist him or her throughout the first year. Coaches should have received training about the experience of moving from individual contributor to manager and about how best to develop new managers. They should initially be proactive in making themselves available, initiating interactions in an attempt to establish rapport with the new manager. Over time, the coach should allow the new manager to be the primary instigator of their conversations. The new manager should also be "assigned" to a new manager support group. Ideally, this would be the group with which the new manager goes through formal training.

In the classroom, new managers should be introduced to basic managerial concepts and techniques, the tools they will need to make sense of the situations they face on the job. As more basic ones are mastered, the new managers are exposed to evermore complex and refined frameworks with which to understand their new role. Hence, classroom training works best if it takes place periodically, perhaps in four multiple day sessions, throughout the new managers' first year.

The classroom training would be supplemented with a practicum of some sort; for instance, working as a group on a specific problem that one of the new managers has encountered, or on a strategic issue that senior management deems important (White, in his chapter on the "Job as Classroom," outlines ways in which assignments can be used to leverage managerial development). The instructors in the program would be available during these exercises to answer questions and facilitate the process when necessary. But basically, the new managers would be allowed to proceed on their own. Such experiences would provide the new managers with a chance to test the concepts and skills they had acquired in the classroom and identify difficulties they might have applying them on the job. And time should be set aside to allow the new managers to interact informally in their support group and to meet with appropriate others from various parts of the corporation.

Admittedly, these recommendations are expensive and assume some reordering of corporate priorities. However, if one compares the cost of such endeavors to the costs, both financial and human, of managerial failure and turnover, they seem most reasonable. If forecasts are correct, the transition from individual contributor to manager will become more treacherous as the managerial role becomes more complex and demanding (e.g., Drucker, 1988). As companies face serious shortages of managerial talent, they are beginning to institute programs like those proposed above. Practices that once were seen as infeasible are being redefined as investments in the corporation's future vitality. Helping new managers become the best managers they can become is not a magical undertaking; it is a straightforward exercise that deserves the commitment of senior management.

ENDNOTES

1. Unless otherwise noted, all quotations in this chapter are either direct quotes from the managers in this study or reconstructed from interview notes. Many have been altered slightly to protect anonymity or confidentiality.

2. Notable exceptions include, for example, McCall et al. (1988) and Nicholson and West (1988).

3. The goal of this research was to provide a forum for new managers to recount their experiences. Nineteen new managers were investigated in depth. During the course of their first year, the researcher periodically observed and interviewed each manager. In addition, the researcher interviewed their senior management, representatives of their immediate superiors, subordinates, experienced peer managers, and relevant human resource managers. Selected training programs held for the new managers were also attended. This study was exploratory in nature. Although some systematic research methods (structured interviews, the critical incidents technique, and participant observation) were used, a deliberate decision was made to allow for unstructured observation and to remain open to unfolding events.

4. In their research, Burgoyne and Stuart (1976) reported that "the greater part of learning of managerial skills comes from 'natural' experiential sources — work and other events and experiences not deliberately planned for learning purposes" (pg. 29). They identified nine categories of learning source for managerial skills. In order of importance, they were: doing the job, non-company education, living, in-company training, self, doing other jobs, media, parents, innate. In fact, the new managers in this study cited instances of each of these; however, the three resources discussed in this chapter were viewed as the most critical.

5. Formal training refers to corporate training in this study. None of the new managers in the study had completed an MBA; however, two were taking MBA courses in the evenings.

6. Louis (1980), among others, has noted that too little attention is paid to helping individuals learn the cultures of their organizations.

7. Trice and Morand (1989) argued that such rites of passage or rites of integration, to use their terminology, can play an important role in an individual's socialization into an organization.

8. For example, Johnston and his associates (1986) made the following observation:

    Dramatization is a powerful device for creating the feel of managerial experiences, for acquainting students not just with the factual outlines of specific situations but with the sensations and stresses of the executive's life.... At its best, the teaching case should heighten students' awareness of managerial consciousness of self (pg. 152).

9. McCall et al. (1988) made the following observation about the pivotal role of the immediate superior in a manager's development:

    It is nearly always the immediate boss who passes on the organization's attitude toward mistakes. But because bosses each have a uniquely personal response to mistakes, this is akin to handing out shotguns randomly laced with either buckshot or flowers. For every story of a boss helping a subordinate to learn from mistakes, there is one of a boss who cruelly metes out punishment and scorn (pg. 110).

10. In the book there is considerable detail about the critical lessons new managers had to learn and the most common mistakes they tended to make. Because this information is not provided in detail in this chapter, only broad recommendations about content are delineated here.

11. Weick (1974) came to a similar conclusion:

> To the teacher the advice reads: get away from cognitive learning and train your students instead in eight basic managerial skills (for example, peer skills, resource-allocation skills, skills of introspection). Scientists are advised to provide managers with better descriptions of their jobs, treat induction as a topic rather than resource of research, and relax your aversion to quick and dirty analytic techniques (pg. 118).

12. Whetten and Cameron (1984) summarized some of the research on training program effectiveness:

> Education that involves teaching behavioral guidelines but provides no opportunity for practice ignores the precarious link between knowledge and application.... Similarly, training programs that do not provide a broad conceptual understanding of skill topics and instead emphasize rote behavior modeling overlook the need for flexible application (pg. 3).

13. Medcoff (1985) extolled the benefits of a program for new research and development managers in which they met once a week for a number of months to discuss their problems with fellow managers. Over time their level of sophistication as well as their awareness of themselves as managers improved.

BIBLIOGRAPHY

Bandura, A. and Wood, R. Effect of Perceived Controllability and Performance Standards on Self-Regulation of Complex Decision Making. *Journal of Personality and Social Psychology,* 1989, 56: 805–814.

Burgoyne, J. and Stuart, R. The Nature, Use, and Acquisition of Managerial Skills and Other Attributes. *Personnel Review,* 1976, 5: 19–29.

Drucker, P. The Coming of the New Organization. *Harvard Business Review,* 1988, 66: 45–53.

Flamholtz, E. and Randle, Y. *The Inner Game of Management,* New York, New York: American Management Association, 1987.

Hall, D. *Careers in Organizations,* Santa Monica, California: Goodyear, 1976.

Hall, D. Dilemmas in Linking Succession Planning to Individual Executive Learning. *Human Resource Management,* 1986, 25: 235–265.

Johnston, J., Jr., Burns, S., Butler, D., Hirsch, M., Jones, T., Kantrow, A., Mohrman, K., Smith, R. and Useem, M. *Educating Managers,* San Francisco, California: Jossey-Bass, 1986.

Louis, M. Surprise and Sense-making: What Newcomers Experience in Entering Unfamiliar Organizational Settings. *Administrative Science Quarterly,* 1980, 25: 226–251.

McCall, M., Jr., Lombardo, M., and Morrison, A. *The Lessons of Experience,* Lexington, Massachusetts: Lexington Books, 1988.

Medcoff, J. Training Technologists to Become Managers. *Research Management,* 1985, 28: 18–21.

Mintzberg, H. The Manager's Job: Folklore and Fact. *Harvard Business Review,* 1975, 53: 49–61.

Sonnenfeld, J. Demystifying the Magic of Training. In *HRM Trends and Challenges for the 1980s.* R. Walton and Lawrence, P. (eds.) Boston, Massachusetts: Harvard Business School Press, 1985: 285–318.

Trice, H. and Morand, D. Rites of Passage in Work Careers. In *Handbook of Career Theory.* Arthur, M., Hall, D., and Lawrence, B. (eds.) Cambridge, England: Cambridge University Press, 1989: 397–416.

Whetten, D. and Cameron, K. *Developing Management Skills,* Glenview, Illinois: 1984.

Weick, K. Review of Henry Mintzberg's *The Nature of Managerial Work. Administrative Science Quarterly,* 1974, 19: 111–118.

Chapter 10

JOB AS CLASSROOM:
USING ASSIGNMENTS TO
LEVERAGE DEVELOPMENT

RANDALL P. WHITE

To compete effectively in the years ahead, organizations must begin to consciously use job assignments to develop two groups of managers. One group, currently the recipient of most developmental opportunities, is the high potential managers, those likely to become future leaders of the organization. The second group, the organization's solid citizens, comprises the bulk of managerial talent in large organizations. But as organizations become flatter and these technical/functional managers plateau at earlier ages, organizations need to use on-the-job development to challenge them. Using developmental job assignments productively will have positive benefits for both the individuals and the organization.

The idea that one learns from experience is neither novel nor a revelation. In the past several years organizations have started looking at the types of experiences available for developing future leaders. This examination of experiential learning is an outgrowth of a rediscovery that experience is an invaluable, if not the best, teacher of leadership. Given two patterns currently emerging in U.S. based businesses—the lack of bench strength in many executive teams and the flattening of organizations resulting in less hierarchy but more horizontal span—understanding the role of experience-based learning becomes a necessity in organizations preparing for a competitive future.

As we shall see, rotation from one functional area to another (e.g., from manufacturing to sales), as has been practiced for years, can be hit and miss in regard to developing leadership versus technical skills. Human resources professionals working in tandem with senior line executives can better leverage executive development efforts by:

a) understanding the types of experiences from which people tend to learn;

b) understanding the types of learning that result from various experiences;

190

c) targeting specific experiences as developmental opportunities, and in turn practicing good stewardship of those opportunities; and

d) helping candidates learn from developmental experiences with coaching both prior to and after the experience.

Background

A series of studies has been conducted at the Center for Creative Leadership focused on interviews with executives to more fully understand how individuals learn, grow, and change on the way to becoming senior managers. An inductive approach was used to categorize each executive's response to the following:

> When you think about your career as a manager, certain events or episodes probably stand out in your mind—things that led to a lasting change in you as a manager. Please jot down some notes for yourself identifying at least three 'key events' in your career, things that made a difference in the way you manage now. When we meet with you, we'll ask you about each event: What happened? What did you learn from it for better or for worse?

There was no preconceived framework that these stories—key events—needed to fit.

There were discernible themes to these stories, and this was later confirmed in various survey replications and in a follow-up study with executive women. The themes crossed organizations and individuals. They tended to cluster around and serve as both context and linking commentary for the critical leadership challenges faced by the executives. The challenges, in turn, tended to be linked to learnings.

> I became managing director of a new company, out-of-country. There was lots I'd never done before. I was representing minority shareholders and had to build a plant and an entire community out of nothing. There were major political and social issues, and I had a real concern for my family. This was a tremendous challenge; I had opportunities to develop and test skills totally on my own. My area chairman was an outstanding individual, but this project was minor to him.
>
> I learned that the leadership role makes a big difference in the performance of a company, for example, in racial issues. The location was primitive and mostly black, and we had to impact white professionals. I saw my responsibility as bringing those people together, counter to cultural norms; I wanted equal opportunity for everyone and tried to provide an example of how this could be done.
>
> I also learned from the chairman an uncompromising view of high standards and maintaining them even when resources are limited. I learned how to

maintain excellence when resources are primitive and scarce. This involves spending time working with and helping people who don't know how to do it.

Over a period of months hundreds of such stories and thousands of lessons were collected and sorted into 16 broad types of critical experiences and 34 lesson categories. Most important during this process was the discovery that job assignments—five of the 16 critical events—were most often mentioned as triggers for learning, growth and change.

Five broad types of assignments mattered:

Fix it/turn around —managers had the task of repairing, restructuring, or selling a foundering business. Sometimes managers lacked the authority to make all the changes necessary to fix the business.

Starting from scratch —building a new plant, business enterprise, or product line where none previously existed.

Scope change —put in charge of an existing business or piece a business but with more people, products, markets, and/or profit-and-loss responsibility for the first time.

Line-to-staff —moving from line to a staff role; in many cases an "assistant to" role, reporting to someone as much as four levels higher.

Special project/task force —a special assignment, usually as a head of a team; sometimes involving formal negotiation with external parties.

Executives reported significant learning experiences stemming from hardships (5 of the 16 categories) and learning from other people, both the revered and the hated, mostly bosses in their past (2 of the 16). But when closely scrutinized, the greatest point of developmental leverage involves the assignments an organization has to offer. Human resources professionals, as well as the line executives they support, need to realize that other people—good and bad bosses—also serve as sources of development. Likewise, hardship experiences such as dealing with subordinate performance problems, being demoted, and making a business mistake are developmental—yet unplanned—experiences.

It was found that there are different challenges involved in each assignment type; fixing a business had different leadership challenges than starting a business. While not a one-to-one correspondence, different types of assignments teach different lessons. For example, "starting from scratch" tends to teach standing alone, being in charge, discovering what one really wants to do, getting cooperation from people one has no control over, and understanding other people, among others. "Special projects and task force" assignments, on the other hand, teach very different lessons of comfort with ambiguity, knowing how to work with executives, and negotiation. A more complete comparison of the major lessons from each of the five assignments is presented in Table 10-1.

Table 10-1. Developmental Assignments and the Lessons They Can Teach.

Lessons/Skills and Perspectives	Scratch	Fix-It	Projects	Scope	Line/Staff
Resourcefulness					
• comfort with ambiguity			x		x
• seeing organizations as systems					x
• knowing what executives are like					x
• knowing how to work with executives			x		x
• knowing how to use systems to manage		x		x	
Doing whatever it takes					
• perseverance		x			
• standing alone	x	x			
• discovering what one really wants to do	x				x
Quick study					
• technical knowledge				x	x
• how the business works	x	x			x
Decisiveness	x	x	x		
Leading subordinates	x	x		x	
Setting a developmental climate	x	x		x	
Confronting problem subordinates		x			
Team orientation				x	x
Hiring talented staff	x	x		x	
Building and mending relationships					
• negotiation with external parties		x	x		
• getting cooperation	x	x			x
• understanding other people	x				
Straightforwardness and composure			x		
Acting with flexibility		x			

Human resources professionals can use the implications of these findings to:

a) Audit developmental jobs in the organization—What developmental jobs are there, and what do they teach?

b) Draw conclusions about the organization's culture based on the current executive crop—What types of developmental jobs have these executives held, and what lessons have they learned?

c) Project the skills/lessons needed in the future leaders of the organization and, using the audit, place people in developmental positions to increase the likelihood that they will be exposed to those lessons.

d) Change the culture by doing "c" above.

e) Recognize that more jobs are developmental than is usually assumed.

f) See that development can also be accomplished in place, for both line and staff.

Developmental Audits

In most organizations, there are assignments that exist to challenge even the hardiest of souls—going to the Amazon 5000 miles away from corporate headquarters to start a new plant is not for the faint-hearted. Surely these types of situations are rare enough that they are easily identified as developmental, although as will be pointed out, if the wrong individual is placed in the job, it becomes less developmental or not developmental at all. But how about the task force the chairman forms to study new ways to do performance appraisal or the staff assistant role that the Vice President of New Products wants filled? These are developmental assignments too. In fact, all of the assignments in a system are developmental for someone because the developmental potential of a job is a function of an individual's ability to do that job. As the ability, knowledge, skills, values match what it takes to do the job, the developmental potential of the job diminishes, so much so that if an individual can presently do the job one would say there is little developmental potential in that job for that person.

This conceptualization of the developmental potential of jobs allows every job to be developmental for someone. However, this notion runs smack into an important issue from the business side of organizations: the aversion to taking risk. As the developmental potential of the job increases (for example, it has many elements that are new and/or unfamiliar skills, abilities, values, attitudes, knowledge to be applied), the risk to the business (the risk of failure resulting in lost time, money, productivity, etc.) likewise increases. Since most businesses operate in a risk-averse or at best in a balanced risk-taking stance, many potential developmental assignments go to candidates who can already do what is required to get the job done. For example, there are major problems at one of the company's plants; someone will be sent who has fixed things before. This practice often results in an organization developing a cadre of single-experience leaders—they have one year of experience repeated twenty times. Or, most leaders in the organization know how to run smoothly operating businesses, but not how to fix a business.

For these single-experience leaders there is a concomitant dilemma of being developed as a specialist in certain types of leadership situations—fix it or start up—and only knowing those skills. When there are no longer those situations facing the organization, the single-experience leader becomes obsolete, a loss for the organization as well as the individual.

A more complete determination of the developmental potential of an assignment, then, rests with evaluating the abilities and track record of the candidate against the types of learning likely from that assignment. In other words, the developmental potential of the job changes given the candidate for the job. Obviously, for a candidate who can already do the job, there is little or no potential for further development. And for someone who cannot, the developmental potential, and concomitant risk to the business, is very high.

This may help to explain why so few women, when given the opportunity to describe their most significant career events, described no "start from scratch" events and about one-third the number of "fix it/turn arounds" as the men. The implication here is that white male executives have the propensity to give potentially developmental assignments to people who look like and act like them and who they judge stand the greatest likelihood of successfully completing the assignment with the least risk to the business. Hence, women and other minorities are either excluded from the opportunities or are given much safer and potentially less stretching developmental opportunities.

Ways to proceed

Organizations would be wise to look at all the assignments being offered so that better leverage could be applied to developmental efforts. This can be done in a couple of ways:

1. Organizations can survey a number of individuals at various organization levels to get information on the developmental aspects of the jobs represented, the backgrounds/track records of those holding the jobs, the current leadership challenges and what, if anything, is being learned from these challenges.

2. Organizations can interview the senior management team to determine which assignments proved to be most memorable developmentally and what was learned. The results of this analysis might even shed light on the leadership strengths and weaknesses of the current management team. These results can also serve as a cultural audit—What lessons, skills, and values does the senior management team seem to exemplify/personify? Are these different from what they should be for future success?

A Case in Point

Illustrative of the forgoing is the case of a large Midwestern manufacturing firm which in the mid 1980s became interested in establishing an executive development effort to carry its management staff into a challenging and uncertain future. The effort, undertaken by a small staff using materials and guidance from the Center for Creative Leadership, was easily accomplished and is still guiding management development efforts today. A step-by-step examination of this process will more fully illustrate the use of on-the-job assignments for development.

This organization can be characterized as an "up through the ranks," long tenure system where most key leadership positions are filled from within. It was not unusual for key executives to have worked their entire careers for only this organization. Hence, bringing in outsiders for senior positions, while not impossible, would prove rather difficult for all parties. To develop additional leadership competencies, then, required that this organization identify future competencies necessary and specify what the behavioral component(s) might look like (see Table 10-2).

Parallel with this effort was a survey of 100 key managers in the organization. These managers, while at various performance levels, constituted the pool of future executives in the fairly closed system of this organization. The survey was identical to the open-ended question in the original Center for Creative Leadership data collection effort.[1]

The results of the study were eye-opening for the senior management team. Those parts of the business that had in the past produced leaders were found to be providing an overwhelming number of special project/task force assignments. In this organization, these project/task force assignments were not additional developmental assignments; instead, they were used as a way of carrying out many managerial missions — even to the extent of sending a *team* to fix a business, or a team — where there was shared authority — to start up a business.

Using teams to such a great extent in this part of the business produced such leadership strengths as comfort with ambiguity, negotiation, and a high degree of team orientation. Unfortunately, the lessons of take-charge leadership, one of the key ingredients in the development of future leaders that senior management felt lacking, was not being systematically offered.

Interestingly, another segment of the organization involved self-contained units, units where the managers were clearly in charge of an entire business. While the manager had a team of direct reports, he/she nonetheless was

---

[1]A survey instrument called the Job Challenge Profile has been under development since 1988 to provide more systematic detail of the developmental aspects of jobs. This instrument, currently being validated, should be available in 1991 or 1992.

Table 10-2. Recommended Executive Development Experiences.

Knowledge/Skills/Abilities	Scratch	Fix-It	Projects	Scope	Line/Staff
Visionary thinking	x			x	
Long-range planning and organizing	x		x	x	
Managing for results		x	x		
Systems thinking		x	x		x
Openness to innovation	x	x	x		x
Knowledge of organization's external environment			x		x
Knowledge of organization	x	x			x
Technical competence				x	x
Decisive leadership	x	x	x		
Organizational motivation	x	x		x	
Executive image					x
Skill in attracting and developing talent	x	x			x
Influencing and negotiating skills	x	x	x		x
Networking skills			x		x
Commitment to treat others fairly and equally		x			
Interpersonal responsiveness		x			x
High-impact delivery skills	x		x		x
Skill in critiquing written documents			x		
Skill in conducting/facilitating/participating in meetings	x	x	x	x	x
Self-organization and delegation	x			x	x
Handling pressure	x	x			

fully accountable for every aspect of the business. Somewhat surprisingly senior management didn't see the developmental potential of these assignments, while managers who were actually in these assignments did. In this part of the business managers were learning to stand alone and be in charge, strategic lessons in how the business works, and decisiveness—the lessons of leadership. Unfortunately managers from this side of the business rarely made it into the executive ranks. Also, future executives from the other side of the business rarely, if ever, moved to the side where individual leadership skills would be challenged and stretched, especially at lower levels where making a mistake would affect fewer people and have a smaller impact on the overall bottom line.

The results suggested steps in developing some of the people already in the system, but they also suggested steps that could be taken to develop people not yet in the system, namely new hires. First, it was obvious that teamwork was a critical ingredient in this organization's culture. It was something to be preserved, yet it was too ingrained in the way assignments were constructed. People seldom talked about teamwork, yet it was central to how they went about doing their jobs. They began to ask how to hold on to the strengths of teamwork as a cultural norm without encountering some unfortunate downsides when every challenging assignment is performed in teams. Such disadvantages include:

- confusion over who is in charge,
- lack of timeliness in delivery of product/service, and
- lessened opportunity for testing/developing leadership qualities in any one team member.

It was agreed that while many assignments would still be done in teams, some of the more challenging opportunities for testing individual leadership had to be allocated to individual managers. They would purposely resist the first impulse to assign a team.

Second, they discovered a series of individual leadership opportunities on the "less favored" side of the business that potentially provided a great leadership proving ground. By being more careful stewards of these experiences, they could develop and test leadership competencies one plant manager at a time. Quite interestingly, the first switch brought a more entrepreneurial manager into the traditionally team-oriented side of the business. The happy result was a more team-oriented entrepreneur who was teaching the factory council and anyone else who would listen how to be more aggressive in getting product out the door.

A final and potentially longer-lasting result of auditing this organization's developmental assignments involved the building of an experience-by-competency matrix. As each competency was identified, it was correlated with the survey results to produce a matrix that addressed the following questions:

If I have a particular type of developmental experience, what am I likely to learn in this organization?

or

If I want/need to learn a particular skill, perspective, value, what experience is likely to teach it in this organization?

Table 10-2 represents a general example of such an experience-by-learning matrix. Here the organization can ask where various broad based knowledge, skills, and abilities are most likely to be learned. It is possible to refine either the developmental experiences or the lessons (knowledge, skills, abilities, values) or both into a more detailed analysis of what an organization's developmental experiences teach. Table 10-3, drawn directly from the Center's analysis of all 16 developmental events and 34 lessons learned in six major corporations, is representative of this more detailed analysis. Even more detail is possible.

Most important, however, is how such a matrix can be useful to the organization. Individuals inside the organization can see what competencies, skills, values, and knowledge current leadership thinks will be necessary for competitive success in the future. Individuals can quickly see where these attributes might be tested/developed within the organization—"Oh, so if I take that task force assignment, I might learn to . . . "

Bosses, those who might directly oversee development plans, have a better idea of valid developmental steps as a result of the evaluation of a candidate's strengths and weaknesses. Bosses can, by using such a matrix, help candidates target alternative ways to build strengths and counter leadership weaknesses on-the-job.

This point, of course, runs counter to two practices often used by organizations for development. Practice 1: "Let's send 'X' to a course." This is the easiest developmental option because it requires only money and time; little real thought and effort need go into this decision to evaluate whether the skill building hoped for will result from having attending a course. In fact, executives suggest that coursework is helpful only in certain instances and teaches a very focused, often technical, set of lessons.

And, Practice 2: "Let's rotate 'X' into sales to gain understanding of the technical aspects of the sales business." Again, rotation for building technical skills limits the value of the rotation. Rotating a manager into sales, or any other department, to learn more about that piece of the business is effective in many ways, but to be more effective, the rotation should also expose the candidate to a leadership challenge that needs developing, say, managing former peers or bosses. So a developmental matrix helps organizations—bosses and subordinates—understand how and where development occurs in a systematic way. The use of such a matrix, increases the awareness of the developmental potential in every assignment.

Preparations for Development Assignments

At the conclusion of any assignment, time should be provided for a short period of reflection—a "walk on the beach"—and questions to guide this reflection might be posed to both the incumbent and the boss. The focus of these questions, much like those contained in the appendix, should be on the development that took place in the last assignment: What were the biggest challenges? What mistakes produced learning? What strengths were developed? What weaknesses were countered? What strengths and weaknesses emerged?

It is important, too, to continue to assess whether the candidate is open to

Table 10–3
EXECUTIVE LEADERSHIP QUALITIES AND THE EXPERIENCES ASSOCIATED WITH THEM

LEARNING EXPERIENCES: DEVELOPMENTAL EVENTS

LEARNING CONTENT: LEADERSHIP QUALITIES	Assignments					Hardships					Other People		Other Events			
	Scratch	Fix It	Projects/ Task Forces	Scope	Line to Staff	Business Failures	Lousy Jobs	Subordinate Performance Problem	Breaking a Rut	Personal Trauma	Role Models	Values Playing Out	Course Work	Early Work	First Supervision	Personal
Setting and Implementing Agendas																
1. Specific technical knowledge					█								█			
2. How the business works	█			█												
3. Standing alone, being decisive	█		█													
4. Seeing organizations as systems					█									█		
5. Solving and framing problems														█		
6. Building/using structure and control systems		█	█													
7. Doing, not talking about it		█		█												
Handling Relationships																
8. Directing and motivating others					█											
9. Dealing with people's perspectives	█					█										█
10. Politics is part of organizational life	█		█									█				
11. Getting cooperation: non-authority relationships	█		█													
12. Working with executives			█											█		
13. Strategies for negotiating			█											█		
14. Confront subordinate work performance problems			█					█								
15. What executives (and managers) are like									█		█			█		
16. Management vs. technical work								█						█		
17. Developing your people					█		█									
18. Managing people with more experience than you (former bosses, etc.)							█								█	
19. Dealing with conflict			█													
20. Management models and theories			█													
Basic Values																
21. Basic values: trust, integrity, credibility																█
22. Human values: sensitivity to needs			█	█				█								
Executive Temperament																
23. Can't manage it all by yourself			█													
24. Self-confidence in skills and judgment			█			█							█			
25. Comfort with ambiguity, stress, uncertainty													█			
26. Perservering under adverse conditions								█		█			█			
27. Learning to be tough							█				█					
28. Coping with situations beyond your control																
Personal Awareness																
29. Using, and not abusing, power						█										
30. Recognizing personal limits and weaknesses						█	█									
31. Learning which jobs are and aren't enjoyable	█					█	█									
32. Taking control of own actions: career							█									
33. Perspective on life and work													█			
34. Being prepared for opportunities									█							█

From Developing Executives Through Work Experience by McCall, 1988.

learning. Involving the boss can help to give the developing manager the opportunity for specific behavioral feedback on strengths and weaknesses demonstrated in the assignment.

Administering an instrument to collect data from peers, subordinates, customers, and clients (both internal and external) can be helpful at this stage, too, as this data can serve as a checkpoint on development in the last job and as a reminder or rediscovery of areas to develop in the next job. The candidate is now ready to meet with the new boss and subordinates for briefings on strengths and weaknesses and for the new boss to offer a road map for what is most important—what the biggest challenges are—in the new assignment. It's a chance for the organization, through the boss, to let the candidate know the types of development that are being sought. And it's a chance for the candidate to think through the best approach to this next assignment given the recent assessment of leadership strengths and weaknesses.[2]

Caveats

There are some important caveats to using assignments for development.

1. Individuals who are chosen for a developmental assignment ought to be told why they are getting the assignment. Furthermore, some support system ought to be put in place. For example, in the case study presented, the entrepreneur moving into the team environment was watched and coached by the vice president of manufacturing and a senior human resources expert from corporate. They were there to help if the targeted manager got into trouble. Recall, this was not only a switch for the individual but also in the way things normally got done in the organization. In a sense, the greater the developmental move for the person and the more counterculture for the organization, the more support should be provided.

2. Developmental moves won't fix every weakness nor will they build leadership in everyone. The best example of this came from an early sponsor for this research. The executive vice president for a major division had purposely rotated a key functional specialist to a foreign posting for some broadening and technical development. The person being replaced was in turn posted to the U.S. but was viewed as a place-holder; that is, the person was going nowhere but was competent enough to do the job. But when the target of the development returned to the U.S. and was asked, "What did you learn?", the response was, "Nothing—lots of problems out-of-

---

[2]Human resources professionals are often aware that bosses may be unwilling or unable to give constructive feedback to aid in a subordinate's development. Here is yet another opportunity for the savvy HRD professional to step into the process in an ongoing effort to ensure development.

country, family disliked the assignment, just a waste of time." When the "place-holder" was asked, it was quite a different story: That person learned how U.S. executives thought, got a better understanding (a more strategic one) of how the business operated, and got involved in setting in motion a major change in the way the business was conducted. He grew as a leader.

Early on, this situation reinforced a key consideration in using job assignments for development: **The fact that it might be possible to learn something from an assignment doesn't mean it will be learned.** Therefore, simply giving someone an assignment is a guarantee of nothing. But, if the assignment might test/build strengths the person needs to develop *and* if the person is open to learning, the likelihood that development might take place is increased. And, if this is done often enough, then a more systematic approach to development results.

3. Most organizations don't have enough big assignments to develop all the leaders they'll need in the future. But there are ways to develop people that don't involve sending them to start an operation in Timbucktoo or to shut down a factory in Tanzania. Developing them in place, by providing additional (and often, targeted) responsibilities can provide development. This strategy can be particularly useful when organizations lack the "big" developmental assignments or when a candidate can't, for one reason or another, make a major developmental move. It's also valuable for those solid performers who want to stretch and grow but for whom the organization may not have more senior level positions in mind. Every activity from running the company picnic to being a loaned executive on a United Way campaign can qualify as development in place.[3]

Remember, every assignment is potentially developmental for someone. But a critical step in the process is to involve the target of development—the individual—in the process.

HRD professionals and their organizations will benefit now and in the future by becoming more aware of the developmental potential of jobs. Too often jobs are assigned with little thought to the potential development that might occur if the right candidate is placed in that position. The strategic use of on-the-job development may be the competitive advantage of the coming years.

---

[3]Technical reports 136 and 144, listed in the references, provide detailed information.

APPENDIX

Career Interest and Self-Assessment

Assessment

1. In your last assignment, what stands out as performance accomplishments and disappointments? Be as specific as possible in describing them. Please indicate tangible bottom-line operating results as well as longer-term strategic accomplishments.
2. Describe and assess how you have fulfilled the major functions of leadership and where you missed opportunities to do so. Be specific in telling what you did and the observable impact.
   a. Creating a vision:
   b. Creating understanding and ownership of the vision:
   c. Implementing the vision, achieving outstanding business results:
3. Describe and assess your *strengths* and *areas needing development* according to this company's Leader Characteristics. Give examples.
4. Assess and give examples of how you have managed learning and growth over your career.

Interests

1. What are your career objectives?
2. In light of your self-assessment and career objectives, what are your major developmental needs?
3. What sequence of positions would be of interest to help meet your career objectives?
4. What will it take for you to perform in the positions effectively? How will the positions contribute to meeting your developmental needs?
5. What other developmental opportunities are you considering (e.g., special projects, task forces, training programs)?
6. Have you discussed the feasibility of these plans with your manager and others?
7. What will you do to get agreement and commitment to these plans?
8. What language skills do you have: a) speak b) read?
9. Are you willing to relocate? If so, do you have location preferences? special needs? constraints?

Individual Assessment From Boss

Assessment

1. We'd like to get a picture of the performance track record of this individual. Over the last several jobs, what stands out as performance accomplishments and disappointments? Be as specific as possible in describing them. Please indicate tangible bottom-line operating results as well as longer-term strategic accomplishments.

2. Describe and assess how the individual has fulfilled the major functions of leadership and where he/she has missed opportunities to do so. Be specific in telling what the individual did and the observable impact.
   a. Creating a vision:
   b. Creating understanding and ownership of the vision:
   c. Implementing the vision, achieving outstanding business results:

3. Describe and assess strengths and areas needing development according to this company's Leader Characteristics. Give examples.

4. Assess and give examples of the individual's motivation to continuously learn and grow.

Career Implications

The attached should be used as an input form from multiple sources — including peers and subordinates of the candidate — or as your summary of information from those sources. After completing the assessment questions, consider the following for discussion at a Review Meeting.

1. What is the individual's unique potential?

2. In what roles (e.g., general manager, functional manager) would the individual make the best contribution? (For what should we ultimately develop the individual?)

3. How flexible and adaptable is the individual to new situations, people, cultures?

4. What does the individual still have to learn in the current position?

5. Given that potential and the individual's experiences thus far, what internal and external development programs would be appropriate? What else will it take from us to support the development of the individual's unique potential?

6. What should be the next two types of position(s) or assignment(s)?

7. Of our current leaders, who would be the best role model for this person? Does the person have a mentor?

8. Does this plan fit with the individual's expressed interests? Should other moves or opportunities be considered?

FURTHER READING

The following represents some of the more helpful pieces of writing on executive learning from ten years of work at the Center for Creative Leadership.

McCall, M.W. Jr., Lombardo, M.M. & Morrison, A.M. (1988). *The lessons of experience: How successful executives develop on the job.* Lexington, MA: Lexington Books.
Book details learning, growth, and change that took place in the executives interviewed in several major corporations. The idea that different types of experiences teach 'different lessons is presented in detail.

Lindsay, E.H., Homes, V. & McCall, M.W. Jr. (1987). Key events in executives' lives (Report no. 132). Greensboro, NC: Center for Creative Leadership.
The nuts-and-bolts description of each of the sixteen key events discussed by executives, as well as detail on each of the more than 30 lesson categories. Statistical analyses and tables regarding two questions: a) If an executive needs to learn "X," where—under what circumstances—might it be learned? What type of critical event might teach the lesson? b) If an executive has the opportunity to have a particular type of developmental experience—starting a new business, for example—what will most likely be the leadership challenges faced and the lessons learned?

Morrison, A.M., White, R.P. & Van Velsor, E. (1989). *Breaking the glass ceiling: Can women reach the top of America's largest corporations?* Reading, MA: Addison-Wesley.
An examination of the critical events and lessons reported by executive women at 25 large corporations. This work also compares success and derailment characteristics of men and women.

Van Velsor, E. & Hughes, M. (1990). Gender differences in the development of managers: How women managers learn from experience. Greensboro, NC: Center for Creative Leadership. (Technical Report 145)
A comparison of men's and women's key events and lessons, this technical report takes the data bases from *Breaking the glass ceiling* and *Lessons of experience* and continues them in an effort to see if male and female managers learn the same leadership lessons from the same key events.

The following literature deals directly with learning from on-the-job experience.

McCauley, C.D. (1986). Development experiences in managerial work: A literature review (Technical Rpt. 126). Greensboro, NC: Center for Creative Leadership.
A review of the literature that deals with learning on the job.

McCall, M.W. Jr. (1988). Developing executives through work experience (Technical Rpt. 133). Greensboro, NC: Center for Creative Leadership.
A summary of the major themes that successful executives learn from on-the-job experience. The report details the meaning of job challenge.

Lombardo, M.M. & Eichinger, R.W. (1989). Eighty-eight assignments for development in place: Enhancing the development challenge of existing jobs (Technical Rpt. 136). Greensboro, NC: Center for Creative Leadership.
The authors identify other avenues for developing leaders in organizations aside from full job change. They examine the idea that individuals can develop leadership skills through a series of add-ons to current assignments.

Eichinger, R.W. & Lombardo, M.M. (1990). Twenty-two ways to develop leadership in staff managers (Technical Rpt. 144). Greensboro, NC: Center for Creative Leadership.
A companion piece to "Eighty-eight Assignments," these 22 suggestions foster development in staff and functional specialists.

Chapter 11

CAREER ANCHORS AND JOB/ROLE PLANNING: THE LINKS BETWEEN CAREER PLANNING AND CAREER DEVELOPMENT

EDGAR H. SCHEIN

The fundamental problem that all organizations face when they attempt to plan for their human resources is that they have to match the ever-changing needs of the organization with the ever-changing needs of the employees. When one considers that most organizations today exist in a highly dynamic environment in which technology, economic conditions, political circumstances, and social/cultural values are changing at an ever more rapid rate, it becomes almost impossible to think clearly about the planning process.

Can and should organizations invest in career development systems that will allow them to build a stable employee pool or should they seek a whole new set of concepts for "contracting" with employees that allows for easier entry and exit as circumstances change? In order to answer such a question one must have a better understanding not only of the changing nature of work, but of the dynamics of the "internal career," the self-image that employees develop of their own work life and its relationship to their personal and family concerns (Schein, 1978, 1985, 1987, 1990).

Two concepts and activities are described in this paper that help to deal with these problems—the concept of *career anchors* and the concept of *job/role planning*. Each concept is described in general terms and the practical activities that organizations can undertake to utilize the concept are described.

Career Anchors

The concept of "career anchor" grew out of several decades of longitudinal research to capture some of the essential components of how career occupants define themselves in relation to their work. A person's career anchor is the evolving self-concept of what one is good at, what one's needs and motives are, and what values govern one's work-related choices. One does not have a career anchor until one has worked for a number of years and has

207

had relevant feedback from those experiences. But once a career anchor evolves, roughly five to ten years after one has started work, it becomes a stabilizing force in the total personality that guides and constrains future career choices.

The word "career" is used here in the general sense of the set of occupational experiences and roles that make up a person's work life. In this sense everyone has a career even if the work is mundane and "nonprofessional." So everyone develops a career anchor, but in many occupations there is insufficient flexibility in the work situation for the anchor to be expressed at work. Thus production workers have career anchors but such anchors may exhibit themselves more readily off the job (in hobbies, for example).

Types of Career Anchors

To get a better understanding of the dynamics of the career anchor concept it will help to analyze the major types of anchors that have been identified thus far. These reflect some of the basic personality issues that all humans face and some of the social values that occupational structures the world over seem to generate.

The categories are based originally on a 13-year longitudinal study of 44 early sixties alumni of the MIT Sloan School Masters Degree Program in Management, supplemented by early and mid-career interviews of several hundred managers, teachers and members of various other professions and occupations to see if the categories applied to them (Schein, 1978, 1985, 1987). These interviews, and related research by Derr (1980), revealed the need to add several other categories.

In creating a typology, it is important to specify the scientific and practical function of that typology. A research goal in this study was to better understand the internal career. In the interviews similarities among the various people interviewed were observed and attempts made to capture these similarities. The reliability of the categories was measured by comparing the classifications of several readers of the interviews. By this criterion they are highly reliable in that two independent readers agreed on 40 of the original 44 cases. In subsequent interview studies similarly high levels of agreement were always attained.

New categories were created if at least two cases were found that resembled each other and that could not be fitted into the existing categories. By this criterion it is possible that with further interviews other anchor categories may surface.

The function of the typology is another issue. There was no attempt to develop a selection tool that would allow others to label career occupants. Instead, while dealing with the internal career, the goal was to create a typology that would help a person decipher his or her own work priorities. Since the ultimate goal was to help individuals develop the kind of self-insight that would enable them to negotiate better with organizations in the management of their own career, the typology had to be primarily oriented toward inducing self-understanding. This meant that the individual might not be able to classify him or herself cleanly in terms of categories discovered thus far, but would still benefit from the exercise of attempting to do so in that it would produce a greater level of self-awareness. These categories are presented in a diagnostic form to stimulate this kind of self-awareness.

One of the most fundamental issues that all career occupants have to resolve is the balance between autonomy and security. For some people one or the other extreme of this dimension becomes the overriding factor in integrating self-image and thus becomes a career anchor.

1. **Security/Stability:** If this is your anchor it means that you are *primarily* and *always* concerned about jobs and work that will make you feel economically secure and stable. You will worry less about the content of the work you do and more about the degree to which your employer offers you "tenure," good benefits, generous retirement, and so on. The so-called "golden handcuffs" is exactly what you are looking for. You may have a variety of talents and values, but none of these are more important to you than feeling secure and stable.

2. **Autonomy/Independence:** If this is your anchor it means that above all else you want your worklife to be under your own control. You resist organizational routines, rules, uniforms or dress codes, hours of work, and all other forms of regimentation. You probably would prefer to work as a teacher, consultant, or independent businessperson, but some kinds of organizational jobs might suit you such as field sales, or professional staff jobs such as research and development. But you would become unhappy if you were promoted into headquarters where you lost your autonomy even if that was a "bigger," better paying job.

A second major issue for all career occupants is how much to develop their unique craft, the set of special skills that provide them employment in the first place versus broadening themselves, learning a variety of skills, and, ultimately, moving into administration and management. Extreme positions along this dimension produce two other career anchor categories.

3. **Technical or Functional Competence:** If this is your anchor it means that your self-concept is built around your particular talents or skills, and that the exercise of those talents and skills at ever higher levels is your primary means of "being yourself." You seek higher levels of challenge within your skill area, and may go into administration or management *in that skill area,* but you resist general management because that would require you to drop the exercise of your skill. You seek recognition primarily from others who

can appreciate your skill and you will quit jobs that do not challenge you unless, for economic reasons, you must keep the job. In this case you would endeavor to exercise your skill off the job by moonlighting or developing a hobby in that area. The biggest danger for you in most organizations is that your skill will lead you to being promoted into general management which you will not like and will not be good at.

4. **General Management Competence:** If this is your anchor it means that you want to rise to a high level in an organization where you can measure your own competence by the performance of the organization that you manage. You view technical or functional skills to be necessary to climbing the ladder, but you will not feel you have made it until you are a general manager integrating the other functions. You will have learned that to succeed as a general manager you will need some combination of high motivation, skills in analyzing and synthesizing information, interpersonal skills, and emotional skills in the sense of being able to make tough decisions day after day without becoming debilitated by them. Your basic identity and sense of success will come through the success of the organization for which you work.

What is to be noted so far is that these four types of people use different criteria for determining whether or not they are successful, they have different attitudes toward economic rewards, they will respond to different kinds of rewards and incentives, and they will often have difficulty understanding each other. Most organizational career systems are built around the security/stability type and the general managerial type. To the extent that the needed talent resides in technical/functionally and autonomy anchored people, we can predict difficulties in attracting and retaining such people.

Even more problematic is the tendency to move the technically/functionally-anchored types onto career ladders that eventually lead to general management and to watching such people fail, either because they cannot do the work of general management or they are not really motivated to do it. They are the true victims of the Peter Principle because they would not have wanted such jobs in the first place if multiple career ladders were more available in organizations.

A small number of people in each of the studies conducted showed clear tendencies to want to create something entirely their own. They were genuinely different from others in how they structured their internal career, though their pattern of jobs in the early external career looked quite conventional.

5. **Entrepreneurial Creativity:** If this is your anchor you have always wanted to create a business or product or service of your own, where your success was entirely due to your own creative effort. You probably launched new enterprises when you were in school, and you think about such enterprises

all the time, even while you might be employed in a more traditional kind of job. You want to make a lot of money eventually but the money is not the goal in itself; rather it is a measure of how successful you are in creating something new. The new enterprise is an extension of yourself so you will often give it your own name. You would work for a company if it allowed you to develop your own enterprise and gave you control over it, or if it allowed you to keep your own patents, but you are not willing to be a minority share holder or to share credit with others for what you have done.

From the point of view of this career anchor, the debate about "intrapreneurship" is irrelevant. If a person is really anchored in this way it is inevitable that he or she will start their own enterprise sooner or later. On the other hand, companies can certainly attempt to use these individuals in the early stages of their career, so long as they are aware that they will not retain them.

The other issue is whether or not the emphasis on creativity implies that the other anchor groups are less concerned about creative efforts. The way to think about this is that in each group the creative impulse manifests itself differently. The technical/functional types certainly want to be creative in how they manage. The point about entrepreneurs is that they are obsessed with the need to create on a large scale and as an extension of themselves.

The next anchor category is, in a sense, at the opposite extreme in highlighting concern for others, for a cause, for a dominant ideal or value.

6. **Service/Dedication to a Cause:** If this is your anchor, you see your career entirely in terms of some core values that you are trying to achieve through the kind of work you do. Those values could be such things as "making the world a better place in which to live," "creating a more humane workplace for people in organizations," "inventing products that will save lives or cure starvation," and so on. You will only remain in a job or organization if it allows you to fulfill the values you hold.

A good example of an individual in this category is an ex-professor of forestry in Australia who had been hired by an aluminum company to plan their mining in such a way that the environment would be minimally disturbed. He was not merely to stay within the law, but to actively promote environmental preservation. He was responsible for areas that had been reforested, cited statistics showing that animals had already returned, and discussed his system for minimizing negative impact. He also made it quite clear that he would resign if the company in any way interfered with his plan.

One is tempted to correlate this anchor with entire occupations such as social work, the ministry, personnel management, and the like, but, in fact, one finds service-anchored people in every occupation. On the other hand, any given occupation will have most of the anchors represented in it. In other words, some people go into social work because they enjoy it as a craft, some want the supervision and management, some want the chance to pursue an autonomous practice, some find it a secure career, and so on. Similarly, one will find among doctors or lawyers or police officers, the full range of anchors described here.

A small and unusual group of people seemed to care less about what they did and more about the degree to which their work tested them on a daily basis.

7. **Pure Challenge:** If this is your anchor you require the kind of work that will always permit you to feel that you are overcoming "impossible" barriers, meeting very difficult challenges or winning over tough competitors. The kind of work you do is less important to you than the fact that it allows you to win out over opponents or problems. You tend to define situations in terms of winning or losing, and you only get true satisfaction when you win.

This group was originally identified by Derr (1980) in his study of naval officers. He found a set of Navy flyers who were totally concentrated on training themselves to a level of perfection that would allow them to win in combat if and when that opportunity arose. Similar concerns are evident in some athletes, in salesmen, and in other occupations where "head to head" confrontation occurred. Some engineers thrive on solving impossible problems, some strategy consultants are only motivated if the company they are helping is extremely bad off, and some managers only enjoyed turna-round situations in which everyone else had failed.

The final anchor group is probably a reflection of changing values in society and structural changes in the labor force resulting from larger numbers of women in organizations and the corresponding increase in dual careers. Increasingly it is found in men as well and at all ages.

8. **Life Style:** If this is your anchor you feel that your work life and career must be integrated with other aspects of your total life—your family situation and your personal growth needs. You will therefore seek situations that allow you to make that integration even if that means some sacrifices in relation to the career. The situation comes up most clearly for you if you have a career-involved spouse and the two of you need to make joint life-style decisions. You will decide how each of you will balance personal and professional needs, where you will live in terms of joint job opportunities, whether or not and when to have children, and how to handle situations where your organizational careers might require one or both of you to make a career compromise. But you will tend to seek integrative solutions rather than letting career concerns dominate the decision.

Research so far shows that these eight categories encompass all people interviewed in a variety of occupations. Other kinds of anchors may be found in future research, but so far all the cases fit into one of the eight categories. The relative frequency of the anchor types varies by occupation, by socioeconomic level, and other variables.

From a theoretical point of view, one wonders why some obvious categories of anchors did not show up. For example, why is pure power not an anchor. One hypothesis about this is that we all have power needs and they get expressed sufficiently in various occupations through the other anchors. Perhaps if one examined specific occupations such as politics or elementary school teaching where pure power can be expressed, one would find some members of those occupations with power anchors.

Some people have speculated that variety should be a career anchor, but here again it appears that needs for variety come to be ultimately expressed through autonomy or general management or pure challenge anchors. Organizational membership and the identity it provides could have been found to be an anchor in its own right, but it appears to be expressed more in terms of security/stability needs or general management needs.

Practical Application. Career anchors can be determined by career occupants through a self diagnostic exercise. The core of the exercise is to work with a partner and to do a mutual career history interview leading to a career anchor determination (Schein, 1985, 1990). Such an exercise is most appropriate under the following conditions: (1) When a crucial career choice has to be made, such as when a person is offered a promotion or a transfer; (2) When the career occupant feels the need of a change, such as when he or she is not happy in the present situation and is seeking something different; (3) When the organization requires career data for their human resource inventory and each career occupant has to provide some written career plans; (4) When the career occupant is facing a career counseling session with his or her supervisor, an activity that is increasingly required by organizations as part of their career development system; and (5) when in a dual career situation choices have to be made about how best to maximize the potential of both careers.

Job/Role Planning

Most human resource planning systems have components such as succession planning, career pathing, and programmed development activities oriented to getting specific people ready for higher level jobs. Most often these systems start with a pool of people and *plan for the people*. That is, the organization manages the career and decides how best to deploy its people so that jobs will be filled as needed and people will develop as needed.

There are two fundamental flaws in this model. First, the organization makes assumptions about the motives, needs, and values of the people that may not fit reality. In other words, the career anchor may not match the

planned career path. Second, the organization does too little job/role planning (Schein, 1978) and therefore miscalculates what kind of person with
what sets of skills and anchors it will need in the future.

In a dynamic environment, the organization should concentrate primarily on figuring out what needs to be done for the organization to survive,
grow, and innovate. What kinds of tasks will face the organization in the
future, and how those tasks will be accomplished. The *human resources*
needed can only be determined if there is a good understanding of what
work needs to be done.

At the senior management levels this is the job of strategic planning, but
at every level such strategic thinking should be supplemented by formal
planning for every job that currently exists in the organization. This activity
carried out for all jobs throughout the organization is job/role planning.

For example, the job of plant manager is evolving and changing to such a
degree that if one pulled out the job description for plant managers even
a few years ago, one would find that those descriptions do not at all fit
current realities. Specifically, whereas in most industries the role of plant
manager used to be technical, it has in many cases evolved into a role that is
much more political, where the plant manager relies on a technical staff
for most of the operational problems while he or she negotiates with the
government around occupational safety and health issues, the local community around issues of pollution and employment and the union around
everything.

In principle, all jobs should be periodically analyzed from this planning
point of view. Any given organization can, of course, first identify which
particular jobs are going to change most in response to environmental
changes and strategic changes in the organization, and concentrate on job/role
planning just for those jobs.

Practical Application. Job/role planning is easiest to implement around
succession planning. For every key job in the organization where a back-up
person is to be identified and where a career development track is to be
considered, the first step is for a group consisting of some present occupants
and some managers one level higher to spend a couple of hours doing an
"open systems analysis" of how the job will evolve over the next several years
(Schein, 1978; Beckhard & Harris, 1987).

(1) What demand systems or other roles is the job connected to inside and
outside the organization, (2) How will those demand systems change, and
(3) What will this mean for future occupants of that job in terms of the kinds
of skills, attitudes, values and career anchors they will have to have.

Only after such an analysis is it appropriate to consider the names of
individuals who might fill that job. Doing the analysis in a formal way and
writing up the results has a second payoff. For candidates who are being

considered (if the organization is using open job posting), or for incumbents who have already been given the job, giving them the actual job/role analysis completed by the group turns out to be far more helpful than giving them the job descriptions. Somehow the job/role planning process gets at the essence of a job in a way that formal job descriptions do not, and that makes it easier for the candidate to judge whether or not his or her own career anchor fits with the future requirements of the job.

Effective job/role planning makes it possible for career occupants to concentrate primarily on their own career planning and development, and facilitates an effective dialogue between the organization and the individual that permits better matching of what the organization needs and what individual career occupants need. If that dialogue is to work, individuals need to be more self-aware and more skilled in negotiating with their employers to insure a career path that fits their anchors, and the employer needs to be more aware of the realities of the organization's work as it moves into an uncertain future.

A Brief Look Into the Future

In contemplating the increasingly turbulent environment in which organizations will have to operate in the future, can one foresee any trends either for career anchors or for key jobs and roles in organizations? Several observations can be made along these lines:

1. **The Effect of Globalization.** Career anchors exist in every culture, but the priorities among them, how careers are perceived, how work and family concerns are balanced vary from culture to culture. Career development systems, therefore, have to be culture specific. It is very doubtful that any multi-national organization is able to use the same systems in all of its country subsidiaries, but the structure of creating a dialogue by doing job/role planning and helping people to figure out their own anchor is necessary in all of them.

Job/role planning will become even more important because jobs with the same titles will be different in different cultures. One will not be able to assume that if someone has been a successful plant manager in the U.S., he or she will be able to do the same job in a European or Asian country. In fact job/role planning may be a very important tool to identify cultural variations and thus to avoid making inappropriate assignments.

2. **The Effect of Technological Change.** All futurists seem to agree that technical change is accelerating in all aspects, especially information technology. The main effect of this trend is that every organization will need more specialists and that the rate of people becoming technically obsolete will increase. People with a technical/functional anchor will, therefore,

become more important to organizations and career systems will have to evolve that can meet the needs of such specialists.

At the same time, job/role planning will reveal that many such people become obsolete within their own career span so provisions must be made both by individual career occupants and organizations for retraining and reeducation. Whether this is done inside organizations or through educational subsidies of various sorts is not clear, but what is clear is that given specialities will probably not be needed over the entire span of a career.

There will also be a change in the basic structure of organizations that will make the integrative managerial job substantially different. Information technology will make it possible for organizations to create networks that will either displace, shrink, or change the nature of hierarchies. The job of general manager will become much more one of facilitating, negotiating, integrating, and process consulting (Schein, 1985b, 1987, 1988).

If organizations become flatter, as seems to be happening in some industries. there will be fewer senior management jobs of an integrative nature, but, at the same time, with flatter organizations will come more project activity which will require more general managers at lower levels. It remains to be seen how this will impact on the nature of these jobs and whether or not they will require people with anchors other than general manager ones. Another related impact will be that functional units will become more important and functional managers will find themselves in more senior positions of influence. With such restructuring the opportunities for technically/functionally anchored people increase as organizations flatten.

This will have an impact on those individuals who have general management anchors in that it will be less and less clear whether or not they can have the individual level of accountability and authority that they may feel they need. They will be more dependent on their specialist subordinates and will have to learn how to influence without authority (Bradford & Cohen, 1990).

3. **The Effect of Changing Sociocultural Values.** Though this is happening at very different rates in different countries, it seems clear that we are entering a period of the world's development where people expect more and are less willing to settle for autocratically mandated lives. There will be more people with autonomy anchors, life-style anchors, service anchors, and entrepreneurial creativity anchors.

Organizations will probably be more fluid and the nature of the psychological contract between employers and employees will be much looser and dynamic. Security issues will obviously remain a concern, but the concept of who is responsible for making someone feel secure may shift away from employing organizations toward the individual and toward new social institutions that have not yet been invented. In the more developed countries neither the individual career occupant, nor the employing organization will want to commit to golden handcuffs or lifetime employment.

Whatever else happens, the more people know about their own needs and the more organizations can understand the realities of how their work is changing and what kinds of human resources they will need to manage an uncertain future, the better off they will be.

CONCLUSION

The purpose of career anchor research is to help individuals to become more self-aware so that they can negotiate better with their organizations around career pathing and career development. Organizations attempting to maintain effectiveness in increasingly dynamic environments will need to improve the process by which work is matched to people. In that matching process they will increasingly be dependent upon career occupants being open and clear about their own career anchors, so it is in the best interests of both the individual and the organization to stimulate self-awareness and to create a climate in which employees can be more open in stating their career priorities and anchors.

At the same time, this dialogue can only work if organizations become more clear about the nature of the work that is to be done, and learn to communicate clearly to future career occupants what they are to do and what they will face. To generate such information organizations will have to do more job/role planning and will have to be more open in sharing the information generated by this process.

What this means, ultimately, is that organizations and management should manage the work of the organization, and that individual career occupants should manage their own careers.

REFERENCES

Beckhard, R. and Harris, R.T. *Organizational Transitions: Managing Complex Change.* Reading, Ma.: Addison-Wesley, 1987.

Cohen, A.R. & Bradford, D.L. *Influence without authority.* N.Y.: Wiley, 1990.

Derr, C.B. (Ed.) *Work, family, and the career.* N.Y.: Praeger, 1980.

Schein, E.H. *Career dynamics.* Reading, Ma.: Addison-Wesley, 1978.

Schein, E.H. *Career anchors.* San Diego, Ca.: University Associates, 1985.

Schein, E.H. *Organizational culture and leadership.* San Francisco: Jossey-Bass, 1985b.

Schein, E.H. Individuals and Careers, Jay Lorsch (Ed.) *Handbook of Organizational Behavior.* Englewood Cliffs, N.J.: Prentice-Hall, 1987. pp. 155–171.

Schein, E.H. *Process consultation. Vol. 2.* Reading, Ma.: Addison-Wesley, 1987b.

Schein, E.H. *Process consultation. Vol. 1 (Rev.).* Reading, Ma.: Addison-Wesley, 1988.

Schein, E.H. *Career anchors (Revised Edition).* San Diego, Ca.: University Associates, 1990.

Part C
The Maintenance Stage

Chapter 12

DEVELOPMENT THROUGH MENTORING:
A STRATEGIC APPROACH*

KATHY E. KRAM AND MADELINE C. BRAGAR

The increasingly difficult challenges that businesses face in the next century heighten the need for individuals at every career stage to regularly develop new skills and adapt to rapidly changing work environments. It is also strikingly evident that relationships that support learning and development are not sufficiently available to those who can benefit from them. The purpose of this chapter is to assess the value of planned mentoring programs, and to present a broader approach to improving the quality and availability of developmental relationships that is directly linked to key strategic concerns and consistent with current management practices. Formal mentoring programs present only one alternative with considerable limitations that must not be overlooked. This chapter outlines a strategic approach to mentoring—which may or may not include formal programs—that is aligned with key business concerns and based on a "continuous improvement" paradigm. This approach systematically considers a range of Human Resource systems and practices that significantly impact the mentoring process.

Mentoring is now widely recognized as an important source of development for individuals at every career stage. Relationships between juniors and seniors that provide a variety of developmental functions, including coaching and counseling, enable both parties to build new skills, prepare for advancement and other growth opportunities, adapt to changing organizational circumstances, and/or build self-esteem and self-confidence (Kram, 1986; Kram, 1988). Other kinds of relationships with superiors, peers, and subordinates can also substantially aid development, even though they are more limited than mentoring alliances in terms of level of involvement and depth of impact (Thomas & Kram, 1987; McCall et al., 1988; Zemke, 1985).

With increased attention to the role of relationships in development, it has become strikingly evident that supportive alliances are not sufficiently available to those who can benefit from them. This is particularly troublesome as we witness the increasingly difficult challenges that businesses face: challenges that heighten the need for individuals to regularly learn new

*We gratefully acknowledge the helpful comments of Marilynn Miles Gray, Chris Shinkman, Tim Hall, Morgan McCall, David Montross, and Kent Seibert on an earlier draft of this chapter.

skills and adapt to rapidly changing environments. The purpose of this chapter is to assess the value of planned mentoring programs, and to present a broader approach to improving the quality and availability of developmental relationships that is directly linked to key strategic concerns and consistent with current management practices.

An examination of the current business context reveals forces which simultaneously demand more of individuals at every career stage, and create obstacles to building developmental relationships that would enhance learning and adaptability. American businesses now—and even more so in the year 2000—are facing unprecedented uncertainties in market structures, dramatic changes in technology, increasing domestic and foreign competition, changing customer needs, and an increasingly diverse workforce in terms of cultural background, personal values, expectations, and skills (see Fig. 12-1). These forces, combined with the fact that the U.S. World Market share has dropped more than 50 percent in the last ten years in 20 major industries, and about 40 U.S. Fortune 500 companies have gone bankrupt since 1982 (Peters, 1987), are testimony to the magnitude of the challenges posed by the world economy.[1]

To cope with these forces, successful organizations in a variety of industries are internalizing the concept of continuous improvement as essential to survival and achievement of key strategic objectives (Harrington, 1987; Peters, 1987). The emphasis on building problem-solving capabilities that will consistently and incrementally improve overall quality and service to customers is being incorporated into both vision statements and operational management systems and practices. There is a fundamental shift occurring in the way organizations are structured and managed, and in the way their members are expected to go about their work. A clear focus on total quality improvement is now considered of paramount importance, even if short-term results must be sacrificed in order to achieve long-term collaborative problem-solving capabilities.

In turn, HRD practitioners and scholars have recognized that these fundamental shifts in management philosophy and practice demand dramatically different skill sets among employees, and over the longer term, require that individuals regularly learn new methods to adapt to changes in both technology and organizational culture (Johnson & Packer, 1987; Fombrun et al., 1984; Hall, 1986). For example, downsizing and restructuring are becoming commonplace in most industries; these major changes magnify problems of obsolescence and plateauing. Similarly, demographic trends clearly indicate that individuals are increasingly faced with more demanding situations at home and at work as dual income families become the norm, and individuals are expected to accomplish more at work with fewer resources and to collaborate with people who may be culturally quite different from themselves.

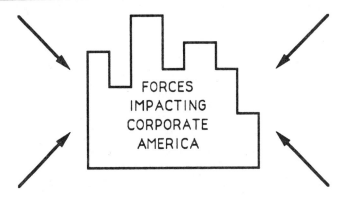

NEW COMPETITION

Foreign
* Developed (e.g. Japan, Germany)
* Newly Industrialized (e.g. Korea)

Domestic
* Smaller firms resulting from entrepreneurial explosion
* Downsized units within big firms

WORKFORCE 2000

* Changing Demographics (e.g. 85% of new entrants to work force will not be white males)
* Increase of two wage earner families
* Increasing demand for more highly skilled workers
* Rising average age of workers
* Shrinking labor pool

FORCES
IMPACTING
CORPORATE
AMERICA

GENERIC UNCERTAINTY

* Mergers, divestitures, joint-ventures
* Maturing U.S. industries
* $1 trillion in developing country debt
* Record business and bank failures and record start-ups

TECHNOLOGY REVOLUTION

Design
* Fast collection of customer data, reduced time to manufacture

Manufacturing
* Smaller, more flexible factories

Distribution
* Electronic linkages to customers

Figure 12-1.

Thus, in parallel and in concert with the concept of total quality and continuous improvement, the capacity for continuous learning is essential (Hayes, 1985; Hall, 1986). In the near term, individuals are confronted with having to learn new technical and interpersonal skills and to find effective ways to define themselves in relation to work and family responsibilities. In the longer term, the capacity to adapt to change and to periodically redefine one's identity will be critical. It is unlikely that the rate of change will decrease, and it is certain that personal needs will change as individuals' careers (and lives) unfold. Since relationships are a critical factor in enabling both task and personal learning, the need to improve the quality and availability of mentoring and other developmental relationships has become an urgent one.[2]

Paradoxically, those forces that have resulted in an urgent need to improve the quality of relationships have also created conditions that undermine the trust and rapport that are the foundation for effective alliances. First, competitive pressures are demanding that individuals do more with less; as a consequence, the energy and time available for relationship building and coaching others are dramatically reduced. In addition, the uncertainties and rapid pace of change undermine self-confidence and personal security which are key to individuals' psychological availability to mentor others. Finally, and of equal importance, increasing diversity in the workforce—evidenced by the prediction that in the year 2000, 85 percent of new entrants into the labor force will be other than native white males—presents obstacles to effective communication and collaboration which must be transcended if people from a variety of backgrounds are to have meaningful access to mentoring and other developmental relationships.

Recent attempts to improve the quality and availability of mentoring have included, primarily, the establishment of planned mentoring programs in which juniors and seniors are matched with each other for the principal purpose of supporting the less experienced individual's development. We begin with an extensive critique of these efforts in order to highlight when they are likely to have worthwhile benefits, and what practitioners can do to maximize their value. This critique leads us to surmise that formal mentoring programs represent only one alternative with considerable limitations that must not be overlooked. We conclude by proposing a strategic approach to improving mentoring—which may or may not include planned mentoring programs—that is aligned with key strategic concerns. This approach takes into account current and future work force needs and requirements, and systematically considers a range of other HR systems and practices (including rewards, performance appraisal systems, job assignments, education and training, and cultural change efforts) as factors that significantly impact the quality and availability of developmental relationships.

PLANNED MENTORING PROGRAMS

Until the early 1970s, mentoring was left to chance in most companies, with a few exceptions, e.g., The Jewel Companies; AT&T (cf., Phillips-Jones, 1982; Zey, 1984; Kram, 1988). Development activities were generally limited to a range of training and educational programs, job rotation experiences, and some career coaching as part of performance evaluation in preparation for future advancement. Mentoring tended to spontaneously occur only for an elite group of high potential exempt managers who hoped to advance to senior management, and who were most like those who already occupied such positions. As a developmental tool, then, mentoring was readily available to a very small population.

Several factors contributed to the first attempts to actively plan formal mentoring relationships. With increasing numbers of women and minorities in other than blue-collar jobs, and the creation of EEOC and Affirmative Action Programs, organizations became increasingly concerned with how they might best create advancement opportunities for other than majority group members. At the same time, advances in our understanding of adult development, career development, and human resources management all pointed to the importance of relationships in supporting individuals' capacities to learn new skills and effectively meet the challenges of successive life and career stages (cf., Levinson et al., 1978; Hall 1976; Schein, 1978; Dalton et al., 1977; McCall et al., 1988). These early programs were generally designed to promote mentoring relationships for selected groups of women and/or minority group members, or for recent college graduates for whom effective relationships with more senior colleagues would facilitate learning the ropes and establishing a new career (Lean, 1983; Phillips-Jones, 1983; Zey, 1984; Kram, 1988). In all instances, the assumption underlying such efforts was that without formal arrangements, such relationships were unlikely to emerge.

During the 1980s, we have witnessed a proliferation of such programs, not only for women and minority group members, but also for all high potential managers who are slated for middle and senior management (cf., *International Journal of Mentoring*, Vol. 3, #1, #2, 1989). The most current research on managerial learning, emphasizing the critical role of relationships in development (e.g., McCall, Lombardo and Morrison, 1988; Hall, 1986; Kram, 1988; Dalton and Thompson, 1986), and the difficult competitive challenges facing organizations in both private and public sectors, have prompted senior executives and HR professionals to look towards formal mentoring programs as a key tool for developing the talent that is so necessary for survival.

The purpose here is to highlight the conditions under which planned mentoring programs seem to work and what can realistically be expected from such efforts. *Formalizing the mentoring process—in order to make it readily available to those who otherwise don't find it easily—must not result in yet another panacea for growth and development that results in disappointment, frustration and other unintended negative consequences.* There is enough data now to indicate that planned programs may be beneficial to those who participate; however, they frequently have a number of unintended negative consequences.

Core Components

There is a clear consensus among those who have designed, implemented. and participated in planned mentoring programs that a number of core components are essential to their effectiveness (Zey, 1989; Alleman, 1989; Gray, 1989; Kram 1986; Phillips-Jones, 1982). These include specific objectives of the program that define the target population, as well as the intended benefits of participation; a selection process that maximizes voluntary participation and the likelihood that matched pairs will find value in their relationship; orientation and training that provide knowledge, skills, and support for participants to benefit from their involvement; a communication process that informs both participants and nonparticipants about the intent and parameters of the program; a monitoring and evaluation process that determines whether objectives are achieved and how the program might be strengthened; and a coordinator, usually located in the Human Resources function, who manages the program and provides ongoing support and counsel to participants (see Fig. 12-2).

While the exact nature of these components will vary depending upon the developmental needs of participants and the particular context in which it is implemented, experiences with programs implemented in the 1970s and 1980s offer three important lessons that are generalizable to a wide range of situations.[3] As with so many developmental programs, the need for up front planning that insures a good fit with other policies and practices is essential. In addition, any attempt at expediency which minimizes planning or reduces the orientation, training, and monitoring components is likely to undermine programs' effectiveness. Finally, given the nature of mentoring relationships, program flexibility and voluntary participation are critical regardless of specific objectives or organizational context.

When planned programs are clearly linked to the business strategy and are consistent with other personnel policies and practices, they are more easily accepted and actively supported by both senior management and potential participants. For example. programs designed to make mentoring more available to high

PLANNED MENTORING PROGRAMS
CORE COMPONENTS

OBJECTIVES

* Target population(s)
* Desired outcomes
    - for Mentors
    - for Mentees
    - for the Organization

GUIDELINES

* Selection and matching process
* Responsibilites of each participant
* Potential obstacles and opportunites
* Suggestions on getting, started, managing
  and ending relationships

TRAINING/EDUCATION

* What mentoring is and is not
* Self-assessment
* Interpersonal skill training
* Implications of workforce diversity
* Expectation-setting for pairs and
  supervisors

COMMUNICATION STRATEGY

* With participants
* With participants' peers and supervisors
* With senior management
* With general population

MONITORING/EVALUATION

* Qualitative and quantitative data
  through interviews and questionnaires
* Subjective and objective measures
* Linkages to business strategy and HR
  strategy

COORDINATOR ROLE

* Third-party consultant to pairs
* Manager of program
* Evaluator of program
* Link to senior management

Figure 12-2.

potential women and minority group members have gained acceptance and have had positive impact in organizations where increasing diversity in management has been an explicit and real objective, and other efforts are simultaneously undertaken to support such a major cultural change. The same is true for planned programs designed to help newcomers learn the ropes, or for those with the objective of preparing high potential junior managers for middle and senior management. When these target populations have been viewed as essential to meeting organizational objectives, and other practices are in place to support their development (i.e., training and education, effective supervision, and meaningful assignments), planned efforts to provide mentoring have been viewed as relevant and effective.

The most vivid examples of this point can be observed by comparing programs designed to enhance the development of high potential women and minority group members.[4] In some of these programs the majority of participants are positively engaged in building meaningful mentoring relationships. In others an equal proportion of participants are frustrated by the superficiality of the "matched" relationships, or are marking time until their official commitment is over. In the former, a great deal of up-front work has been done to insure that developing workforce diversity in management is a shared objective that is part of the overall strategy, participants are assisted in learning how to build meaningful alliances across gender and racial boundaries, and managers are recognized and encouraged for taking the time to develop their junior colleagues.

In contrast, there are as many instances where programs with the same purpose have resulted in more negative outcomes than beneficial ones. Here, whether it be manufacturing, insurance, or high technology, a genuine commitment to building work force diversity is lacking, and little is done beyond setting up a formal mentoring program to encourage effective alliances. In these instances the culture tends to reward short-term, bottom-line results to the exclusion of long-term, developmental activities; discourages open exploration of the barriers to building strong relationships with those who are different; and fails to provide the necessary education, training, and personnel practices to support overall objectives. Not surprisingly, many participants are alienated from the program and the organization, resources have been wasted, and the Human Resource staff responsible for the design and implementation loses credibility. It's just "another fad" with little concrete payoff.

When core components of planned programs — guidelines and expectations, selection criteria and process, training and education, monitoring and evaluation processes, and a strategy for communication about the program — are designed with effectiveness rather than expediency in mind, positive outcomes will be maximized. This is not easy to keep in mind in cost-cutting and downsizing environments, where the tendency is to minimize training expenses and/or investments of time and money in activities which seem to have little immediate tangible benefit. Under the pressure to do more with less, the HR staff responsible for designing a mentoring program may want to get the initiative launched as soon as possible, and at minimum cost. This approach, however, has repeatedly resulted in negative outcomes: participants are confused about their responsibilities in the program, or feel inadequately prepared to assume them; nonparticipants and/or supervisors of participants are poorly informed and thus become resentful or threatened; and there are inadequate feedback mechanisms in place to modify the program when necessary, or to assess the program's impact.

Decisions about the kind of orientation and training that is offered to program participants illustrates this point clearly. In the interest of saving money and time, some program designers have limited participant orientation and training to a half-day seminar. Program objectives and guidelines are reviewed, and questions are answered. There is minimal, if any, education on the process of mentoring, or self-assessment and interpersonal skill training that would enhance self-awareness and competence in building new developmental relationships. It appears that while some do go on to establish satisfying relationships because they already have the necessary self-awareness and interpersonal skills, others experience substantial anxiety, and feelings of incompetence or disappointment which cause them to psychologically, if not officially, withdraw from the program.

Sufficient experience with education and training related to mentoring now exists to offer program designers a number of alternatives (Kram, 1986; Gray, 1988; Alleman, 1989).[5] As with other core components it makes sense to poll potential participants to accurately diagnose what is necessary and appropriate for a given target population. For some, intensive self-assessment and skill training will be necessary to enable individuals to know what they need and have to offer in new relationships with juniors or seniors. For others, structured and facilitated meetings with their matched partners (and/or immediate supervisors of the mentees) will be crucial to help clarify expectations and initiate new relationships. And, in programs designed to promote interracial and cross-gender alliances, it is very likely that focussed work on the management of cultural differences and gender dynamics will be essential preparation in order for meaningful alliances to develop (Thomas & Kram, 1988; Thomas, 1989; Thomas & Alderfer, 1989; Morrison et al., 1987).

Similar care is required when developing guidelines, communication strategies and monitoring/evaluation processes. As with the orientation and training components, shortcuts in these areas incur associated risks of misunderstanding, resentment, and lack of program credibility. The unintended consequences of efficiency can be great. In most instances, it would be better not to implement a mentoring program than to pursue a low-cost plan which neither adequately prepares participants nor informs others about the intent and impact of the effort.

Given the nature of mentoring relationships, voluntary participation, and flexible guidelines are critical to the success of a planned program — subtle (or not so subtle) pressures to participate, and uniform requirements that overlook differences in participants' needs will have dysfunctional consequences. Indeed, most internal and external consultants agree that these are essential characteristics for a successful mentoring program. Yet in the interest of getting started on a timely basis, these are often compromised. In one company, for example, while voluntary participation was stipulated, when too few experienced managers offered to be mentors, the HR staff begin to "sell" the idea and urge the CEO to identify and "strongly encourage" his subordinates to participate. Rather than examining the reluctance to participate, which would have surfaced the fact that current conditions in the firm left upper-middle managers feeling underappreciated and overburdened, arms were subtly twisted. It was not surprising, when six months later these individuals had met quite infrequently with their matched mentees, and the latter were disillusioned about the intent of a program presumably designed for their benefit.

In an equally stressful environment at another company, a different recruitment strategy was used which seemed to minimize the pressure to participate involuntarily. Here, a seminar was offered to potential mentors and potential mentees simultaneously with no expectation that individuals would have to make a decision on the spot to participate. Instead, individuals were invited to attend a follow-up orientation session or to contact the coordinator at a later date should they be interested in getting involved. In this particular context the matching of mentors and proteges was left to potential participants — juniors and seniors were encouraged to reach out to each other, and were given a list of those who had expressed interest in the program. In this instance, the HR staff coordinator forfeited control over how many pairs emerged and between whom, but anecdotal data suggested that many were positively engaged in increasingly useful alliances six months after these initial sessions.

Parallel examples concerning the nature of program guidelines abound. In an attempt to provide clarity of expectations and assistance in getting started, guidelines sometimes err in the direction of requiring uniformity among participants who have unique needs and interpersonal styles. There is sufficient data on both informal and formal mentoring relationships to suggest that both kinds of relationships get started in a variety of ways, and that the particular developmental functions that they serve vary with the career stage and personal needs of the individuals involved (Noe, 1988a; Kram, 1988).[6] Guidelines which allow for these variations and also provide enough information to help participants define roles and actions for themselves are likely to be most effective. In practice this means that participants are offered a range of alternatives and assistance (through self-assessment methods) for making informed choices, rather than a succinct list of "how to's" which may only be right for a few, and surely not for all.

Such flexibility allows for maximum involvement by encouraging individuals to tailor expectations and actions to their particular needs. For example, in one program, some mentors assessed that they were able and willing to provide coaching to newcomers but were not in a position to sponsor, counsel or give challenging assignments to their mentees. Others, after self-reflection, found that they preferred to be role models and counsel mentees on personal and professional dilemmas. These two groups systematically reflected different career stages—the former were younger and in the advancement stage of their careers; the latter were more seasoned managers interested in sharing their personal experiences and not particularly concerned with upward mobility. Similarly, some of the mentees were seeking career functions (e.g., challenging assignments, exposure, coaching) which would aid promotional opportunities, while others were seeking psychosocial functions (e.g., role modeling, counselling, support, friendship) which would help build self-confidence and self-worth. Guidelines and training which encourage self-exploration successfully support a wider range of potential participants.

Benefits and Limitations

When planned mentoring programs are designed and implemented with the above principles in mind, they will have a number of benefits for both participants and organizations. Indeed, both qualitative and quantitative data obtained from interviews with program participants and employee surveys indicate positive outcomes including learning new skills, developing self-confidence and professional direction, realizing new opportunities for advancement, and making greater commitment to one's career and organization (cf., *Mentoring International*, Vol 3, no 1, 1989; Zey, 1984). An equally important benefit is the formation of relationships that might not otherwise occur, particularly those that cross gender and/or racial boundaries. Both mentors and mentees derive benefits, and in some instances these benefits have been linked to objective measures of retention, turnover, and promotion (cf., Alleman, 1989; Gillespie, 1989; Gray, 1989; Land, 1989; Shaw, 1989).

The actual benefits found in a particular setting will depend on the original objectives, for in some instances skill development is emphasized where in others, building self-confidence or preparing for advancement are the primary aims.[7] Much to the surprise of program coordinators, benefits do accrue to both mentors and mentees even though original objectives tend to be framed in terms of what the junior participants will gain. On average, self-report data collected to assess programs' effectiveness indicates that 95 percent of matched pairs feel that their relationships have been beneficial.

On closer inspection, however, these positive outcomes are tempered by several limitations. First, the number of participants that a planned program can accommodate is quite small, suggesting that the costs of implementation may outweigh the benefits derived for a small population. Second, the relationships that are developed through planned programs appear to be more limited in depth, scope, and impact. Finally, there are a number of unintended and often hidden negative consequences. For example, even in the best of programs substantially dissatisfying experiences have been reported by, on average, 5 percent of matched pairs. In addition, programs may produce resentment or disillusionment among nonparticipants and participants' immediate supervisors, although for different reasons (see below). Equally important is the implicit message communicated through planned programs that one mentoring relationship will suffice in enhancing participants' development.

On average, planned mentoring programs tend to accommodate twenty pairs per year. In part, this is due to the limited availability of mentors, but also to the training and monitoring efforts that are required to effectively support these new relationships. In most organizations this is a very small percentage of the total population in need of mentoring. Thus, many developmental needs will go unmet, unless mentoring is encouraged informally. Some organizations (c.f., AT&T—Indianapolis, Shaw, 1989) have eliminated this constraint by minimizing the formal structure and defining various types of mentors with more limited responsibilities, making it possible for more individuals to participate. This, however, begins to look more like a networking program, making a great number of short-term and superficial alliances available to whoever takes the initiative to contact those who have put their names on a list of "technical" and "interpersonal" mentors.

Even in programs where participation is limited to a relatively small and select group, personal accounts indicate that the majority of these relationships do not achieve the depth, scope, and level of commitment comparable to what is experienced in informally developed mentoring alliances. Formal relationships tend to be more task focussed (providing career functions) rather than more broadly defined to encompass psychosocial functions as well (Thomas & Kram, 1987; Kram, 1988). As a consequence, one could argue that what is created are coaching relationships rather than mentoring relationships. While these are beneficial, they do not have the long-term impact on self-esteem and identity that more intimate mentoring alliances do (see footnote 4 for the factors accounting for this important difference). Although in some instances these formally arranged pairs lead to deeper relationships, it has been argued that planned programs should define more realistic coaching objectives for the populations they are serving (Keele, et al., 1987), rather than perpetuate the myth that fully developed mentoring alliances can be expected.

Reports of substantially negative experiences in matched pairs are of concern because of the potential to undermine individuals' careers and self-esteem. Although these only account for 5 percent in well-managed programs, they are still qualitatively significant. In these instances, individuals report alienation, feelings of inadequacy, resentment, and anger. Juniors can feel quite disillusioned, particularly if communication with their assigned mentors remains superficial and expectations for the relationship are far from met. Even worse, if assigned mentors are not embracing the new role or are preoccupied with other matters, they may become resentful of these arranged alliances. Such unintended consequences may result from poor matches in the first place, or more likely from lack of adequate training in the process of mentoring, "forced" participation, difficulties encountered in cross-gender or interracial pairs for which individuals have not been prepared ahead of time, or lack of rewards and recognition for taking the time to participate. Program coordinators must be available to actively intervene in these situations to minimize the destructive consequences. If third party intervention does not improve the situation, such relationships should be terminated and replaced.

The unintended impact on participants' peers and immediate supervisors can be costly. Peers who see the program's possible benefits may feel deprived of a valuable developmental opportunity and may be increasingly pessimistic about their own futures. And supervisors, if not somehow included in establishing expectations for participants during the first phase of a mentoring program, may perceive their formal authority to be undermined. This is not surprising since, in effect, both mentors and supervisors may coach and counsel subordinates on various work and nonwork issues. Without clarifying the boundaries of each party's responsibilities, supervisors who enjoy these aspects of their role will feel as though formal mentors are doing part of their job. Indeed, at several companies supervisors have been included in advisory groups established to help define expectations and to monitor the program's impact. This provides an opportunity to address supervisors' concerns, to differentiate roles of mentor and supervisor, and to obtain their support. While steps can be taken in the communication strategy to reduce some of these ill effects, it is doubtful that they can be eliminated entirely.

Finally, and perhaps most importantly, all planned mentoring programs convey the message that establishing one mentor relationship—rather than a system of developmental relationships with seniors, peers, and subordinates—is key to enhancing one's development. The most current research on relationships and career development clearly indicates that individuals benefit from a variety of relationships, only some of which approximate the duration and intimacy of the classical mentor relationship (McCall et al., 1988; Thomas & Kram, 1988). It is clearly a disservice to individuals and to organizations concerned with developing their human resources to perpetuate this misconception. Instead, it is essential that individuals be encouraged to build a number of alliances which will support them. This approach is key to development and to the process of mentoring.

Although planned mentoring programs can be worthwhile, they are not without considerable limitations and unintended negative consequences. A consolidated list of myths and realities serves to highlight the context in which planned programs are most useful (see Fig. 12-3). Ultimately, those which are consistent with the principals outlined earlier can have value, particularly when they are implemented as part of a broader strategy designed to create an organizational culture which encourages effective teamwork, meaningful collaboration, and sufficient trust for mentoring to flourish naturally. This, of course, is an essential strategy for organizations facing increasingly difficult competitive pressures, rapid technological and environmental changes requiring constant learning on the job, and a work force characterized by increasingly diverse backgrounds and needs. These challenges, and the developmental needs they imply, cannot be met by planned mentoring programs alone.

BEYOND FORMAL PROGRAMS: A STRATEGIC APPROACH

Given the limitations of planned programs, and the significant challenges now facing organizations and individuals, it is critical to take a broader approach to enhancing the quality and availability of developmental alliances. Fortunately, this aim is consistent with recent efforts to strengthen the impact of Human Resource practices, to achieve total quality, and to create learning organizations. We now know something about which factors underlie the success and failure of these initiatives. Several key learnings inform the strategic approach is outlined here.

First, it is now widely acknowledged that HR programs and practices will only be effective if they are directly linked to and supportive of strategic business concerns (Devanna et al., 1984; Hall, 1984; Ulrich, 1987). Strategic Human Resources Development—explicitly relating development practices to business objectives—involves taking a long term perspective (3–5 years minimum), identifying work-force requirements in terms of skill mix

PLANNED MENTORING PROGRAMS

<u>MYTHS</u>	<u>REALITIES</u>
MOST MATCHED PAIRS EXPERIENCE EFFECTIVE <u>MENTORING</u> ALLIANCES THAT OFFER BOTH CAREER AND PSYCHOSOCIAL SUPPORT	MOST MATCHED PAIRS EXPERIENCE EFFECTIVE <u>COACHING</u> RELATIONSHIPS THAT ARE LIMITED TO TASK-RELATED SUPPORT. ABOUT 5% EXPERIENCE DESTRUCTIVE RELATIONSHIPS.
ALL ENVIRONMENTS CAN BENEFIT FROM FORMAL PROGRAMS TO SOME DEGREE.	IN CONTEXTS CHARACTERIZED BY MINIMAL REWARDS FOR DEVELOPING OTHERS, LOW TRUST AND FEW OPPORTUNITIES (OR SKILLS) FOR COLLABORATION, OUTCOMES OF FORMAL PROGRAMS WILL BE LARGELY NEGATIVE.
IF PROGRAMS ARE DESIGNED CORRECTLY, THE COMPLEXITIES OF INTERRACIAL AND CROSS-GENDER RELATIONSHIPS WILL BE MANAGED EFFECTIVELY.	ONLY IF THE CULTURE GENUINELY SUPPORTS OPEN EXPLORATION OF COMPLEXITIES CREATED BY DIVERSITY, WILL SUCH DYNAMICS BE MANAGED EFFECTIVELY.
PLANNED MENTORING PROGRAMS ARE THE MOST DIRECT AND EFFECTIVE WAY TO ENCOURAGE THESE DEVELOPMENTAL ALLIANCES.	PLANNED MENTORING PROGRAMS SHOULD BE VIEWED AS A SPRINGBOARD FOR LEARNING HOW TO BUILD DEVELOPMENTAL ALLIANCES BEYOND THE MATCHED RELATIONSHIP.

Figure 12-3.

and learning needs, and deliberately organizing HRD programs and practices around critical business issues such as quality or productivity (Louis, 1989).

In practice, this means that actions to improve the quality and availability of relationships should only be defined after key strategic business concerns and objectives have been identified, and there has been a careful assessment of the skills needed now, and in the future, to meet anticipated challenges. Otherwise, it is likely that formal mentoring programs, education on the process of mentoring, and other attempts to enhance the role of relationships in development will be isolated from key business concerns and perceived as, if not in fact, irrelevant. Just as practitioners are encouraged to think in terms of strategic staffing, strategic appraisal, strategic rewards, and strategic development (Devanna et al., 1984; Hall, 1984), it is essential for those concerned with enhancing the role of relationships to take a strategic approach as well.

Second, from the recent efforts to enhance total quality through continuous improvement, we have learned that a systematic and collaborative problem-solving approach is essential for insuring that relevant and effective actions are taken, and that they are championed and supported by senior line managers (Harrington, 1987; Peters, 1987). Companies have been successful in their quality programs when they have embraced a planning method that insures attention to process as well as end results, is customer-driven, involves employees in planning, doing and evaluating their own work, and includes ongoing benchmarking of the impact of new activities.

The method used most often in continuous improvement is the PDCA cycle (Deming, 1981). Simply put, PDCA stands for *Plan, Do, Check* and *Act*. [8] As a planning process it pushes managers and HR practitioners to ask key questions to insure that adequate information is obtained to effectively align development activities with strategic business needs, and to involve all those who will be affected by and must support such initiatives. There is clearly an emphasis on facts and data, rather than on intuition and "gut hunches." The steps in the cycle tend to create breakthroughs in thinking and results. In terms of a strategic approach to improving relationships, this means that a wide variety of action alternatives will be considered, and senior management, as well as others who will be affected by new programs, will be involved in the process of determining the best course to follow and in regularly evaluating the impact of new initiatives.

Finally, we now know from attempts to create learning environments (Hall, 1986; McCall et al., 1988; Fiol & Lyles, 1985; Levitt & March, 1988) and attempts to improve overall organizational effectiveness (Peters, 1987) that both formal and informal aspects of an organization must be taken in to account in planning for change. This means that Human Resource practices, including staffing, compensation, appraisal and development, as well as the leadership and culture of an organization are possible levers for meaningful change. Too often, efforts to improve the quality of mentoring are limited to the obvious — formal programs, education and training — rather than considering how changes in rewards, changes in job assignment practices, or cultural interventions might also significantly impact the quality and availability of developmental relationships. In fact, these other factors frequently pose substantial obstacles to managers embracing the mentoring role (Kram, 1988).

The strategic approach to mentoring consists of four major steps which, like the PDCA model utilized in continuous improvement/quality programs, is intended to be cyclical (see Fig. 4). This means that, over time, there will be a need to revisit each step to stay abreast of changes in the strategic direction of the firm, or in the learning needs of various employee groups within the organization. And, as such changes occur, there will be a need to revisit alternative actions involving both formal and informal practices.[9]

Aligning Development Efforts with Strategic Business Needs

To insure that efforts to improve the mentoring process are relevant and effective, it is essential to link them to the key strategic concerns of the business. In practice, those concerned with improving the quality and availability of developmental relationships must first identify core strategic concerns and what they suggest about the task and personal learning that will be required of various employee populations in order for the company to be successful. In the 1990s, we know that companies in all industries face some of the following challenges: downsizing/restructuring, rapid technological change, globalization, total quality improvement, and work force diversity (See Fig. 12-1).

Each of these has profound implications for development. For example, in companies that are downsizing and restructuring, employees are faced with having to leave their companies entirely when their jobs are eliminated. After the stock market crash in 1987, Merrill Lynch's Advanced Office Systems Group designed a career mentoring program to help leverage staff skills and training, to provide support in positioning staff for realistic success, and to retain valued staff who would otherwise search for career opportunities in nondownsizing corporations (Lawler, 1989). In these same settings, middle managers are having to assume greater responsibilities and span of control. The traditional role of manager, i.e., to plan, motivate, lead, and control, is changing dramatically. The rate of change, the volume of information, and the number of technological advances makes doing business each day different and more demanding. Managers are required to delegate more, to negotiate, to manage conflict and to drastically alter their

A STRATEGIC APPROACH TO MENTORING

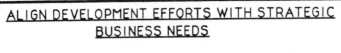

ALIGN DEVELOPMENT EFFORTS WITH STRATEGIC BUSINESS NEEDS

- Core strategic concerns (e.g. Quality, Technological Innovation, Downsizing/Restructuring, Globalization)

- Workforce requirements (e.g. Skills mix, Learning needs, Work/family issues)

ASSESS THE IMPACT OF CURRENT PRACTICES

- Formal (e.g. Performance Appraisal, Succession Planning, Rewards, Training and Management Development, EEO Planning)

- Informal (e.g. Cultural values regarding management of differences, learning, relationships, trust)

IDENTIFY AND CHOOSE ACTION ALTERNATIVES

- Natural learning opportunities
- HR systems to encourage mentoring
- Planned mentoring programs
- Cultural interventions

MONITOR, EVALUATE, AND FOLLOW-UP

- Assess results
- Communicate with management and target populations
- Correct, maintain, or improve

Figure 12-4.

style to get work completed in an ever fluid environment. The ability to learn how to learn, adapt to change, and work collaboratively are fast becoming standard expectations of all employees. As reported recently in a Harvard University study (Bragar, 1990), the ability to develop other people's talents in these areas has become an expertise expected of middle managers.

Similarly, in companies engaged in total quality improvement efforts, individuals at every level and career stage are being asked to learn new technical, interpersonal, and teamwork skills that are essential to addressing important business problems on a timely basis. Finally, in those organizations where globalization is necessary for competitive survival, and/or increasing workforce diversity is inevitable, the ability to understand and communicate across cultural boundaries — to manage differences effectively — is no longer desirable, but rather is absolutely critical.

Realistically, not all needs can be met through developmental relationships, and, in all likelihood, some needs are more pressing than others. It is also true, however, that efforts to improve the mentoring process usually serve the needs of several populations. For example, at one financial services organization, there was a need to improve the retention and performance of new college graduates, many of whom were minority and/or female. Education and training on mentoring, combined with a number of structured opportunities for these newcomers to interact with middle managers in their departments early in their tenure with the company, fostered the formation of developmental alliances that helped them learn the ropes quickly, and feel valued and welcomed. These same relationships also revitalized the middle managers who got involved, and taught them a great deal about coaching people who are different from them in terms of age and cultural background.

If such efforts are to have substantial impact, individuals must be encouraged, supported, and rewarded for getting involved in the first place. Whether the target groups are newcomers in a financial services company, high potential managers in a telecommunications company, plateaued middle managers in a manufacturing environment, or minority group members in entry level sales, it is critical to create opportunities as well as incentives to get involved in relationship building activities. Thus, as steps two and three of the strategic approach suggest, planned mentoring programs are not sufficient. Certainly, rewards, education and training, and other Human Resource practices will be essential to any efforts designed to improve the mentoring process.

Aligning development efforts with strategic business needs is a critical and difficult diagnostic task. It cannot be done without collecting data from several "internal customers." Senior managers need to be tapped for their understanding of core strategic concerns, and at the same time invited to shape, support, and possibly participate in forthcoming development efforts. For example, if they anticipate increasing globalization, then some individuals in the firm will have to become more international in focus and be supported in overseas assignments. Alternatively, if they anticipate new business requiring different technologies, certain employees will need to develop new technical skills. And if globalization, new business and/or new technologies requires a different organizational structure and more collaboration, individuals will need to learn new people skills including conflict resolution, negotiation, and teamwork. Not only can executives help to define these developmental needs, but they may also have a critical part in serving as role models, coaches, and counselors for those who have much to learn.

Individuals at various career stages and levels should also be asked about their career development needs and concerns to determine where developmental relationships are lacking, and who might be available, and currently underutilized, to mentor others. And, by asking various populations to identify significant challenges that they face, and how the organization might support them in accomplishing key objectives, learning needs can be identified. As part of the same diagnostic effort, various populations could also be asked how they might serve as mentors or coaches for others. Existing data should be examined for insights into current developmental needs; indeed, organizations generally have reams of data which are regularly overlooked (e.g., ongoing attitude surveys, complaint logs, seminar attendance, performance appraisals; skills inventories, etc). Finally, as the PDCA model suggests, at this early point it is useful to survey the best practices in other companies to see what has worked elsewhere to meet similar development objectives.

There are a number of ways to collect these data, and appropriate methods depend on what mechanisms already exist, available resources in terms of time and money, and the cultural context. For example, attitude surveys offer one vehicle for collecting data from a wide range of employees. However, they will only be effective if there is sufficient trust in the organization to assume that the data will be seriously considered. In addition, surveys are limited in the depth of understanding that they can provide. Usually face-to-face interviews with individuals or groups provide more insight into the factors shaping the quality of relationships. Finally, task forces that bring together individuals from different target populations provide an opportunity for data collection and for dialogue among those representing different concerns. This vehicle often produces creative insights and ideas for action which are not as likely to surface from the other methods. Good examples of this are found in companies that have created a multicultural task force of managers at different levels and career stages to define strategies for effectively developing female and minority talent. Frequently these groups have produced innovative actions including planned mentoring programs, developmental assignments, other on the job learning events, formal classroom experiences, and changes in the reward system to actively encourage cross-gender and interracial mentoring.

A combined approach seems to work best. If attitude surveys already exist in a company, questions can be added to shed light on the development concerns of various employee populations. However, it is only in interviews that the most sensitive concerns, such as the difficulties encountered in building relationships across gender or racial boundaries, are surfaced. And, the task force seems to be the most effective mechanism for attaining the commitment and involvement of the various groups who are integral to creating a learning environment.

Assessing the Impact of Current Practices

The diagnostic process suggested in the first step of the strategic approach will clarify which target populations have critical learning needs, and the extent to which mentoring is available to support their development. It is quite common to assume at this point that a planned mentoring program for select groups should be promptly established. Yet, for many of the reasons outlined earlier, this action is premature and possibly unwarranted altogether. First, it is necessary to examine the formal and informal practices already in place to foster both individual development and effective teamwork. It is likely that some of the existing Human Resource practices already provide opportunities for individuals to build supportive relationships with bosses and peers. Other practices may present obstacles to building supportive relationships, and will have to be altered before meaningful relationship building can happen.

For example, in a division of a high technology firm, a survey of engineers and scientists indicated considerable dissatisfaction with career development practices. Juniors wanted more coaching and mentoring from their senior colleagues in order to better prepare themselves for advancement. Seniors felt undervalued by the organization and blocked in terms of their own development. A natural next step might be to set up a mentoring program in which senior researchers and managers would be matched with those junior to them who had an interest in learning new technical and organizational skills. It was assumed that both would benefit from such arrangements, as would the company. If the matches worked, both groups would develop new skills, feel more appreciated, and be more productive.

However, in one-to-one interviews we discovered that performance appraisal interviews were done in a very cursory and ineffective manner. Juniors were very unclear about what they needed to do to be eligible for new assignments, and seniors felt unrecognized for their efforts to develop subordinates. It became clear that a number of factors had to change before individuals would willingly engage in developmental relationships. Instead of setting up a formal mentoring program, a decision was made to alter other Human Resources practices which were impeding the mentoring process. A Career Development program was established which provided information on career opportunities as well as education in self-assessment and career management for exempt employees who wanted to further their development. And, all supervisors and managers were required to attend career planning and counseling workshops in which coaching and counseling skills were practiced, and performance appraisal and development discussions were reviewed.

Two additional actions were taken that were critical to improving the quality and availability of mentoring in this setting. Job assignments were made on the basis of technical expertise, as well as career stage and developmental needs. Juniors and seniors were placed together on project teams not only because of the technical skills they brought, but also for the opportunity to build developmental relationships with each other. At the same time, a conscious decision was made to modify the reward system so that seniors would be recognized on a regular basis for their efforts to develop junior colleagues. Within two years, a considerable increase in coaching and counseling had occurred, and individuals at every career stage reported increased satisfaction with the developmental opportunities that were available to them. In the end, a formal mentoring program was never established, yet the quality and availability of mentoring had improved.

In a number of other settings, assessment of current practices has indicated that the culture—rather than formal systems and practices—would have to change before mentoring could flourish. Performance appraisal systems, job assignment practices, EEO Planning, and the like, were in place, but the informal organization prevented their effective utilization with particular employee groups. Sometimes the bottom-line, short-term results-orientation created a culture in which immediate concern for productivity tended to drive out time for building relationships and addressing developmental needs. Equally often, with an increasingly diverse workforce, individuals have encountered great difficulty in building effective alliances that cross gender or racial boundaries.

In these instances, cultural interventions are needed to create conditions that enable necessary mentoring to flourish. More often than not, these have taken the form of educational experiences with a strong personal growth orientation, in combination with frequent opportunities for making the relevant cultural values discussible, and then alterable. Recently, several companies including high technology, pharmaceutical, financial services, and manufacturing firms have introduced education on mentoring and/or diversity management. This is designed to call into question the basic assumptions that limit relationship building, and to offer interpersonal skill building opportunities as well.[10] In combination with such educational forums, most of these companies have also supported the formation of women and minority managers' networks which empower members of particular groups to build supportive relationships with others who face similar workplace challenges.

These efforts to alter the informal organization will only have sustained impact if a company's leadership endorses and models the cultural changes that are intended. Otherwise, there is a likelihood that participants in educational forums will become frustrated and/or cynical when work in the classroom is undermined back on the job. Ideally, senior managers will participate themselves, early in the implementation process. This sends the message that learning how to build developmental relationships and how to manage a culturally-diverse work force is essential for people at all levels within the organization. At a minimum, conscious attempts must be made to have some champions within senior management ranks. The only way to insure an infrastructure that is supportive of learning and development is to engage senior level managers in this assessment process.

As in the first step of the strategic approach, there are a number of ways to capture the attention of senior management. Briefings on current practices and how they are impacting the development of various employee populations, and their ability to achieve business objectives, will inform them of the need for changes. One-to-one discussions or group meetings will provide opportunities for them to influence and build ownership for particular action plans. And, sometimes, it is beneficial to bring in outside experts who can provide information about other companies efforts to address similar issues. This can both legitimize the need to move forward and provide some of the expert resources required to do so.

Identifying and Choosing Alternatives

Ultimately, the actions taken to improve the mentoring process should bring both formal and informal practices into alignment with current strategic concerns and employees' learning needs. Thus in choosing among alternatives, it is essential to assess whether a particular action will create better conditions for mentoring and other developmental relationships, and also fit with other initiatives. There are a range of possibilities to choose from (see Fig. 12-4).

Natural learning opportunities are created through assignments to task forces, project teams, internal consulting projects, and lateral moves to other functional areas. They not only offer opportunities to develop new skills, but also provide ready access to people who might serve as mentors or coaches. Using job assignments to encourage developmental relationships is generally unrecognized as an explicit development strategy. This, in fact, is a relatively easy and low cost way to foster new relationships. If the corporate culture supports learning on the job and recognizes the value of "developmental assignments" this alternative has great possibilities. As in the high technology example discussed above, project teams can foster developmental alliances between individuals at complementary career stages.

The assessment of current practices may indicate a need to modify existing Human Resource systems or a need to introduce new ones. In recent years, for example, companies have begun to work on the succession planning process to improve its role in developing managerial potential (Hall, 1986). Similarly, there are numerous examples of career development programs aimed at empowering individuals to take charge of their own learning (Leibowitz, Farren & Kaye, 1986; Hall, et al., 1986; London & Mone, 1988). Clearly, such actions are more intrusive, requiring senior management approval, the involvement of those responsible for designing and monitoring the HR systems, and the acceptance of line "customers." However, such actions may be appropriate, particularly if current practices are undermining relationship building. This is most evident in companies where performance appraisal systems are no more than a paper and pencil exercise which produces disappointment and resentment.

Planned mentoring programs may make sense, particularly if there is an immediate need to create coaching relationships that will not otherwise occur naturally. Recent college hires, for example, greatly benefit in the first year of employment from active guidance provided by a more experienced colleague. In some contexts this happens naturally, but in others it has to be engineered. If retention or socialization of these newcomers is problematic, then a planned program may offer a good solution. Similarly, if a particular group is requesting that a planned mentoring program be established, this alternative should be seriously considered. In several companies where work force diversity is problematic, groups of women managers have made such requests on their own behalf.

Frequently, however, the request for a planned mentoring program is symptomatic of obstacles to relationship building created by the corporate culture. If this is the case, then a planned mentoring program will not result in meaningful coaching or mentoring relationships. Clearly, as indicated before, these obstacles have to be addressed before such initiatives can have positive impact. Efforts to change the culture can take a number of forms, and in all likelihood should encompass a number of initiatives. Training and education on mentoring, workshops on managing diversity, and Total Quality Management programs are three approaches frequently utilized in today's corporate environment. Each focusses on changing basic assumptions (regarding relationships, managing differences, the importance of meeting customer needs) and developing interpersonal skills that are needed to address contemporary strategic challenges.

As in the first two steps of the strategic approach, and consistent with the PDCA model, all relevant constituencies (internal customers) should be consulted in deciding how to proceed. At this point in the process, however, it is likely that a task force or Human Resource advisory board has already been established to assess current developmental needs, and formal/informal practices. It is critical that senior management, potential mentors, and those in need of developmental relationships all be consulted to insure that the chosen course of action is acceptable, relevant and feasible.

Monitoring and Evaluating Actions to Enhance Relationships

All too often, systematic evaluation of new initiatives is not anticipated at the outset, and, as a consequence, one or two years later there is little clarity regarding the benefits of these earlier initiatives. Periodic assessments through focus groups, one-to-one interviews and/or surveys can illuminate what is working, what needs to be improved upon, and at the same time build and maintain the credibility of those who have championed efforts to improve the mentoring process.

It is not easy to assess the impact of actions taken to enhance the quality of mentoring and other developmental relationships. More so than with some other change efforts, there is a need to rely on subjective experiences of target populations because the impact on objective measures like performance and advancement only becomes clear if at all, over a longer time period. This is particularly troublesome if subjective measures are not valued. Most companies have begun to substantially alter their measurement approaches, recognizing that an exclusive focus on quantifiable and short-term, bottom-line results is very costly in the long term. In addition, there is a growing appreciation for the value of qualitative assessments of both customers' and employees' perceptions and experiences.

The methods used to assess impact will depend on what actions have been taken and what mechanisms already exist for monitoring Human Resource practices. Clearly, any monitoring systems that are already in place and have credibility should be utilized. Thus, periodic attitude surveys, Human Resource Advisory Boards, and focus groups can be used to help set targets and to assess how well particular initiatives have fared. One will also have to judge whether the feedback mechanisms that do exist are sufficient to assess both the process and the results of actions that have been taken. For example, if a formal mentoring program has been established, the only way to assess how well it is working may be to interview program participants with questions tailored to the experiences of the matched pairs.

Equally important is to be explicit about what is being monitored. Indeed, companies should be interested not only in the *results* of particular initiatives, but also in the *processes* that have been instituted. For example, in the case of a planned mentoring program, we would want to know how matched pairs feel at the end of the first year, what actually transpired between individuals as they attempted to build developmental alliances with each other, and how well support mechanisms such as orientation and training, written guidelines, and the HR coordinator role serve participants' needs. Similarly, if education on mentoring has been introduced, or a performance appraisal system has been modified to encourage developmental discussions and relationship building, then evaluation efforts should elicit data on both the outcomes of particular education events or appraisal discussions, as well as the processes that occurred in the classroom or in boss-subordinate discussions. The latter will suggest ways to improve and sharpen new initiatives over time.

As the PDCA model suggests, follow-up to these monitoring efforts can take one of three forms: maintain, improve, or correct. First, if a new program is working well, then action should be taken to reenforce and celebrate the successes to insure that positive results and processes are sustained over time. Several companies have explicitly rewarded managers for actively developing subordinates as a way to encourage more mentoring and coaching behavior. Not only has this become an explicit objective to be assessed in annual appraisals of performance, but awards have been established to publicly recognize excellence in this domain. For example, each year the Honeywell Corporation gives the Lund Award (cash) to publicly recognize a manager who is identified as an outstanding developer of others. This has been institutionalized and named after a valued executive who had a reputation as an excellent mentor. In addition, many companies are now including the ability to develop others in the listed criteria for assessing middle and senior management potential. By including this in the appraisal process, and sometimes soliciting feedback from subordinates, efforts to develop others are monitored and reinforced.

Frequently, the early monitoring of new initiatives will suggest ways to improve both process and outcomes. For example, in assessing the impact of a revised appraisal process, it was discovered that managers were lacking in the interpersonal skills needed to provide effective feedback and coaching. As a consequence, they would make appraisal discussions as brief as possible, and all parties concerned would experience the process as superficial. The result of the year-end evaluation was a decision to offer training in coaching and feedback skills to all supervisors and managers. Similarly, at the end of the first year of a planned mentoring program, those involved in cross-gender and interracial relationships reported less frequent contact and more difficulty in building rapport than those in homogeneous alliances. A decision was made to offer workshops which would address the complexities of working with people of the opposite gender and different cultural backgrounds.

In some instances, an initiative designed to foster developmental relationships may need to be substantially modified if data indicate unintended negative processes or results. Such corrective actions are often required in situations where formal mentoring programs have been implemented without the requisite infrastructure to support them. In these instances participants are consistently disappointed and frustrated with the superficial nature of arranged relationships, nonparticipants are newly disillusioned about their own developmental opportunities, and/or immediate supervisors feel undermined by their subordinates' participation in the program. Each of these consequences is symptomatic of the need for some corrective action. Sometimes better communication is all that is necessary. More often, however, significant cultural changes are necessary to create an environment that is supportive of learning, relationship building, and cultural diversity.

In this last step of the strategic approach, it is critical that the results of monitoring efforts be communicated and discussed with representatives of the target populations and senior management (i.e., the "internal customers"). In fact, it is equally important to communicate with "nonparticipants" to insure that other learning needs, not yet addressed, are at least recognized. These discussions will serve to inform various groups about the results of new initiatives, to reenforce successes, and to identify needed improvements or corrective actions. And, as mentioned at the outset, this monitoring process should regularly return to step one of the models to insure that efforts to improve the quality and availability of developmental relationships are linked to current strategic challenges and workforce requirements.[11]

CONCLUSION

In this chapter our purpose has been to assess the value of planned mentoring programs, and to present a broader approach to improving the quality and availability of developmental relationships. We have argued that planned mentoring programs can be beneficial, particularly if they are implemented with careful attention to selection, training, and monitoring processes. However, given the limitations of these matching efforts a strategic approach is strongly recommended — one which may or may not include a formal mentoring program. This four-step process is based on a "continuous improvement" paradigm, and it is designed to make sure that development efforts are aligned with key business concerns, responsive to individuals' learning needs and consistent with current management practices.

Given the strategic challenges that most organizations are facing, requests for substantial improvements in the quality of relationships at work will multiply in the coming years. Not only are individuals facing immediate expectations to learn new skills and to adapt to changing circumstances, but organizations are facing challenges which demand that their members collaborate effectively and creatively in order to remain competitive in the year 2000. Thus, while mentoring is not an antidote to shrinking markets, lack of strategic initiative, or sexism and racism, it is a critical developmental process which can strengthen individuals' learning and performance as well as increase overall organizational effectiveness.

Our understanding of how individuals learn in work settings has shaped our recommendations in important ways. We now know that relationships play a central role in learning, and individuals at every career stage benefit from a variety of alliances, only some of which may approximate a classical mentorship (McCall et al., 1988; Thomas & Kram, 1988). In practice, this means that planned mentoring programs, even if implemented effectively, are too limited in scope—they reach only small numbers of people, and they emphasize forming one developmental alliance rather than a system of relationships that can support both short-term and long-term learning. As noted previously, in the right circumstances planned programs can have some benefits for a particular target population, but it is unlikely that such initiatives will ever suffice.

Starting with key strategic issues insures that any efforts to improve the mentoring process are not made in isolation, but rather in explicit support of immediate and future business objectives. Then, the four steps insure regular involvement of "internal customers" (i.e., senior executives, potential mentors, individuals with particular learning and relationship needs), consideration of both formal and informal practices, ongoing benchmarking of processes and results, and continuous improvement as the steps are revisited. Ultimately, in using this approach, one might decide to implement a planned mentoring program. But this would happen only after a full range of alternatives has been considered, and a supportive infrastructure is clearly in place.

The examples used in this chapter have been carefully delineated to highlight the potential pitfalls that practitioners too often encounter when faced with pressures to reduce costs and demonstrate immediate results. The strategic approach can serve as a guide to those who are asked to improve the mentoring process in their organization. By involving members of senior management in each step, by carefully assessing the impact of current practices, and by considering both formal HR practices as well as the corporate culture as levers of change, it is possible to counteract pressures which produce superficial and costly results. For example, when the environment is plagued with gender and racial stereotyping that interferes with effective relationship building, the correct hard choice is to introduce work-shops on managing diversity and to work on creating a more supportive culture—prior to, or perhaps instead of—setting up a formal mentoring program intended to promote cross-gender and interracial mentoring.

A wide range of possible actions can be taken to foster mentoring develop-mental relationships. When faced with the challenge of creating opportuni-ties for new relationships to form, we suggest that job assignments, rewards, performance appraisal systems, succession planning systems, training and education, as well as cultural change efforts should be considered in conjunc-tion with the more obvious and circumscribed programmatic efforts. In some instances, low cost strategies can have great impact—as with job assign-ments which are made with the clear objective of encouraging interaction among individuals at complementary career stages. In other instances, initiatives in related but different areas (i.e., Diversity Management, Total Quality Management) can unintentionally provide forums for learning the interpersonal and team skills necessary to build developmental alliances, as well as opportunities to begin new relationships.

Finally, given demographic, economic and social trends, learning needs will grow and change at a rapid pace. Initiatives of today are likely to be insufficient in the near future. Therefore, it will be critical to recycle through the four step process on an annual basis. Tom Peters recently wrote "Most quality programs fail for one of two reasons: they have system without passion, or passion without system. You must have both" (Peters, 1987; p. 90). The strategic approach presented here will enable those concerned with the mentoring process to ask critical diagnostic questions, involve all of the relevant internal customers, and consider a range of creative alternatives. In doing so, they are likely to achieve the success factors that Peters describes. Both individuals and organizations will be better prepared to meet the dynamic challenges they face.

ENDNOTES

1. These data are taken from two sources: *Thriving On Chaos,* by Tom Peters (1987) and *Workforce 2000,* by W.B. Johnston and A.H. Packer (1987). The latter not only provides a wealth of demographic and economic projections, but also delineates the core challenges facing public policy makers, business executives, educators, and Human Resource practitioners.

2. The emphasis here is on both *task* and *personal* learning. Tim Hall (1986, 1976) has pointed out in his discussions of types of learning that too often there is a tendency to focus on task learning (acquiring knowledge and skills related to job performance) to the exclusion of personal learning (acquiring self-awareness about attitudes and identity that enable resolution of personal

conflicts that predictably surface at each career stage). In his model of learning he also emphasizes the importance of attending to both short-term and long-term learning. See also his chapter with Kent Seibert in this book.

3. The intent here is not to delineate specific guidelines for building a program or to review the various forms that core components might take. There are now a number of resources available for these purposes. The International Centre for Mentoring in Vancouver, B.C., publishes *Mentoring International* on a quarterly basis which includes articles by practicing consultants, HR professionals and line managers that offer practical advice and guidelines for building programs in both private and nonprofit settings. The American Society for Training and Development workbook entitled, *Design Productive Mentoring Programs* offers an outline and set of questions for making key design decisions. See also Kram (1986), Zey (1984), Phillips-Jones (1982).

4. The examples that follow are drawn from prior or current relationships with client systems in a variety of industries including manufacturing, financial services, high technology, and pharmaceuticals. The firms are not identified in order to respect the confidentiality of these consultations and research collaborations. As indicated above in footnote #3, there are numerous public accounts now available on specific mentoring programs. The intent here is to generalize from a wide array of experiences, using specific, yet anonymous, examples to illustrate key points.

5. Among those who have designed and implemented education and training related to mentoring there is a consensus that experiential workshops (generally 1–3 days long) make a difference in enabling participants to benefit from planned mentoring relationships. Through self-assessment activities, role plays, case studies, and peer consultation, participants develop the self-awareness and interpersonal skills necessary to initiate and manage developmental relationships over time. For specific examples of such materials see Gray (1988), *Mentoring International* (1990), Alleman (1989), and Kram (1986).

6. To date differences between formally arranged and naturally occurring mentoring relationships have not been empirically delineated. But Noe (1988) and Kram (1988) do suggest that formally arranged relationships may be more limited than naturally occurring ones in terms of depth of commitment, level of intimacy experienced, and range of developmental functions provided. Several factors may account for these differences: a lack of personal chemistry and identifications in prearranged relationships; the limited time frame of 6 months to 2 years imposed in planned mentoring programs; and, the public (rather than private) nature of formally arranged relationships which are in the service of organizational objectives (e.g., developing particular talent to meet future staffing requirements), rather than solely to meet participants' personal needs. Of course, formally arranged relationships serve a good purpose if program objectives are linked to key strategic concerns. The ideal is to foster informal mentoring as well, so that the benefits of both kinds can be realized.

7. In fact, these potential benefits will be diluted when objectives are not clear. For example, in one company advancement opportunities were very limited, and the original intent of the mentoring program was to provide opportunities for skill development and enrichment within participants' current jobs. However, participants were under the misconception that involvement in the mentoring program would also lead to new promotional opportunities. When the latter did not occur, there was considerable frustration and disappointment. As a consequence, both HR staff and senior management lost credibility.

8. The PDCA Cycle assumes that individuals and teams should go through the entire cycle as they work on problems and projects to insure that a range of important factors (e.g. process *and* results, customer needs, success factors, etc.) are considered. This process stands in sharp contrast to traditional management models in which planning and doing activities are segregated. Deming (1981) has demonstrated how separating the four activities leads to inefficiencies, poor quality, and lack of innovation.

9. The framework presented here builds on the Organizational Change Approach outlined in Kram (1988), Kram (1986), Kram (1985) and Thomas & Kram (1988). However, several critical differences should be noted. First, the strategic approach emphasizes the need to align development efforts with key business concerns, whereas the earlier model did not consider this important linkage. Second, senior management must be consulted and involved regularly, to insure their support and meaningful participation, as well as the perceived relevance of any actions taken. Finally, from the PDCA model several internal customers are incorporated (e.g., senior management, potential mentors, potential proteges, supervisors and Human Resource professionals) as populations whose needs must be considered.

10. These types of programs are most effective when they are held away from the office for several days, they employ experiential methods and systematic self-reflection, and a trusting climate that insures confidentiality is established. Most often, these conditions are achieved in collaboration with outside consultants who bring the requisite process skills as well as multicultural backgrounds to address workforce diversity concerns. Outsiders also have the unique ability to discuss the indiscussible precisely because they are not part of the culture. Thus, they can model behavior that heretofore has been absent from the corporate culture and provide the psychological safety for participants to explore new ways of building relationships that cross gender and cultural boundaries.

11. Given the rapid rate of change, the alignment of development efforts with strategic business needs and workforce requirements must be assessed annually. It is very likely that this can be incorporated into ongoing planning activities. Regularly checking in with senior management on the strategic direction of the company not only insures the relevance and effectiveness of Human Resource initiatives, but also serves to insure key executives' continued awareness, support and involvement.

BIBLIOGRAPHY

Alleman, E. "Two Planned Mentoring Programs That Worked," *Mentoring International*, Vol 3, 1, 1989, 6–12.

Bragar, J.L. *Effective Leadership Practice for Managers: Balancing Interdependence and Autonomy*, Harvard Graduate School of Education, Doctoral Dissertation, 1990.

Crosby, P.B. *Quality Is Free*, New York: McGraw-Hill, 1979.

Dalton, G., Thompson, P. *Novations: Strategies for Career Management*. Glenview, IL: Scott, Foresman, 1986.

Dalton, G., Thompson, P. and Price, R. "The Four Stages of Professional Careers — A New Look at Performance by Professionals," *Organizational Dynamics*, Summer. 1977, pp. 19–42.

Deming, W.E. *Japanese Methods for Productivity and Quality*. Washington D.C.: George Washington University, 1981.

Devanna, M.A., Fombrun, C.J., Tichy, N.M. "A Framework for Strategic Human Resources Management." In Fombrun, C.J., Tichy, N.M., Devanna, M.A. (Eds.) *Strategic Human Resource Management*, New York: John Wiley & Sons, 1984, pp. 33–51.

Dyer, L. "Bringing Human Resources into the Strategy Formulation Process." *Human Resource Management*, Vol 22, 1983, pp. 257–271.

Fiol, C.M., Lyles, M.A. "Organizational Learning," *Academy of Management Review*, Vol 10, 4, 1985, pp. 803–813.

Fombrun, C.J., Tichy N.M., Devanna, M.A. *Strategic Human Resource Management*, New York: John Wiley & Sons, 1984.

Gillespie, D.B. "Implementing a Mentoring Program in Life Insurance Companies." *Mentoring International*, Vol 3, 1, 1989, pp. 13–18.

Gray, W.A. "Situational Mentoring: Custom Designing Planned Mentoring Programs." *Mentoring International*, Vol 3, 1, 1989 pp. 19–28.

Gray, W.A. "Developing A Planned Mentoring Program to Facilitate Career Development," *International Journal of Mentoring*, Vol 2, 1, 1988, pp. 9–16.

Hall, D.T. and Associates, *Career Development In Organizations*, San Francisco, CA: Jossey-Bass, 1986.

Hall, D.T. "Dilemmas in Linking Succession Planning to Individual Executive Learning," *Human Resource Management*, Vol 25, 2, 1986, pp. 235–265.

Hall, D.T. "Human Resource Development and Organizational Effectiveness." In C. Fombrun, N. Tichy, Devanna, M.A. (Eds.), Strategic Human Resource Management, New York: John Wiley & Sons, 1984, pp. 159–181.

Hall, D.T. *Careers in Organizations*. Santa Monica, CA: Goodyear, 1976.

Hall, D.T., Goodale, J.G. *Human Resource Management: Strategy, Design, and Implementation*, Glenview, IL.: Scott, Foresman, 1986.

Harrington, H.J. *The Improvement Process: How America's Leading Companies Improve Quality*. New York: McGraw-Hill, 1987.

Hayes, R.H. "Strategic Planning — Forward or Reverse?," *Harvard Business Review*, November–December, Vol 63, 1985, pp. 111–119.

Johnston, W.B., Packer, A.H. *Workforce 2000: Work and Workers for the 21st Century.* Indianapolis, IN: Hudson Institute, 1987.

Juran, J.M. *Quality Control Handbook,* New York: McGraw-Hill, 1979.

Kaplan, R., Drath, W., Kofodimos, J. *High Hurdles: The Challenge of Executive Self-Development,* Greensboro, NC: Center for Creative Leadership, Technical Report No. 25, 1985.

Keele, R.L., Buckner, K., Bushnell, S.J. "Formal Mentoring Programs are No Panacea," *Management Review,* Vol 76, February, 1987, pp. 67–68.

Kram, K.E. "Creating Conditions That Encourage Mentoring," in *The 1985 Annual: Developing Human Resources,* San Diego: CA, University Associates, 1985.

Kram, K.E., Isabella, L.A. "Mentoring Alternatives: The Role of Peer Relationships in Career Development," *Academy of Management Journal,* Vol 28, 1, 1985, pp. 110–132.

Kram, K.E. "Mentoring In The Workplace." In D.T. Hall (Ed.) *Career Development In Organizations,* San Francisco, CA: Jossey-Bass, 1986, pp. 160–201.

Kram, K.E. *Mentoring At Work: Developmental Relationships in Organizational Life.* Lanham, Maryland: University Press of America, 1988.

Land, T. "Mentoring at Motorola: High Touch in High Tech," *Mentoring International,* Vol 3, 1, 1989, pp. 29–35.

Lawler, James. "Are Career Mentoring Programs Useful in a Downsizing Environment?," *The Career Center Bulletin,* The Center for Career Research and Human Resource Management, Columbia University, Vol 6, 4, 1990, pp. 8–12.

Lean, E. "Cross-Gender Mentoring—Downright Upright and Good for Productivity," *Training and Developmental Journal,* May 1983, pp. 60–65.

Leibowitz, S., Farren, C., Kaye, B. *Designing Career Development Systems,* San Francisco, CA: Jossey-Bass, 1986.

Levinson, D.J., Darrow, D., Levinson, M. and McKee, B. *Seasons of a Man's Life,* New York, NY: Alfred Knopf, 1978.

Levitt, B., March, J.G. "Organizational Learning," *Annual Review of Sociology, 1988,* 14:319–40.

London, M., Mone, E. *Career Growth and Human Resource Strategies,* New York, NY: Quorum Books, 1988.

Louis, M.R. "Systems Support for Strategic HR: Is There a Role for OD?," *Human Resource Planning,* Vol 12, 4, 1989, pp. 277–299.

McCall, M., Lombardo, M., Morrison, A. *The Lessons of Experience,* Lexington, MA: Lexington Books, 1988.

Mentoring International Journal. *Mentoring—A Business Perspective,* Vol 3, 1, Vancouver, BC, Canada, 1989.

Mentoring International Journal. *Mentoring An Educational Perspective,* Vol 3, 2, Vancouver, BC, Canada, 1989.

Morrison, A., White, R., Van Velsor, E. *Breaking The Glass Ceiling,* Reading, MA.: Addison-Wesley, 1987.

Noe, R.A. "An Investigation of the Determinants of Successful Assigned Mentoring Relationships," *Personnel Psychology,* 1988a, Vol 41, 1988a, pp. 457–479.

Noe, R.A. "Women and Mentoring: A Review and Research Agenda," *Academy of Management Review,* 1988b, Vol 13, pp. 65–78.

Peters, T. *Thriving On Chaos: Handbook For A Management Revolution,* New York, NY: Alfred Knopf, 1987.

Phillips-Jones, L. *Mentors and Proteges,* New York, NY: Arbor House, 1982.

Shaw, Y. "Mentoring at AT&T," *Mentoring International,* Vol 3, 1, 1989, pp. 41–47.

Schein, E. *Career Dynamics: Matching Individual and Organizational Needs,* Reading, MA: Addison-Wesley, 1978.

Thomas, D.A. "Mentoring and Irrationality: The role of Racial Taboos," *Human Resource Management,* Vol 28, 2, 1989, pp. 279–290.

Thomas, D.A., Alderfer, C.P. "The Influence of Race on Career Dynamics: Theory and Research on Minority Career Experiences," In M. Arthur, D.T. Hall, and B. Lawrence (Eds.) *Handbook of Career Theory,* New York, NY: Cambridge University Press, 1989, pp. 133–158.

Thomas, D.A., Kram, K.E. "Promoting Career-Enhancing Relationship in Organizations: The Role of the HR Professional," In M. London and E. Mone (Eds.), *Career Growth and Human Resources Strategies,* New York, NY: Quorum Books, 1988, pp. 49–66.

Tichy, N.M., Fombrun, C.J., Devanna, M.A. "Strategic Human Resource Management," *Sloan Management Review,* Vol 23, 2, 1982, pp. 47–61.

Ulrich, D. "Organizational Capability as a Competitive Advantage: Human Resource Professionals as Strategic Partners," *Human Resource Planning,* 10, 1987, pp. 169–184.

Zemke, R. "The Honeywell Studies: How Managers Learn To Manage." *Training,* August 1985, pp. 46–51.

Zey, M. *The Mentor Connection.* Homewood, IL: Dow Jones-Irwin, 1984.

Zey, M. "Building a Successful Formal Mentor Program," *Mentoring International.* Vol 3, 1, 1989, pp. 48–51.

Zey, M. "A Mentor For All," *Personnel Journal,* Vol 67, 1988, pp. 46–51.

Chapter 13

STRATEGIC MANAGEMENT DEVELOPMENT: LINKING ORGANIZATIONAL STRATEGY, SUCCESSION PLANNING, AND MANAGERIAL LEARNING[1]

Douglas T. Hall and Kent W. Seibert

Most careers unfold in an organizational setting. Therefore, to understand adult career development processes, it is necessary to understand how organization processes and systems influence the development of individuals. In this chapter, the authors examine career learning in organizational settings, with a focus on managers and executives. More specifically, succession planning is examined as an organizational activity designed to promote continuity of leadership by preparing future generations of executives. As such, succession planning should logically be related to the future direction (strategy) of the organization, as well as to the learning and development of young managers. However, in practice, these links often do not exist. A major reason for these "disconnects" is the top-down, mechanistic (single-loop) process which is generally used to conduct succession planning. This chapter describes research, theory, and practices aimed at tightening the links between strategy, succession planning, and managerial learning. In contrast to the traditional top-down strategic approach, a continuous improvement process based upon self-learning and organizational learning is advocated.

Strong and Weak Links

A recent survey conducted for the Executive Development Roundtable at Boston University examined the perceived relationships between business strategy, management development strategy, and managerial career development activities in a group of 25 companies with progressive human resource

[1]The authors gratefully acknowledge the helpful comments of Michael Arthur, Kathy Kram, David Montross, and Chris Shinkman on earlier drafts of this paper. Partial support for work on this paper was provided by the Executive Development Roundtable and by the Human Resources Policy Institute of the Boston University School of Management.

255

practices (Seibert, Hall, and Kram, 1991). When asked about the strength of relationships between these entities, respondents indicated that in their companies there was a strong relationship between the business environment and the business strategy. In other words, the business strategy seemed clear and relevant. The link between the strategy for developing managers and the actual developmental activities was seen as moderate. However, the main problem came in the link between the business strategy and the management development strategy, which was seen as weak. And, as some participants observed while discussing these results, "If there's little fit between the business strategy and our management development strategy, can we even say we *have* a strategy for developing managers?" An earlier literature review and discussion found similar "disconnects" between business strategy and individual development of managers (Hall, 1986).

These findings are similar to a major issue that has existed in the research literature for many years on organizational careers: the separation between organization-based *career management* activities (such as human resource planning and succession planning) and individually-oriented *career planning* activities (Hall, 1976; Hall and Associates, 1985; Gutteridge, 1985). The organizational careers literature has essentially split into "macro" and "micro" camps, with specialists working in their own subfields. There is a real need within organizations to integrate these approaches. Some corporate career practitioners may be making more progress than academics in discovering a unified approach to organizational career development. This chapter will report some of this progress.

Typology of Succession Planning

Organizations engage in a variety of activities to ensure continuity of their management resources. In practice, all of these activities are usually referred to by the organizations that use them as "succession planning." But, in reality, not everything that is *called* succession planning really is. According to a typology of management continuity activities developed by Hall (1986), these activities generally fall into one of three categories: one-shot staffing decisions; replacement planning; and genuine succession planning. The activities are discussed below in order of increasing sophistication. Note also that as the sophistication of the activities increases their prevalence in organizations decreases.

The least sophisticated of all management continuity activities is the *one-shot staffing decision.* It involves finding the best qualified individual to fill an existing vacant position. This activity is a reactive one which is initiated only after a critical position has become open through a departure, retirement, etc. Little attention is given to developing a candidate, because there is no time to do so. Candidates must already be capable of meeting the demands of the vacant position.

Replacement planning, where the focus is on filling anticipated future openings, is a more advanced approach to management continuity. It entails having senior executives periodically review their top managers and those in the next-lower echelon, and agree on two or three back-ups for each top management slot. Replacement planning is done for a large number of positions and on a regular time schedule, instead of waiting for individual job vacancies to arise. Thus it has the advantage over one-shot staffing of being proactive. It is often done subjectively, however, without established job descriptions or related knowledge, skill, and experience requirements. Since objective criteria are not employed by the relevant decision makers, the typical result is inaccurate or incomplete replacement plans. And it is usually discovered that too few people have been developed to be ready to move into higher management positions. Therefore, the challenge with replacement planning is likely to be a shortage of prepared management talent, developed and ready to assume greater responsibility.

In *succession planning,* as it is typically practiced, the focus is on both positions and candidates. There is usually an *assessment* process to identify high potential young managers and to profile their strong and deficient areas. This assessment of individuals then flows upward into an *organizational talent review,* to identify back-up candidates for key management positions. In addition, *development plans* are created to improve the person's skills and to provide needed future experiences to get him or her ready for target slots. Often, however, the development piece is weaker and has less accountability and follow-up than the assessment activity (Hall, 1986). An effective succession system should contain an *assignment management* process to ensure that the planned developmental moves in fact take place.

Succession planning obviously is a sophisticated management continuity activity. However, succession plans are often given little attention for several reasons (Hall, 1986). Accustomed to working with quantitative data, many senior executives are uncomfortable with the more subjective evaluations of people that are contained in management reviews, and hence the reviews are discounted. Many executives are also uncomfortable selecting successors who differ substantially from themselves, even though different executives may be just what success in the future requires. In addition, as indicated earlier in this chapter, the link between business' strategic plans and their management development strategies is weak. Thus, little confidence may be placed in estimations of future management positions and associated skill requirements which are largely divorced from future business plans. And even if this link were strong, predicting the future is inherently precarious. Consequently, while succession planning represents a clear improvement over one-shot staffing decisions and replacement planning, it has its own significant limitations.

Like many other organizational activities, work on succession planning can take place at three levels: strategic, managerial, and operational. An additional limitation of most succession planning is that it occurs primarily at the operational level. What is missing is work at the other two levels. Ideally, at the top, or *strategic* level, there should be an effort to set organizational policies or values which relate to how people are managed over the course of their careers. If supportive policies regarding human resources are established at the top, the details of implementing succession planning become far easier. Examples of such supportive policies are cross-functional or cross-business movement, promotion from within, full employment, linking subordinate development to managerial rewards, minimum and maximum job tenures, focus on high potentials (or a wider group), and CEO involvement. The more clarity and support there is for policies such as these from top management, the more successful succession will be.

At the *managerial* level are the specific systems and programs which are designed to support succession activities. Examples of managerial level activities are training for managers in career coaching and mentoring, administrative structures for cross-functional mobility of young managers, designing assessment methods, and career training and development programs.

Finally, once these systems and programs are in place, specific *operational* succession activities can be created. These are the "nitty gritty" details such as conducting assessments and performance appraisals, mentoring, working with consultants, administering executive tracking systems, and so forth.

The problem in many organizations is that these operational activities are defined as *the* succession process, rather than working at the strategic or managerial levels. Far too much attention is focused on the operational level, and far too little is devoted to strategic-level succession matters. The reason for this is that it is much *easier* to change the operational details than it is to influence top management policy. But as long as operational details alone are the focus of succession work, little real progress will be made. This is why some organizations seem to be forever struggling to create an effective succession process, and they never seem to learn how to do it. (See Hall, 1989, for an example of one such nonlearning organization, "PowerInc".) And thus the gap between the desire for effective managerial succession and its actual practice continues to grow. Effective succession is not so much a matter of finding the right answers as it is asking the right questions.

What Is Strategic Management Development?

Succession planning as it is currently practiced in many organizations is inadequate. What is needed is a management continuity activity that starts at the strategic level and then works to link business strategy, succession planning, and managerial learning. Such an approach is *strategic management development.* In strategic management development the focus is on anticipated *future* management positions, the expected skill requirements of those positions, *and* developing the people who might be candidates to fill the positions. Organizations are becoming increasingly aware of the need to plan to staff *future* management positions. Such positions often bear little resemblance to the positions held by existing top managers. Hence, planning to simply succeed existing managers when they vacate positions is often no longer sufficient. Ideally, potential future positions are derived from the business' strategic plan. Each strategic plan has definite implications for the types of positions that will be required to implement that plan. In addition, strategic management development involves the identification of the expected skill requirements of anticipated positions and the associated developmental needs of candidates. It also emphasizes the deliberate management of candidates' learning and development.

Strategic management development, therefore, consists of the following elements:

1. The identification and
2. Growth of
3. Needed managerial knowledge, skills, abilities, experiences, attitudes, and identities
4. For the intermediate and long-term future
5. In support of explicit corporate and business objectives.

What seems so striking about this definition is its obviousness—and its simplicity. When each of the elements is considered separately, it seems clear that we know how to do each part. Regarding identification, assessment center technology, as well as management group profiling methods, behavioral observation methods, and biographical methods, to name a few, are all well-validated ways of identifying management potential. Growth and development methods have been identified in a variety of studies such as those by the Center for Creative Leadership (McCall, Lombardo and Morrison, 1988) and AT&T (Howard and Bray, 1988). Recent studies have begun to establish some of the emerging skills that will be essential for the executive of the future (Korn/Ferry International and Columbia University Graduate School of Business, 1989; Jacques, 1989). Strategic business planning is practiced in most leading corporations, so that intermediate and long-term objectives are known. And good sources of guidance for carrying out many of these activities, such as the work of Mahler and Drotter (1986), Friedman (1986), Hall (1986), and Jacques (1989) already exist. More specifically, Hall and Foulkes (1990) discuss how to tailor the succession process to the design of a particular organization (e.g., focused strategy vs. diverse strategy). So all that needs to be done is to put all of these elements together. It seems very simple.

In fact, nothing could be more difficult. Senior line and human resource (HR) managers report that when they try to get together to discuss linking business planning with human resource planning, each group feels that the other is speaking a foreign language. Line executives report that HR managers do not understand the "real world" of business, that pressing operational needs take priority over developing managers, that there are no rewards for developing managers, that management development is fuzzy and hard to measure, and that HR processes for developing managers are unnecessarily bureaucratic.

HR managers, on the other hand, report that line managers care little about long-term issues, that they are too focused on the bottom line, that they do not understand how developing people can strengthen their organization, and that it is inconsistent to invest in R&D, marketing and capital equipment, but not to invest in young managers. In fact, Friedman (1986) has found that strategic management development is related to organizational effectiveness (as measured by financial performance and ratings by executives in other firms). However, this process is executed most effectively where there is top level support, in the form of the CEO's time and involvement. Thus, ironically, an organization has the opportunity to see the performance payoff for strategic management development when top management is already committed to it.

Top-Down vs. Organizational Learning Process

Top management commitment to the succession planning process is *necessary but not sufficient* to make strategic management development possible. If top management chooses to implement the succession process in a formal, top-down manner, with little informal discussion and upward communication at all levels, the system will be just a "paper process." Managers will fill out the necessary forms, send them up to the next level, and that will be the end of the process. An alternative approach, the learning organization approach, is described later in this chapter. The essence of this approach is to start with the business needs of managers at a particular level of the organization and to have those managers meet to discuss business plans and ways to implement those plans. Part of this discussion would be about how best to develop key individuals to strengthen the organization. Managers also discuss "player swaps" and other creative ways of both meeting staffing needs and individual development needs. The main idea, then, is to make management development a user-driven process, rather than a top-down formal system. The system is made more systematic and formal as it evolves through this more informal, bottom-up system.

A Model of Managerial Learning

The Nature of Management Learning

As indicated earlier in this chapter, the development piece of succession systems is often weaker than the assessment activity. A major reason for this is that the assessment process has been better understood, and thus more easily managed, than the process of management learning and development. From a strategic management development perspective, management learning needs to be linked to business and succession planning. And in order for that to happen, understanding of management learning must be substantially increased.

Hall (1976) has proposed two types of learning which are necessary as a manager develops. The first, which is most generally associated with management development, is *task learning:* improving the knowledge, skills, and abilities necessary to perform higher level jobs effectively. The second, infrequently discussed in the succession and management development literature, is *personal learning:* the mastery of the socioemotional tasks associated with a person's stage in life. Most of the succession and management development literature ignores this facet of learning, thus completely overlooking the fact that managers are adults who continue to grow and develop. More specifically, these two types of learning relate to four dimensions of career growth and effectiveness: performance, adaptability, attitudes, and identity (Hall, 1976). Performance and adaptability refer, respectively, to short-term and long-term facets of task mastery. Attitudes and identity deal with short-term and long-term aspects of socioemotional mastery, respectively.

These four dimensions of career effectiveness are displayed in Table 13-1. As more strategic management development systems facilitate all four dimensions of career growth, they become more effective. Indeed, the four dimensions can be viewed as the desired outcomes of effective management learning.

Seibert (1989) has proposed a comprehensive model of experiential management learning and development in order to organize the major factor involved in on-the-job management learning.[2] The model represents a starting point for considering the development piece of a strategic manage-

---

[2]The help of Kathy Kram and Meryl Louis in the development of this model is gratefully acknowledged.

Table 13-1. Types of Learning.

		Focus of Learning	
		Task	*Self*
Time	Short-term	Performance	Attitudes
Span	Long-term	Adaptability	Identity

ment development approach to management continuity. Specifically, the model does two things. First, for the researcher, it provides a conceptual framework for identifying areas in need of investigation in order for management learning to be more fully understood. Second, for the HR manager, it provides an outline of the key components of the management learning and development process. While the model is a useful starting point for HR managers interested in guiding the management learning process in their organizations, it is not intended to provide detailed "how-to" advice for handling specific situations. Figure 13-1 presents a simplified version of the model. It has three major components: the Inputs managers bring to their job; the Content of management learning; and the Outcomes of management learning.

Management Learning Inputs

Managers do not learn in a vacuum. Accompanying each learning situation is a host of variables each of which has the potential to significantly impact learning. The five variables which appear in Figure 13-1 as Inputs are hypothesized to be most influential. The first variable is *life stage*. Ironically, the vast majority of management development literature has neglected the fact that managers are people who face all the developmental life tasks normally associated with the life stage in which they find themselves. People's needs differ across the various stages of adult life (Levinson, 1978), and those needs affect the type of management learning an individual is able to experience at any given point in time. Managers' learning is also influenced by *career stage* and its associated developmental tasks. Task and socioemotional needs vary from early to middle to late career (Hall, 1976). Management learning occurs, thus, in the context of an individual's overall career. Not only should life and career stage be important to management learning, but so too should what Schein (see Chapter 10) has called the *career anchor*. A person's career anchor is a combination of his or her self-perceived abilities, motives, and values. The career anchor serves to guide, constrain, and stabilize a person's career. According to Schein, a number of anchors exist, one of which is "managerial competence." Conceivably, persons with this anchor will be more prone to learn and develop in the role of manager.

Learning style is the fourth variable. Kolb (1984) has demonstrated that not everyone learns in the same way. For example, some individuals take an active approach to learning, while others are more reflective. Kolb has identified four distinct styles of learning and, according to his research, most managers exhibit a preference for styles that emphasize action. Managers' learning styles have obvious implications for how they learn to manage. Lastly, a manager's *gender* (Van Nelson and Hughes, 1990) and *personality* are likely to impact his/her learning. Personality variables relevant to management learning include: locus of control (Spector, 1982), self-efficacy (Gist, 1987), hardiness, flexibility, tolerance of ambiguity, dominance, independence, motivation for advancement, and basic personality predisposition (Hall, 1986). Generally, the manager who feels capable of learning new and different things will be in a good position to accomplish such learning.

Management Learning Content

The content of management learning, depicted in the center of the model, represents the model's core. It consists of two dimensions. Four potential *sources of management learning and development* are depicted along the horizontal dimension. The first, Training and Education, refers to formal, primarily classroom-based management learning activities. These include university-based MBA and executive programs, as well as classroom-oriented corporate training and development programs. Formalized managerial training has traditionally been the primary means of fostering management learning (and continues to be used extensively), although its ultimate value remains questionable (Burke & Day, 1986).

Recent research has shown the vital importance of on-the-job experiences to management learning and development. The most thorough study of the contribution of experience to management learning and development was completed by McCall et al. (1988) of the Center for Creative Leadership. Three types of experience emerged as significant in their research: specific job assignments, other people, and hardships. These three types of experience, along with formal training and education, comprise the four potential sources of management learning shown in Figure 13-1. According to McCall et al., job assignments are the primary source of learning for managers. Challenge, and more specifically, diversity and adversity are what all developmental assignments seem to have in common. After job assignments, McCall et al. found other people to be the next most important source of learning for managers. In their study, 90 percent of the people described as influential were bosses. Good bosses provided most of the learning, primarily by serving as role models. Additional people, for example mentors, have been shown by other researchers (e.g., see Chapter 11.) to also be influential in managers' learning. The third class of developmental experiences discovered by the Center for Creative Leadership involves what are called hardships. Executives reported that learning from hardships, most of which consisted of failures, involved taking a hard look inside themselves. Those who struggled through hardships emerged with a clearer view of themselves and what was important to them in life. They also gained a dose of humility as a tempering agent to the confidence developed from the successful completion of job assignments. Clearly, personal learning (i.e., attitude and identity development) was the primary outcome of weathering hardships.

FIGURE 1.   TWO-DIMENSIONAL MODEL OF MANAGEMENT

LEARNING AND DEVELOPMENT

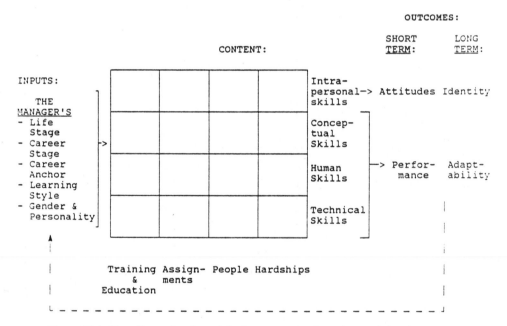

Figure 13-1. Two-dimensional model of management learning and development.

The specific experiences that McCall and other researchers have found to contribute to management learning are summarized in Table 13-2. Since research on the contribution of on-the-job experiences to management learning is still relatively new, Table 13-2 should be viewed as a preliminary list of potentially relevant experiences.

The vertical dimension of the grid in Figure 13-1 shows four classes of

Table 13-2. Types of Experiences That Contribute to Management Learning and Development.

Training & Education	People	Hardships	Job Assignments
• University based MBA and Executive Programs	• Bosses	• Personal Trauma	• Project Work
	• Superiors other than Bosses	• Career Setbacks	• Task Force Assignments
• In-house corporate training programs			• Line to Staff Switches
	• Mentors	• Changing Jobs	
• Corporate sponsored external seminars	• Peers	• Business Mistakes	• Start-ups
• Public Seminars	• Subordinates		• Fix-Its/Turn Arounds
		• Subordinate Performance Problems	
	• Family and Friends		• Leaps in Scope of Responsibility
	• Customers and Clients		• Early Leadership Responsibility

SOURCES: Baird and Kram, 1983
Carnevale and Gainer, (undated)
Clawson, 1980
Davies and Easterby-Smith, 1984
Hall and Louis, 1988
Kram, 1988
Kram and Isabella, 1985
Louis and Hall, 1987
Manz and Sims, 1981
Margerison and Kakabadse, 1984
McCall et al., 1988
Seibert, 1989

skills which may be acquired or refined through engagement in managerial learning. They include the three developable skills of a manager identified by Katz (1974): technical skills (specialized knowledge, analytical ability within a speciality, and facility in the use of the tools and techniques of a specialty); human skills (working as a group member and building cooperative effort within a team as its leader); and conceptual skills (seeing the enterprise as a whole and making decisions to act in ways that advance the overall welfare of the organization). To Katz's three skills are added a fourth, intrapersonal skill: awareness of one's own identity, strengths and limitations, and the ability to change those aspects of the self.

Management Learning Outcomes

The acquisition of technical, human and conceptual skills results in task learning. The outcomes of task learning, improved performance in the short term and enhanced adaptability in the long term, have already been discussed above. In a similar fashion, intrapersonal skill acquisition leads to personal learning, with the associated short-term outcome of attitude formation and the long-term outcome of identity development, which were also presented earlier. Successful management learning, thus, produces skills which lead to positive changes in all four career outcomes.

The Model's Operation and Implications

According to Figure 13-1, managers bring their unique inputs to their managerial position. The model illustrates that a manager develops technical, human, conceptual, and intrapersonal skills through a combination of training and education, assignments, people, and hardships. The outcomes of intrapersonal skill acquisition are attitude formation and identity development. And the outcomes of technical, human and conceptual skill acquisition are improved performance and enhanced adaptability. All the outcomes feed back and change the inputs the manager will bring to subsequent learning situations. Indeed, it is this change that represents growth and development.

The model provides a convenient framework for more in-depth examination of the phenomenon of management learning. For example, the cell in the lower left hand corner of the grid (Fig. 13-1) lists those training and educational activities which contribute to managers' acquisition of technical skills. What needs to be considered here is the *importance* of technical skills to a given managerial position and the *specific types* of training and education that contribute the most to technical skill development. These same two basic issues—the importance of a given skill to a particular managerial position and the specific types of training, assignments, people, or hardships that contribute the most to skill acquisition—are what are at issue in each of the other 16 cells comprising the grid.

Clearly, managers' learning is greatly affected by where they are located in the management hierarchy. It is important, therefore, not to lump all managers' learning together, but to consider how it differs across the levels of management. The same *process* of learning will occur at all levels of management, although the *content* of the learning will differ. The addition of a third dimension, *management level,* transforms the grid into a cube with 64 cells, as shown in Figure 13-2. The content of each cell is unique, representing the contribution of a specific source of management learning to the acquisition of a particular set of skills at a given level of management.

That there are 64 cells indicates the complexity of the management learning process, from the perspective of the organization trying to manage it.

This learning model raises more questions than it answers. This is because research on the contribution of on-the-job experiences to management learning, particularly across levels of management, is still in its infancy. Thus, the actual content of each of the 64 cells is yet to be determined. Moreover, traditional management development efforts have been aimed almost exclusively at the performance outcome. Little is known about how to affect changes in adaptability, attitudes, and identity. Yet in the future such changes will likely be an essential part of management learning. *Broadly viewed, the model points to the need for managers to become self-learners.* There are two primary reasons for this. First, the complexity of the management learning process makes it extremely difficult for organizations to give adequate attention to all managers' developmental needs. Consequently, managers must take responsibility for their own learning. Second, faced with dynamic organizations and environments, managers have no choice but to continue to learn and change. And no one is in a better position to manage this growth than managers themselves. Indeed, the ability to be a self-learner may well become one of the most important characteristics of the manager of the future.

Manz & Sims (1989), in their aptly-titled book, *SuperLeadership,* have suggested that attention be directed toward those behaviors and thoughts that people can use to influence themselves. They recognize that using these behaviors and thoughts, or engaging in superleadership as they call it, is something that must be learned. Behaviors that they believe foster self-leadership include self-set goals, management of cues, rehearsal, self-observation, self-reward, and self-punishment. Relevant thoughts include building natural rewards into tasks, focusing thinking on natural rewards, and establishing constructive thought patterns. Self-learning likewise must be learned. And the most effective way for that to occur is for managers and organizations to become partners in the development of self-learning skills. Such an approach is required if management learning is to be optimally managed.

Building Learning Into the Organization

The previous section focused on *individual* learning. The strategic management development perspective recognizes, however, that successful management learning entails more than understanding and managing individual learning; it requires attending to issues of *organizational learning.* This can be done at three levels.

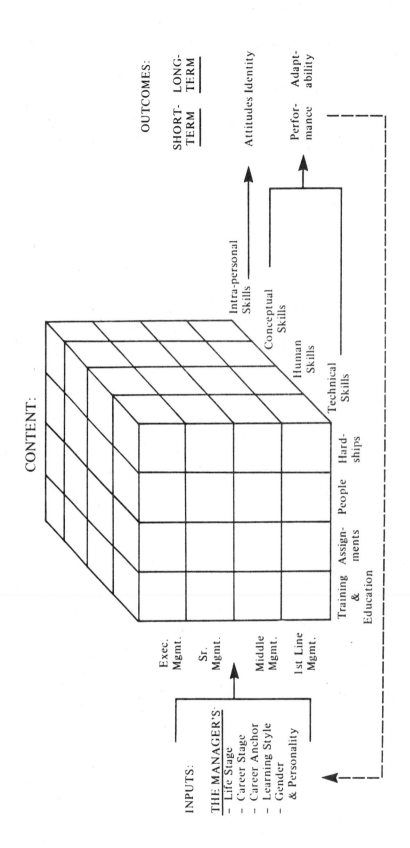

Figure 13-2. Three dimensional model of management learning and development.

At the Strategic Level

The key to corporate competitiveness is learning. The right question here is not, How can we make learning happen more quickly and responsively? If we try to *make* learning occur, we will never be able to fully anticipate all the various future needs for learning and devise delivery systems that will be quick enough. Rather, the right question is, How can we *make* learning a part of the basic fabric of the operation of the organization? *How can the organization, in the course of its everyday operational activities, be sufficiently in contact with the needs of its environment, especially customers, and be developing internal resources for change so that it is always learning and adapting?*

Another way to get at this is to distinguish between the two types of learning described earlier: task learning and personal learning. With task learning, the focus is on developing specific skills, knowledge, and abilities to enhance performance related to certain job activities. The emphasis, then, is on *development for mastery*. Although such development is necessary, it is far from sufficient.

What is proposed, instead, is an emphasis on personal learning, the enhancement of identity and adaptability so that one can learn how to learn. The goal is for the person to become more self-directed as a learner. The emphasis is on *development for adaptability*. That is, to develop skills for capitalizing on the uncertainty that is inherent in managing in the next century.

At the organizational level, such learning means a continuous improvement process. One method of creating development for uncertainty is found in the current technologies for quality and productivity improvement. Another approach is the "double loop learning" methodology of Argyris and his colleagues (e.g., Argyris, Putnam, and Smith, 1986). Here critical self-examination of the basic interpersonal decision making processes of top management becomes part of the culture of the organization.

With a focus on development for uncertainty, the culture thus comes to value deviant ideas and behavior, seeing them as stimulating and constructive, rather than threatening (Kiesler and Sproull, 1989). The attempt is to help key managers seek and learn from constant feedback not only on the outputs of the firm but also on the internal processes by which it operates. Such learning organizations do not need restructuring or redesigning, as they have become *self-designing systems* (Weick and Berlinger, 1989). Thus senior management self-examination and personal learning are the critical ingredients for the learning organization at the strategic level.

Pepsico: Linking Individual Learning to Business Planning

How can individual managerial learning be integrated with organizational strategy? Much of Pepsico's corporate success is related to the fact that the development of managers is built into the corporate culture (Dumaine,

1989). CEO Wayne Calloway attributes the company's marketing excellence to what he calls the three P's: "people, people, people." The stress is on rigorous evaluation of and feedback to managers, encouragement of risk, and big rewards for excellence.

More specifically, management development occurs through what Pepsico calls the "Human Resource Game Plan," which combines management development and business planning. The first step is "Development Feedback" for the individual manager. The manager and his or her boss assess that manager against 15 key skills and think about developmental options. Then they meet to discuss these assessments. Based on this discussion, the boss comes up with a one-page summary for that subordinate manager. This summary contains the "career call" (next steps), strengths, needs, performance, career summary, developmental progress, and the *key question* about the person's career outlook. This latter point seems unique to Pepsico, and is a useful way to communicate to higher management the central issue in that person's career that needs to be addressed.

The next step is the boss's analysis of his or her unit, based on all of the individual manager assessments. What are the unit's key business objectives for the year, and how does the unit's management staff measure up to the skills and experience needed for these tasks?

The aggregate of this information is presented to the executive at the next higher level in a session called the "Game Plan." This process was recently revised, using an organization development process, based on feedback from 60 managers. In the past the game plan was described as a "big show," a "command performance," with perhaps 25 or 30 people in the room. Now the game plan is held off site, attire is casual, and there are never more than five people in the room. Participants are usually the unit manager (designated as the "Discussion Leader"), his or her boss (called the "Senior Leader"), the head of Employee Relations, and a representative of the Management Development function. As the role designations imply, the manager whose unit's Game Plan is being discussed is in charge of the discussion, with the Senior Leader acting as a coach and consultant. The topics to be covered include:

- individual and organizational strengths
- development needs
- staffing
- key organizational/business issues, and
- cultural issues.

An important aspect of the Game Plan process is that assessment and *planning* (problem solving) are both accomplished at the same time. And both types of planning, organizational planning and management development planning, are carried out together. Thus the links between business strategy, management development strategy, and management learning activities are strengthened.

At the Managerial Level

Building learning into an organization also requires taking concrete steps at the managerial level. A recent study by the American Society for Training and Development and the U.S. Department of Labor provides several relevant recommendations (Carnevale and Gainer, undated):

1. The CEO must make training and development a priority.
2. The head of human resource development must be part of the top management team.
3. Individual line managers must be held accountable for developing their subordinates.
4. 4 percent of payroll, up from the current 1.4 percent, should be the goal for employer-based training expenditures.

In addition, Kiesler and Sproull (1989) discuss how information technologies can stimulate and broaden people's thinking. "Soft" information technologies can create contact with new people and new ideas (e.g., bulletin boards, distribution lists, and conferences using electronic mail). They discuss the example of the question, "Does anybody know . . . ?" used over electronic mail. Such a question can cover a wide distribution, yielding inputs from a much more diverse set of informants than the asker might have asked individually. It also provides new contacts, a wider network to the asker. Also, by simply having the question posed to everyone on the system, even people who do not respond have their thinking stimulated and their awareness broadened.

Furthermore, as Kiesler and Sproull (1989) point out, such a query can also generate *secondary learning*. If the answers, as well as the questions, are broadcast to the entire network, everyone on the system, not just the inquirer, can learn from the responses. Also, if the answers are stored as plain text archives, they will be accessible to future learners. And if the text contains the questions as well as the answers, the answers can provide refinement of the questions. Also, as Kiesler and Sproull (1989) point out, these information technologies can increase openness, as they reduce barriers to communication such as nonverbal behaviors, status differences, social desirability, and social context (see, Kiesler and Sproull, 1986, and Dubrovsky, Kiesler, and Sethna, 1989).

At the Operational Level

At the level of the individual manager, the key to the learning organization is managers who have acquired the "meta-skills" of learning: adaptability and identity learning. A previous section described how this personal learning can be facilitated through experiences at work. What is critical here is simply giving more *focus* to personal learning for managers and executives. More effective means of harnessing the learning potential of work experiences need to be found as well as the need to help individuals recognize, label, and value personal learning.

The current interest in promoting work/family balance will contribute to creating more personal learning and more qualities of the learning organization (Hall, 1990). The concept of "balance" means not only balance between two roles, work and family. It also means internal balance, balance between one's psychological involvement in work and his or her involvement in home roles (Kofodimos, 1990). This inner balance entails personal values and identity, and improving balance in a serious way requires deep examination of those values and that identity. Thus, if individuals and organizations work on the issue of work/family balance seriously and pursue it to its logical extreme, this will also promote the creation of learning organizations (Hall, 1990).

CONCLUSION

This chapter has focused on the purpose of career development. The purpose which the authors feel needs increased attention is preparing managerial talent to meet the future strategic needs of the organization. The task is at once very simple and very complex: how to link assessment, development planning, and development action to future success profiles to meet intermediate and long-term strategic objectives.

This chapter has presented the concept of strategic management development as a means of linking business strategy and individual learning to critical organizational outcomes. An attempt is made to bridge the traditional macro-micro split in the career literature. If the needed "learning organization" of the future is to in fact take shape, it will have to be built on the aggregate individual learnings of its members.

REFERENCES

Argyris, Chris, Putnam, Robert, and Smith, Diana (1986). *Action Science.* San Francisco: Jossey-Bass.

Baird, L. and Kram, K. (1983). "Career dynamics: Managing the superior/subordinate relationship." *Organizational Dynamics,* Spring, 46–64.

Burke, M.J. and Day, R.R. (1986). "A cumulative study of the effectiveness of managerial training." *Journal of Applied Psychology,* 71, 232–245.

Carnevale, Anthony P., and Gainer, Leila J. (Undated). *The Learning Enterprise.*

Washington, D.C.: The American Society for Training and Development and the U.S. Department of Labor.

Clawson, J.G. (1980). "Mentoring in managerial careers," in C.B. Derr (ed.). *Work, Family, and the Career.* New York: Praeger.

Davies, J. and Easterby-Smith, M. (1984). "Learning and developing from managerial work experiences." *Journal of Management Studies,* 21(2), 169–183.

Dubrovsky, Vitaly, Kiesler, Sara, and Sethna, Beheruz (1989). "Expected and unexpected effects of communication media on group decision making." *SIG Chi Bulletin,* 21.

Dumaine, Brian (1989). "Those highflying Pepsico managers." *Fortune,* April 10, 78–86.

Friedman, Stewart D. (1984) *Succession Systems and Organizational Performance in Large Corporations.* Unpublished doctoral dissertation, University of Michigan. (Revised version published as monograph, 1985): *Leadership Succession Systems and Corporate Performance.* New York: Carter for Career Research and Human Resource Management, Columbia University.

Friedman, Stewart D. (1986) "Succession systems in large corporations." *Human Resource Management.* 25, 191, 214.

Gist, M.E. (1987). "Self-efficacy: implications for organizational behavior and human resource management." *Academy of Management Review.* July, 472–485.

Gutteridge, Thomas G. (1985). "Organizational career development systems: The state of the practice." In Douglas T. Hall and Associates, *Career Development in Organizations.* San Francisco: Jossey-Bass, 50–94.

Hall, Douglas T. (1976). *Careers in Organizations.* Glenview, IL: Scott, Foresman.

Hall, Douglas T. and Associates (1985). *Career Development in Organizations.* San Francisco: Jossey-Bass.

Hall, Douglas T. (1986). "Dilemmas in linking succession planning to individual executive learning." *Human Resource Management.* 25, 235–265.

Hall, Douglas T. and Louis, Meryl R. (1988). "When careers plateau." *Research Technology Management.* 31(1), 41–45.

Hall, Douglas T. (1989). "How top management and the organization itself can block effective executive succession." *Human Resource Management.* 28, 5–24.

Hall, Douglas T. (1990). "Promoting work/family balance: An organization-change approach." *Organizational Dynamics,* Winter, 18, 5–18.

Hall, Douglas T., and Foulkes, Fred K. (1990). "Succession planning as a competitive advantage." In Lawrence W. Foster (Ed.), *Advances in Applied Business Strategy,* Greenwich, CT: JAI Press, In Press.

Hayes, R.H. (1985). "Strategic Planning—forward or reverse?" *Harvard Business Review,* 63, 111–119.

Howard, Ann, and Bray, Douglas W. (1988). *Managerial Lives in Transition: Advancing Age and Changing Times.* New York: Guilford Press.

Jacques, Elliot (1989). *Requisite Organization: The CEO's Guide to Creative Structure and Leadership.* Arlington, VA: Coson Hall.

Katz, R. (1974). "Skills of an effective administrator," *Harvard Business Review.* September-October, 90–102.

Katz, D. and Kahn, R. (1966). Response effects in the electronic survey. *Public Opinion Survey,* 50, 402–413.

Kiesler, Sara, and Sproull, Lee (1986). Response effects in the electronic survey. *Public Opinion Survey,* 50, 402–413.

Kiesler, Sara, and Sproull, Lee (1989). *Information Technology and Intraorganizational Learning.* Working Paper, Carnegie Mellon University.

Kofodimos, Joan (1990).

Kolb, D.A. (1984). *Experimental Learning: Experience as the Source of Learning and Development.* Englewood Cliffs, NJ: Prentice-Hall.

Kram, K.E. and Isabella, L. (1985). "Mentoring alternatives: The role of peer relationships in career development. *Academy of Management Journal,* 28, 110–132.

Kram, K.E. (1988). *Mentoring at Work.* Lanham, MD: University Press of America.

Levison, D.J. (1978). *The Seasons of a Man's Life.* New York: Alfred A. Knopf.

Louis, Meryl R. and Hall, Douglas T. (1987). "On taking project work seriously: Effects on workers' experiences and career effectiveness." Working Paper, School of Management, Boston University.

Manz, C.C. and Sims, H.P. (1981). "Vicarious learning: The influence of modeling on organizational behavior." *Academy of Management Review.* 6(1), 105–113.

Manz, C.C. and Sims, H.P. (1989). *SuperLeadership: Leading Others to Lead Themselves.* New York: Prentice-Hall.

Mahler, Walter, and Drotter, Stephen J. (1986). *The Succession Planning Handbook for the Chief Executive.* Midland Park, NJ: Mahler.

March, J. and Simon H. (1959). *Organizations.* New York: Wiley.

Margerison, C. and Kakabadse, A. (1984). *How American Chief Executives Succeed.* New York: American Management Association.

McCall, Morgan W., Lombardo, Michael M., and Morrison, Ann M. (1988). *The Lessons of Experience: How Successful Executives Develop on the Job.* Lexington, MA: Lexington Books.

Morgan, G. (1988). *Riding the Waves of Change: Developing Managerial Competencies for a Turbulent World.* San Francisco: Jossey-Bass.

Schein, E.H., (1985). *Organizational Culture and Leadership.* San Francisco: Jossey-Bass.

Schein, E.H., (1978). *Career Dynamics: Matching Individual and Organizational Needs.* Reading, MA: Addison-Wesley.

Seibert, Kent W. (1989). "Using experience to transform managers: A fresh look at management development." Working Paper, School of Management, Boston University.

Seibert, Kent W., Hall, Douglas T., and Kram, Kathy E. (1991). "Management learning and the bottom line." Working Paper, School of Management, Boston University.

Spector, P. (1982). "Behavior in organizations as a function of employee's locus of control." *Psychological Bulletin.* 91(3), 482–497.

Van Velsor, Ellen, and Martha W. Hughes (1990), "Gender differences in the development of managers: How women learn from experience." Greensboro, N.C.: Center for Creative Leadership, Technical Report Number 145.

Weick, Karl E., and Berlinger, Lisa R. (1989). "Career improvisation in self-designing organizations." In Arthur, Michael B., Hall, Douglas T., and Lawrence, Barbara S. (Eds.), *Handbook of Career Theory*. Cambridge, England: Cambridge University Press, 313–328.

Part D
The Disengagement Stage

Chapter 14

CAREER AND RETIREMENT COUNSELING FOR OLDER WORKERS

JANE E. MYERS

The graying of America is well-documented in recent professional literature and public media. Some reports of population changes imply drastic, negative consequences of current trends, which will materialize sometime during the 1990s or early in the 21st century. Other reports note the current state of affairs and project significant changes for the future which even could be positive. What these reports share in common is a recognition that America is in a state of transition with respect to its older population.

Concurrent with increases in the older population are changes in the proportion of older workers in the labor market. Statisticians and futurists are predicting even greater labor force participation among older people in the years ahead. Federal and state laws, rules, regulations, employment and corporate policies are changing in response to demographic fluctuations. Further, rapid changes in the nature of work, workers, and the job market (stimulated by new technologies) require new adaptations by persons wanting to enter or remain in the labor market for a prolonged period. At the same time, retirement incentive programs are proliferating, and workers are encouraged to leave their employment at earlier ages in order to enjoy the benefits of "the golden years." As a normal stage in the career development process, retirement decisions are complicated by phenomena which may or may not be under the control of the prospective retiree—some older persons remain in the labor market by choice, some leave by choice, and others remain or leave against their desires.

A major role for counselors has been to assist persons in planning for and achieving satisfying lives, both in employment and in leisure time and personal relationships. Although the work of counselors traditionally has focused on work with younger persons, social and demographic changes demand that the counseling profession help older workers (and employers) prepare for and respond to the emerging realities of the work world. This chapter reviews the challenges for counselors in planning for and working with an aging work force in a greying population.

The first section reviews demographic data which define the American population and workforce, as well as changes which have occurred and are projected to occur in the future. The meaning and value of work to older persons is discussed, including an overview of late-life vocational development theories. The meaning and impact of the retirement transition is explored. Implications for counselors are provided in terms of employment, retirement, and life-career counseling.

Demographic Changes and The World of Work

Trying to determine who is an older person can be confusing. Statistics on the older population differ markedly depending on which of a number of available definitions is used. Some commonly used definitions are provided in this section, followed by demographic information about older persons in general and older workers. Past, current, and future population statistics are presented.

Older Persons and Older Workers Defined

Who is an "older person?" That depends on who you ask. The U.S. Administration on Aging, the agency which administers the federal Older Americans Act (OAA), defines "older" as age 60 and above. The Social Security Administration refers to persons as "older" when they are 62, if they want "reduced retirement" benefits. Full retirement benefits may be received at the age of 65, or at any age should one become disabled. For purposes of receiving Supplemental Security Income (SSI), persons are "older" when they reach the age of 62, or at any age when they acquire a disability.

The American Association of Retired Persons (AARP) recently lowered its minimum age for membership from 55 to 50. Commercial airline pilots are required by federal law to retire at the age of 60. College professors now may work until 70, while U.S. Supreme Court justices, U.S. Presidents, and federal workers have no mandatory retirement age. The Rehabilitation Services Administration defines "working age" for adults as 16 to 64. Meanwhile, the Department of Labor offended many persons concerned about growing older by officially defining an "older worker" as one who has reached the age of 40.

Clearly, any review of demographic and statistical information cannot be made without careful attention to definitions. To assure consistency of interpretation, the statistics presented here on the older population follow the U.S. census category of age 65 and above, unless otherwise indicated.

Demographics of the Older Population

When America declared its independence in 1776, a mere 2 percent of the population or one in fifty persons (1:50) were aged 65+. That number had increased to only 4 percent (1:25) at the turn of this century. In 1980 older persons comprised more than 11 percent (1:9) of our population, and by 1985 more than 12 percent (1:8). Between 1980 and 1985 the over-65 population increased by 11 percent while that under 65 increased by only 4 percent. The trend is clear, reflected in a rise in the median age from 23 in 1900 to 30 in 1980 (American Association for Retired Persons (AARP), 1986).

People are living longer, to the average age of 75 compared to only 47 in 1900. Women may expect to live longer than men: 77 years compared to 73 years. Since older persons are survivors, statisticians remind us that the longer one lives the longer they may expect to live. A woman who is 65 today may expect to live an additional 19 years while a 65-year-old man can expect to live another 15 years (AARP, 1986). Differential life expectancies are reflected in an overall sex ratio among older people of 147 women for every 100 men. About 77 percent of older men are married while only 40 percent of older women are married. In contrast, 51 percent of older females are widowed, while only 14 percent of older men are widowed. Older men tend to remarry; the average American woman can expect to remain a widow for 25 years (Special Committee on Aging, 1983).

Life expectancy differs according to ethnic origin as well. In 1900, non-whites could expect to live to be almost 34, while by 1976 that figure had increased to 68. Recently the expected lifespan for black females surpassed that of white males, leaving black and other minority males with the shortest American lifespans. Not surprisingly, older minority males are least likely of any group to be in the labor market.

The median years of education completed by older persons rose from 8.7 to 11.7 between 1970 and 1985, a trend which is expected to continue. Education differs markedly according to ethnic origin, with Caucasians averaging 12 years of schooling, blacks only eight, and Hispanic individuals only seven years. Both minority status and lower levels of education correlate highly with disability rates. It is estimated that one-third of all functionally disabled persons are over the age of 65 (Rehab Group, 1979). Disability rates tend to increase significantly with age after age 40 for all individuals, and employment rates decrease correspondingly.

Older Americans in the Labor Force

Participation rates for older workers have changed significantly during this century. In 1900, two out of three older males were working. In 1980, only one in five were in the labor market, and one in 12 females over age 65.

(Labor force participation statistics include persons employed full or part time as well as those seeking employment.) Between 1960 and 1980 the female work force doubled, including an 85 percent increase for women aged 45 and older. Between 1950 and 1980, the percent of women aged 55–64 in the labor force increased from 27 percent to 42 percent, while participation among older men decreased from 88 percent to 64 percent.

Participation in the civilian labor force peaks between the ages of 25 and 35, and marked declines begin to occur after age 55. Whereas over 91 percent of men are in the labor force between the ages of 45–54, this drops to 70 percent for those aged 55–64, to 27 percent for those in the 65–69 age bracket, and to 17 percent for those aged 70–74. A total of 62 percent of women aged 45–64 are in the labor market, 41 percent of women between 55 and 64, 15 percent aged 65–69, and only 7.5 percent aged 70–74 (Yankelovich, Skelly & White, 1985).

A major reason for employment in old age is the need for additional income. Most persons experience a one-half to two-thirds drop in income after retirement, resulting in about one in five older persons being classified as poor or near poor (AARP, 1986a). Almost half of the income received by older persons comes from retirement benefits, including Social Security and public and private pensions, while almost a third comes from employment earnings (Cook & Stewart, 1985). Multiple risk factors, such as being an ethnic minority, having no work history or working only in low-paying jobs, or being disabled tend to increase the risk of poverty in old age.

Future Projections

Trends in labor force participation reveal an increasingly smaller proportion of older workers compared to the total work force in the future. The size of the older work force is shrinking relative to the total work force. In 1976, over 19 percent of the work force was comprised of older workers (e.g., over age 65) while in 1986 this number had dropped to just over 15 percent (National Alliance of Business, 1985). In 1985, it was estimated that 38 percent of workers were over age 40. This number is projected to increase to 50 percent by the year 2010, meaning that the greatest number of workers will be between the ages of 40 and 65.

As the median age of the population increases, there will be a corresponding increase in the proportion of older workers (40 and above) in the work force. But, at the same time, there will be a reduced proportion of workers among the older population itself (65 and over). The median age of workers is expected to rise from 32 to 42 by 2030 (AARP, 1987). This trend will be accompanied by fewer persons aged 18–24 available to enter the labor force (Mitchell, 1987).

Thus, statisticians project chronic job shortages in the future. It seems reasonable to expect that more older persons could and/or should be encouraged to remain in or reenter the labor force to meet the need for workers. At the same time, some authors suggest encouragement of early retirement as a possible solution to high unemployment (Mirkin, 1987). The situation is anything but simple. Counselors can assist in responding to needs of the labor force—and older individuals—if they understand the nature of work and retirement, and incentives for each.

Meaning and Value of Work to Older People: Theoretical and Empirical Perspectives

For persons of any age, work serves as a source of income, accomplishment, and identity (Tolbert, 1980). It also provides a sense of status, and is a source of social contacts and self-esteem (Okun, 1984). Work provides an inherent time management structure. For older persons, work also provides a means to stay active and independent. It is rewarding, promotes good health, and contributes to a sense of usefulness and purpose in life.

Changes in mandatory retirement ages combined with the results of inflation have increased the desire of many older persons to remain in or reenter the labor market (Kieffer, 1980). Results of a recent study indicate that half of todays' older workers would continue to work even if they had no financial need simply because they enjoy working. However, more than two-thirds of older persons would prefer part-time employment to full retirement after age 65 (National Alliance for Business, 1985). In addition to knowledge of the labor market and the availability of both full- and part-time job opportunities, counselors need to be aware of factors affecting career choices in the later years. Other than demographic factors, such as the need for income, what might cause an older person to choose to work? Theories of human development and career development may offer some guidelines.

Human Development in Later Life

Erikson (1963) suggested that the central psychosocial crisis of later life is the search for ego integrity. The process of life review is an essential means of achieving integrity, or the sense that the life one lived is the best one could have lived. A failure to achieve this sense of well-being leads to despair, since it is now too late to make the changes which might have resulted in a sense of satisfaction with one's life.

Havighurst (1972) defined a number of life tasks which must be met if older persons are to age successfully and happily. These include adjusting to retirement, adjusting to reduced income, and adjusting to declining

strength and health. These and other tasks imply the need to make significant life changes if the later years are to be lived with a sense of well-being.
Havighurst did not define a search for new employment or a new career as a
central task of later life.

Other theories of human development offer similar perspectives; the
later years of life are a time for changes in life style, for greater inner-
directness, for slowing down, and for evaluating the totality of one's life
span. Erikson wrote at a time when people did not live as long as they do
today, leaving him to define the period of later adulthood as that over age
50. Since people now live one-fourth to one-third or more of their lives as
older persons, some reexamination of Erikson's theories is timely. In fact,
the results of recent research suggest that the search for integrity is largely
completed during the sixth decade, leaving older persons with the time,
resources, and even energy to make significant life changes and to set new
goals (Riker & Myers, 1990).

The theories of Havighurst and others may be similarly questioned, with
similar outcomes. People today may live "in retirement" for roughly the
same number of years that they worked. They certainly have the opportunity to create life styles which may or may not involve a continuation of
prior work and leisure pursuits, and they have an opportunity to set and
achieve new goals. Such goals could include the chance to enter a new
career, expand a hobby to a full- or part-time employment endeavor, or
pursue a new career training opportunity. Riker and Myers (1990) recommend a series of developmental tasks for each of the decades of life beginning at age 60. With a positive perspective on roles, relationships, and the
possibility of continued growth throughout the later years of life, it seems
that physical health and attitudes may be the primary personal factors
which limit career choice in the later years.

Career Development in Later Life

Career development theories, unfortunately, offer little assistance to
counselors in understanding vocational choices and development specifically for older people. Most view retirement as "the 'end' of the career
development process" (Okun, 1984, p.361). Such theories could be extended
to include older persons, although any attempt to explain vocational development of older persons needs also to incorporate their basic physical
and psychological needs and changes, dynamics of normative life stages and
tasks, and analysis of common transitions. Tiedeman (in Tolbert, 1980)
suggests that the resolution of Eriksonian tasks leads to more suitable vocational choices for older people. Counselors can facilitate this resolution.

Super associates old age with a period of vocational decline which begins
around the age of 65 with a deceleration of work demands (Miller, 1984).

Super's (1980) Life Career Rainbow can be used to help explain basic needs for children, young, and middle-aged adults. The rainbow concept needs to be more fully explored in regards to older persons, whose life roles may or may not expand—or may not expand *voluntarily*—to fill the void left by work, thus resulting in depression rather than role adaptation. The concept of retirement, in general, can be integrated more fully with Super's rainbow to assist career counselors in working with older people.

Meaning and Value of Retirement

Retirement is a naturally occurring event in the occupational life cycle which many older persons eagerly anticipate and choose to pursue. A twentieth century phenomenon, retirement was touted for many years as a desirable time of life. Persons approaching retirement age were lured with promises of the "golden years." Employers initiated retirement incentive programs to encourage older workers to step aside and allow younger workers to enter and advance in occupations. Recent studies have shown many of the virtues of retirement to be a modern myth (Atchley, 1977; Hitchcock, 1984; Kieffer, 1986; Riker & Myers, 1990).

Retirement can be viewed as a high-impact life event. The loss of employment at retirement can be equally as devastating to the older individual as job loss at *any* time in life. Haynes and Nutman (1981) describe job loss as a psychosocial transition. Self-esteem is greatly impacted, the individual becomes immobilized, often depressed, and must go through a psychologically painful process of grieving and adjustment.

Even for persons who look forward to retirement, the cessation of work presents a "crisis in the meaningful use of time" (Havighurst, in Kleemeier, 1961). Whereas work provides a time management structure for most persons for most of their lives, the sudden availability of large amounts of time can be a dramatic shock, especially in the absence of advanced planning (McDaniels, 1982). The need for adjustment is made much more difficult when retirement is forced rather than chosen.

A 1974 study revealed that 41 percent of retired women and 32 percent of retired men were forced to retire (Harris & Associates, 1974). A follow-up study of retirees in 1979 showed that 46 percent of older retirees would prefer to be working, while 50 percent preferred not to return to paid employment. More than half of all older persons currently employed want to continue working, and more than 90 percent of all employees surveyed indicated that no one should be forced to retire if they are able and choose to continue to work (National Alliance for Business, 1985). This finding is best understood in the context of the meaning of retirement.

Atchley (1977) defined retirement as simultaneously a process, an event, and a role. As a process, it involves separation from a job role (or withdrawal), the end of a close relationship between one's life style and one's job, and the acquisition of a "retired" role. Unfortunately, that role is far more ambiguous, has far fewer positive role models, and far less social approval than the role of "worker." As an event, retirement is an informal rite of passage which signifies the end of employment and the beginning of a jobless life. Social status decreases.

As a role, retirement provides the right to an income without working and to autonomy of time management (whether one is prepared or not after 30–60 years of work-regulated time schedules, and whether one is accustomed to decision making or not with respect to one's time). There is an expectation that the retired individual will maintain preretirement modes of interacting with significant others, in spite of greater free time, will automatically increase his or her decision making capabilities for use of available time, and will manage a retirement income without difficulty or complaint.

All this occurs simultaneously with a loss of identity and consequent loss of a sense of power over one's life and decisions. The ability to determine one's personal direction suffers considerably, especially if retirement is forced, or if chosen, the choice was made because of health reasons. A study of retired men made in 1963 showed that more than half (53%) retired for health reasons (Atchley, 1977). Additional factors have been examined which correlate with adjustment to retirement.

The major factor affecting retirement adjustment seems to be attitude, with positive attitudes helping to assure positive adjustment. Most studies reveal the strongest correlate of adjustment to be higher income, with advanced planning a distant second place. Opportunities for counseling, education, discussions, and exposure to news media correlate with more successful retirement transitions. These opportunities share in common ways of broadening the number and types of out-of-work priorities, leading to expansion of nonwork roles. Positive adjustments correlate with being male, having adequate income, working in a semiskilled job, having good health, and having higher education (AARP, 1988). Additional correlates of retirement adjustment include the ability to adapt to change, positive expectations, self-satisfaction, and positive family attitudes (AARP, 1986b).

Negative adjustments to retirement are found in greater proportions among females, mid- and upper-level employees, and persons with strong work commitments. About one-half of retirees have a poor adjustment, and 40 percent of their problems are related to income. Additional negative correlates include poor health, recent widowhood, and retirement earlier than expected. Forced retirement has been found to have a negative effect on health, longevity, and life satisfaction (Lowry, 1985).

Attitudes toward retirement are further explained by studies of older persons who are working. More than two-thirds of men and women report that they work because of the needed income it provides as well as because they enjoy it. Major positives on the job include fellow employees, the organization, the type of work, and the challenge work provides (AARP, 1988). While more than a third of retirees would like to work, almost 80 percent find that employer discrimination limits their ability to find jobs (National Alliance for Business, 1985). Hence the question arises, for older persons as well as counselors, . . . :

Employment or Retirement? What Choice for Older Persons?

Rosen and Jerdee (1985) presented a model of the individual retirement decision process which incorporates government policies, individual, family, and community circumstances, and organizational policies. The outcome is a decision for early retirement, retirement at age 65 (or some other age-based employer policy), or postponed retirement. Each of the three areas to be considered mitigates for or against the decision. An important factor which affects all three inputs into the decision is employer bias against older workers. Even those who choose to continue working may be unable to do so.

The importance of this model lies in its ability to facilitate the decision making process. What must be stressed is that the retirement decision, regardless of outcome, is more easily accepted and results in more positive adjustments with prior planning (Hunter, 1973; Riker & Myers, 1990). The act of making the decision, rather than accepting retirement as a natural consequence of age or circumstances, allows retirees to maintain an internal locus of control and sense of power in their lives (Abel & Hayslip, 1987). Adjustment is optimum when retirement is the culmination of careful planning over a period of years (McDaniels, 1982).

Partial rather than full retirement from work is increasingly becoming an option for older persons. More than two-thirds of adults aged 55–64 favor such options, which include job sharing, work at home, part-time work, and flexible work hours (AARP, 1987; National Alliance of Business, 1985). Corporate attitudes toward older workers are changing in positive directions (Yankelovich, Skelly & White, 1985). Alternative work arrangements and flexible schedules are seen as appropriate responses to the changing nature of the work force (Barocas & Morrison, 1985). Strategies such as retraining or job modification are increasingly being implemented to encourage older workers to remain in the labor market (Czaja, 1986; Sheppard, 1986). At the same time, retirement planning programs increasingly are viewed as part of comprehensive employee benefit packages (Fever, 1985). As the range of options expands, older persons may increasingly benefit from assistance in sorting out their choices. Such assistance is well within the purview of the counseling profession.

Counselor's Roles and Responses

There are numerous benefits to older persons of continuing to work, as well as many benefits for those who choose to retire. With so many older persons wanting or needing to work, and so many others wanting or needing to retire, and the possibility for negative or positive adjustments in either case, potential roles for counselors are urgently needed and at the same time not clearly defined. Hitchcock (1984) emphasized the need for counselors to be aware of and responsive to the needs of older workers. Myers (1980) and Cahill and Salomone (1987) explored strategies counselors can use to overcome barriers and help older persons seeking employment. Riker and Myers (1990) emphasized needs of older persons and strategies for facilitating successful adjustment to retirement.

Tremendous flexibility is required in responding to the employment-retirement needs of older individuals (Blyton, 1984). Perhaps counselors need to look beyond the immediate situation and develop a broad philosophical approach to working with older adults. The "busy ethic" proposed by Ekerdt (1986) is one example. Ekerdt suggested that retirement is ligitimized on a day-to-day basis in part by an ethic which values active lifestyles, whether the activity be work or leisure. Another example is provided by Burr (1986), who suggests that older adults should be helped to discover new, more satisfying life styles after the age of 50. Perhaps, as Bolles (1978) so aptly suggests, we need to get out of the three boxes of our lives and integrate education, work, and leisure across the life span.

Kieffer (1986) suggested that we cannot afford to promote early retirement, while Mirkin (1987) considered early retirement a possible solution to problems of unemployment. In a complex world, solutions are not simple and unidimensional. Counselors still are best guided by the needs of the individual client. Whether it is called life-career (Miller-Tiedeman, 1986), work-life planning (Bolles, 1978), or preparation for retirement (Hunter, 1973), or employment counseling, the fact remains that counselors who take an holistic approach to work with older people, considering their needs as well as social and personal resources, ultimately will be most helpful to persons in their later adult years.

REFERENCES

Abel, B.J. & Hayslip, B. (1987). Locus of control and retirement preparation. *Journal of Gerontology, 42*(2), 165–167.

American Association of Retired Persons. (1986a). *A profile of older Americans.* Washington, DC: Author.

American Association of Retired Persons. (1986b). *Work and retirement: Employees over 40 and their views.* Washington, DC: Author.

American Association of Retired Persons (1987, September/October). *Working Age.* 3(2).

American Association of Retired Persons. (1988, January/February). *Working Age,* 3(4), p.2.

Atchley, R.C. (1977). *The social forces in later life* (second edition). Belmont, CA: Wadsworth.

Barocas, V. & Morrison, M. (1985). Employee, retiree options for an aging work force. *Business and Health,* 2(5), 25–29.

Blyton, P. (1984). Older workers, retirement, and the need for flexibility. *Employee Relations,* 6(2), i–iii.

Bolles, R. (1978). *The three boxes of life.* Berkeley, CA: Ten Speed Press.

Burr, E.W. (1986). What next after 50? *Journal of Counseling and Development,* 13(2), 23–29.

Cahill, M. & Salamone, P.R. (1987). Career counseling for work life extension: Integrating the older worker into the labor force. *The Career Development Quarterly,* 35(3), 188–196.

Cook, P. & Stewart, E. (1985). *Meeting guidance needs of older adults.* Columbus, OH: The National Center for Research in Vocational Education.

Czaja, S.J. (1986). Retraining middle aged and older workers. Invitational conference on work, aging, and visual impairment. Washington, DC, February 22–25, 1986.

Ekerdt, D.J. (1986). The busy ethic: Moral continuity between work and retirement. *The Gerontologist,* 26(3), 293–94.

Erikson, E. (1963). *Childhood and society.* NY: Norton.

Fever, D. (1985). Retirement planning: A coming imperative. *Training,* 22(2), 49–53.

Harris, L. & Associates. (1974). *The myth and reality of aging in America.* Washington, DC: National Council on the Aging.

Havighurst, R.J. (1972). *Developmental tasks and education.* NY: McKay.

Hayes, J. & Nutman, P. (1981). *Understanding the unemployed.* New York, NY: Tavistock.

Hitchcock, A.A. (1984). Work, aging, and counseling: Current trends. *Journal of Counseling and Development,* 63(4), 258–259.

Hunter, W.W. (1973). *Preparation for retirement.* Ann Arbor, MI: University of Michigan-Wayne State University.

Kieffer, J.A. (1980). Counselors and the older worker: An overview. *Journal of Employment Counseling,* 17(1), 8–16.

Kieffer, J.A. (1986). Kicking the premature retirement habit. *Journal of Career Development,* 13(2), 39–51.

Kleemeier, R.W. (Ed.). (1961). *Aging and leisure: A research perspective into the meaningful use of time.* New York, NY: Oxford University Press.

Lowry, J.H. (1985). Predictors of successful aging in retirement. In E.B. Palmore (Ed.), *Normal aging III* (pp.394–404). Durham, NC: Duke University Press.

McDaniels, C. (1982). *Leisure: Integrating a neglected component in life planning.* Columbus, OH: The National Center for Research in Vocational Education.

Miller, J.V. (1984). *The family-career connection: A new framework for career development.* Columbus, OH: The National Center for Research in Vocational Education.

Miller-Tiedeman, A. (1986). *How to NOT make it- and succeed: The truth about your LIFECAREER.* Los Angeles, CA: Lifecareer Foundation.

Mirkin, B.A. (1987). Early retirement as a labor force policy: An international overview. *Monthly Labor Review, 110*(3), 19–33.

Mitchell, K. (1987). The aging work force and the politics of incapacity. *The aging workforce: Implications for rehabilitation.* Alexandria, VA: National Rehabilitation Association.

Myers, J.E. (1980). Counseling the disabled older person for the world of work. *Journal of Employment Counseling, 17*(1), 37–48.

National Alliance of Business. (1985). *New directions for an aging workforce: An analysis of issues and options for business.* Washington, DC: Author.

Okun, B.F. (1984). *Working with adults: Individual, family, and career development.* Monterey, CA: Brooks/Cole.

Rehab Group. (1979). *Digest of data on persons with disabilities.* Alexandria, VA: Author.

Riker, H.C. & Myers, J.E. (1990). *Retirement counseling: A handbook for action.* New York, NY: Hemisphere.

Rosen, B. & Jerdee, T.H. (1985). *Older employees: New roles for valued resources.* Homewood, IL: Dow-Jones-Irwin.

Sheppard, H.L. (1986). Work and Aging. Invitational Conference on Work, Aging, and Vision. Washington, DC, February 22–25.

Special Committee on Aging, U.S. Senate. (1983). *Developments in aging, 1983.* Washington, DC: U.S. Government Printing Office.

Super, D.E. (1980). A life-span, life-space approach to career development. *Journal of Vocational Behavior, 16,* 282–298.

Tolbert, E.L. (1980). *Counseling for career development* (second edition). Boston: Houghton Mifflin.

Yankelovich, Skelly & White, Inc. (1985). *Workers over 50: Old myths, new realities.* Washington, DC: American Association of Retired Persons.

SECTION III
RESOURCES AND INTERVENTIONS

INTRODUCTION TO SECTION III—
RESOURCES AND INTERVENTION STRATEGIES

DAVID H. MONTROSS

In the previous section, we looked at a range of issues and programs associated with particular career stages. In this section, the focus shifts to those resources and methods of intervention which are either relevant to a particular population, or which cut across the full spectrum of those having career concerns.

In Chapter 15, Sywak describes emerging areas for career development professionals—outplacement and career consulting. As we have seen throughout this book, there is increasing turmoil in the workplace, and one direct result of that is the need for a new type of career assistance for employees whose careers are disrupted by organizational "right-sizings" and other unanticipated events. Similarly, organizations are seeking expert guidance on how best to manage the careers of their employees, resulting in additional opportunities for the experienced career professional.

Souerwine provides a new view of the role of the manager in the career development process. He suggests that there are limits regarding the role of the manager in providing career counseling for employees, and he offers a model which will enable practitioners to design appropriate counseling strategies for persons with a range of career concerns. Liebowitz, Feldman and Mosley break new ground with a description of the types of resources which should prove helpful to employee populations that heretofore have received minimal or no career assistance—the blue collar and support staffs in organizations.

Savickas offers an analysis of the types of assessment approaches available to the career practitioner, including the latest advances in approaches to assessment which focus more on the subjective aspects of career decision-making. Harris-Bowlsbey follows with an update on the way computer systems have evolved to support career decision making and development from the middle school through retirement planning. Based on Super's career stage model, she describes how the computer is now able to help individuals deal with the developmental issues faced in the successive stages.

Chapter 15

THE CAREER DEVELOPMENT PROFESSIONAL*

MARJORIE SYWAK

The continuous change that characterizes contemporary work environ- ments is disrupting careers more than ever, sending increasing numbers of adults and the organizations they work for in search of professional assistance to handle these career transitions effectively. Responding to this need, there has been a significant increase in the number of professionals working in the career development fields in the last decade. Little has been written about their growth, however, because as a group, they are still relatively small, new, and loosely defined and organized. While some career work with adults occurs in government, nonprofit and educational settings, this chapter focuses on career trends in the most common market-driven work options — outplacement, organizational consulting, and private practice career coun- seling. The focus is on the current state and emerging trends in these three segments of the field, highlighting similarities and differences. Particular attention is given to the types of clients served, the focus of the services offered, and the educational and professional background of practioners.

A 1990 Gallup poll, "National Survey of Working America," commissioned by the National Career Development Association, indicated that many Americans needed assistance with their careers (National Career Develop- ment Association, 1990). About 44 percent of employed adults were either unsure of their job's future or definitely expected to leave their current employer by choice or forced termination within a year. Another 65% said they would definitely get more information about job options if they could plan their work lives again. The survey also showed that only 4 out of every 10 people had planned their careers. That would seem to be good news for people working in career development.

The bad news, however, is that most people continue to find career help randomly and informally. Forty-two percent went to friends or relatives; 10 percent did not know where to go for help; and 9 percent did not seek any assistance. As these statistics indicate, seeking professional help with one's career is something most people do not consider. While the survey docu- ments a definite need for quality career services for adults, it also points out

*The author would like to gratefully acknowledge the significant research and writing assistance of Ms. Linda Artel, M.A., in the private practice section of this chapter and her keen insights on the general topic.

that the delivery system for these services is only now emerging and brings with it many questions and concerns.

People working in the Career Development field can have many different titles—outplacement consultant, career counselor and strategic human resource planning and development consultant to name a few. Whatever the title, career development practitioners share a common focus of function: facilitating the optimal match between an individual and the work he or she does. This assistance may be offered outside an organization, assisting individuals in determining the kind of work for which they are best suited and strategizing how to find a job doing that work. Or, it can be done internally, assisting organizations in finding the best match between their employees' skills and the work the organization needs to get done.

Another way to look at the field is from the perspective of the purchaser of career development work. A company will sometimes pay for career work for its employees, either because they will no longer have a job there or because something about their job or the organization is changing. Individuals also pay for career work when they want to initiate change in their work and they seek professional help to make that change. This chapter begins with a look at a growing field of career development work initiated and paid for by the organization—outplacement.

Outplacement

From its birth in 1960 when Humble Oil sought assistance for terminated executives, outplacement has grown in 30 years to a $400 million business with 203 licensed firms listed in the current *Directory of Outplacement Firms(1990).* (Kennedy Publications, 1990). Outplacement is a service offered by organizations to terminated employees to provide them with assistance in finding new jobs. The most comprehensive programs consist of counseling on how to deal with emotional issues related to termination, career assessment testing, developing marketing campaigns and written job search materials such as letters and resumes, training in the skills needed to conduct an effective job search, motivational support, clerical assistance and office space from the time of termination until the client is placed in a new job. The fee for this full service ranges from 10 - 15 percent of the client's annual salary. Outplacement firms also offer consulting services on legal, benefit and organizational issues to organizations contemplating a force reduction.

Once considered a perk for senior management, the service is now more commonly offered to mid-management and technical professionals as well. In addition, reflecting the growth of women in management ranks in the past decade, there are also more women as clients of outplacement firms. Precise and concrete documentation of these demographic changes in the client base is not available. As one would suspect in such a new and enterpreneurial industry, there is no general data base describing the specific population served by outplacement firms and how this has changed and grown over the last decade.

A study by the Daniel Yankelovich Group, commissioned by the Association of Outplacement Consulting Firms (AOCF), on the needs and differences of female clients, however, does present an interesting portrait of both male and female clients being served in outplacement today. A survey of 297 men and 140 women using the services found that female candidates tend to be younger (77% of men were over 40 while only 53% of women had reached that age), newer to the work force (62% of men and 34% of women had been working for at least 20 years), and working at lower levels in an organization (38% of men and 67% of women were earning under $60,000) (Daniel Yankelovick Group, 1989).

Client interest in possible career change also showed a sex difference. Women candidates reported being more open to new jobs while men sought to duplicate the jobs they had held previously. Perhaps the most disturbing finding is that men were more skeptical of the reasons for being fired while women were more likely to call the firing justified, indicating a possible need for additional counseling assistance for some women candidates who may be undervaluing themselves. One final note from the study: there was no significant difference between men and women in success in finding new work. Both took an average of 5 months to locate their next position.

In addition to serving a broader range of corporate clients, outplacement firms are seeing clients with different needs. Due to the increasing number of mergers, acquisitions, and layoffs in the last decade, the shock of job loss is not the unexpected and uniquely disruptive event that it used to be. While a major focus of earlier work was helping clients deal with the trauma of termination, today's clients are less likely to be as intensely shaken by losing their jobs.

Instead, clients spend less energy on navigating through emotions and, in recessionary times, are increasingly concerned with getting a job. The fact that a majority of outplacement clients opt to stay in their same field translates to a concern about meaningful assistance in finding a job comparable to or better than the one they had formerly. Specifically, what they want from their outplacement consultant is very sophisticated knowledge of the job market and assistance in marketing themselves in a highly complex and competitive marketplace. Corporate buyers of the service are also more savvy and are concerned with the bottom line question — can you get our people new jobs?

In addition, outplacement as an industry is becoming increasingly competitive. Large national firms have been taking over smaller local and regional firms. Many remaining small local firms are forming into federated groups. Furthermore, outplacement firms have always had a difficult challenge differentiating themselves in terms of their services and approaches and, in some cases, have relied instead on the decor of their offices. While insiders complain of price cutting and the unbundling of services, corporate buyers have learned that most fees are negotiable. Some companies have also instituted the practice of candidate shopping, allowing terminated employees to choose their own outplacement firm or take the outplacement fee in lieu of services.

Reflecting both the increasing competition of the industry and the changing needs of clients, the outplacement practitioner of the future will more likely come from a marketing and business background rather than the more traditional source of industry professionals—counseling and human resources. While every firm will still have a certain number of Ph.D. psychologists on staff or on contract to handle the testing and assessment part of the process and to work with clients having difficulty coping with the termination, the trend is to hire full-time consultants with a business development background.

In a paper titled *The Excellent Practitioner: A Study of Characteristics of Outplacement Consultants (1989),* James Gallagher commented:

> There's not much room in the Outplacement field these days for the traditional practitioner. That's the old "counselor" type, the person who joined the field because it provided the opportunity to do good things for other people. That's the person who was more versed in psychology than in business, who found rewards in clients interactions and considered selling the service a great problem associated with the job . . .
>
> . . . the reality is that the consultants evaluated by their supervisors as most effective at their work these days are more business and less social-service directed, . . . left-brained, numerically, mechanically and technically oriented . . . and more like their senior executive clients in temperament, interest patterns and vocational suitability.
>
> In fact, the Outplacement consultant of the future is more likely to be a former bank president than the teacher, consultant or corporate human resource officer who currently make up the bulk of practitioners.

More recently, Gallagher summarized his conclusion stating that the ideal outplacement consultant of the future would be "A Harvard M.B.A. with 10 to 12 years of business management experience—and a heart left."

In summary, the field is moving from its origins in a counseling model into a more business-oriented marketing model. A recent profile of outplacement professionals gave testimony to where the field has been (Gallagher, 1988). In a survey of 279 outplacement professionals including 202 males and 77 females, results showed that the typical practitioner was a 48.5-year-old male with 2 degrees—one in business and one in psychology and an accumulation of 22 years' experience in at least 3 careers. The most common background was human resources followed closely by consulting. The typical practitioner had worked in outplacement for 7 years.

Outplacement has traditionally been a male-dominated career. The 1988 survey reported that 74 percent of practitioners are men. In addition, men in the field tend to have more business experience and tend to have worked longer in outplacement. While men and women are equally well educated, men's degrees tend to be more in business while women's are more likely to be in the social sciences. An important finding is that men in the field significantly out earn women—the salaries of men average $83,000 while women's average $48,000. There are no existing data on the ethnic composition of professionals, though observation would indicate that there is a preponderance of Caucasians in the field.

Another major variable in compensation differences is between owners and employees. Compensation of owners averaged $114,930 in 1989 while that of nonowners averaged $58,479. Since most owners are male and the survey included 74 owners or partners, this may also impact the male-female earning difference.

This same report indicates that practitioners spend about two-thirds of their time doing one-to-one counseling with clients and that they find this both the most rewarding and the most difficult part of their work. They carry an average case load of 15 clients at any given time and start an average of 4 new cases per month. The rest of their time is spent marketing, the least attractive part of the job for more counseling-oriented professionals. Given the trend toward hiring consultants with a marketing background and orientation, however, this aversion to selling the service will no doubt change.

Another important professional issue is the minimal training practitioners receive—the greatest amount of preparation reported was 41.8 hours. This issue is especially acute in one of the fastest growing parts of the industry, group outplacement services. Group services are often provided by part time contract employees, hired by firms to deliver seminars as part of a large group contract. On occasion this has led to criticism of the industry for using unqualified part timers and giving them little training before allowing them to work with candidates. The survey also shows that full-time practitioners receive little direct supervision. They report that most of their feedback comes from their clients or client companies.

Like the shoemaker's attitude towards his barefoot children, the outplacement industry appears to have given little attention to the career development needs of its own members and to ensure standards of quality and professionalism in the field. At this point, professionals in the field looking for development go to a variety of related professional organizations and individual seminars. The practioners survey reported that 4 out of 5 members belonged to the Society for Human Resource Managers (SHRM) and 70 percent are members of the American Society of Training and Development (ASTD).

Pressure has been building from both inside and outside the industry to develop standards of professionalism. The Association of Outplacement Consulting Firms, the industry association, has focused its attention on the quality control issue by requiring licensing standards for member firms. These include at least 2 full-time professionals on staff and no executive search or retail career counseling business.

Distancing outplacement services from retail firms is a continuing issue in the industry. Retail firms, which often call themselves outplacement companies, differ from association licensed firms by taking clients who pay their own fees. The services they promise are basically the same as those offered by company paid firms. Retail firms charge a flat fee for their services, usually several thousands of dollars, and they are difficult to describe as a group because they have no association which speaks for them. There have been several national chains that have run into legal problems with lawsuits by consumers claiming the firms promised more than was delivered.

Until very recently, there has been no professional association for the individual outplacement professional. At the second annual conference of the AOCF in 1989, a professional association for outplacement practitioners was born—the International Association of Outplacement Professionals (IAOP). The purpose of this group is the on-going continuing education, training, and development of professionals in the outplacement field. This association will serve both new people entering the field and experienced practitioners who need to update their skills. In addition, AOCF has set a goal of developing a credentialling process for all professionals in the field by 1994. This will involve sponsoring research, identifying a body of knowledge one needs to know in order to be an effective outplacement professional, and developing standards of quality.

As industry competition increases, as the volatile job market makes prospective clients more vulnerable to quick fix promises, and as marketing and sales become a stronger focus of all firms, the potential for abuse by unscrupulous practitioners is obvious. This potential is especially present when compensation is linked to sales, as it is in some firms. These trends and practices makes the self-regulation discussed above an important objective of the profession.

There are two other important questions these trends in outplacement raise for the career development profession. The first has to do with adapting marketing lingo and frameworks to discuss career development. While marketing savvy and an in-depth awareness of changes in the economy are a critical part of the business, some practitioners are taking it one step further and talking about a client's visibility as a problem of them needing more "shelf space" or of their firms problems in "moving inventory."

Secondly, it is also important to question how well the business-oriented practitioner of the future will handle clients for whom job loss represents serious life crisis. Will this practitioner have the skill or the interest to counsel clients through a major career redirection or mid-life reevaluation? Will they know how to differentiate job loss blues or career indecision from subtle signals that additional help is needed? Outplacement is clearly not therapy, but if it is not the place to work with people on major career identity shifts, where is that work going to done? In a world where careers and jobs are changing very rapidly and where career continues to be a core part of an individual's identity, these are important questions for the outplacement profession.

Organizational Career Development Consulting

A further development in the outplacement industry provides a bridge to the next topic—career development consulting. Industry observers note that many outplacement firms are becoming more like general human resource consulting firms offering services in the areas of career, management and employee development, selection and interview training, and strategic human resource planning and development. Some say this is due to the increased competition in the industry and the need to diversify to survive—a way to stay in business in both expanding and contracting economies.

Others see the diversification as a logical extension of the work. As Jim Gallagher states, "It is like the resident doctor in an emergency ward who sooner or later begins to champion gun control. You can't stay in this business too long before you want to get involved in prevention. You want to move up-stream in an organization and work on the issue of matching people and jobs and developing people in their careers. Over the years we have been giving away lots of consulting in trying to get at the reasons why terminations happen. Some firms have decided to build on that side of their business."

While some of this work is happening through outplacement firms, there are other career development professionals who are working both internally and as external consultants in assisting organizations with the career issues of their employees.

There are three kinds of career work being done in organizations—individual counseling, training, and human resource systems development. Individual work, sometimes called inplacement, is based on the one-to-one career counseling model and involves working with key individuals to deal with current career issues. In some organizations, outside consultants are being brought in to do this work because of the greater assurance of confidentiality and lack of time available from the existing human resource staff. The desired outcome is to assist the employee to move to a more satisfying internal position or to the realization that the individual can best advance his or her career in another organization.

Training often takes the form of a career planning workshop for a particular group. This might be people impacted by a reorganization who need to find new positions, a high potential group, or a group of individuals who have voluntarily chosen the seminar because of various career issues they are facing. Training is also offered to managers to develop their skills as career coaches for their direct reports. With the increasing challenge of retaining top performers in an era of lean, flat organizations, the career conversation with the manager has become an important management tool. Many organizations are realizing that managers needs special skills to work with their people to help them see opportunity for growth at the organization, especially when this growth means developing in place.

The third area of consulting involves incorporating the first two into the design and implementation of broad human resource systems—the direction in which the field appears to be moving. The trend in organizational career development is away from one-shot, stand alone counseling and training interventions towards the development of an integrated career management system. Professional consultants in this area, both internal and external to organizations, are being asked to tie individual career development concerns with strategic human resource planning and development by integrating human resource planning, performance appraisal, succession planning, and management and executive development systems. And, as in human resources in general, the thrust is to tie this work into the organization's overall business strategy by developing and retaining the talent the organization needs to master the challenges of the next decade.

Professionals working successfully as consultants in this field tend to come from a background in business and human resource systems with a solid knowledge of performance appraisal, succession planning, human resource planning, and management and executive development. Those interested in systems work most often belong to the Human Resource Planning Society while practitioners more involved in training belong to the American Society for Training and Development.

ASTD has a Career Development Professional Practice Area with 2,500 members, a number that has remained stable over the last 5 years. The current director, Lynn Slavenski of Equifax in Atlanta, Georgia, says she feels that it is the most misunderstood of the Professional Practice Areas. "Most people think practitioners in this area are only doing career counseling. But we bring in a perspective of the total human resource development system" (1991).

Given the need to bring this broad background to organizational career consulting, it becomes clear why there are only a small number of people doing it successfully. For those who are, it is dynamic, interesting, and well paid work.

Individual Career Counseling

Most individuals who receive assistance with career concerns from company-sponsored programs, such as outplacement or in-house career seminars, do not seek out the service. In contrast, people who personally look for career counselors are usually experiencing some distress in their lives related to their jobs or careers. They are looking for advice and counsel, and they are paying for it themselves.

Most people working as career counselors are self-employed individuals who derive their income from seeing clients in one-to-one sessions. Since many career counselors in private practice work independently, and since no accreditation or licensing is required, there are few indicators of how many career counselors are currently practicing. The small number who have gone through the national licensing process adds further proof to the fact that, at this point, anyone can call him or herself a career counselor and open up a business. The interesting paradox of this work, however, is that while there appears to be a large need for this kind of service, few people are able to make their living as full-time career counselors.

According to the National Board of Certified Counselors, only 938 individuals have fulfilled the requirements to be a National Certified Career Counselor, and many of them are working in California (14%), New York (10%) and Texas (9%). Records are not kept on how many of these licensed professional are working as private practitioners. However, Al Hafer, chair of the 270 member National Career Development Association's Private Practice Special Interest Group, noted that it is safe to assume that many who have gone through the certification process have done so to enhance their credibility as private practitioners (1991).

Almost all private career counselors come to the field from another profession. Since no one professional degree qualifies people to work in the field, private practitioners have training in a variety of disciplines. Frequently they hold a Masters degree in counseling. Only two institutions, John F. Kennedy University in Orinda, California, and the College of New Rochelle in New Rochelle, New York, offer a Masters degree in Career Development.

Private practitioners typically see clients for 4–10 one-hour sessions. Services offered include self-assessment testing, guided career exploration and career decision making. Some counselors also help clients develop and implement marketing and job search strategy. Several observers of the field have noted that it is really two different professions needing two different sets of skills: one focuses on assessment and requires strong counseling skills and an in-depth knowledge of assessment tools. The second requires job market knowledge and the skills of the marketing strategist. In general, career counselors have been criticized, especially by outplacement, for being strong on the former and weak on the latter. Career counselors, in turn, have criticized outplacement professionals for lacking the skills or concern to deal with more in-depth career assessment issues.

In looking at the different emphasis in these two aspects of the profession, it is important to remember that there is usually a major difference in how one begins using each of these services. Individuals usually do not choose to be terminated. For most outplacement clients, the desired outcome is another job in the same career. In contrast, people usually choose to go to career counseling out of a need to change something about their career or job. They therefore need assistance in figuring out what else they can do.

Even though clients begin in a different place, career services should be offered as a continuum, going from assessment to focusing to job search strategy. All practitioners should appreciate the importance of the full spectrum of services, know where their strengths are and when to refer clients to other professionals for additional help. Clients are not ethically served when they are encouraged to continue in a profession for which they are not suited just to ensure a rapid placement. The same can be said when clients are encouraged to identify a career that would be a perfect match for their interests, skills, and values without being given assistance in translating that goal into reality.

Starting and maintaining a career counseling practice is a difficult business proposition. While a generalized need for the service may exist, there is little understanding of what career counselors can do for clients. Some clients expect a quick fix—three sessions and an answer, a new career direction that will be fun and profitable. For clients new to career counseling, some up-front time needs to be spent clarifying expectations. Another problem is translating the need for the service into a stream of actual, paying clients. This is especially true since the service offered is short term, and it rarely generates repeat business. And, most significantly, there are few sources of third party payment.

At this point, third party payment options are limited to spousal relocation programs paid for by a corporation and spousal assessment and counseling required by the judicial system. In the former, corporations offer counseling to the "trailing spouse" as a benefit to encourage employees in dual career marriages to relocate. In the latter, the judicial system provides referral and payment for spousal career assessment to determine a financially dependent spouse's potential employability. The counselor conducts an assessment and makes a recommendation on the spouse's needs related to retraining and employment.

Despite the difficulties mentioned above there are a number of professionals engaged in successful career counseling practices. Fees range from $30 to $100 per hour. Some counselors offer their services in packages; a sample career assessment and testing package can range from $200 to $900.

Those who have the most lucrative practices seem, from anecdotal evidence, to have been a successful professional in another field and to have used this credibility and their contacts with former colleagues to build a referral base. Some started with a particular speciality — reentry women, lawyers, mid-career professionals and have subsequently branched out. They also seem to have developed strong referral sources from other professionals — lawyers, executive recruiters, human resource departments of companies, or therapists. As with most self-employed professionals, the first few years are the most difficult. Over time, a practice builds and grows from word of mouth by satisfied clients.

Successful practitioners appear to be energetic, persistent, and strategic networkers. Common marketing activities include teaching adult education classes, speaking on career issues to community groups, and writing books or articles for newspapers. Those who are most successful have built these activities into their careers, so they no longer feel the burden of marketing. They write, teach, and give speeches because that is part of the work they like to do. In fact, most successful career professionals in private practice have what is often labelled a "composite career." They do some consulting or contract work for outplacement firms, some teaching, and some career counseling. In individual conversations, some report limiting their counseling as it can become too draining or repetitive.

To avoid the burden of marketing and running a business, some self-employed counselors work as independent contractors for private group practices or nonprofit career centers. Counselors working in this manner, however, earn significantly less per client hour.

While the last decade has seen the emergence of various career specialities focusing on working with adults on their career issues, the future of these careers remains uncertain. One important question is whether the need for these services will grow? Some postulate that the baby boom generation, more comfortable with paying for mental health services and familiar with career services from college career centers, will use career counselors more frequently and will demand that their companies provide these services as they try to navigate their careers through the stormy waters ahead. Others feel that individual career services will only become widely used if third-party payment becomes generally available, an unlikely trend given the pressure to keep spiraling benefit costs under control.

On the other hand, trends such as the tight labor market for highly-trained professionals and the rapidly changing work environment and its disruptive impact on careers may motivate organizations to continue to provide more career counseling, outplacement and spousal relocation assistance to their employees.

A second question is the important issue of defining, regulating, and licensing the profession. Will the professional groups discussed in this chapter find effective ways to assure ethical, quality service through credentialing licensing or some other means? If they do, will this bring broader understanding and exposure, clearer client expectations, and a more professional status to the field? Or will the career development field remain an open game that any convincing practitioner can play?

The next decade, which promises to bring vast changes to all professions, will be an interesting one for the career development profession as well.

Acknowledgments

I would like to gratefully acknowledge the professionals interviewed for this article who gave very freely of their time and expertise: Sue Aiken, David Bacharach, Leonard Bachleis, Rogene Baxter, Marilyn Bechtold, Joyce Beckett, Elizabeth Branstead, Marilyn Buckner, Cheri Butler, Janice Chiappone, Priscilla Claman, Nicole Falk, Howard Figler, Sharon Gadberry, James Gallagher, Lorraine Gazzano, Mark Guterman, Al Hafer, Elaine Kaback, Richard Knowdell, Mildred McClosky, Jo Meissner, David Montross, Connie Palladino, Mark Pope, Lynn Slavenski, Sharon Truex, Diane Wexler.

BIBLIOGRAPHY

Daniel Yankelovich Group. "Women in Outplacement National Effectiveness Study." Parsippany, N.J.: Association of Outplacement Consulting Firms, 1988.

Gallagher, James. "A Baseline Survey, Practitioners of Outplacement." Unpublished paper presented to AOCF Conference, 1988.

Gallagher, James. "The Excellent Practitioner: A Study of Characteristics of Outplacement Consultants." Unpublished paper presented to AOCF Conference, 1989.

Hafner, Al. Telephone interview. May, 1991.

Kennedy Publications. An Analysis of the Outplacement Consulting Business in the U.S. Today. Fitzwilliam, N.H., 1989.

Kennedy Publications. Directory of Outplacement Firms. Fitzwilliam, N.H., 1990.

Mulligan, Michael, Ph.D. "What Does It Take To Be An Effective Outplacement Counselor" in Directory of Outplacement Firms. Kennedy Publications. Fitzwilliam, N.H., 1989.

National Career Development Association, "National Survey of Working America, 1990." Alexandria, VA: NCDA, 1990.

Slavenski, Lynn. Telephone interview. April, 1991.

Chapter 16

THE MANAGER'S ROLE IN CAREER COUNSELING

Andrew H. Souerwine

This chapter will cover the following topics relating to the manager's role in the career development process of employees: (1) shifts that have occurred during the past decade that will influence the manager's priorities in the career process; (2) some basics of career development that have not been influenced by these recent changes; (3) distinctions between the role of the manager in career counseling and the role of a career counselor and why these distinctions are important within the realities of a work organization; (4) the importance of self-management to the success of career development; (5) the climate needed in an organization for success in career development and the paradoxes with which the manager must deal; (6) the complexities of dealing with the perceptions of managers and employees regarding performance, growth potential, and motivation for development; and (7) what the manager needs to do to prepare for his/her role in a career development discussion with an employee.

Some Changes

Much has happened in the world of work since a similar chapter on this topic was published in 1981. Some events will have a direct effect on the career development process and therefore on the manager who has much of the responsibility for its implementation and effectiveness. These changes are mentioned here to clarify the environment in which managers are expected to help employees develop their careers:

Demographic Changes

The baby boomers are entering middle age. Increased longevity and a declining birth rate mean a rapidly aging work force. New waves of immigration and the voices of minorities are bringing new values and new languages into organizations. Single parent families and working mothers are giving new meaning to career planning. Each of these groups presents different challenges for management in their role as career developers. These challenges are discussed in separate chapters in this book.

Technological Changes

Computer networks and other technological advances are integrating functions in ways which require project orientation by teams. This demand suits those who are well-educated and computer-literate, but it puts greater stress on those with lesser skills. Organizations will therefore continue to have a large task in educating the work force. Deciding who gets educated, and on what subjects is a large responsibility for managers in the career development of employees.

Competitive Changes

Merger mania of the past few years and the more competitive worldwide economic picture have proved to be unsettling for the American worker. Concepts of rapid turnover, downsizing, outplacement, and the like have led many employees to question their loyalty to a firm and to have fostered a short-term extrinsic reward orientation. Added to that is the question of the presence or absence of ethical standards in business and the apparent greed that motivates some business decisions. For many employees it raises questions about how to handle a career over a long-time span. For example, can workers rely on the services and integrity of management which supposedly is there to assist in each person's career development?

Human Resources Management Changes

The years ahead will call for new strategies in dealing with issues of profit and self-preservation for organizations. A key to these strategies will be the relationship between management and employees. Corporations are talking about being more flexible and adaptable, about restructuring to reduce hierarchies, bureaucracy, and static. Employee-involvement, collaboration, teamwork are more acceptable concepts. For example, self-managing teams used by few companies in the 1960s and 1970s began a rapid spread in the mid-to-late 1980s, and appear to be the wave of the future. (2)

For that to happen a broad redesigning must occur over an entire organization. Such changes are subject to resistance, suspicion, and time delay because of educational and attitude-change requirements. How managers handle this shift in their role as coach and counselor becomes critical for success of the restructuring. This chapter deals with some of the major concerns of managers in achieving this shift.

Some Basics That Have Not Changed

While these changes bring new attention to some aspects of career development, some principles and practices of career development remain fundamentally the same:

1. The need for "information systems that will permit an integration of data relating to management succession, human resources development and human resources planning."(14) Such systems are still lacking in many organizations. Their absence prevents managers from making good considered judgements about individuals and their careers and prevents the necessary linkage among performance review data, personal career information, succession planning, and corporate strategies.

On the other hand, computer-based data systems have become available to assist individuals in gaining more information about jobs and about potential career moves. Many organizations have responded to these advancements by providing appropriate software for employees' use. Nevertheless, their overall effectiveness is lost without a total system for career development and planning.

Whatever the system in place, it can be potentially threatening. It can be unpleasant for the manager who now has employees who have access to more data and know a lot more about career possibilities than they once did. They come armed with more questions and they have available to them more options with which managers must deal.

For the employee, it can be frustrating to have information and not know how to use it, or to be blocked in proper use of data by an indifferent organization or manager.

2. The need for dialogue between the individual and the manager for performance feedback, guidance on standards and procedures, and coaching on how to do what needs to be done.(14) While earlier comments suggest that U.S. corporations are moving in the right direction in developing these relationships, there is evidence that there is a long way to go. Many employers are still struggling with work cultures that disregard some fundamental management practices. Showing little regard for feelings, creating auras of suspicion, making unrealistic and insensitive demands, creating feelings of guilt and disloyalty for unacceptable decisions—the list from disillusioned workers with unenlightened bosses is a long one.(16)

3. The growing linkage between personal and work life. While career development professionals have long suggested the relationship (4, 13), its toll in terms of stress is gaining greater recognition (15). "Over the last decade, work has become an integral part of more and more lives . . . for many people, career and identity are inextricably bound up: Indeed, they are almost equivalent." Classic symptoms such as anxiety, depression, rage, indecisiveness, and excessive use of drugs and alcohol can be a reaction to problems at work. Not surprisingly, then, more and more Americans are seeking help from people who understand their work. (15)

This, of course, can place extreme burdens on managers who must work with such employees. Can a manager counsel a worker at this personal level? This chapter deals with that question.

4. The importance of management support for the establishment of proper climates and cultural values. In an earlier work, Souerwine (13) suggested that while top management support is often difficult to find, a lack of support "does not deny the initiation of at least bits and pieces of the process." He further suggested that the personnel specialist has a responsibility "to initiate the kind of change process that will ultimately gain the overt or covert support of top management."

Because of earlier reference to shifts in demands for human resources management, the wholehearted support of management becomes even more necessary. Bits and pieces won't do anymore; neither will covert management support. At the moment, organizations are doing more talking than acting on such matters as participative management and self-directed teams. As Kuttner (6) reports: "A naively hopeful fable is making the rounds, celebrating a new enlightened self-interest of ordinary hard-nosed leaders . . . The trouble is that the fable is just that. . . . business is not yet playing seriously." Nevertheless, management enlightenment in the affairs of society and its workers must gain momentum. "The business of America may be business, but it's not just business. It's also citizenship."(6)

Such value systems strike at the very heart of career development in organizations. Support requires more than mere words in carefully chosen speeches and places. It requires day-to-day actions over a three to five year period — and the, of course, continually. It requires that specific policies and procedures be practiced as a priority target for all who are responsible for the leadership of the organization. Without that dedication, the activities that make up career development will rapidly erode. Bits and pieces, now and then will not do the job.

The Manager and the Counselor

Other chapters in this book discuss the manager's role in mentoring, in assessing potential, in succession planning, in preretirement planning and outplacement, in working with high-potential or plateaued employees, with women and minorities. Implied in these discussions is the manager's use of a set of skills which foster openness, trust, and responsible employee self-direction. These skills are commonly known as the skills of counseling. They differ markedly from many of the skills which managers are prone to use to get work done.

There are real differences between the role of the manager and that of the counselor. While professional practitioners encourage as much overlap as possible in these two roles, there is serious question whether managers can, in fact, play the role of counselor.

At this point it is useful to make the distinction between the two roles and the contexts in which they are played.

The manager's role is one that requires getting things done through an objective "business-like" approach to problems. That person is a planner, controller, trainer, coach, recruiter, outplacer, rewarder, allocator of resources, a person hired to achieve a certain agreed-upon or not agreed-upon result. These things are done in a fairly structured, controlled, and formal system of relationships and responsibilities, where organizational values and objectives dictate vested interests. In these circumstances the manager is therefore more judgmental, more problem-centered, and gives more direction than the counselor. (5) In short, there is a marked power relationship between the manager and the subordinate in this role.

The counselor's role, on the other hand, has as its objective to help people to help themselves. The counselor is more concerned with the "being" of the client, his/her emotions and feelings, the diagnosis of issues that lead to self-acceptance, integrity, change, empowering by the client. (8) The counselor does this in a context of developing personal and confidential relationships, of being responsive to the client's interests and objectives, and helping the client learn how to solve problems for him/herself. The counselor is, therefore, more nonjudgmental, nondirective, discovery-oriented, and person-centered than the manager. In a problem-centered interview the counselor is in less of a power relationship than is the manager. (7)

These two roles overlap in the *skills* they both use to achieve these different objectives. These skills are, in their simplicity of design and complexity of doing, key to what organizations and managers need to perfect: open-ended questioning, active listening, nonevaluative listening, reflection, silence, establishing and maintaining rapport, observing posture and gestures. (13)

Second, a distinction must be made as to when and by whom these skills are used. Milne (7) suggests that while these *skills* can and should be used by line managers, human resource specialists, and professional counselors, there is a difference between *using* counseling skills and *being* a professional counselor. This spectrum leads to three levels of skills to be used in an organization.

At level 1, the line manager uses counseling skills for better listening and observing, rapport building, and activities which enhance a culture of openness and trust. These skills serve the manager well in recruiting, performance appraisal interviews, coaching activities, and in day-to-day interpersonal relations with employees. Such activities take, on average, about 65 percent of the manager's time. When those skills are not used or used poorly, it is costly to organizational effectiveness. Furthermore, using these skills well will make the manager sensitive to the need to refer some employees to a more highly trained person, at level 2.

Milne (7) suggests that level 2 people have a less power-oriented relationship with the employee and have more professional training in the use of counseling skills in work settings. They are usually found in staff functions in human resource departments, management development, succession planning, employee assistance programs, or employee health functions. As such, they assist the organization in redeployment counseling, personal and career counseling, and management and executive development. Their in-depth training allows them to know when to refer an employee to a counselor at level 3.

At level 3 are the independent professional counselors who function outside the organization and typically see clients outside the work setting. These referrals usually occur when the organization sees counseling as too time-consuming for in-house attention, or when the employee wants or needs to discuss an issue with people outside the organization, or when issues become too critical for or beyond the expertise of the level 2 counselor. In some cases, the independent outsider is used for executive counseling purpose, to maintain organizational confidentiality or to prevent certain issues from becoming known internally.

These three levels are depicted in figure 16-1, with the shaded area indicating where each level functions.

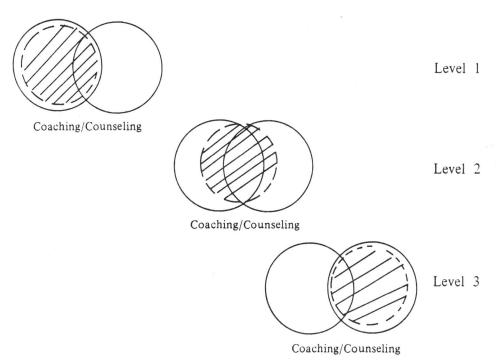

Coaching/Counseling   Level 1

Coaching/Counseling   Level 2

Coaching/Counseling   Level 3

Figure 16-1.

Why These Distinctions Are Important

These distinctions between the manager and the counselor and among the three levels of counseling make sense within the realities of work organizations. These realities include:

1. *A power relationship, implied or actual, between the manager and subordinate:*

Hore (5) reports that, even in role playing training exercises where trainees (all managers) are instructed "not to act out the manager role but rather to achieve the best results possible through the use of counseling skills," and where trainees had successfully learned how to use those skills effectively, the "managers" and "workers" immediately adopt superior/ subordinate postures with "the 'workers' donning their powerless, submissive posture as naturally as the 'managers' take to their dominant position." (5, p. 10) What's even more to the point is that trainees are "often unaware of their changed behavior. . . . we start behaving like managers and the role *not the job to be done* is the major determinant of our actions." (5, p. 10)

2. *Organizational demands and the reward process:*

Organizations reward managers for results and rarely are results defined in terms of "soft" acts, such as career development, because they have no apparent direct relationship to revenues or profits. (13) The traditional cutting of training expenses when costs must be lowered, or the outplacement of masses of personnel when organizations decide to become more "efficient," are testimony to this mentality.

3. *The increasingly hectic role of the manager:*

Vaill (17) describes the role of the manager as "the dynamism, fluidity, extraordinary complexity, and fundamental personalness of all organizational action. . . . permanent white water, . . . the pace, complexity, novelty, danger, and nonstop challenge of the modern environment." (17, p.xiv) Into that world, the introduction of any process that is perceived to take more time, require new skills, or create more confusion for the manager is almost always automatically rejected. It is a difficult task to make the practical, helpful linkage between the use of counseling skills and the frantic pace toward results that the job demands.

In addition, the manager's job requires attention to brief, nonsequential episodes of activity (9) while counseling demands a shift to longer episodes of relative passivity and nondirective behavior by the manager. (13) No wonder management resists counseling except to deal with immediate issues and concerns. No wonder, then, that levels 2 and 3 make good organizational sense.

4. *The personal nature of the career development process:*

As a person becomes more involved in the career development process, it becomes difficult to separate work issues from nonwork life. "Most people who have worked for some years in any structured organization have been aware of a protective wall around them. They are unsure of what is "out there" on the other side of the wall, and sometimes experience real fear about this." (8)

Sooner or later, the person confronts (or should confront) questions such as "Who am I?" and "What can I take with me on my career journey in the way of strengths, values, interests, and skills?" Answers develop best through interaction with someone who understands personality structure and dynamics. This helps the person to confront issues of self-awareness and self-confidence, issues which are frequently difficult to discuss with management and if discussed, difficult for managers to handle. And yet, the manager must have the counseling skills to be able to draw out these issues and to recognize when such issues are better handled by someone else.

These realities lead to the conclusion that managers *should* use counseling *skills* in order to encourage a climate of openness and trust. They are charged with obtaining optimum return on resources, and people resources are becoming increasingly the most expensive and the most valuable of these resources. Any barriers to creativity, problem solving, decision making and action, and personal development by definition lock up the employee's initiative and energy, skills and talents to perform in the best interests of self and/or of organization. Counseling fosters self-esteem, and that in turn fosters motivation and commitment. (5)

Can managers counsel? In the professional sense of performing in the role of counselor, the answer is "no." Managers do not have the time, the training, nor the internal organizational system to assume such a role. But they *can use* counseling skills. They can be taught these skills in a matter of days (8, 12). And when these skills are reinforced by the organization through a system of clearly stated objectives and standards, performance appraisal, and reward structure, managers can be encouraged to use them consistently within the organizational setting. They *can* and *should* use these skills in their role as coach, mentor, recruiter, trainer, and evaluator. Managers who understand that, are less reluctant to assume a rightful niche in the career development process and are ready to deal with the classic career concerns which most employees have.

Issue: The Self-Management Aspect of Career Development

In this era of increasing self-management within work organizations, the influential role of the manager in career development is not wholly the manager's responsibility. Counselors, coaches, mentors, sponsors can help an employee think through the issues, but the ultimate choice is the employee's, not the manager's. Events over the life span, from the establishment of a career through mid-career transitions to impending retirement, can create stresses for an employee; and a manager, consciously or unconsciously, can help to create those stresses. Whatever the cause, an employee shoulders some of the responsibility for the outcome.

Table 16-1 shows how the influence shifts as the employee progresses in the organization and/or in career.

TABLE 16-1

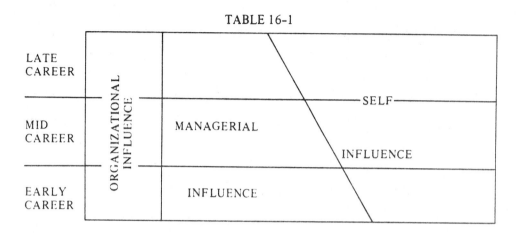

All three entities—the organization, the manager, and the individual—have influence on the career development process. While the organization's influence remains fairly constant, the manager's role diminishes over the span of the career while the individual's influence expands. It is during these early stages that the organization and the manager have an opportunity to teach/coach/counsel the employee on the basic behavioral patterns necessary for making appropriate choices in a career. What the person learns (or does not learn) in these early stages will have a marked effect on the transition into and through subsequent career stages.

As Table 16-1 shows, the organization can influence the career development process at any career level. The organization is, of course, management, especially top management, and it is their policy and practices, their value systems and priorities, what they say and do that sets the stage for effective career development.(14) In his work on effective self-management, Hackman (3) mentions five conditions which are essential for support of self-management teams. While Hackman's conditions apply primarily to performing units of employees, they provide insights into the role of the organization in a career development system which encourages the employee to become involved in the self-management of his/her career. The areas of influence for the organization and management, on the one hand, and for the employee, on the other, are different, and the manager needs to recognize those differences.

At any level of career, the organization will influence the career development process by:

1. establishing a set of cultural values, and pressing them at every

opportunity, encouraging individuals to do career planning and to seek activities which will enhance career growth;

2. establishing a set of policies and practices which permits individuals career growth without advancement, without movement into management, and which recognizes that effective career can exist even when workers plateau or are down-graded;

3. providing training and development opportunities and appropriate tools, for people at all levels, which encourage self-awareness, the development of skills and abilities, and the development and execution of personal career plans;

4. providing employees with information regarding jobs and families of jobs which cut across departments and functions, so that workers understand more clearly what their options might be;

5. providing an effective system for performance evaluation which gives employees current and valid feedback on performance and its implications for career effectiveness and which defines the behaviors necessary for positive evaluations;

6. establishing an integrated system of human resources management which makes certain that the various human resource functions—recruiting and selection, compensation, training and development, succession planning— all work in a direction supportive of corporate values (which hopefully are also supportive of worker, market, and societal values);

7. making available expert coaching and consultation beyond one's own manager for discussion and resolution of personal career issues;

8. providing a performance structure that fosters good job design and appropriate people and material resources to enhance work effectiveness and optimum personal growth.

Issue: The Culture Needed for Self-Management

The manager must create first an appropriate environment for optimizing desire for self-direction and the building of self-worth through knowledge and acceptance of oneself.

The following paradoxes are not easy for managers to understand or to implement, but they need to be present in *spirit* as basic managerial values and in *practice* as basic behavioral motivations of those who manage.

1. *Encourage autonomy through interdependence.*

A major value orientation for most people is to gain a certain amount of independence, freedom to choose, to make decisions. Indeed there is a tendency to encourage that in children from the day they are born. But such a goal denies the very nature of an employee's need to accomplish and to grow. That can only be done by relying on others for certain resources— their materials, skills, time. Relying on others—in teams, in networks—

becomes a crucial avenue toward one's own independence. Managers who encourage that involvement with others create an environment that leads to self-direction.

2. *Develop security through instability.*

Managers who structure too carefully, who set up rigid guidelines that minimize an employee's ability to choose and to make decisions, do the employee a disservice. Under such circumstances, the employee learns to rely on management for structure and guidance, and does not learn to cope with the changes that inevitably occur in the workplace. It is impossible to establish rules for every conceivable event. Hence, feelings of security in employees occur when management permits ambiguity and helps the employee to learn how to handle it. Management's role is to be supportive, to use appropriate coaching and counseling skills to help employees deal with uncertainty, and not to prevent it from occurring by trying to maintain a stable, unchanging environment.

3. *Encourage growth through failure.*

This is a corollary of the security-instability paradox. Learning/growth is synonymous with career development. Understanding one's own strengths *and* limitations is critically important to establishing realistic goals. While successes give an employee cues regarding strengths, interests, and skills, they do little to help the employee understand limitations that could make certain career goals unrealistic. Indeed, the success syndrome—a history of never experiencing failure, of believing that "I can do anything, aspire to do or be anything I want"—leads people into positions where failure is inevitable. They are left without critical mechanisms learned to cope with such failure. It follows, then, that managers need to permit employees to fail and to learn from that failure. It is through such learning that the manager creates an environment in which employees know their limitations and know, therefore, when to rely on other resources for their own achievement and growth.

4. *Develop rationality through emotion.*

It is false to believe that to be "business-like" means to be objective, to deal only with the "facts." It is false to believe that to be rational is to avoid emotion and feelings. To be aware, to be lucid, one must deal as much or more with the emotional side of events as with the objective events themselves. Those emotions are, after all, events in their own right.

Managers who understand that and who encourage themselves and their employees to deal with those feelings permit themselves and others to get closer to reality. And that is essential if one is to make "rational" decisions about one's career growth. To deny feelings, values, emotions is to discount an important piece of the jigsaw puzzle that complete the picture of man.

With how much of that "feeling side" can a manager deal? As was indicated earlier, the probabilities are high that dealing with personal feelings, (especially those that come close to an employee's sense of self worth), must be left to those who are more detached from determining the ultimate career destiny of the employee. The employee, too, must recognize that and understand to whom to go in order to get a more objective perspective on feelings and how they influence career decisions. Mentors and counselors play an especially important role in that regard.

5. *Encourage structured flexibility through specificity.*

This is another corollary of the security/instability paradox and may appear to be a contradiction of it. Managers need to structure, to provide guidelines so that employees understand what the boundaries are for rewards and failures. The security/instability paradox simply states that those guidelines must be broad enough to permit employees to learn how to cope with change as it occurs, without relying on authority to establish all of the rules.

The flexibility/specificity paradox suggests that employees need to learn that they usually have many options in their career development, and those options can be dealt with only by being specific in their definition and implementation. To be vague about a goal literally reduces an employee's options, because the goal can mean everything and nothing. As such, its vagueness does not permit the employee to test out its reality. When the goal becomes specific in terms of standards for accomplishment and in plans for achieving it, the employee learns much more about self and the goal's validity. It is that kind of learning that helps the employee to be flexible within the structure of reality.

Managers can do a lot to provide data to employees regarding the realities of careers and career prospects within the organization. It is within that structure that employees can learn how to function by testing out specific and realistic options.

6. *Encourage long-term orientation through immediate results.*

The very concept of "career" suggests a series of jobs or positions over time all of which together constitute a "career." It requires, therefore, a long-term orientation spanning many years. Souerwine (13) reports that it is not unusual for employees to become disillusioned and frustrated as the years go by with little or no apparent progress being made toward long-term career goals. He further reports that the more ambiguous those goals are, the greater the potential frustration.

Again, the setting of specific goals, with standards of performance, and the achievement of those goals helps to develop self-confidence. In the career development process, it is important that short-term goals are not ends in themselves, but rather means to the achievement of other, next-in-line short-term goals. It is through this process of gaining immediate results (all of which have a bearing on the next goal in the sequence) that an employee keeps motivated in his/her career and also maintains a long-term orientation. To focus solely on the achievement of short-term results without an awareness of how those results relate to future career goals potentially minimizes the effectiveness of the career development process.

Furthermore, focusing on immediate results which are means to other ends helps the employee to give more meaning to his/her career goals. If immediate performance is effective, it encourages pursuit of the goal. If it is ineffective, it may suggest review of longer-range goals and possible revisions.

7. *Maintain power by giving it up.*

This paradox is really a statement of the basis of self-motivation. We alluded earlier to the negative impact that a sense of loss of personal control may have on developing effective manager-employee relationships. Also important is the personal nature of career choices. Nevertheless, some managers worry that encouraging employees to give personal direction to their careers diminishes the control the manager has over them. They reason that it is the manager's responsibility to place people in jobs, to decide who will be moved into what positions and when, that giving the employee opportunity for input into these matters will lead to chaotic personnel management. They argue that to give up the power to decide, to choose, to give direction is to abandon their role as managers.

When a manager imposes his/her power over an employee so that the employee feels thwarted in his/her desire for self-management, it may lead to resentment, fear, anger, hostility, suspicion, and/or lack of trust. It does not lead to optimum efficiency and effectiveness in personal productivity and development. Under these circumstances, the employee wants "out" of the environment.

Employees who are encouraged to take on responsibility for their own behavior, for the choices they make in problem solving situations tend to be more productive, solve problems more creatively, enhance the function for which the manager is responsible. When an employee has these positive experiences, the employee wants "in." Such leadership practices convince an employee to support the manager and keep him/her in power.

These seven paradoxes of managerial behavior, when carefully and consciously applied, help to create a proper catalyst for an employee's self-direction in a career. To be autonomous, to feel secure, to accept failure and to seek achievement, to be rational, to be specific, to accomplish the planned immediate, to assume control—these are worthwhile commandments for the person interested in developing a career.

For the manager, the issue is not so much the outcome as it is how the employee learns to get to those outcomes. The manager can be very helpful here by providing appropriate environmental support and cues that encourage process as well as results.

Issue: Manager and Employee Perceptions of Performance and Motivation

The manager's role in the career development process is not an isolated one. Equally involved is the employee. Perceptions of the manager and the employee create a complexity that demands attention in helping the employee to develop. At the very least, these perceptions require attention:

1. The manager's perception (judgment) of the employee's performance.
2. The manager's perception of the employee's growth potential (movement up, down, sideways, or not at all, into technical or managerial positions).
3. The employee's perception of his/her performance in present or future positions.
4. The employee's perception of his/her desire for career growth (again: up, down, sideways, or not at all, into technical or managerial positions).

The manager can perceive the employee's performance as either high or low; the employee's growth potential as either high or low. Likewise, the employee can perceive his/her performance and growth potential as either high or low. (Of course, there are many other possibilities, but these few will serve to demonstrate the complexity of career development for both the employee and the manager.)

The following chart lists some, not all, of the possible combinations for these variables:

	Abe	*Bea*	*Cleo*	*Dan*	*E*	*etc.*
Mgt. Perception of Growth Potential	Hi	Hi	Lo	Lo	Lo	
Mgt. Perception of Emp. Performance	Hi	Hi	Lo	Hi	Lo	
Emp. Perception of Motivation for Growth	Lo	Hi	Lo	Hi	Hi	
Emp. Perception of Performance	Hi	Hi	Lo	Hi	Hi	

The problems for the manager are different as s/he deals with each of these employees. And these problems would change for employees at different stages of their careers. Without discussing all of the possible combinations (the scope of this chapter does not permit such detail), a look at a few will emphasize the managerial task.

In the example above the manager is high on Abe's performance and potential for growth. Abe, on the other hand, believes that he is performing well, but has low motivation for further growth in the job. Assuming that all perceptions are valid, the manager must ferret out from Abe that lack of desire for growth. Until that happens, the two may be on a collision course.

Without the use of appropriate counseling skills and without the appropriate climate which encourages openness and trust, it may be difficult for Abe to confess to a desire to remain in his present position or a similar one. Without that climate, it may also be difficult for Abe to resist the manager's desire for further growth and the manager's putting Abe into assignments which encourage movement. To move Abe into greater responsibility without knowing about his low motivation for growth is to risk possible inefficiencies for the organization and certainly frustrations for Abe.

Of course, since either party or both could be wrong in their perceptions, it behooves each to use appropriate communications skills to determine the validity of their judgments.

Most managers will have little difficulty in working with Bea. The manager judges Bea's performance to be high as is her potential for growth in the organization. Bea, too, sees her performance as high and has high motivation for growth in the organization. Assuming that all perceptions are reasonably valid (that assumption should be tested by both parties), and assuming that they both can agree on what they mean by "growth" (another relative term that needs clarification), Bea will give her career development activity a priory and the manager will support it within the context of organizational practices.

In many organizations Cleo is easily dealt with. After establishing a suitable "record" that Cleo's performance is indeed low, she will be "outplaced"; and depending on her level and length of service, Cleo will be provided with some professional outplacement counseling service to assist her in her career development.

Such action for Cleo is appropriate if her performance and motivation are not a function of placement in the wrong position, or poor training, or poor managerial practices. There have been too many cases in which employees who have been "outplaced" have been found to be perfectly adequate for the organization which has done the outplacement. The independent level 3 counselor is able to discover those strengths which are not apparent to level 1 or 2 people.

Dan represents a delicate problem for his manager, the organization, and of course, Dan himself. Dan's is not an unusual situation. High performers are often declared by management to have low growth potential because more than mere performance enters into the judgment criteria for growth. That is especially true when management and the organization construe growth to mean movement upward in management positions. Developing effective interpersonal relationships, building networks, and being accepted by upper management, all enter into growth potential judgments.

Dan, on the other hand, believes that he has high potential, is performing well, and wants to grow. When boss and employee disagree on that potential, it sets the stage for a classic conflict. How Dan's manager handles that is important to Dan's future performance in the organization, whether growth does or does not occur. Both must resolve the difference in the appraisal of growth potential by building up a series of experiences that support or deny the manager's or Dan's perceptions. Until it is resolved to both parties' satisfaction, it can make the difference between Dan's being a "star" or a "solid citizen" or just plain "deadwood."

These few examples emphasize that resolution of differences between manager and employee in perceptions of potential, ability, and motivation require good skills of listening and observing by both parties, and also good management skills to create the kind of work environment that encourages appropriate discussions.

Issue: After Skill Development and Climate-Building, Preparation for Career Development Discussion

Managers need to give careful attention, as well, to the quality of the discussions they will have with employees regarding career development. Such discussions require preparation and an assurance by the manager that s/he has relevant information to assist in the career development process. Preparation includes answers to the following questions:

- Do I know enough about the employee to warrant a career discussion? Do I know what s/he wants from work and the organization? Do I know what kind of work s/he wants and what kind of work would best fit his/her strengths and interests? Do I know whether s/he wants to work alone or with others; as a technician or a manager?
- What do I know about the organization, its direction, its plans, growth patterns for employees? What options does the employee have in the organization? How much information can I realistically give the employee? What problems, if any, do I create for the employee and the organization by giving the information to the employee? If there are problems, how do I resolve them?
- Do I really understand myself well? Do I understand the career development process and my role in it? Do I have the time to deal with the process? And if I do, do I want to take the time? Does the organization want me to play that role, or does it have other priorities for me? Do I have the necessary skills to deal with the issues as I see them developing with this employee?
- Have I done a good job of reviewing with the employee mutually-understood expectations with respect to the job duties, projects, goals, standards, and other predetermined performance factors? Does the employee have honest feedback from me regarding his/her per-

formance? In providing feedback, have I avoided bias and prejudice and undue influence by my own experiences and aspirations?

SUMMARY

In a previous work, Souerwine (13) wrote about "the manager as a career counselor." The title of this chapter, while a sequel to the previous work, is different and reflects a new condition that the manager, the organization, and the career development professional need to recognize in the role of the manager in the career development process.

After reflecting on the various changes that are occurring in the work environment that have a direct bearing on careers and the career development process, this chapter emphasizes a real distinction between practicing counseling skills and being a counselor. A manager should do the former and leave the latter to those who are more professionally qualified.

Beyond that, the manager can use counseling skills to create a culture which enhances the probabilities of success of the career development process. How that culture is created and what the dimensions of that culture need to be are described in detail, including focus on self-management techniques and why they are important.

The chapter concludes with discussion of some specific situations with which the manager is confronted in an attempt to deal with the career development of employees.

A major message of this chapter is that the manager will have difficulty in being successful in the career planning process unless s/he focuses first, along with the entire organization, on the creation of a culture which enhances the basic premises behind career development. Understanding the career process and learning skills to implement it will be of little avail without the culture to reinforce it.

REFERENCES

1. *Business Week*, "The New America", September 25, 1989, pp. 91–179.
2. *Business Week*, "The Payoff from Teamwork", July 10, 1989, pp. 56–62.
3. Hackman, J. Richard "The Psychology of Self-Management In Organizations". From M. S. Pallak and R. Perloff (Eds) *Psychology and Work: Productivity, Change, and Employment*. Washington, D.C.: American Psychological Association, 1986.
4. Hall, Douglas T. *Careers in Organizations*. Pacific Palisades, CA: Goodyear, 1976.
5. Hore, Ian D. "Can Managers Counsel?" *Counselling*, No.48, May, 1984, pp. 7–13.
6. Kuttner, Robert "U.S. Business Isn't About To Be Society's Savior". *Business Week*, Nov. 6, 1989, p. 29.

7. Milne, A. R. "An Approach to Setting Up an In-House Counselling Service" *Counselling News for Managers,* December, 1988, pp. 4–6.

8. Milne, A. R. "Executive Career Counselling" *British Journal of Guidance and Counselling,* Vol. 16 No. 3, September 1988, 277–285.

9. Mintzberg, Henry *The Nature of Managerial Work.* New York: Harper & Row, 1973.

10. Moses, Barbara and B. J. Chakiris "The Manager as Career Counselor", *Training and Development Journal,* July 1989, pp. 60–65.

11. Osipow, Samuel H. "Career Issues Through The Life Span". From M. S. Pallak and R. Perloff (Eds), *Psychology and Work: Productivity, Change, and Employment.* Washington, D.C.: American Psychological Association, 1986.

12. Souerwine, Andrew H. *Career Strategies: Planning for Personal Achievement.* New York: AMACOM, 1978.

13. Souerwine, Andrew H. "The Manager As Career Counselor: Some Issues and Approaches" D. H. Montross and C. J. Shinkman (Eds) *Career Development in the 1980s: Theory and Practice.* Springfield, IL: Charles C Thomas, 1981.

14. Souerwine, Andrew H. "Career Planning: Getting Started with Top Management Support" From D. H. Montross and C. J. Shinkman (Eds) *Career Development in the 1980s: Theory and Practice.* Springfield, IL: Charles C Thomas, 1981.

15. Sandroff, Ronni "Is Your Job Driving You Crazy?" *Psychology Today,* July/August, 1989, pp. 41–45.

16. "Terrible Boss Stories" *Northeast magazine, The Hartford Courant,* December 17, 1989, pp. 8–13.

17. Vaill, Peter B. *Managing As A Performing Art: New Ideas For A World Of Chaotic Change.* San Francisco, CA: Jossey-Bass, 1989.

Chapter 17

CAREER DEVELOPMENT FOR NONEXEMPT EMPLOYEES: ISSUES AND POSSIBILITIES*

ZANDY B. LEIBOWITZ, BARBARA H. FELDMAN, AND SHERRY H. MOSLEY

In these fast-paced times it is not difficult to find organizational career development programs that address the increasingly varied career needs of executives, managers, technical and administrative professional employees. and others who constitute the "exempt" population—that is, salaried employees who are not paid overtime wages. The career-related concerns of this population have been closely scrutinized by career development specialists who have tailored numerous imaginative and effective programs to address this group's needs.

The same cannot be said, however, of the nonexempt population in many organizations—the host of clerical and support staff, technicians, and others who are paid on an hourly or weekly basis, are entitled to overtime, and are sometimes union members. These employees' career development concerns have not typically been the focus of intensive examination by HR professionals; indeed, the tacit assumption in many organizations appears to be that this population has no significant long-term aspirations that need to be addressed by the organization's career development staff.

This situation raises several provocative questions. Is it possible to arrive at some meaningful generalizations about the career-related preoccupations of this group of workers—and about how their concerns differ from those of the exempt population? What are the implications of such differences for career development programming in organizations large and small? With such questions in mind, this chapter takes a close look at the attitudinal and cultural traits of nonexempt employees. Through interviews with human resource professionals at several large organizations in diverse industries an attempt was made to obtain the practitioner's perspective on nonexempt employees and the challenges inherent in devising meaningful career development programs for this population.

---

*Portions of this chapter were adapted from Leibowitz, Z.B., Feldman, B.H., and Mosley, S.H., "Career Development Works Overtime at Corning, Inc.," *Personnel*, April 1990, pp. 38–45.

In this chapter the results of those interviews are presented first, to set the stage for a more detailed investigation of the complex questions surrounding career development for nonexempt workers. An unusual career planning and development program targeted at a 1,500-member nonexempt workforce (administrative and technical employees, or A&Ts) at the headquarters of Corning, Inc. is also examined. Corning is a Fortune 500 company and a leader in specialty glass, telecommunications, health and science technology, and consumer products. The development of Corning's program—why and how it came into being—shows the subtleties of conceiving and implementing a career development system to empower nonexempt employees. This population sometimes suffers from low self-esteem and frustration—difficulties that are unique to most nonexempt employees' place and role within the organization.

What emerges from the Corning story is an important and exciting possibility: namely, that taking an interest in all employees' career development—not just in the development of management and nonexempt employees—can bring large benefits for the entire organization. It can improve morale at all levels, boost productivity, and help the organization become more efficient by encouraging realistic and meaningful matches between people and jobs. Moreover, such a program can reduce turnover (and its costs) and empower the entire workforce to realize its full potential.

Nonexempt Employees: Aspirations and Expectations

To understand what nonexempts want (or do not want) from their careers, it is helpful to look at the attitudes and culture of these employees, outlining the contours of their general experience as workers. Before doing so, however, it should be noted that nonexempt workers in most large organizations are a varied group, and their career aspirations and concerns are not always homogeneous. Some of these employees are unionized, some not; some are paid on an hourly basis, some weekly; some are linked, by way of their technical, administrative, or operational functions, with exempt professionals with whom they interact frequently and closely—and with whom they thus have certain cultural bonds.

These important distinctions notwithstanding, however, the career development professionals interviewed shared certain views on the nonexempt population—beginning with the fact that historically, this sector has not been adequately served by most career development programs. Other assessments of nonexempt employees encountered during the interviews were these:

- For nonexempts, job satisfaction often derives from the quality of work relationships and interactions more than from the nature of the work itself—which in many cases is unarguably repetitive and/or unchallenging. Support staff tend to value the social environment of their work; they are more concerned than many technical or managerial employees about the atmosphere of their workplaces and the "feel" of their collaborations with other employees (both salaried and nonexempt).

- Changing from a union to nonunion, or blue-collar to white-collar, job tends to involve a major personal investment and a significant cultural adjustment on the part of the nonexempt employee. This is the case for several reasons. White-collar jobs usually require a higher educational level and different skill level than are needed in blue-collar jobs. Union jobs offer security in terms of promotion on a seniority basis, training, and wages—none of which are automatically present in most nonunion or white-collar jobs. And even if a nonexempt worker does succeed in crossing the "collar line," he or she may be in for a rough cultural transition, one in which support from coworkers may not be forthcoming to the degree needed.

- Because their options for vertical movement within organizations have traditionally been limited, many nonexempts experience a higher level of frustration in their work lives than do their exempt counterparts. Some nonexempts enter the organization with the expectation that vertical mobility is possible, and they are disappointed and discouraged when they discover that making such a transition is quite difficult—for cultural reasons as well as reasons having to do with actual technical or educational deficits.

The "collar line" affects perceptions on both sides. In one interview, Ken Ideus of British Petroleum (BP) noted that nonexempts' frustration increases when they perceive that managers or other exempt workers tend not to consult them for ideas on how to get things done. Many organizations, Ideus stated, fail to recognize these employees for their vital contributions or accomplishments—which only adds to their discouragement. His statements verify what is acknowledged in many HR circles: the fact that there is a significant morale problem within this sector of the workforce. That problem is unlikely to stay within borders; it will inevitably affect morale throughout the organization. This situation suggests that it is a mistake for managers to overlook the career-related concerns of the nonexempt worker—a point to be examined in detail in this chapter.

An HR professional who is a strong supporter of career development programs for nonexempts also stated that these employees are often frustrated. They are unclear about ways to make career transitions, particularly to the exempt level. Complicating matters, their managers are not always well-equipped to serve as their mentors in this area and to give them practical assistance in breaking through the barriers that they feel are separating them from exempt jobs.

Another HR professional with the same company pointed out that for many nonexempts, work is a job, not a career. Long-term aspirations and expectations are simply not as relevant or pressing for this sector of the work force because these people do not typically think in terms of developing expertise—and career options—over a period of years. In fact, he said, some nonexempts rule out altogether the possibility of becoming exempt employees; this option is simply not a part of their thinking. Clearly, such attitudinal features have implications for career development programming; what works for the exempt population may well be less efficacious for nonexempts. Goal-setting exercises, for example, may well be difficult to undertake with nonexempts because such activities may be viewed as fundamentally irrelevant.

In discussing career development issues for nonexempts, one HR consultant stated that the stigma of beginning work as a nonexempt employee lingers even if such a worker manages to cross over into the salaried group. She cited employee frustration as an inevitable consequence of limited opportunities for upward mobility. The consultant argued for "extra attention" to the nonexempt population (and especially to its feeling of being stigmatized, which weakens corporate morale overall).

All of the professionals we interviewed expressed concern about the problem of educational level as it affects the nonexempt employee's prospects for promotion into an exempt position. Ideus, noting that exempts at BP generally have at least a BA and often a master's degree, stated that many support employees at the company enter with the expectation that they will advance as a result of gaining significant work experience within BP and are then frustrated to find that they need advanced education. Night school is an option chosen by some employees facing this dilemma; however, Ideus argued that the most efficient way to overcome the obstacle is to leave the company, devote full-time effort to procuring a college degree, and then seek employment once again at BP—thereby securing "a more strategic position," as Ideus put it, than other college graduates lacking hands-on knowledge of the company and its business. The organization is responsive to such displays of commitment and planning, according to Ideus—although such an approach obviously entails a large expenditure of time and energy and a certain amount of risk.

Designing Career Development Programs for Nonexempts

When asked about specific programs to address the needs of the nonexempt worker, interviewees had some interestingly similar responses to the issues and challenges of such programming. Because of the existence of limits on advancement options for nonexempts, job enrichment was cited as a major focus of the career development activities of several companies with respect to these employees. Ideus said that in counseling all BP employees, and nonexempts in particular, the first emphasis is on enhancement of the present job. Two other interviewees spoke of the need to encourage nonexempts to think in terms of taking the initiative in addressing possibilities for job enrichment as well as for advancement. The question of the advisability of bringing together exempts and nonexempts in career development workshops or other programs elicited divergent opinions. One person argued in favor of such a mixing of groups because it allows nonexempts to see that exempt employees also struggle with issues of self-esteem, anxiety about the future, getting ahead, and so on. His colleague, however, cautioned against combining the two categories of employees in one workshop or program setting. He felt that the interactions among employees were better when the groups were separated and that nonexempts tend to become inhibited when listening to discussions of issues that for them appear to be irrelevant. Their company initially separated the two groups on the theory that nonexempts might experience frustration at being in a mixed setting; at present, however, the company offers an optional all-nonexempt workshop and also provides opportunities for members of both groups to share information, ideas, and experiences in the context of a career development workshop. Offering both kinds of workshops appears to have enhanced the popularity of the program overall.

An HR consultant maintained that the career development process is the same for both groups but conceded that there might be a need for a special workshop addressing the needs of nonexempts who are making the transition to a salaried position. She cited one Fortune 500 corporation that found that some of its nonexempt workers experienced heightened frustration after going through a career development workshop in the company of exempt employees because they saw clearly the increased opportunities and options that these individuals enjoyed (and from which they felt excluded). A tradeoff obviously exists between the benefits of information-sharing and the costs of nonexempts' disappointment and sensation of being immobilized by their position within the organizational structure.

Addressing the Needs of Nonexempts: Challenges and Resources

Several themes threaded consistently through interviews with HR professionals. *Self-esteem* is evidently important in dealing with nonexempt employees' career development needs. Caught in the real or perceived binds of hierarchy and undeniably constrained, in many workplaces, by their lack of higher education, nonexempt employees often suffer from a sense of helplessness. The first challenge for the career development specialist working with this population is thus to empower nonexempts to take responsibility for their own future. As those people interviewed indicated, bringing about such attitudinal changes is not easy; however, it must be initiated if the problem of self-esteem is to be addressed in a deep-seated, long-lasting way.

Once nonexempts have recognized and accepted their crucial role in shaping their own future, the next task is to assist these employees in thinking in terms of options: of job performance and job enrichment as well as vertical mobility. With these notions comes an understanding of how a satisfying career is built—not as an inevitable ascension up a preordained "ladder" but rather as a continuous, flexible plotting of a pathway whose terminus is not solely or necessarily an adequate salary.

Another thematic thread uncovered in the interviews is that of *managerial responsibility* in both acknowledging and dealing practically with the blocks experienced by many nonexempts. Managers accustomed to using terminology and behavior that reinforce class barriers within the organization (i.e., "I'll get my girl to do it") are unlikely to do more than foster an unhealthy combination of dependence and ongoing frustration in their nonexempt workers. Intentional changes in corporate culture and climate—transformations initiated and supported by top management—help many managers supply the kind of guidance that can genuinely enhance the career opportunities and choices of nonexempts.

In the companies of the professionals interviewed, career development programming emphasizes *networking, information sharing,* and *taking responsibility for one's career* as crucial for all employees, nonexempt as well as salaried. In another large organization, Lockheed Marine of Seattle, Washington, the career development process devised in the mid-1980s for nonexempts entailed an effective mix of career/life planning classes, a career resource center offering diverse literature and workbooks, and a "lifelong learning program" that involved employees, together with their families, in continuing education. Weekend seminars and full tuition reimbursement for work-related coursework were among the offerings of Lockheed's program, which markedly increased the internal promotions of nonexempts into salaried positions (Russell, 1984).

Such a model and set of principles bears imitating, but getting from a commitment to helping nonexempts develop personally and professionally to an effective program for career development is not a simple undertaking. Naturally, there is no one blueprint for success, but certain processes and activities clearly enhance the prospects for a useful program. A career planning and development program devised and refined by Corning during the 1980s—a program highlighting some of the major questions that must be asked by career development professionals charged with addressing the special needs of the nonexempt population—is still a model for the corporate world.

The Corning System: Objectives and Design

The original impetus for Corning's career development efforts on behalf of its nonexempt workforce was its "Total Quality" program, through which the company articulates its commitment to identifying and meeting the requirements of both its customers and its employees. The Corporate Values Statement, initiated in 1983, contained a statement regarding the value of the individual at Corning with important implications for nonexempt employees: "Each employee must have the opportunity to participate fully, to grow professionally, and to develop to his or her highest potential."

In more concrete terms, that statement has led to a multidimensional system that helps individuals take primary responsibility for their career planning. The system gives nonexempts a process, tools, information, and skills to enable them to develop their careers in two specific ways:

- By focusing on current job performance and determining how they can enrich their present jobs rather than looking at career planning only in terms of upward movement.
- By working closely with supervisors on formulating a realistic development plan consistent with the overall goals of the organization.

Employees at Corning's upstate New York facility helped design the system now in place—a fact that has undoubtedly added to the quality and degree of employee ownership of the system. A steering committee comprising divisional HR staff helped with system design. Design criteria were related to the roles of the three key players at Corning: the employee, the supervisor, and the organization. All design elements were piloted and evaluated by groups of supervisors and employees. Impelling the entire design process was the recognized need to promote realistic goals for employees and to tie in the career development process with Corning's performance development and review (PD&R) process, which was the existing performance appraisal system.

Corning's management had already acknowledged and decided to exploit the natural links between the PD&R process and career planning. However, the process was handicapped by:

- Lack of employee participation in the appraisal process.
- Lack of sufficient time for appraisal interviews.
- Lack of sufficient career information and consequent lack of realism in employee career planning.
- Lack of understanding of the placement process.
- Lack of employee ownership of developmental objectives.

Without a clear developmental component, the PD&R process had become too appraisal-oriented. The new Career Planning and Information System brought new vitality to the performance appraisal process and introduced a needed retraining and development focus.

The System's Components

The system consists of a computer software package, three videos, information books, and two days of supervisory training. Included in the software package are four programs that each address a question employees often ask about their career development. *Who Am I?* deals with the employee's skills, values, and interests as they relate to his or her career. *How Am I Seen?* discusses the perceptions of colleagues and supervisors and their implications for the employee. *What Are My Goals and Alternatives?* addresses the realism of career goals in the Corning context. And *How Can I Achieve My Goals?* deals with formulating a realistic development plan to help the employee attain his or her goals.

The videos, designed in conjunction with the software, assist each employee through the steps of self-assessment, goal setting, and action planning. *Your Career Is Up to You* defines career planning at Corning and identifies tools available to help the employee plan his or her own career. *Career Directions at Corning* highlights the career opportunities in the five functional areas open to nonexempt employees. *How to Use All You've Learned to Plan Your Career* reviews the planning process, clarifies the employee's role in that process, and explains how career planning fits into the performance appraisal process. It also outlines the range of tangible and intangible educational and training factors that affect career planning and offers information regarding the move from nonexempt to exempt status.

The information book entitled *The Career Planning Matrix Book* lists all nonexempt positions in the Corning, New York, area by title and salary grade. It also includes a skills inventory for functional areas along with model job descriptions for each salary grade in each functional area. In addition, the book gives this information for entry-level exempt positions—

for use by high-level nonexempts who may seek to move to the exempt group. *The Career Information Book* offers information on demographics and trends in employment, including career statistics, sample career paths, and data to help in career planning.

The one-day supervisory training course helps managers link the career planning process to the PD&R process. This training ensures that managers have the requisite knowledge and skills to hold effective career discussions with their employees. It is organized around four managerial roles and associated skills: coach, appraiser, advisor, and developer.

Implementing the System

To make the new system broadly available to its employees, Corning's management decentralized the system's implementation. After the design work had been completed, each division introduced the program in its area. The corporate HR department trained the trainers and provided the materials needed to market the system internally. Each division selected its own methods of introduction and implementation; this flexible approach enhanced the sense of ownership and employee participation that each division sought for the new system. Typical introductions to the system entailed a formal presentation to the division's top management, followed by a written announcement to divisional employees and their supervisors, along with group informational meetings.

Initially, the company created 14 career planning and information system sites. Each was overseen by a coordinator—a nonexempt employee who performed this role in addition to other duties. These sites were in effect small career resource centers; each offered the software package, videos, and information books as well as supporting materials. The coordinator's role was to explain the career planning and development process to employees, assist with technical difficulties, answer questions, and direct employees to relevant resources. Coordinators also served as troubleshooters who could notify the corporate HR staff of any problems in the process. Coordinators took pride in their role, noting that they had been given increased responsibility and status.

Updating the System

Corning's management conceived the Career Planning and Information System as an evolving process responsive to internal and external changes. Since initial system implementation in 1985, the system's software has been upgraded; each year, the information books are revised. In 1987 a placement service for nonexempts was introduced. It provides information on job openings through a telephone bulletin-board service. Corning made use once again of a participative process to design this placement service, gathering feedback from employees at all corporate levels. Management piloted the program for 10 months and then began listing all nonexempt positions in the Corning, New York, area through the service. Positions are listed weekly (unless organizational restructuring results in a displacement of nonexempt employees).

Recognizing the informal aspects of the hiring process, the service now also allows managers to make lists of potential applicants and integrate that list with a formal listing. The corporate HR department administers the service and passes on all applications to the appropriate hiring manager.

Each week the service lists between one and five openings and receives approximately 500 calls from nonexempt employees—who know that their applications are private and confidential. At present, 30 percent of those employees who have used the service have indicated that they have also used other elements of the Career Planning and Information System.

System Outcomes

In the Corning facility, roughly 600 of 1,500 employees have completed all elements of the system. Moreover, all 700 supervisors have received training in the system. Responses to the system from both employees and supervisors have been enthusiastic. Employees have commented that the system "facilitated discussions with supervisors" and helped them prepare for PD&Rs and focus more clearly on the development of their careers. Supervisors reported that the process helped them "do a better job in giving feedback" and gain a "more in-depth understanding of a person's career development."

A 1989 survey of employees indicated that career planning was the area that had improved most for nonexempts. Of those A&Ts with access to the career development system, more than 30 percent responded favorably to a survey question about the availability of information on career opportunities at Corning. Before the system was implemented, only 15 percent of all A&Ts responded favorably to a similar question posed in a 1984 survey of employees. The A&Ts at Corning's headquarters reported that they felt more positive about making career plans because they understand and can participate in the planning process: it has become one about which they feel considerable ownership. This outcome is particularly welcome in light of the fact that in 1984, these employees responded to a similar survey by reporting that they had little information and few opportunities to develop their careers. Not surprisingly, Corning is now expanding the system to include all its exempt employees.

CONCLUSIONS

Career development programs for nonexempts, such as the processes implemented by Corning, Lockheed Marine, and other pioneering companies, are based on certain shared premises. Chief among these is the belief that addressing the career-related concerns and aspirations of nonexempt staff will have inevitable and positive consequences for the entire organization.

Such a belief has empirical foundations. The chronic frustration of the nonexempt population is apparently costly; it erodes enthusiasm and performance, increases turnover, and spills over sooner or later into other ranks. In an era when "working smart," flexibility, and efficiency are prized characteristics of any workforce (blue-collar or white-collar, manufacturing or service), organizations cannot afford not to examine more closely the career development needs of their nonsalaried workers.

In a mid-1980s study, Harvard sociologist Jerry Jacobs, studying the relationship of economic sectors and career mobility, came to the conclusion that the "collar line" has a greater effect on career mobility than do industrial or economic sectors. Differences in educational requirements between white- and blue-collar jobs, stated Jacobs, "reduce the likelihood of moves in both directions" (1983, p. 420). Interestingly, channels of information and patterns of information exchange may be responsible, according to Jacobs, for modest sectoral differences in mobility between jobs requiring similar skill levels. This implies that the ways in which workers find out about career opportunities and job openings may affect their willingness to explore new options—although education-level barriers must still be crossed, and the "collar line" may be an insuperable obstacle for many nonexempts.

Clearly, despite the real and perceived obstacles to upward career mobility, there are many exciting career-enhancement possibilities for the nonexempt population. Networking, information sharing, career workshops, tuition reimbursement—all are important and effective aids. So, too, are the sophisticated, multi-dimensional programs of companies such as Corning. It would seem that the first step for career development specialists is to recognize the genuine value of cultivating a nonexempt workforce that is prepared to help improve its own prospects: to begin a process of empowerment that will bring about lasting changes in attitude, morale, and productivity.

REFERENCES

Jacobs, J. "Industrial Sector and Career Mobility Reconsidered," *American Sociological Review 48* (1983), pp. 415–421.

Russell, M. "Career Planning in a Blue-Collar Company," *Training and Development Journal 38* (1984), pp. 87–88.

Chapter 18

NEW DIRECTIONS IN CAREER ASSESSMENT

Mark L. Savickas

This chapter discusses current developments in career assessment. In particular, the chapter describes new assessment models and measures that can be useful to career counselors. The chapter consists of three sections. The first section, "Assessment of Career Themes," describes the emergence of narrative psychology as an important model for career assessment. It also explains how the model may increase interest in relatively obscure measures of career development. The second section of the chapter, "Assessment of Career Decision Making," deals with measures that assess the decision-making process among adolescents and young adults who are making career choices. The third and final section, "Assessment of Career Adaptability," addresses measures of the vocational development process in working adults.

Assessment of Career Themes

Most vocational psychologists and career counselors base their work on the philosophy known as logical positivism (Brown and Brooks, 1990). Because positivism focuses attention on objective reality, it has produced career development theories and interventions that emphasize verifiable action. Thus in doing vocational appraisals, career counselors use assessment models and measures that deal with clients' manifest behavior and quantifiable traits. After measuring clients' interests and abilities, counselors use these objective observations of clients to identify "realistic" occupational alternatives. This practice may occasionally prompt some counselors to unintentionally treat clients as objects. For example, a counselor can objectify clients by counting their interests and abilities as traits that clients possess rather than learning how clients use their interests and abilities to suit their purposes and express their life pattern.

Although logical positivism still shapes how counselors view career assessment, some counselors have recognized the usefulness of taking a second perspective on career assessment. Rather than replacing positivism, they add the view offered by phenomenology. Accordingly, these counselors complement their objective perspective on clients' careers with a subjective perspective. In assessing subjective experience, counselors apprehend clients' conceptions of their personal experience. The phenomenological perspective leads counselors to help clients understand their own experience. When operating from the phenomenological perspective, counselors elicit clients' conceptions of themselves and their world. Then counselors act as interpreters to help clients understand themselves and the meaning that they give to their lives. When counselors take the phenomenological perspective on assessment, they do more than use the trait theory of individual differences to identify occupations that match clients' interest and ability profiles. They go beyond the view of trait theory and seek to comprehend the meaning of clients' interests and abilities as a part of a life pattern. From this perspective, counselors view interests and abilities as solutions to problems in growing up, not just as quantifiable characteristics. The phenomenological perspective enriches career assessments because counselors can count the interests and abilities that a client *possesses* as well as understand how that client *intends* to use these interests and abilities in fashioning a career.

Why Add the Subjective Perspective?

Three reasons motivate counselors to add the subjective perspective to their objective observations of a client. First, they have learned from research that the phenomenological perspective can increase the predictive accuracy of career assessments. A substantial body of literature about interest assessment indicates that expressed interests either equal or exceed the predictive accuracy of inventoried interests. Moreover, predictive efficiency increases when counselors use objectively inventoried interests in tandem with subjectively expressed vocational aspirations (Holland, Gottfredson, & Baker, 1990). Thus, a comprehensive assessment of a client's interests might combine an examination of the client's occupational daydreams (Touchton & Magoon, 1977) with an objective inventory of the client's interests.

Some counselors have adopted the subjective perspective on career assessment for a second reason. They believe that assessing a client's subjective experience helps counselors to increase their own job satisfaction. Many career counselors have reported their dissatisfaction in providing traditional interventions. They complain that the objective application of the matching model emphasizes the delivery of authoritative guidance and concentrates exclusively on the client's role as worker. These counselors sometimes feel bored as they provide services such as workshops, interest inventory interpretations, occupational information, and computer-assisted guidance. Adding the subjective perspective to their career assessments allows these counselors to reduce the artificial distinction between career and personal counseling. It also emphasizes the counseling relationship rather than the delivery of a service (Slaney & MacKinnon-Slaney, 1990). By attending to a client's subjective experience, these counselors enlarge the arena of career counseling beyond the work role. A counselor who understands a client's life themes and tensions can assist the client in preparing to play multiple roles at work, in the home, and throughout the community. In addition, counselors may use life-theme insights to become therapeutically involved in the lives of their clients (Slaney & MacKinnon-Slaney, 1990).

A third reason has also motivated counselors to add the subjective perspective to their career assessments. Advances in other specialties within psychology have prompted career counselors to think about models and methods for assessing how clients subjectively experience their careers. Counselors have enriched their perspective on career assessment by learning about "life narrative psychology" as it has been articulated by developmental psychologists (Mandler, 1984; Whitbourne & Dannefer, 1986), social psychologists, (Gergen and Gergen, 1986; Scheibe, 1986), cognitive scientists (Lehnert, 1981) and personality theorists (McAdams & Ochberg, 1988). In considering this literature, counselors quickly concluded that they can use client narratives to access the subjective experience of self and career. Stories that people tell about their education, work history, and vocational aspirations reveal recurring situations, characters, and plots. Counselors can analyze these story elements to uncover the characteristic themes and tensions that shape clients' lives. In assessing career stories, counselors can also make connections that enable clients to recognize the meaning of their behavior. For example, by connecting scenes from the past with potential scenarios for the future, counselors can help clients to answer questions such as: Who am I? Where did I come from? Where am I going? Who is my enemy? What must I struggle against? Therapeutic dialogue between counselor and client occurs when together they reinterpret the text of the client's career to make better sense and to allow choice or change. Because people change their ways by changing their stories, the narrative psychology approach to career counseling can legitimately be called career therapy (Blustein, 1987).

Assessment Models

Counselors who seek to recognize life themes must act as biographers who interpret lives in progress rather than as actuaries who count interests and abilities. To learn biographical methods, counselors may consult a growing literature on the phenomenology of careers. Classic articles about life-theme models for career assessment emerged from Super's (1954) work on career pattern theory and Csikzentmihalyi and Beattie's (1979) work on the origin of life themes. More recent life-theme models have been offered by Carlsen (1988), Cochran (1990), MacGregor and Cochran (1988), Miller-Tiedeman (1988), Savickas (1988, 1989), Watkins and Savickas (1990), Young (1988), and Young and Collin (1988). These writers emphasize the importance of understanding the meaning that clients invest in their careers. They each suggest that the essence of assessing a client's subjective experience consists of analyzing life stories to identify themes.

Typically, the clinical assessment methods associated with life-theme models are more like structured interviews than objective psychometric inventories. Kvale (1983) described three phases of an assessment interview and three levels of assessment interpretations. During the first phase of an assessment interview, clients describe their experiences and feelings in response to the counselor's open questions about their lives. The counselor listens to narratives and asks clients to elaborate important or ambiguous aspects of a story. During this initial phase, the counselor does not offer any interpretations of the narratives. In the second phase of an assessment interview, the counselor prompts clients to recognize new relationships among the activities and feelings described in their narratives. Making connections creates new meaning for the client. The assessment interview concludes with a third phase during which the counselor condenses and interprets the meanings in clients' narratives and asks clients to correct mistaken interpretations. After concluding the assessment interview, the counselor analyzes interview notes or transcripts to identify a client's life themes and to formulate three types of interpretations dealing with private meaning, public meaning, and therapeutic meaning. First-level interpretations consist of conclusions about what their experiences mean to clients. Second-level interpretations extend that personal meaning by using common-sense to read between the lines and explicitly connect loosely attached ideas. Third-level interpretations use a personality theory to go beyond the client's self-understandings and commonsense meanings.

Assessment Measures

Counselors who want to assess a client's subjective experience use many different methods to elicit life narratives. The four most popular methods are autobiographies, early recollections, structured interviews, and card sorts. These methods are not new; clinical psychologists have used them for years. However, the application of these methods to career assessment is relatively new. The increasing use of these methods by career counselors coincides with their new-found interest in comprehending subjective careers.

Autobiographical Methods. As counselors search to recognize life themes, the client's life history is the central unit to be assessed. Thus, it is little wonder that many counselors use autobiographies to access clients' subjective experience of career. While listening to client narratives about episodes in their lives, counselors can identify themes or particular patterns of interaction with the environment and then uncover recurring plots. Counselors who wish to learn more about autobiographies as an assessment tool may consult Daily's (1971) *Assessment of Lives.* This book provides clear directions on how to conduct a career assessment starting with the simple injunction, "Tell me about your life." Annis (1967) offers a second source of specific questions and interpretive procedures in his review of how counselors use autobiographical techniques. He includes several sets of stimulus questions used by career counselors.

The newest development in autobiographic methods integrates the objective and subjective perspectives on career assessment. The "self-confrontation method" combines an autobiographic interview with objective inventory methods to yield a well-structured survey of a life in progress (Hermans, Fiddelaers, deGroot, & Nauta, 1990). The method consists of three parts. The assessment starts with an interview to identify "valuations." A valuation is a unit of meaning such as a pivotal memory, difficult problem, significant person, personal ideal, or influential experience. The counselor elicits valuations by questioning clients about their past, present, and future (e.g., "Was there something in your past that has been of major importance or significance for your life and which still plays an important part today?"; "Is there in your present life something that is of major importance for, or exerts a great influence, on your existence?"; "Do you foresee something that will be of great importance for, or of major influence on, your future life?"). During the second part of the assessment, the counselor has the client rate each valuation from 0 to 5 on a standard set of 16 affective words (e.g., joy, trust, disappointment). These procedures result in a matrix in the form of a valuations column and an affect row. From this matrix, counselors compute indices for positive affect, negative affect, general experience, affect expressing self-enhancement, and affect referring to contact with other people. During the third part of the assessment, the counselor discusses the results with the client to deepen self-exploration and create meaning by making new connections at both manifest and latent levels. The counselor and client use the resulting self-knowledge to generate new ideas and plan a life direction.

Early Recollections. Several career counselors have constructed structured interviews that seek biographical data particularly relevant in assisting clients to make a career choice. McKelvie (1979) and McKelvie and Friedland (1978, 1981) devised "career goal counseling" to implement Alfred Adler's ideas about career choice. Adler (1964) believed that "choice of the occupation is foreshadowed by some dominant interest of the psychic prototype." McKelvie and Friedland based career goal counseling on the Adlerian concept of life style. Counselors who use this approach begin with an assessment technique that elicits clients' early recollections about their lives. Counselors analyze the early recollections to uncover the individual's life story and its ruling motive. In particular, counselors identify the goals that guide clients' vocational behavior, the obstacles or mistaken ideas that hinder movement toward career goals, and the behaviors that heighten obstacles. Counselors then use this assessment information to help clients recognize and clarify goals, identify obstacles that thwart goal attainment, and develop new strategies to hurdle obstacles and move toward goals.

Structured Interviews. Another approach to identifying life themes is to ask clients a short list of questions about their vocational and educational experiences. Three structured interviews for career assessment have been devised to integrate the objective and subjective perspectives on clients' vocational lives. Savickas' (1989) career-style interview uses eight questions to elicit a client's subjective perspective on career choice. The interview manual describes how to combine this assessment of subjective experience with the results of objective interest inventories such as the Vocational Preference Inventory or the Self-Directed Search. Kurtz (1974) integrated the objective and subjective perspectives for career assessment by combining Strong Interest Inventory results with a structured interview based on the Transactional Analysis model. Clawson, Kotter, Faux, and McArthur (1985) provide a workbook modeled after the "Self-Assessment and Career Development" course in the MBA program at the Harvard Business School. By answering the questions and performing the exercises that constitute the workbook, individuals learn to understand and manage their careers using both the objective and the subjective perspectives. All three of these structured interviews assess the interests and abilities that a client possesses and how the client uses them to establish a suitable and viable occupational choice.

Card Sorts. Another technique that may combine objective and subjective perspectives is card sorts. Sorting tasks have been shown to reveal clients' individuality (Tyler, 1961). Vocational card-sort techniques use a deck of cards in which each card states a vocational or educational stimulus such as occupational titles from the Strong Interest Inventory and Holland's RIASEC typology, basic interest groups from the Strong Interest Inventory, descriptions of Holland's RIASEC types, leisure activities, and community organizations. Recently constructed card sorts have used work tasks categorized by data, people, things, and ideas (Career Systems, 1985) as well as occupational titles grouped by gender type and prestige level (Brooks, 1988). In using a card sort, counselors ask clients to sort the cards into groups of "like," "dislike," and "no opinion." Counselors may choose to designate different categories for the groups and to use more than three groups. As clients engage in the sorting task, counselors ask clients to think aloud. Counselors then use probing questions to explore pivotal choices by asking clients to further articulate their reasoning or describe episodes from their lives that explain their choices. Analyzing a client's decision-making process and reasons for choices allows the counselor to discern the client's personality pattern and life themes. With these assessment data, counselors can identify what clients affirm and deny as they navigate their life course and design their careers. Detailed instructions on how to use vocational card sorts can be found in Gysbers and Moore (1986) or Slaney and MacKinnon-Slaney (1990).

Assessment of Career Decision Making

As noted above, the assessment of career content now pays more attention to subjective experience. This movement has not produced novel assessment measures or methods. Rather, counselors' interest in assessing clients' subjective experience of vocational development content has increased the popularity of methods that have long been available. In contrast, counselors' increasing interest in the vocational development process has produced many new measures for assessing how clients advance their careers. This section deals with new ways of assessing the decision-making process of high school and college students. The next section deals with assessing career adaptability in adults.

Career counselors have always recognized that clients who seek help with decision making may benefit from different interventions. The originator of the matching model for career counseling suggested that counselors use developmental assessments to guide differential treatment of clients. In describing the goals of an initial counseling interview, Frank Parsons advised counselors to classify clients into two types.

> First, those who have well-developed aptitudes and interests and a practical basis for a reasonable conclusion in respect to the choice of a vocation. Second, boys and girls with so little experience that there is no basis yet for a wise decision (Parsons, 1909/1967).

In the following decades, counselors tried to heed Parson's advice to assess client readiness to make career choices. They devised many diagnostic schemes in unsuccessful attempts to identify types of clients who would benefit from different career interventions (Crites, 1969).

During the 1970s, counselors turned their attention to using client differences in decidedness to predict outcomes of career treatments (Fretz & Leong, 1982). Before that time, researchers had used just two categories—*decided* and *undecided*—to classify a client's decisional status. By the mid 1970s, many researchers and practitioners had learned to view decisional status as a continuum rather than a dichotomy. The prototypal work performed by Osipow and his colleagues helped to popularize the process view of decidedness. Osipow, Carney, Winer, Yanico, and Koschier (1976) constructed the Career Decision Scale (CDS) to measure indecision. The

CDS allowed counselors to quickly assess high school and college students' degree of indecision. Osipow, Carney, and Barak (1976) then used the CDS to identify four dimensions within the problem of indecision. Subsequently, numerous researchers have tried to identify stable dimensions of career indecision and have suggested corresponding CDS subscales for use in differential diagnosis. Vondracek, Hostetler, Schulenberg, and Shimizu (1990) recently reported on the status of this line of inquiry.

Indecision Measures: The Second Generation

The first generation of instruments to assess career indecision included the Career Decision Scale, Vocational Decision Scale (Jones & Chenery, 1980) and the Vocational Decision-Making Difficulties Scale (Holland, Gottfredson, & Nafziger, 1973). These three instruments engendered extensive research on the differential diagnosis of indecision. Recently, several researchers have contributed to this research stream by constructing a second generation of career indecision measures. These measures are more complex because they operationally define career indecision as a multidimensional construct. Each of the four measures described below provides a way to differentiate clients by career choice status and potentially answers the attribute-intervention question, "Who gets which intervention?"

Commitment to Career Choices Scale. The Commitment to Career Choices Scale (Blustein, Ellis, & Devenis, 1989) measures two dimensions of the commitment process. The "Vocational Exploration and Commitment" subscale uses 19 items to measure commitment to career choices. The items deal with perceived self-knowledge, occupational knowledge, awareness of obstacles, need to explore, and confidence about and commitment to a specific occupational preference. The "Tendency to Foreclose" subscale uses 9 items to measure how one commits to career choices. The items deal with willingness to consider more than one occupation at a time, the belief that more than one occupation can suit an individual, and tolerance for ambiguity in making career commitments. Individuals who foreclose their career choices make early commitments to career choices without thorough exploration or provisional commitment. The theoretical constructs measured by these two subscales are carefully discussed and documented in the monograph that introduced the measure (Blustein, Ellis, & Devenis, 1989). The theory behind the Commitment to Career Choices Scale and its impressive psychometric characteristics both recommend the scale for future research on differential diagnosis and treatment of career indecision.

Fear of Commitment Scale. Many researchers who have considered the dimensions of indecision have suggested that indecisiveness differs qualitatively from undecidedness (Crites, 1969; Jones, 1989; Tyler, 1961). Undecided students encounter difficulty in making a career choice but do not experience impaired decision making in other life domains. By contrast, indecisive students seem to have pervasive difficulty in making decisions in most life domains. This difficulty stems from personality problems such as low self-esteem, high anxiety, dependency on other people, external locus of control, and behavioral inhibition. To date, counselors who wish to screen career clients for indecisiveness face two unattractive choices. On the one hand, counselors can assume that extreme scores on indecision measures (e.g., Career Decision Scale) indicate indecisiveness. Defining indecisiveness as extreme indecision confuses multifaceted career undecidedness with generalized indecisiveness. This quantitative definition misses the qualitative distinction between career indecision and pervasive indecisiveness. On the other hand, some counselors have used a profile of scores from career indecision, anxiety, and self-esteem inventories to screen for indecisiveness. Unfortunately, these assessment batteries typically are too time consuming and expensive for routine use in screening career clients.

An innovative measure constructed by Serling and Betz (1990) attempts to advance our understanding and treatment of indecisiveness by constructing a measure to distinguish career indecision from pervasive indecisiveness. They constructed the Fear of Commitment Scale (FOC) to measure the relatively stable disposition to respond to choices in many important life domains with impaired decision making. The impaired decision making stems from anticipation of negative outcomes such as (a) performing poorly, (b) losing options, (c) making wrong choice, (d) displeasing significant others, (e) being disliked, (f) fearing success, and (g) acknowledging imperfections. Because of its theoretical coherence and sound psychometric characteristics, the FOC scale has the potential to significantly advance our understanding of indecisiveness and to provide a practical way to differentiate undecidedness from indecisiveness.

Career Factors Inventory. The Career Factors Inventory (Chartrand, Robbins, Morrill, & Boggs, 1990) provides a multidimensional measure of career indecision. Its authors reasoned that "informational and personal-emotional factors interact to either facilitate or to inhibit the career decision-making process." Thus, they constructed two informational and two personal-emotional scales. The two information scales measure "Need for Career Information" (6 items) such as facts about occupations and "Need for Self-Knowledge" (4 items) about personal qualities such as capabilities and interests. High scores on these two scales indicate a need for either more vocational exploration and experience or more self-definition and discovery. The two personal-emotional scales measure "Career Choice Anxiety" (6 items) attached to the vocational decision-making process and "Generalized Indecisiveness" (5 items) even when the conditions necessary for making a choice are present. High scores on these two scales indicate a need for anxiety reduction or decisional training. Counselors formulate differential career interventions based on profiles of the four scale scores. For example, counselors might treat a student with high informational and low personal-emotional scores with cognitive intervention and treat a student showing the opposite pattern with supportive counseling.

Career Decision Profile. The Career Decision Profile (CDP; Jones, 1989) assesses a client's degree of decidedness, degree of comfort with decisional status, and reasons for being decided or undecided. The CDP "Decidedness" scale consists of two questions that deal with occupational field and occupational choice. "Comfort" is measured by two items about being at ease with or worried about one's career choice. Four 3-item scales measure the reasons dimension. The "Self-Clarity" scale deals with self-knowledge about interests, ability, and personality. The "Knowledge About Occupations and Training" scale deals with information about occupations of interest and their educational requirements. The "Decisiveness" scale deals with ability to decide without unnecessary delay, difficulty, or reliance upon other people. The "Career Choice Importance" scale deals with the client's feelings about the importance of work and making a career choice. The scores on the "Decidedness" and "Comfort" scales can be used to identify a client's decisional status as decided/comfortable, decided/uncomfortable, undecided/ comfortable, or undecided/uncomfortable. Counselors can then examine the client's scores on the reasons scales to learn the antecedents of the client's decisional status. Describing the client's decisional status and the reasons for that status prepares the counselor to prescribe unique interventions that facilitate the client's vocational decision making and career choice.

Assessment of Career Adaptability

In conducting a career assessment with high school or college students, counselors typically concentrate on decision-making problems because students usually want help with making career choices. Because counselors assume that the problem is the need to make a choice, they use measures that assess how clients cope with that problem. Note that the measures described earlier in this chapter each dealt with diagnosing problems in decision making.

In conducting a career assessment with adults, counselors cannot concentrate on just decision-making problems because adults also seek help with problems of career adaptation. Adults in the work force face a heterogeneous set of problems in adapting to changes in work or working conditions. Therefore, in performing career assessments with adults, counselors must first find the source of the client's career problem. Accordingly, they need measures that identify the problem *and* measures that appraise coping responses to that problem.

The homogeneity in career choice problems faced by high school and college students made the development of decision-making measures easier. By assuming that the problem was career choice, test constructors could concentrate on measuring decision-making difficulties and resources. By contrast, the heterogeneity in career problems faced by adults has hindered development of career adaptability measures (Super & Knasel, 1981; Savickas, Passen, & Jarjoura, 1988). In constructing adaptability measures, researchers chose to first deal with identifying career problems. Thus, the first measure of career adaptability, the Adult Career Concerns Inventory, dealt only with identifying career problems. Subsequent measures, such as the Career Mastery Inventory and the Occupational Stress Inventory, attempt to both identify career problems and appraise coping repertoires. Each of these three innovative inventories of career adaptability provides unique career assessment information because each one uses a different model to comprehend adult vocational development.

Adult Career Concerns Inventory. The Adult Career Concerns Inventory (ACCI; Super, Thompson, & Lindeman, 1988) indicates the type of career development problem that concerns an individual. However, it does not reveal whether the concern is prompted by requirements or opportunities for developmental task coping, adaptive problem solving, or occupational change. For example, a client's ACCI profile may indicate a concern with vocational exploration. This concern could be prompted by the need to declare a college major, specify a career choice, orient oneself to a new career stage, explain one's job failure and dissatisfaction, or recycle to a different occupational field.

The ACCI measures concerns associated with four stages in Super's model of vocational development: exploration, establishment, maintenance, and decline. Each career stage is represented by three 5-item subscales that measure a unique concern. The three exploration stage concerns are *crystallizing* preferences for an occupational field and level that matches one's interests and abilities; *specifying* a particular occupational choice within that field and level; and tentatively *implementing* that choice by securing an entry-level position in that occupation. The three establishment stage concerns are *stabilizing* oneself in an occupational position, *consolidating* one's hold on that position, and *advancing* to the next position in that occupation's career path. The three maintenance stage concerns are *holding on* to the position that one has attained, *updating* the knowledge and skills used in that position, and *innovating* new ways of doing the work involved in that position. The three disengagement stage concerns are *decelerating* one's career by reducing the work load, *retirement planning,* and *retirement living.*

Clients respond to the five items in each subscale on a 5-point Likert scale that ranges from no concern to great concern. Higher scores indicate greater concern. By plotting a client's subscale scores on the profile sheet, the counselor can assess how involved the client is with each of the 12 types of concerns. In considering the profile as a whole, counselors can discern the maturational and adaptive tasks that preoccupy the client. For example, if a 40-year old client expresses great concern with specifying and advancing, then the counselor may surmise that the client needs to explore the next steps on the career path in his or her current organization or consider seeking a higher level position in a different organization.

The ACCI can be used for more than just individual career counseling. It also provides an excellent means for surveying employees' career development status and needs. Specialists in organizational development have used ACCI surveys to plan in-service workshops and to diagnose productivity and morale problems. The ACCI can also be used as a lesson plan to teach career theory to graduate students or to orient students and employees to the maturational tasks that they should anticipate and the coping attitudes and behaviors they should cultivate.

Career Mastery Inventory. The Career Mastery Inventory (CMI; Crites, 1990) consists of two parts. Part 1 measures degree of coping with the maturational tasks of adult vocational development. Part 2 measures work adjustment mechanisms that adults use to solve problems at work. Counselors can use the first part to identify the client's career problems and the second part to appraise how the client copes with those problems.

Part 1 of the CMI consists of six scales which measure coping with six vocational development tasks of the career establishment stage: (1) Organizational Adaptability, (2) Position Performance, (3) Work Habits and Attitudes, (4) Coworker Relationships, (5) Advancement, and (6) Career Choice and Plans. Each scale contains 15 items. Clients respond to the items on a 7-point Likert scale. Higher scale scores indicate greater task mastery. A profile of the six scale scores portrays a client's progress along the continuum of vocational development tasks that define the three phases of the establishment stage.

As described in the foregoing section on the ACCI, Super's model of career development defines three major phases for the years from occupational entry to midcareer (i.e., establishment stage). Each phase is characterized by concerns about stabilizing, consolidating, and advancing one's occupational position. The CMI scales for "Position Performance" and for "Organizational Adaptability" indicate how well clients have coped with the stabilizing phase of early establishment. Poor performance or conflict with organizational values prevents stabilization and generally forces an individual to find a more fitting position within the same occupation or to enter a new occupation.

Once individuals stabilize in their positions, they should attend to consolidating their job by forming cooperative relationships with coworkers and sustaining positive work habits and attitudes over the long haul. The CMI scales for "Coworker Relationships" and for "Work Habits and Attitudes" measure the degree to which an individual has become a dependable producer with a positive attitude. Failure to deal effectively with interpersonal problems on the job is the most frequent reason for leaving a position during the consolidation phase of the establishment years. Mastery of the twin tasks leading to consolidation prepares people to enter the advancement phase of the establishment stage.

The CMI scales for "Advancement" and for "Career Choice and Plans" measure the degree to which an individual has mastered the tasks of career advancement. The "Advancement" scale looks to the intermediate future and indicates the degree to which individuals know about the career paths in their organizations and know how to move to the next position. The "Career Choice and Plans" scale looks to the long-range future and indicates the degree to which individuals know how they want to spend the rest of their working lives. Often, people who are actively coping with the career planning task are viewed as having a "midcareer crisis." However, not all workers suffer a crisis as they face this task. Many workers, after a period of reflection, move smoothly into the maintenance stage (i.e., the years from midcareer to retirement) and deal with the tasks of holding, updating, and innovating their positions. Workers who spend significant time dealing with the task of career planning at midlife may be in a renewal stage (Murphy and Burck, 1976; Williams & Savickas, 1990). During a period of renewal, people thoroughly reassess their careers and lives. They dream about alternative futures, examine their direction in life, reorganize their priorities, and consider changing occupations. The reassessment may result in (a) reaffirmation of the present occupational position through updating and innovating, (b) reordering priorities to devote more time to family and leisure while holding on to the present position, or (c) redirecting oneself into a different occupational field and recycling through the tasks of stabilizing, consolidating, and advancing in a new occupational position.

Part 2 of the CMI deals with problem solving and complements Part 1 (problem identification). The second part of the CMI contains 20 multiple-choice questions that deal with strategies for resolving problems at work. Each question consists of a stem that describes a typical problem which may arise at work. After reading the stem, clients select a behavioral response from three alternatives. The three options purport to represent (1) Integrative, (2) Adjustive, and (3) Nonadjustive mechanisms for dealing with problems.

Because an integrative response is accurate and socially reasonable, it produces a change in the objective situation or solves the problem. Crites defines an integrative response as one that removes thwarting conditions and reduces tension or anxiety.

An adjustive response deals with problems by changing the subjective situation to safeguard self-esteem. These responses reduce anxiety or tension but they do not remove the thwarting conditions. Adjustive responses accomplish subjective relief by some conscious negation or unconscious distortion of the objective situation. Adjustive responses include coping mechanisms (Menaghan & Merves, 1984) such as restricted expectations (e.g., work is not supposed to be fun), optimistic comparisons (e.g., I am luckier than most people), and selective attention (e.g., for every bad part there is a good part). Some problems create more anxiety than an individual can handle with conscious coping mechanisms. In these situations, individuals may resort to using unconscious defense mechanisms such as displacement, regression, projection, and reaction formation. Adjustive responses succeed when they buy the time that allows the objective situation to change or the individual to develop an integrative response. Adjustive responses fail to help individuals when they become repetitive and perpetual. The continual shoring up of defenses against anxiety and tension produces a false equilibrium sustained by behavioral rigidity and compartmentalization of life.

Nonadjustive responses are alternatives to integrative problem solving or adjustive coping and defense. According to Crites, nonadjustive responses neither remove thwarting conditions nor reduce tension and anxiety. Nonadjustive responses exacerbate the problematic situation and increase tension and anxiety. Eventually, most individuals withdraw from the problem into mental illness, malingering, quitting, running away, psychophysical illness, or substance abuse.

In scoring the work adjustment section of the CMI, integrative responses earn 3 points, adjustive responses earn 2 points, and nonadjustive responses earn 1 point. The total score may range from 20 to 60. Presumably people with higher scores (more integrative) experience greater job success and satisfaction because they solve work problems as they arise. Individuals with lower scores are more likely to fail at work and feel dissatisfied. In terms of counseling, higher scores indicate a need for encouragement and reinforcement of current adjustment mechanisms. Middle scores indicate the need to learn how to formulate integrative responses and how to tolerate more stress without resorting to adjustive mechanisms. Counselors can help clients learn to problem solve and relax through training workshops, support groups, and individual counseling. Low scores suggest a need for confrontation by supportive colleagues or a need to change environments (e.g., new job, hospitalization, vacation).

The current version of the CMI resulted from 15 years of research on its predecessor, the Career Adjustment and Development Inventory (CADI; Crites, 1975, 1982). The work adjustment section of the CADI differs in format from its corresponding section on the CMI. As described above, the CMI measures adjustive strategies using 20 multiple-choice items. The CADI measures adjustive strategies using the same item stems but not in a multiple choice format. Instead, they serve as sentence completion stems. The multiple choice alternatives used in the CMI are based on responses clients had written to the CADI incomplete sentences.

Obviously, the CMI multiple-choice format works better for research, screening, and surveys. Yet, the CADI sentence-completion format seems to be particularly useful for career counseling with individuals and for career development training with small groups or large classes. Using the sentence-completion format with individuals allows the counselor to see idiosyncratic responses that reveal the subjective world of the client. These responses provide the counselor with access to a client's life themes. When working with groups or classes, counselors can use the sentence-completion form as a lesson plan. After the participants respond individually to the stems, they can work together to construct "ideal" responses to the 20 problems. The process of constructing ideal responses and thinking about them expands the problem-solving repertoire of each participant.

Taken together, the two parts of the CMI give a comprehensive picture of a client's work problems (Part 1) and problem-solving repertoire (Part 2). Because the two parts of the CMI address distinct issues, each part uses a different conceptual model. Part 1 of the CMI operationally defines developmental tasks in the tradition of developmental psychologists such as Havighurst (1953) and Super (1957). Part 2 of the CMI applies the traditional conception of problem solving articulated by clinicians who specialized in the psychology of adjustment (Shaffer and Shoben, 1956). A different perspective on the source of career problems has emerged from social psychology leading to a third measure of career adaptability that uses the psychology of social roles to comprehend adult vocational development.

Occupational Stress Inventory. Osipow and Spokane (1987) constructed the Occupational Stress Inventory (OSI) to measure adaptation to work role stressors that may disrupt person-position fit or exacerbate an existing misfit. The OSI applies to all occupations because it measures generic pressures inherent in occupations as work roles, not the specific pressures pertaining to a particular occupation such as nursing or engineering. The OSI implements a conceptual model of stress that links perceived job stress to experienced psychological strain. According to the model, both the activating stress and the consequent strain can be alleviated by coping behaviors that reestablish homeostasis. Therefore, the OSI also measures coping resources for countering the effects of occupational stress and strain. The OSI operationalizes its stimulus-organism-response (S–O–R) model with three sets of scales that measure occupational stress, psychological strain, and coping resources.

The Occupational Roles Questionnaire (ORQ) measures six types of occupational stress with six 10-item scales. Because stress is primarily viewed from the social-role perspective, five of the scales measure role stress (Overload, Insufficiency, Ambiguity, Boundary, Responsibility). The sixth scale in the ORQ measures stress that arises from toxins or extreme conditions in the physical environment where work occurs. Each ORQ scale contains ten items that assess the frequency, intensity, and duration of a particular type of stress.

The Personal Strain Questionnaire (PSQ) measures psychological strain with four 10-item scales. The "Vocational Strain" scale deals with problems in work output and quality as well as boredom and absenteeism. The "Psychological Strain" scale assesses intrapersonal problems such as depression, anxiety, irritability, and sleep disturbance. The "Interpersonal Strain" scale addresses interpersonal problems such as argumentativeness and withdrawal. The "Physical Strain" scale measures motivational changes and physical complaints such as lethargy and tension.

The Personal Resources Questionnaire measures coping resources with four 10-item scales. The "Recreation" scale measures the extent to which clients use rest, relaxation, and recreation to repair the damage done by occupational stress and psychological strain. The "Self-Care" scale indicates the extent to which clients engage in good health habits with regard to nutrition, sleep, and exercise. The "Social Support" scale measures the extent to which clients feel succor from at least one sympathetic person. The "Rational/ Cognitive Coping" scale indicates the extent to which clients use their intellectual resources to deal with problems at work.

In addition to its use in career counseling to improve occupational adaptation, the OSI can be used to assess organizational culture. Such assessments may guide redesign of a work context or job tasks. Sometimes the identified stressors cannot be changed. In these situations, counselors may orient workers to the occupational stress peculiar to that job or work unit and describe ways that workers can reduce their vulnerability to psychological strain.

CONCLUSION

In approaching the 21st century, counselors seem to be moving career assessment in three new directions. First, counselors are showing more interest in assessing how clients' subjectively experience their careers. An increasing number of counselors elicit life-story narratives by using autobiographies, early recollections, structured interviews, and card sorts. Analyzing narratives enables counselors to identify the life themes and tensions that pattern a client's career. Second, counselors have intensified their efforts to diagnose decisional problems. These efforts have produced a new generation of career indecision measures and provided ways to study important constructs such as pervasive indecisiveness and foreclosure in career decision making. Third, counselors have begun to overcome obstacles that have thwarted the measurement of adult vocational development. Separating the identification of career problems from the appraisal of problem-solving mechanisms has enabled counselors to construct innovative measures of career adaptability. These novel measures deal with adult career concerns, vocational development tasks, and adaptive problems as well as the adaptive mechanisms and coping resources that may resolve these issues. Counselors' increasing interest in subjective experience, types of indecision, and career adaptability should innovate the practice of career assessment as we approach the 21st century.

REFERENCES

Adler, A. (1964). *Problems of neurosis: A book of case histories.* New York: Harper & Row (Originally published, 1929).

Annis, A. (1967). The autobiography: Its uses and value in professional psychology. *Journal of Counseling Psychology, 14,* 9–17.

Blustein, D. L. (1987). Integrating career counseling and psychotherapy: A comprehensive treatment strategy. *Psychotherapy, 24,* 794–799.

Blustein, D. L., Ellis, M. V., & Devenis, L. (1989). The development and validation of a two-dimensional model of the commitment to career choices process. *Journal of Vocational Behavior, 35,* 342–378.

Brooks, L. (1988). Encouraging women's motivation for nontraditional career and lifestyle options: A model for assessment and intervention. *Journal of Career Development, 14*(4), 223–241.

Brown, D., & Brooks, L. (1990). Introduction to career development: Origins, evolution, and current approaches. In D. Brown, & L. Brooks (Eds.), *Career choice and development* (pp. 1–12). San Francisco, CA: Jossey-Bass.

Career Systems, Inc. (1985). *Deal me in.* Silver Springs, MD. Career Systems, Inc.

Carlsen, M. B. (1988). *Meaning-making.* New York: Norton.

Chartrand, J. M., Robbins, S. B., Morrill, W. H., & Boggs, K. (1990). Development and validation of the Career Factors Inventory. *Journal of Counseling Psychology,* *37*(4), 491–501.

Clawson, J., Kotter, J., Faux, V., & McArthur, C. (1985). *Self-Assessment and Career Development* (Second Edition). Englewood Cliffs, NJ: Prentice-Hall.

Cochran, L. (1990). *The sense of vocation.* State University of New York Press.

Collin, A., & Young, R. A. (1986). New directions for theories of career. *Human Relations, 9,* 837–853.

Crites, J. O. (1969). *Vocational psychology: The study of vocational behavior and development.* New York: McGraw-Hill.

Crites, J. O. (1975). *A comprehensive model of career development in early adulthood* (Occasional Paper No. 12). Columbus, OH: Ohio State University National Center for Research in Vocational Education.

Crites, J. O. (1982). Testing for career adjustment and development. *Training and Development Journal, 36,* 21–26.

Crites, J. O. (1990). The Career Maturity Inventory: A measure of career development in adulthood. In M. Savickas, & E. Watkins, Jr. (Chairs), *Emerging directions in career assessment.* Symposium conducted at the meeting of the American Psychological Association, Boston.

Csikszentmihalyi, M., & Beattie, O. V. (1979). Life themes: A theoretical and empirical exploration of their origins and effects. *Journal of Humanistic Psychology, 19,* 45–63.

Dailey, C. (1971). *Assessment of lives.* San Francisco, CA: Jossey-Bass.

Fretz, B. R., & Leong, F. T. L. (1982). Career development status as a predictor of career intervention outcomes. *Journal of Counseling Psychology, 29*(4), 388–393.

Gergen, K. J., & Gergen, M. M. (1986). Narrative form and the construction of psychological science. In T. R. Sarbin (Ed.), *Narrative psychology: The storied nature of human conduct* (pp. 22–44). New York: Praeger.

Gysbers, N. C., & Moore, E. J. (1986). *Career counseling, skills and techniques for practitioners.* Englewood Cliffs, NJ: Prentice-Hall.

Havighurst, R. J. (1953). *Human development and education.* New York: Longmans.

Hermans, H. J. M., Fiddelaers, R., deGroot, R., & Nauta, J. F. (1990). Self-confrontation as a method for assessment and intervention in counseling. *Journal of Counseling and Development, 69*(2), 156–162.

Holland, J. L., Gottfredson, G. D., & Baker, H. G. (1990). Validity of vocational aspirations and interest inventories: Extended; replicated, and reinterpreted. *Journal of Counseling Psychology, 37*(3), 337–342.

Holland, J. L., Gottfredson, G. D., & Nafziger, D. H. (1973). *A diagnostic scheme for specifying vocational assistance* (Rep. No. 164). Baltimore: The Johns Hopkins University, Center for Social Organization of Schools.

Jones, L. K. (1989). Measuring a three-dimensional construct of career indecision among college students: A revision of the vocational decision scale—The Career Decision Profile. *Journal of Counseling Psychology, 36*(4), 477–486.

Jones, L. K., & Chenery, M. F. (1980). Multiple subtypes among vocationally undecided college students: A model and assessment instrument. *Journal of Counseling Psychology, 27*(5), 469–477.

Kurtz, R. R. (1974). Using a Transactional Analysis format in vocational group counseling. *Journal of College Student Personnel, 15*, 447–451.

Kvale, S. (1983). The qualitative research interview: A phenomenological and a hermeneutical mode of understanding. *Journal of Phenomenological Psychology, 14*(2), 171–196.

Lehnert, W. (1981). Plot units and narrative summarization. *Cognitive Science, 4*, 293–331.

MacGregor, A., & Cochran, L. (1988). Work as enactment of family drama. *Career Development Quarterly, 37*, 138–148.

Mandler, J. M. (1984). *Stories, scripts, and scenes: Aspects of schema theory.* Hillsdale, NJ: Erlbaum.

McAdams, D. P., & Ochberg, R. L. (Eds.) (1988). *Psychobiography and life narratives.* Durham/London: Duke University Press.

McKelvie, W. (1979). Career counseling with early recollections. In H. A. Olson (Ed.), *Early recollections: Their use in diagnosis and psychotherapy* (pp. 234–255). Springfield, IL: Charles C Thomas.

McKelvie, W., & Friedland, B. V. (1978). *Career goals counseling: A holistic approach.* Baltimore, MD: F. M. S. Associates.

McKelvie, W., & Friedland, B. V. (1981). The life style and career counseling. In L. Baruth & D. Eckstein (Eds.), *Lifestyle: Theory, practice and research* (2nd ed.) 552(pp. 57–62). Dubuque, IA: Kendall/Hunt.

Menaghan, E. G., & Merves, E. S. (1984). Coping with occupational problems: The limits of individual efforts. *Journal of Health and Social Behavior, 25*, 406–423.

Miller-Tiedeman, A. (1988). *Lifecareer: The quantum leap into a process theory of career.* Vista, CA: Lifecareer Foundation.

Murphy, P. P., & Burck, H. D. (1976). Career development of men at midlife. *Journal of Vocational Behavior, 9*, 337–343.

Osipow, S. H., Carney, C. G., & Barak, A. (1976). A scale of educational-vocational undecidedness: A typological approach. *Journal of Vocational Behavior, 9*, 233–243.

Osipow, S. H., Carney, C. G., Winer, J. L., Yanico, B., & Koschier, M. (1976). *The Career Decision Scale* (3rd revision). Odessa, FL: Psychological Assessment Resources, Inc.

Osipow, S. H., & Spokane, A. R. (1984). Measuring occupational stress, strain, and coping. In S. Oskamp (Ed.), *Applied social psychology annual 5: Applications in organizational settings* (pp. 67–86). Beverly Hills, CA: Sage.

Osipow, S. H., & Spokane, A. R. (1987). *Occupational stress inventory manual.* Odessa, FL: Psychological Assessment Resources, Inc.

Parsons, F. (1909). *Choosing a vocation.* Boston, MA: Houghton-Mifflin.

Savickas, M. L. (1988). An Adlerian view of the publican's pilgrimage. *Career Development Quarterly, 36*, 211–217.

Savickas, M. L. (1989). Annual review: Practice and research in career counseling and development, 1988. *Career Development Quarterly, 38*, 100–134.

Savickas, M. L. (1989). Career-style assessment and counseling. In T. Sweeney (Ed.), *Adlerian counseling: A practical approach for a new decade* (3rd. ed.) (pp. 289–320). Muncie, IN: Accelerated Development.

Savickas, M. L., Passen, A. J., & Jarjoura, D. G. (1988). Career concern and coping as indicators of adult vocational development. *Journal of Vocational Behavior, 33*(1), 82–98.

Scheibe, K. E. (1986). Self-narratives and adventure. In T. R. Sarbin (Ed.), *Narrative psychology: The storied nature of human conduct* (pp. 129–151). New York: Praeger.

Serling, D. A., & Betz, N. E. (1990). Development and evaluation of a measure of fear of commitment. *Journal of Counseling Psychology, 37*(1), 91–97.

Shaffer, L. F., & Shoben, E. J., Jr. (1956). *The psychology of adjustment* (2nd ed.). Boston: Houghton-Mifflin.

Slaney, R. B. (1988). The assessment of career decision making. In W. B. Walsh, & S. H. Osipow (Eds.), *Career decision making* (pp. 33–77). Hillsdale, NJ: Lawrence Erlbaum Associates.

Slaney, R., & McKinnon-Slaney, F. (1990). The vocational card sorts. In C. E. Watkins, Jr., & V. Campbell (Eds.), *Testing in counseling practice* (pp. 317–371). Hillsdale, NJ: Lawrence Erlbaum Associates.

Super, D. (1954). Career patterns as a basis for vocational counseling. *Journal of Counseling Psychology, 1,* 12–19.

Super, D. (1957). *The psychology of careers.* New York: Harper & Row.

Super, D. E., & Knasel, E. G. (1981). Career development in adulthood: Some theoretical problems. *British Journal of Guidance and Counseling, 9,* 194–201.

Super, D. E., Thompson, A. S., & Lindeman, R. H. (1988). *Adult Career Concerns Inventory: Manual for research and exploratory use in counseling.* Palo Alto, CA: Consulting Psychologists Press.

Touchton, J. G., & Magoon, T. M. (1977). Occupational daydreams as predictors of vocational plans of college women. *Journal of Vocational Behavior, 10,* 156–166.

Tyler, L. E. (1961). Research explorations in the realm of choice. *Journal of Counseling Psychology, 8,* 195–202.

Vondracek, F. W., Hostetler, M., Schulenberg, J. E., & Shimizu, K. (1990). Dimensions of career indecision. *Journal of Counseling Psychology, 37*(1), 98–106.

Watkins, E., Jr., & Savickas, M. L. (1990). Psychodynamic career counseling. In B. Walsh, & S. Osipow (Eds.), *Career counseling: Contemporary topics in vocational psychology* (pp. 79–116). Lawrence Erlbaum Associates.

Whitbourne, S. K., & Dannefer, W. D. (1986). The "life drawing" as a measure of time perspective in adulthood. *International Journal of Aging and Human Development, 22*(2), 147–155.

Williams, C. P., & Savickas, M. L. (1990). Developmental tasks of career maintenance. *Journal of Vocational Behavior, 36,* 166–175.

Young, R. A. (1988). Ordinary explanations and career theories. *Journal of Counseling and Development, 66,* 336–339.

Young, R. A., & Collin, A. (1988). Career development and hermeneutical inquiry Part 1: The framework of a hermeneutical approach. *Canadian Journal of Counseling, 22,* 153–161.

Chapter 19

COMPUTER-BASED
CAREER DEVELOPMENT SYSTEMS
ACROSS THE LIFE SPAN

Jo Ann Harris–Bowlsbey

In 1991, computer-based career planning systems will complete the first quarter of a century of their life span. Over that period of time the medium for their delivery has changed dramatically, the target populations to which they are addressed have broadened immensely, and the number of individuals whom they serve has continually grown. What has not changed dramatically is the system content. Early systems, in the late 1960s, were developed by career development theorists, specifically Donald Super, Martin Katz, and David Tiedeman. A central concept was that the computer could "operationalize" the theory of the theorist, that is, teach it to the user so that he or she would be able to internalize it. Thus, after having learned the theory with the computer's help, the user would be able to practice it again and again as similar decisions and choice points emerged in the career development process. Thus, the concept that a computer-aided career planning system should be undergirded by high-quality theory is deeply imbedded in the history of computer-based systems.

At least four examples (U.S. Dept. of H.E.W., 1969) of this thesis are available. Donald Super, for example, developed with the IBM Corporation a system called the Education and Career Exploration System (ECES). This system embodied Super's concepts related to the use of assessment to identify potential occupations, the value of exploratory behavior in the vocational choice process, and the application of a planful process of decision making to vocational choice. David Tiedeman, in a system funded by the United States Office of Education called the Information System for Vocational Decisions (ISVD), programmed the computer to teach the user his decision-making paradigm and then guide the user through that process while experiencing his or her own career development. Martin Katz, funded by the National Science Foundation, developed the System for Interactive Guidance and Information (SIGI) as a way to operationalize his theory of vocational decision-making. This theory focuses on the overarching role

356

of work values in the decision-making process. As with the other systems, this one taught users the theory and guided them through the application of the theory to their personal vocational planning. Simultaneously, the author, a practitioner at the secondary level, developed the Computerized Vocational Information System (CVIS) and later, DISCOVER, funded by the Illinois and the U.S. Office (then Department) of Education. They are based on an eclectic merger of theory, including the theories of John Holland and David Tiedeman and the classification systems of Anne Roe and the American College Testing Program. These examples show that the computer-based career guidance age had firm roots in career development and choice theory.

The decade of the 1970s was the heyday of the career information systems. Funded by the Department of Labor, Bruce McKinlay developed the Career Information System (CIS) which became the model for the state systems subsequently called Career Information Delivery Systems (CIDS), managed and monitored by the State Occupational Information Coordinating Committees (SOICC) and the National Occupational Information Coordinating Committee (NOICC). These systems were not and are not theory-based. Their purpose is not to teach and monitor a theory-based process of career planning that potentially can be applied again and again across the life span. Rather the purpose is to provide high-quality data with which to make informed vocational decisions. The hallmarks of these systems are (1) the development and delivery of quality, localized occupational and manpower information; and (2) the provision of quick access strategies to identify occupations and their related training. Due to the ample level of Federal and State funding for these systems and the relatively shorter time required for user access, they have seen broader implementation to date than have the theory-based career planning systems. There may be, however, some change in this fact in the next decade due to the development of national guidelines for career guidance and the emphasis on them at the Federal level. These guidelines are based on career development theory.

The Decade of the 90s: Computer-Based Systems with a Life-Span Approach

The Medium. In the next ten years, it appears that the medium for the delivery of computer-based career planning systems will continue to be microcomputers. These will be available with compact disk players capable of storing massive amounts of data, graphics, audio, still pictures, and full-motion video. An alternate hardware configuration will be a compact disk player containing a microcomputer which can use a TV monitor as the display device. This advanced hardware will allow exciting enhancements to computer-based systems, making them more effective with an even wider target population—and giving them entree into the home. Thus, both the medium for their delivery and the milieu that receives them will be changed and broadened.

The Message. The focus of this chapter, however, is on the content of computer-based systems across the life span, and attention will now be turned to that topic. One of the major systems, DISCOVER, offers an almost-complete life span approach. The author of the first chapter of this book, Donald E. Super, has provided the theory (Super, 1963) on which a life-span approach can be based. Figure 19-1 provides an overview of that theory and how it has been applied as a basis for DISCOVER system content. The remainder of this chapter will address Super's life stage and implied developmental tasks and illustrate their use in the DISCOVER product line. Developmental tasks are categorized in three groups: self-information; occupational, world-of-work, and career information; and planning/decision-making information.

Stage 1: Growth (ages 0–15)—Elementary School and Junior High/Middle School

To date computer-based career planning systems have been developed for individuals from age 12 (the middle school/junior high years) through retirement. No systems have been developed for students in the elementary school years. Thus, this section will review developmental tasks, propose content, and describe an ideal system that does not exist.

Super's theory indicates that the following developmental tasks are important in the elementary school years:

- developing a strong, clear, positive self-concept.
- developing a sense of planfulness, and of control of one's life.
- developing a sense of time perspective, that is, awareness that the events of the present have a relationship to the outcomes of the future.
- developing a sense of work as a life role that is a potentially satisfying one.
- beginning to develop an understanding that there are differing interests and abilities, and that these relate to occupations that have differing work tasks.

A system to address these tasks would be presented with a high degree of color, animation, video, graphics, audio prompts, and music. Though it might have instructional segments, the system would rely heavily on gaming and simulation to carry its message. Its content would include the following elements and activities:

- creating a self-picture by selecting pieces that, when put together, form a visual collage. Since each building piece could have a "value," the computer could potentially engage the user in understanding his or her self-statements.

Age →	0		15		25	45	65	?
Life Stages (Super)	GROWTH		EXPLORATION		ESTABLISHMENT	MAINTENANCE	DECLINE	
Related Activity	Elementary School	Middle School	High School	College Work	Graduate School Work	Work / Retirement	Retirement	
Related DISCOVER System	Nonexistent	DISCOVER for Middle Schools	DISCOVER for High Schools		DISCOVER for Colleges and Adults and/or DISCOVER for Organizations		DISCOVER for Retirement Planning	
Developmental tasks				Crystalization/Specification/Stabilization — Implementation/Consolidation				
Developmental tasks related to self	Developing a strong, positive self-concept. Developing a sense of work as a satisfying life role. Knowing the factors to consider when making a choice.		Crystallizing interests, abilities, and values. Further refining the self-concept.		Implementing and balancing additional life roles. Re-assessing interests, skills, and values.	Making smooth transitions as some life roles are lost or substantially modified.	Knowing and applying good health maintenance habits. Identifying interests, skills, and values that can be used in nonwork roles. Maintaining supportive relationships.	
Developmental tasks related to world-of-work and career information	Developing an understanding that individuals have differing interests and abilities and jobs have different tasks. Knowing how the World-of-Work is organized. Exploring the World-of Work broadly.		Specifying a vocational choice. Specifying a plan of education. Acquiring occupational knowledge. Acquiring career information.		Finding and entering a job. or Selecting a program of study and engaging successfully in it. Becoming committed to an occupation and perhaps being promoted, or gaining new work skills.	Identifying a satisfying career path. Acquiring new skills, if needed. Developing a network of supporters. Maintaining a strong niche at work in spite of competition from younger employees.	Making a transition to part-time or non-paid employment. Implementing self-concept by utilizing interests, skills, and values in life roles other than work.	
Developmental tasks related to planning and decision making	Developing a sense of planfulness. Developing a sense of time perspective.		Learning how to make decisions.		Applying decision-making skills to effect changes in vocational choice and/or placement.	Applying decision-making skill to making desired or required occupational change and to planning for retirement.	Having and maintaining a good financial plan. Making and implementing decisions about living arrangements.	

Figure 19-1. Super's life stages and developmental tasks and computer-based systems.

- utilizing games and simulations that would allow the user to plan some future event. There would be multiple outcomes related to this future event, based upon the quality and timing of the effort put into it. The purpose of the game/simulation would be to develop or reinforce the linkage between careful planning and "good" outcomes.
- providing simulations that would allow the user to explore occupations very broadly with audio and full-motion video. The purpose of this exploration would be to create broad awareness of the types of occupations available, the different kinds of work tasks they involve, and the different kinds of interests and abilities possessed by the people who enjoy performing them. This same simulation might encourage the user to "identify" self with one or more of the broad categories (such as Holland's six clusters) that would be presented. The user would have the opportunity to "interview" various workers around a World-of-Work Map for the purpose of learning about occupations in that part of the Map, including the interests, abilities, and values important for each.

The compact disk technology referred to earlier in this section will make these types of activities technically possible.

Super's Stage 2: Exploration (ages 15–25)—High School, College, and Beginning Work Years

This life stage spans three educational levels: the later years of the middle school/junior level, the secondary level, and the postsecondary level. This is the stage that has historically been addressed by computer-based systems. Some systems have provided the same content across these three levels, while others have developed different systems for these levels. DISCOVER offers three different systems, one uniquely designed for the tasks of each level.

The life-stage theory proposes that the following are important developmental tasks for the middle school/junior high level; confirming the belief that, in planning, one may gain some control over one's career:

- continuing to clarify and confirm a positive self-concept.
- beginning to crystallize interests and abilities.
- gaining World-of-Work information, specifically learning a way to organize occupations.
- exploring occupations broadly.
- learning decision-making skills and applying them to the next educational decisions.

- becoming aware of the factors to consider when making a vocational choice.

DISCOVER for Junior High and Middle School students attempts to help students accomplish these developmental tasks through three content modules:

Module 1:   Learning about the World of Work and a Sense of Autonomy. Teaches the four basic dimensions of ACT's World-of-Work Map: working with data, people, things, and ideas and allows users to play a game in which "winning" is being able to accurately relate a work task to one of these four dimensions. At the end of the module users are asked to indicate which one or two of these areas they relate to best.

Module 2:   Learning about Occupations.
Organizes more than 450 occupations by the six clusters (equivalent to Holland's) of ACT's World-of-Work Map and three educational levels. Based on tentative selections from Module 1 or on new selections, the student may select a cluster and an educational level and receive a list of occupational titles produced by those two choices. Upon selection of any occupations on that list, students then receive a short description that includes work tasks, general educational preparation, and general income level.

Module 3:   Planning for High School.
Presents high school course offerings by the same six clusters and three educational levels as in Module 2. Generic course offerings can be replaced by local course offerings as well as local graduation requirements. The user can plan courses for the four years of high school related to one ACT (Holland) cluster and one of three educational plans (no further education after high school, some education after high school, and four years of college). Based on the local school's graduation requirements the system monitors the student's selections and reports discrepancies both to the user and to the counselor, via printed reports.

At the secondary school level, Super's theory involves additional developmental tasks leading to a greater specificity of information about the self, the work world, and decision making/planfulness. Those tasks are:

- Achieving a clear definition of interests and abilities, and at least preliminary development of specific work-related values.

- Specifying one or several occupations for serious exploration (and remaining consistent over time).
- Specifying a plan of education that will lead to potential occupational choice(s).
- Acquiring comprehensive knowledge about the occupations under consideration.
- Acquiring broad "career" information, that is, an understanding of life roles and how the role of Worker interacts with them.
- Developing a more integrated self-concept and a sense of self-efficacy.
- Improving decision-making skill.

DISCOVER for High School Students addresses developmental tasks by devoting specific modules of the system to them, as follows:

Module 1: Understanding the Career Journey.
Describes the career planning process to users and helps them to know where they are in the process.

Module 2: Understanding the World of Work.
Teaches ACT's World of Work Map, complete with its basic work tasks (data, people, things, ideas), its six clusters, twelve regions, and its 23 job families. Allows the user to examine both occupations and school programs of study/majors by its organizing principles.

Module 3: Administers on-line or allows entering scores on inventories and tests of interest, ability, experiences, and values. Interprets measurement of interests, abilities, and experiences by World-of-Work Map tasks and regions, thus giving the user a focus for exploration.

Module 4: Helps the user identify occupations by self-information and/or by important job characteristics.

Module 5: Provides extensive information about occupations the user has identified and more than 450 others. Provides a planful approach for shortening the list.

Module 6: Informs users about the paths available for training for their "short list" of occupations. Also suggests the most closely related programs of study and provides definitions of these.

Module 7: Provides extensive information for implementing educational and vocational choices. Contains searches and information about more than 95 percent of all vocational-technical, two-year, four-year, and graduate institutions in the United States. Also provides extensive information about job-seeking skills and financial aid.

In the later exploration stage Super's theory speaks of the developmental tasks of specification and implementation. Applied to the college years, the following tasks are central:

- crystallizing and specifying interests, abilities, and work-related values.
- selecting and engaging successfully in a program of study related to selected occupations.
- understanding that career is a combination of life roles that all interact and planning toward those of choice.
- entering a job related to the selected occupation.
- continuing refinement of the self-concept.

DISCOVER for College Students and Adults addresses these tasks through the same content used in the high school system, but at a higher concept and reading level. Two additional modules are also offered:

Module 8:   Planning Your Career.
Teaches the roles of Super's "Career Rainbow," namely Child, Student, Worker, Spouse, Parent, Citizen, Leisurite, and Homemaker. Invites user to "draw" graphically his or her present Life Career Rainbow and a desired future one. The computer assists the user in developing an action plan to accomplish the future Career Rainbow.

Module 9:   Making Transitions.
Teaches Schlossberg's theory of transitions (1989) and how to manage them. Asks the user to enter a present or future transition, and by completing an on-line inventory, to measure its impact. If the impact is significant, the system provides some instruction on how to reduce the impact of a transition and helps the user develop an action plan for doing so.

Super's Stage 3: Establishment (Ages 25-45)

Super's theory proposes that individuals normally reach a "settling in" stage at about age 25. This presupposes that individuals have successfully completed all of the preceding developmental tasks, and thus have a high level of vocational maturity that, barring unforeseeable events, has led to a stable career pattern. For these individuals the typical tasks of this stage would include:

- becoming more committed to the chosen occupation.
- gaining in the skills required to do the job well.
- being promoted or given more responsibility.

- progressively making contributions to the field of work in which one is engaged.

Though this pattern holds true for most people, it is by no means a universal pattern. Changes in the labor market, in the values of society, and in the entry of women and other minorities into the work force have made different developmental tasks appropriate. These tasks are:

- re-assessing interests, skills, and values.
- gaining new work skills.
- making shifts in the salience of the several life roles, adopting new ones, and combining more of them.
- exploring new occupations and either transferring skills to enter them, or developing new skills.
- entering work and/or education later than the traditional time line, thus making career entry decisions later than is usual.
- applying decision-making skills to effect changes in vocational choice and/or placement.

Super's Stage 4: Maintenance (ages 45–65)

For those who have made a stable vocational commitment which persists through these years the following set of developmental tasks apply:

- making smooth transitions as some life roles are lost or substantially modified.
- identifying a satisfying career path — moving up in the organization, moving down, moving laterally, or moving out to a similar job in a different organization.
- identifying the kind of skills that need to be acquired in order to make the desired career moves, and learning where and how to acquire these skills.
- creating a network of persons who will assist in career development, including one or more mentors.
- maintaining a strong niche at work in spite of competition from younger employees.

In order to assist individuals in tackling these developmental tasks DIS-COVER for Organizations presents four modules of content:

Module 1:   Reviewing and Organizing what you Know about Yourself. This module provides four assessments (interest inventory, skills inventory, values inventory, and job preferences inventory) on-line and allows the entry of the results of these and other interest inventories (the Self-Directed Search and the Strong Interest Inventory) from having taken them in print form. The results of the interest and skills inventories are used to identify organization-specific positions in Module 2.

Module 2: Learning about Your Organization.

This module offers extensive customization opportunities that may be utilized by the organization to display extensive information about the organization and its policies and to enter the job titles and descriptions of up to 3000 positions. Further, the organization can identify up to 15 characteristics (including the user's interests and skills) by which this file can be searched. Once these characteristics are entered into the system and all positions are "coded" by them, the user can identify positions in the organization to which he or she would like to move. If the "general" occupational file is also retained in the system, users who need or want to move out of the organization can similarly identify "external" possibilities.

Module 3: Identifying Career Moves and Making Plans.

This part of the system defines four types of career moves — up, down, sideways, and out. The user is asked to specify which of these is a desired career move and is asked to specify two or more goals related to this type of move. A forced-field analysis exercise helps the user to identify both positive and negative forces related to the reaching of the goal and to develop an action plan to minimize the identified obstacles and to reach the goal.

Module 4: Putting Plans into Action.

Since many desired career moves require the acquisition of new skills or the upgrading of present skills, this module provides comprehensive data bases of vocational-technical schools, colleges, graduate schools and training available in the organization. It also contains extensive information about networking, resume writing and other job-seeking skills.

Super's Stage 5: Decline (Ages 65 and Above)

Since Super's original proposal of his life stages in the 1950s, concepts about retirement and aging have changed significantly (see Chapter 1). Age 65 is no longer considered the "acceptable" year of retirement from full-time work. Many people retire from a full-time job in their fifties and then pursue more leisure, work part-time, or assume another full-time job. At the same time, a larger percentage of people are working beyond the age of 65 than was true in the 1950s. Improved health maintenance and improved medical technology effect an ever-lengthening life span with more years of good health to use in a myriad of productive and satisfying ways. There are developmental tasks that must be performed prior to this age and at the beginning of this life stage in order to assure that the retirement stage of life is financially, emotionally, and physically stable. Some of these significant tasks are:

- having and maintaining a financial plan (both income and expenditures) that gives financial security to the retirement years.
- knowing and applying good health maintenance and support habits, such as good nutrition, exercise, preventive check ups, and adequate insurance coverage.
- identifying interests and skills that can be used in non-work life roles (i.e., "citizen," "leisurite," "learner," etc.) or in part-time jobs to fill time and find satisfaction previously associated with full-time work.
- maintaining supportive relationships.
- making and implementing decisions about where to live during the retirement years.

In order to help individuals become aware of and cope with these tasks, the last in the life-span series of DISCOVER products, DISCOVER for Retirement Planning, offers the following modules of content:

Introduction—Teaches Schlossberg's theory of transitions (Schlossberg, 1989) and how to cope with them. The two-step process involves 1) taking stock of the self, the situation, and available supports; and 2) taking charge by selecting coping strategies and making an action plan.

Module 1: Mastering Lifestyle: Changed Roles, Relationships and Use of Time.

This module teaches Super's Life-Career Rainbow and asks the user to enter and compare the present life roles and allocation of time to them to a desired future in the retirement years. The important support people related to each of the present life roles are identified. The user may also take inventories of skills, interests, and values. The results of these, the anticipated changes in roles, and the anticipated changes in available support people are combined to give the user a printed summary that can be used as a worksheet for planning use of time during retirement.

Module 2: Mastering Financial Planning.

This module requires the completion of a worksheet prior to coming to the computer. From this worksheet, users enter the line items of an anticipated annual retirement budget in today's dollars. Similarly, they enter the amount of income available from each income-producing asset in retirement years. They also enter a percentage inflation rate and percentage asset growth rates (by type of asset) they wish to use for planning purposes. The computer then displays the presumed financial picture for the first year of retirement and for 15 years thereafter. The user may modify this picture interactively and dynamically by modifying any combination of six assumptions, including year of retirement, inflation rate, and asset growth rate.

Module 3: Mastering Physical Well-being
This module gives the user a questionnaire about personal health maintenance habits. After its completion the computer provides a printed summary that includes the highest-risk causes of death for a national sample of persons of the user's age and sex. This summary indicates what the user might do to reduce these risks based on his or her answers to the inventory questions.

Module 4: Mastering Living Arrangements
This module asks users to describe their "ideal" living arrangement for the retirement years in terms of type of housing, location, amenities, and living partner(s). Then the user compares this ideal with his or her present situation and makes a decision about future arrangements based on that comparison.

SUMMARY

This chapter has reviewed the evolution of computer-based career planning systems including their theory base from the late sixties and the information-emphasis systems of the seventies. In the next decade life-stage theory, specifically Super's, can be used as the theoretical basis for the content of such systems to support development throughout the life span. Important developmental tasks for each of Super's life stages and the content of a computer-based system might serve as an example of system content addressing such developmental tasks.

It would be easy, though inaccurate, to assume that the computer alone could facilitate the accomplishment of these tasks. Though existing research shows that computer-based systems used alone do have positive effects, the same research indicates that their best use is in conjunction with a programmatic effort that includes one-to-one counseling, group work, or both. Helping individuals accomplish developmental tasks is worthwhile since the accomplishment of later lifestage tasks is dependent upon having succeeded at earlier ones.

REFERENCES

Schlossberg, N.K. *Overwhelmed: Coping with Life's Ups and Downs.* Lexington: Lexington Press, 1989.

Super, D.E. in Starishevsky, R; Matlin, N., and Jordaan, J.P. *Career Development: Self-Concept Theory.* Princeton, N.J. College Entrance Examination Board, 1963.

U.S. Department of Health, Education, and Welfare, Office of Education. *Computer-based Vocational Guidance Systems.* Summary of Papers Presented at the Fourth Symposium for System under Development for Vocational Guidance, U.S. Government Printing Office, Washington, D.C., 1969.

SECTION IV
THE FUTURE

INTRODUCTION TO SECTION IV—THE FUTURE

DAVID H. MONTROSS

The major theme that has dominated this book has been change. As we look now to the future, this theme is reiterated even more strongly. The future will see changes in the demographic profile of the work force; changes in the way organizations are structured; and changes in the very pace of change itself. Arthur (Chapter 3) has done an excellent job of highlighting those changes and the impact they are having on career theory. In this section, we focus on the ways organizations will need to shift as a result.

Bailyn (Chapter 20) suggests that the very conditions of work will have to be altered to accommodate the new work force. She argues for changes in policy and procedures which could allow for greater flexibility regarding the degree to which people are committed to their work. She posits that, given the varying demands of family, employees should be permitted to negotiate with their managers for differing levels of involvement in their work. This greater flexibility would be in the best interests of employees, their families, and ultimately our society.

In Chapter 21, Walker argues that notions of stable career paths are largely obsolete. Again, greater flexibility is called for from both employees in managing their career and from organizations in how they are structured. These chapters, combined with Arthur's, suggest dramatic changes in the ways we have come to view an individual's career.

The future, from all indications, will be far less stable and predictable, presenting great challenges for career professionals who assist both individuals and organizations with career planning and career management. Career professionals will be increasingly cast into the role of "change manager," teaching students, employees, and organizations how to best manage change in an ever-changing landscape.

Chapter 20

CHANGING THE CONDITIONS OF WORK: IMPLICATIONS FOR CAREER DEVELOPMENT[1]

Lotte Bailyn

The system of career development in the United States, as much else about the procedures in our organizations, is under attack. As we look to the future we see it as serving neither the organization's goals nor the needs of the employees we now envision as populating the emerging work force. Two sets of pressures create this sense of inadequacy: pressures from the competitive situation in this country and pressures from demographic trends that lead to increasing concern about the U.S. family, particularly its children. Both impel modification of the conditions of work, but their consequences for the individual employee are often contradictory.

The goal of this chapter is to describe changes in the career development system that might resolve this contradiction. Some of these suggestions go against accepted procedures—upheld elsewhere in this book—embedded in our current theories of career. Nothing less could be expected in a rapidly changing world. The chapter emphasizes the link between new pressures in the work environment and career development activity (to use the model developed by Arthur in Chapter 3), and the hope is that out of such an analysis will emerge new and more relevant career theory.

Competitive Pressures

Competitive concerns have led U.S. companies to push for productivity—to get more productive output from each employee. In order to achieve this goal, companies have moved in two directions: greater selectivity in the hiring, training, and movement of personnel, and new more "productive" ways to organize work. Selectivity, brought on also by corporate restructuring, implies reduction of force at all levels and the substitution of machines for

[1]Some of the ideas in this chapter are also discussed in my chapter entitled "Changing the Conditions of Work: Responding to Increasing Work Force Diversity and New Family Patterns," which is to be published in T. Kochan and M. Useem (eds.), *Transforming Organizations*, Oxford University Press. I am grateful to David Montross, Christopher Shinkman, and, especially, to Michael Arthur and Edgar Schein for insightful suggestions on earlier drafts of this chapter. Work on this chapter has been supported, in part, by a grant from the Ford Foundation (grant #890-3012).

people. But, as research in the automobile industry shows (MacDuffie and Krafcik, in press), technology by itself is no guarantee of improved output. And thus the emphasis, instead, is on a new organization of work, based on an increase in employee breadth, responsibility, and involvement (Dertouzos et al., 1989): a postentrepreneurial or high commitment organization (cf. Hackman, 1985; Walton, 1985; Lawler, 1986; Kanter, 1989). Drucker (1988) draws the analogy of an orchestra—a group of people with a common goal jointly working toward its fulfillment.

What are the career implications of these trends? Career development, geared to filling the staffing needs of organizations—for succession and the appropriate distribution of people across skills and locations—is obviously involved in selectivity. But more and more this system is also being asked to serve productivity goals, and what is needed for productivity—according to the newest thinking on organizations—is employees fully committed to organizational goals. To achieve such a work force requires that all employees participate in decision making and that there be coordination of their efforts and delegation of responsibility to the working level. Our traditional selection and reward procedures, however, do not reflect these imperatives. They rely instead on evaluating individual characteristics and on procedures that set up competition among employees—creating winners and losers. In such a system, not even winners are necessarily committed to produce for the organization, as is shown by the evidence on what happens to people who remain in the organization after layoffs (Brockner, 1988).

Further, the use of career development simultaneously to fulfill selectivity and productivity goals runs into another, perhaps even more important complication. By definition, productivity means output—better outcomes from the effort put into work. Output, however, is not easily measured. And so individual input characteristics are used to decide whom to recruit, develop, and promote—characteristics based on fit, hours, and visibility (cf. Jackall, 1988). If people fit the characteristics of those who have previously been successful, they are seen as more likely to be good producers than are those who are different and hence untested—the source of what Kanter (1977) has called "homosocial reproduction." And within the homogeneous group thus identified, employees try to stand out by putting in more hours in order to appear more committed to their work. Indeed, after a century of almost continuous reduction in the number of hours worked, that trend has recently been reversed. Over the last fifteen years, work time in the US has increased 15 percent (Gordon, 1990); among managers the increase is estimated as 20 percent over the last decade (Fowler, 1989). Nearly 24 percent of fully employed Americans spend more than 48 hours per week on their jobs—up from 18 percent ten years ago (Kilborn, 1990). And visibility—

being seen and available at all times—is a further indicator, presumably, of rewardable performance.

These criteria for selectivity are meant to ensure that workers, in the interest of productivity, spend maximum energy on their work and become fully involved in all aspects of their jobs. Such involvement is one of the goals of the "high commitment" organization. It is seen by some as a source of satisfaction that more isolated and routine jobs are unable to supply (e.g., Kanter, 1989), though others have indicated its possibly negative consequences (e.g., Randall, 1987). Energy, perhaps like power, can be generated to some extent (cf. Marks, 1977), but it does have its limits. And time, of course, is necessarily bounded. Thus organizational responses to competitive pressures have significant repercussions for employee time and energy. They create a basic dilemma with the pressures on families that stem from recent demographic changes (see Fig. 20-1).

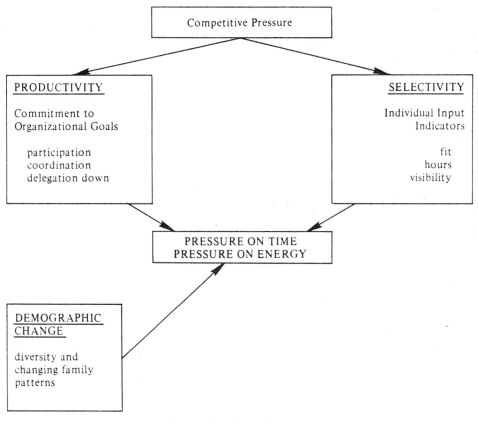

Figure 20-1. Basic dilemma.

Family Concerns

The facts on demographic change are by now familiar. More than half of all mothers with children under one are now in the paid labor force (Hayes et al., 1990); 45 percent of all paid workers are women (Johnston and Packer, 1987). Today, fewer than 10 percent of families follow the pattern of a husband at work and a wife at home caring for the children (U.S. Department of Labor, 1988a). And 28 percent of all households are female-headed (U.S. Department of Commerce, 1989). Further, at present, 60 percent of men in the labor force are married to wives who also hold jobs (U.S. Department of Labor, 1988b). It is not surprising, therefore, that a study by the Bank Street Work and Family Life staff has found that almost 3 out of every 5 employees are having problems managing the often conflicting demands of jobs and family life (Galinsky, 1988). Further, current projections indicate that these changes are likely to be even more dramatic by the end of the century (Fullerton, 1989).

These new patterns of work and family—combined with an aging population, an expected shortage of labor (particularly of well educated, skilled men and women), and an increasing disparity between rich and poor, between employment in "good" companies (usually large, with many benefits) and smaller companies without benefits—lie behind the current concern about the U.S. family, particularly about the welfare of the nation's children (Hayes et al., 1990). The massive movement of women into the labor force, occasioned by economic need and changes in assumptions about appropriate sex roles, is the underlying demographic phenomenon. It raises particularly acute questions in the United States which, almost alone among industrialized countries, has no national family policy to help with the consequences, particularly for children, of this development.

In the absence of government support, some large U.S. companies are beginning to respond. IBM, AT&T, Corning, and Dupont are among a group of forward-looking organizations trying to deal with the family concerns of their employees. Their responses fall into two general categories. First are benefits in the form of services, or financial and information aid in obtaining them, that allow employees with family responsibilities more easily to spend the time and energy now seemingly required by work. Family benefits of this variety do not make U.S. employees less time poor. In fact, because the availability, affordability, and quality of these services are far from adequate, such responses may actually increase the work/family concerns facing American workers.

A second category consists of policies that create flexibility in location and time as well as varying arrangements for personal leave. In essence, these benefits—flextime and flexplace, part-time and job-sharing opportunities, family and medical leaves—are geared to freeing time for employees to attend themselves to family needs. But as long as organizations continue to reward the full commitment of their employees, gauged by the amount of visible time spent at work, flexibility, even when available, will be seen as a liability for the development of one's career. Such benefits, therefore, will reinforce the segmentation of work in the public, economic arena from that in the private, domestic domain. And even though the gendered solution of a specialization of labor between bread-winning and care-taking is no longer seen as optimal, either economically or psychologically, women still seem to be primarily responsible for care. Thus, at the present time, flexible options are more likely to be used by women than by men. And this difference in patterns of use is likely to increase the disadvantages that women already face in the work place through the feminization of poverty, the wage gap, and the glass ceiling. Even in Sweden, which has perhaps the most liberal benefits of this kind (provided, of course, jointly by the state and employers and supported by a high tax rate) occupational segregation by sex is pervasive (Dowd, 1989). Such an outcome, however, conflicts with the American ideology of gender-neutral equality—as was evident in the response to Felice Schwartz's article in the *Harvard Business Review* (1989) suggesting a special family track for women interested both in children and in career.

Implications for Career Development

If it is true that American industry will require the full utilization of all talent—male and female—in order to stay globally competitive, and if we want to achieve this goal within the constraints of our notions of equity and of the needs of future generations, then a reexamination of the assumptions underlying the current conditions of work is in order. No longer can one rely on procedures designed for a more homogeneous work force where 100 percent commitment to work and organization is presumed. On the contrary, a system that provides fairness to both men and women, and meets the needs of their families as well as those of the nation, necessitates a new assumptive base and a different set of career procedures.

Changing Assumptions

To understand the change necessitated by these conflicting pressures on organizations, it helps to start by outlining old, constraining assumptions and juxtaposing new ones more facilitating for employees trying to reconcile the needs of work and family (see Fig. 20-2.)

In the current system, continuous and total commitment is presumed to be necessary for the successful performance of organizational tasks. For some tasks this may be true—but not for all. Nor should commitment to task be gauged by visible time, as is so often the case. In one book, for example, which outlines managerial strategies for obtaining superior performance, commitment is identified as the key (Kinlaw, 1989). It is defined in the following way:

OLD ASSUMPTIONS   NEW ASSUMPTIONS
     (constraining)   (facilitating)

continuous commitment   discontinuity

manage via input;   accountability for results;
before-the-fact approval,   after-the-fact review,
based on control   based on trust

homogeneity in outlook   learning from diversity
and values   (self-design)

Figure 20-2. Need to change assumptions.

Commitment, like motivation, is not something that we can observe directly. We infer that they exist because of what people say and do. There are at least two kinds of behavior that signal employee commitment. First, committed employees *appear* to be very single-minded or focused in doing their work. The second characteristic that we associate with committed employees is their willingness to make personal sacrifices to reach their team's or organization's goals (p. 5, italics added).

So employees, who expect to be evaluated on the basis of these proxy indicators of performance, feel compelled to put work above all else in order to advance their careers. And the importance of such behavior is most critical in the early career years, for, as Rosenbaum (1984) has shown, promotions not achieved during this period seldom occur at a later date. But these early years are generally the ones in which there are the greatest demands from a growing family. Where once this dilemma was resolved by men attending to the needs of career and leaving the needs of family to their wives, the current increase in dual careers necessitates other accommodations. Not to have children or to defer their arrival is one possibility; to buy infant care, sick child care, toddler day care, and after school care—if it exists and is affordable—is another. What is not easily possible, under current assumptions, is to defer the total commitment to career. And yet, there is hardly any convincing evidence to indicate that the premium placed on work in these early years is productive over the long run. On the contrary, we are beset with burnout, plateaus, dead wood, mid-life crises — seemingly unrelated but actually embedded in this emphasis on the early career (cf. Bailyn, 1980). Embedded, that is, to the extent that a career is seen as continuous upward movement in an organizational hierarchy.

It is this presumption of continuity that constrains an employee's ability to reconcile the needs of work and family. In contrast, a new assumption, based on discontinuity, is more facilitating. It would mean dividing the career into independent segments, each with its own distribution of commitments between the public and the private. Low commitment work segments would be judged differently from those with high commitment and would involve different tasks with different levels of reward. The key is that a time of some withdrawal from work would not be considered evidence of failure, or inability to be productive, that would stay with the employee for the rest of his or her career. Such judgments would await a period of high commitment.

A technical employee, for example, can be assigned a routine task or a more complicated, responsible one. The latter fits a period of high commitment, the former meshes better with low commitment. Both kinds of tasks exist in organizations — hence there is no loss in effectiveness — but they must be evaluated in different ways. For the routine task, satisfactory completion is probably a sufficient criterion. For the more complex one, a more elaborate evaluation is called for, one which includes some measures of independence of judgment, awareness of interdependence with other tasks, and so on. What is critical is that such procedures not be uniform, that the criteria for the more complex task not be applied to the simple one, or vice versa.

A second assumption concerns the role of management in the system of authority. The old constraining assumption — based on principles of hierarchy — is that managers must personally control every decision, thus creating elaborate systems of before-the-fact approval. In an oil company, for example, field representatives were not allowed to make pricing decisions for the gasoline stations in their area without going up the line to gain approval (Bailyn, 1988). Expertise and information were assumed to reside at the top, hence managers monitored the way decisions were made, not only their results. There are fundamental difficulties with this assumption, however. Local information is characteristically more available to the working level employee (the field representative in this case), and is probably more critical for the pricing decision than is general expertise. Further, computer technology makes it possible for working level employees to access any general information they may need. Exactly this transition was occurring at the oil company, and the company was undergoing a difficult change; it was slowly moving toward accountability at a lower level with management monitoring the results of decision making, not the process. Such a change from continuous surveillance to after-the-fact review must be based on principles of trust (Gambetta, 1988; Perin, 1991). It has a number of potentially valuable consequences: it creates more involvement on the part of working level employees (thus more commitment) and simultaneously permits more discretion over the way they spend their time, which provides greater control over their lives.

Finally, there is the assumption, despite contradictory evidence (Schein, 1987), that homogeneity in values and outlook is beneficial. Employees are selected according to these criteria or are socialized in this direction. "Misfits," if all else fails, are weeded out. Such procedures, however, can lead to routinization and to lack of innovation and creativity (cf. Van Maanen and Schein, 1979). In contrast, the view that innovative organizations require experimentation, based on a large repertoire of responses (cf. Weick, 1979)—the assumption underlying self-design (Weick, 1977; Weick and Berlinger, 1989)—is better served by diversity.

Diversity in the U.S. work force looms as a key issue for organizations in the coming years. Far from being a problem that needs to be managed, however, such diversity potentially provides the opportunity for an organization to learn about itself and to devise new procedures more in line with changing conditions. Learning from diversity requires one to confront differences, not merely to ignore or to tolerate them (cf. Kristol, 1989). Organizations can use the fact that different people see different things, respond differently to procedures, behave in different ways, and have different needs, to question the way things have always been done and to explore the possibility of improving organizational processes. To realize this potential, however, necessitates linking diversity to organizational issues and not dealing with it only on an individual level. Such a link tends to be missing, even in the most forward looking programs on Valuing Diversity (cf. Thomas, 1990). As of now, most organizations do not see social and cultural differences among their employees as a source of new ideas or as an opportunity for reflecting on traditional procedures. And so diversity does not play a role in their attempts to adopt an active, continuously learning stance.[2]

Changing Procedures

What procedures would flow from these more facilitating assumptions? How would they play themselves out in the reality of organizational life? Three critical changes in career procedures would seem to be necessary. They are not independent of each other. Together they add up to a very

---

[2]There is an interesting parallel here to the Japanese principle of *kaizen*, where continuous improvement is achieved by seeing problems and disruptions not as difficulties to be avoided but as opportunities for learning (cf. MacDuffie, 1991).

different system of career development than is now generally in place (see Fig. 20-3).

CURRENT CHARACTERISTICS
OF CAREER DEVELOPMENT SYSTEM

MATCHING (of individual to job)

CAREER ASSESSMENT
(long-run continuity)

TIGHT COUPLING

Figure 20-3a.

NEEDED NEW CHARACTERISTICS
OF CAREER DEVELOPMENT SYSTEM

PEOPLE CONSTRUCTING JOBS

INDIVIDUAL NEGOTIATION
(discontinuity - career segments)

DISAGGREGATION

Figure 20-3b.

The traditional system is geared to matching an individual to a job that has been carefully defined independently of the person filling it. Hay-type classifications are used to specify tasks and associated rewards, as if work were somehow independent of the people involved in it or of the specific and constantly changing situation in which it takes place. Procedures anchored in such a system reinforce existing ways of doing things at a time when learning to change is considered necessary for organizational survival. So, both researchers and practitioners are beginning to move away from this approach. For example, Schein, in Chapter 11, argues for a shift from job descriptions to job/role planning, an important strategic point. But it is still the incumbent who must operationalize the envisioned role by being actively involved in the construction of his or her assigned job (cf. Miner and Estler, 1985; Miner, 1987).

Elsewhere (Bailyn, 1985), I have distinguished between strategic and operational autonomy in the R&D lab. There it was found that the most effective performance results from strategic guidance combined with operational autonomy, even though this was not the combination usually provided. A similar distinction applies here. After all, despite possibly contrasting claims from artificial intelligence, adaptation and creativity reside only in people. These qualities, however, will only emerge if people are allowed, within overall strategic constraints, to function as people: to experiment and to have control over how to do their work.

A number of consequences flow from this alternative perspective, leading to a second procedural change. If the emphasis shifts away from detailed job descriptions into which employees are plugged and moves toward one more centered on the incumbents of those jobs, then the system cannot be based on career procedures that apply uniformly to all people, whatever their individual situations may be. The constraining effect of such homogeneous systems is beginning to be recognized for functional distinctions. R&D engineers and scientists, for example, could greatly aid the transfer of technology from the laboratory to production if they were allowed to transfer with the technology—as happens, characteristically, in Japan (Westney and Sakakibara, 1988). But it will not happen if in order to stay at the same level and salary the R&D employee in a production unit is required to supervise 50 or 100 people. This barrier existed in a large US manufacturing company and prevented such potentially valuable transfers (Bailyn, 1991). Slowly it is being removed.

It is difficult, however, to envision more individualized treatment for people with differing demands from their private lives. Indeed, homogeneity in systems came about, in part, to minimize the probability of special treatment for certain groups, and is supported by the legal system for just that purpose. But for a diverse work force, with employees in widely differing personal situations, equality in procedures does not necessarily produce equal employment opportunity; it may produce the opposite. It is for this reason that individual career negotiation needs to take the place of organizational career assessment (cf. Bailyn, 1984).

Organizational career assessment is based on long-term planning for an individual's eventual position. It has linear continuity built into it and presumes that the appropriate career direction is up and that what happens at the beginning is a strong determiner of the future. Too often effort is put into early identification of future potential with little concern for the long-range consequences of such decisions. This procedure ignores the possibility that the selection itself may determine the outcome—the self-fulfilling prophecy—and assumes that it is easy to specify the requirements of future work and to relate desired results to particular contributions. Since the pace of change makes it difficult to be clear about future needs, requirements get transformed into prescriptions for behavior, which often center on demands for individual time and visibility. Such demands, then, become apparent work requirements, yet really serve more to impute individual worth in situations where performance needs are difficult or impossible to identify.

Individual negotiation, in contrast, does not assume a linear progression toward some predefined job because it is based on discontinuity—on alternating times of low and high commitment to work. For organizations, such a system is possible because some tasks are necessarily routine, and are probably best performed by people whose involvement in their work and careers at that particular time is less rather than more. For employees, it would permit them to reenter the contest for influential positions, without eliminating them in the early rounds (cf. Rosenbaum, 1984).

A key and final requirement that underlies these suggestions is disaggregation. Our current system tightly couples position, influence, salary, and status with tasks. Such aggregation has long compelled employees able and willing to be technically productive to move into "nonproductive" management jobs. Nor has the dual ladder, because it reflects the same outmoded assumption of continuous linearity (Epstein, 1986), dealt with this issue in a very successful way (see e.g., Gunz, 1980; Roth, 1982; Allen and Katz, 1986; Katz et al., in press). Disaggregation of task from position and pay is necessary if work and compensation are to be attached to people, not to disembodied jobs. It permits more flexibility in the deployment of human resources and encourages the greater adaptability and creativity needed by today's organizations.[3] And though only partial moves in this direction, some initial steps are evident. IBM, for example, no longer has a maximum salary for its engineering positions, thus allowing engineers to increase their compensation without having to shift to nonengineering tasks. And skills-based pay, which is becoming more prevalent in production work, begins to address the same issue.

These suggestions for changes in career procedures would have to be tailored to each organization. Indeed, they are premised on the idea that generalized systems no longer fit current conditions, and that human resource practices must reflect the particular needs of an organization and its individual employees. And though they will not be easy to introduce and to manage, they are necessary if organizations are to compete in a diverse and rapidly changing world and at the same time allow their employees to deal more easily with family concerns. Such changes represent a very different view of career development than we have been used to— one which requires a rethinking of the conditions of work: a reevaluation of what is really needed to do a good job, along with a belief and trust in people's willingness to contribute according to their abilities *and* personal situations. Only by such a revisioning of work and career (cf. Marshall, 1989), will it be possible to integrate U.S. companies' productivity needs

---

[3]It is of interest to note that in flexible production systems, based on the Japanese model, both compensation and seniority are decoupled from task (MacDuffie, 1991).

with the family issues now confronting the U.S. work force. And if one remembers that the nation's children represent tomorrow's workers, citizens, and consumers, their needs present a strong imperative for change.

REFERENCES

Allen, T.J. and Katz, R. The dual ladder: Motivational solution or managerial delusion? *R&D Management, 16,* 1986, 185–197.

Bailyn, L. The slow-burn way to the top: Some thoughts on the early years of organizational careers. In C.B. Deer (ed.), *Work, family, and the career: New frontiers in theory and research.* New York: Praeger, 1980.

Bailyn, L. Issues of work and family in organizations: Responding to social diversity. In M.B. Arthur, et al., *Working with careers.* New York: Center for Research in Career Development, Columbia University, 1984.

Bailyn, L. Autonomy in the R&D lab. *Human Resource Management, 24,* 1985, 129–146.

Bailyn, L. Freeing work from the constraints of location and time. *New Technology, Work and Employment, 3,* 1988, 143–152.

Bailyn, L. The hybrid career: An exploratory study of career routes in R&D. *Journal of Engineering and Technology Management, 8,* 1991, 1–14.

Brockner, J. The effects of work layoff on survivors. In B. Staw and L. Cummings (eds.), *Research in organizational behavior,* vol. 10. Greenwich, CT: JAI Press, 1988.

Dertouzos, M.L., Lester, R.K., and Solow, R.M. *Made in America: Regaining the productive edge.* Cambridge: MIT Press, 1989.

Dowd, N.E. Envisioning work and family: A critical perspective on international models. *Harvard Journal on Legislation, 26,* 1989, 311–348.

Drucker, P.F. The coming of the new organization. *Harvard Business Review,* January/February 1988, 45–53.

Epstein, K.A. The dual ladder: Realities of technically-based careers. Doctoral Dissertation, MIT, 1986.

Fowler, E.M. More stress in the workplace. *New York Times,* September 20, 1989, p. D-22.

Fullerton, H.N., Jr. New labor force projections, spanning 1988 to 2000. *Monthly Labor Review,* November 1989, 3–12.

Galinsky, E. Child care and productivity. Paper prepared for the ChildCare Action Campaign conference, Child Care: The Bottom Line, New York, 1988. Quoted in E. Galinsky and P. Stein, Balancing careers and families: Research findings and institutional responses. Presented at the American Association for the Advancement of Science, Annual Meeting, San Francisco, January 16, 1989.

Gambetta, D. Can we trust trust? In D. Gambetta (ed.), *Trust: Making and breaking cooperative relations.* New York: Basil Blackwell, 1988.

Gordon, S. Work, work, work. *Boston Globe,* August 20, 1989, p. 16ff.

Gunz, H.P. Dual ladders in research: A paradoxical organizational fix. *R&D Management, 10,* 1980, 113–118.

Hackman, J.R. The commitment model: From "whether" to "how". In K.B. Clark,

R.H. Hayes, and C. Lorenz (eds.), *The uneasy alliance: Managing the productivity-technology dilemma.* Boston: Harvard Business School Press, 1985.

Hayes, C.D., Palmer, J., and Zaslow, M. Who cares for America's children: Child care policy for the 1990's. Report of the Panel on Child Care Policy, Committee on Child Development Research and Public Policy. Commission on Behavioral and Social Sciences and Education, National Research Council, Washington D.C., 1990.

Jackall, R. *Moral mazes: The world of corporate managers.* Oxford: Oxford University Press, 1988.

Johnston, W.B., and Packer, A.E. *Workforce 2000: Work and workers for the twenty-first century.* Indianapolis: Hudson Institute, 1987.

Kanter, R.M. *Men and women of the corporation.* New York: Basic Books, 1977.

Kanter, R.M. *When giants learn to dance: Mastering the challenges of strategy, management, and careers in the 1990s.* New York: Simon and Schuster, 1989.

Katz, R.. Tushman, M.L., and Allen, T.J. Exploring the dynamics of dual ladders: A longitudinal study. *Journal of High Technology Managment,* in press.

Kilborn, P.T. The work week grows: Tales from the digital treadmill. *New York Times,* June 3, 1990, section 4, p. 1.

Kinlaw, D.C. *Coaching for commitment: Managerial strategies for obtaining superior performance.* San Diego: University Associates, 1989.

Kristol, E. False tolerance, false unity. *New York Times,* September 25, 1989, p. A-19.

Lawler, E.E. *High involvement management: Participative strategies for improving organizational performance.* San Francisco: Jossey-Bass, 1986.

MacDuffie, J.P. Beyond mass production? Flexible production systems and manufacturing performance in the world auto industry. Doctoral Dissertation, MIT, 1991.

MacDuffie, J.P., and Krafcik, J.F. Integrating technology and human resources for high performance manufacturing: Evidence from the international auto industry. In T. Kochan and M. Useem (eds.), *Transforming Organizations.* Oxford: Oxford University Press, in press.

Marks, S.R. Multiple roles and role strain: Some notes on human energy, time and commitment. *American Sociological Review, 42,* 1977, 921–936.

Marshall, J. Re-visioning career concepts: A feminist invitation. In M.B. Arthur, D.T. Hall, and B.S. Lawrence (eds.), *Handbook of career theory.* Cambridge: Cambridge University Press, 1989.

Miner, A.S. Idiosyncratic jobs in formalized organizations. *Administrative Science Quarterly, 32,* 1987, 327–351.

Miner, A.S., and Estler, S.E. Accrual mobility: Job mobility in higher education through responsibility accrual. *Journal of Higher Education, 56,* 1985, 121–143.

Perin, C. The moral fabric of the office: Panopticon discourse and schedule flexibilities. In S. Bacharach, S.R. Barley, and P.S. Tolbert (eds.), *Research in the sociology of organizations* (special volume on Organizations and Professions). Greenwich, CT: JAI Press, 1991.

Randall, D.M. Commitment and the organization: The organization man revisited. *Academy of Management Review, 12,* 1987, 460–471.

Rosenbaum, J.E. *Career mobility in a corporate hierarchy.* New York: Academic Press, 1984.

Roth, L.M. Critical examination of the dual ladder approach to career advancement. New York: Center for Research in Career Development, Columbia University, 1982.

Schein, E.H. Individuals and careers. In J.W. Lorsch (ed.), *Handbook of organizational behavior.* Englewood Cliffs, NJ: Prentice-Hall, 1987.

Schwartz, F.N. Management women and the new facts of life. *Harvard Business Review,* January/February 1989, 65–76.

Thomas, R.R., Jr. From affirmative action to affirming diversity. *Harvard Business Review,* March/April 1990, 107–117.

US Department of Commerce, *Current Population Reports* (Special Studies Series P-23, No. 159). Bureau of the Census, 1989.

US Department of Labor, *Child care: A workforce issue.* Report of the Secretary's Task Force, April 1988a.

US Department of Labor, *Employment and earnings.* Bureau of Labor Statistics, August 1988b.

Van Maanen, J., and Schein, E.H. Toward a theory of organizational socialization. In B. Staw (ed.), *Research in organizational behavior,* vol. 1. Greenwich, CT: JAI Press, 1979.

Walton, R.E. From control to commitment: Transforming work force management in the United States. In K.B. Clark, R.H. Hayes, and C. Lorenz (eds.), *The uneasy alliance: Managing the productivity-technology dilemma.* Boston: Harvard Business School Press, 1985.

Weick, K.E. Organization design: Organizations as self-designing systems. *Organizational Dynamics,* Autumn 1977, 31–46.

Weick, K.E. *The social psychology of organizing* (2nd ed.). Reading, MA: Addison-Wesley, 1979.

Weick, K.E., and Berlinger, L.R. Career improvisation in self-designing organizations. In M.B. Arthur, D.T. Hall, and B.S. Lawrence (eds.), *Handbook of career theory.* Cambridge: Cambridge University Press, 1989.

Westney, D.E., and Sakakibara, K. Comparative study of the training, careers, and organization of engineers in the computer industry in Japan and the United States. MIT–Japan Science and Technology Working Paper, 1988.

Chapter 21

CAREER PATHS IN FLEXIBLE ORGANIZATIONS

James W. Walker

Employees move through patterned sequences of positions or roles, usually related to work content during their working lives. This is the essence of a career path. As such, career paths do not need to be described in writing in order to exist. They are fact. Everyone has one.

For purposes of career development and other applications in human resource planning, career paths are most useful when they are formally defined and documented. Then, career paths become objective descriptions of sequential work experiences, as opposed to subjective feelings about career progress, personal development, status, or satisfaction. For example, an individual may view increasing responsibilities or changing work assignments within a single job as a career, but this subjective view of a career does not constitute a career path, as defined above.

Most employees want to know about the career opportunities available in an organization to help them set realistic career objectives and plan practical steps for their personal career development. Career development workshops, self-directed materials, and career counseling are often available to help employees manage their careers. However, information available to employees on career paths, including progression possibilities and associated qualifications required, isn't generally available.

Managers, too, want career paths to be defined, so that an adequate number of individuals may be identified and prepared to fill future vacancies. Because employees want to know what opportunities are available to them, career paths and effective career development are positive features that help attract and retain employees, increasingly important in tight labor markets. Also, for the development of senior management talent, career paths are useful as guidelines for career development assignments across functional and organizational lines. Increasingly, senior executives are the product of varied job experiences, including assignments in different units, functions, and countries. Accordingly, many companies have attempted to define career paths for these purposes.

In today's increasingly flat, lean, and global companies, however, paths are more difficult to define. Rapid changes in job content, organization structure, and talent requirements result in shorter-term career planning and step-by-step progression. More flexible approaches for staffing and for guiding career development are used. Employees adapt by becoming more self reliant in defining their career opportunities.

This chapter describes the current use of career paths in organizations from both a management and employee perspective. Suggestions are offered for meeting the needs for information on career opportunities in today's flexible organizations.

Career Paths Are Changing

While the development of career paths has an attractive logic, most employers find that rapid change makes this effort difficult. Organizations have sought to move individuals along defined career paths, in order to develop the capabilities necessary to staff various levels and types of jobs. Accordingly, career paths have traditionally emphasized upward mobility within a single organization unit or functional area of work (e.g., sales, accounting, engineering). In many organizations, paths have meant step-by-step progression geared to years of service. If an individual deviated from the prescribed lock-step pattern and timing, he or she faltered.

Such career paths (or ladders) were developed in the following manner:

- Examination of the paths followed by individuals to the top "rungs of the ladders" in the past
- Identification of entry points in the career path, traditionally at the bottom, and exit points along the way
- Definition of requirements for entry to positions, usually in terms of educational level, specialized skills, experience, and years of service
- Identification of the important job experiences leading to the top rung and benchmark timing for reaching each rung.

This process described a generalized or idealized route for advancement within a unit or function. It made paths explicit.

A typical career path within the sales function, for example, might include five steps: salesman, account supervisor, sales supervisor, district manager, regional manager. Each step in the progression is largely paced by years of service—a tenure considered necessary to master each level of responsibility. Such a simple functional path may be modified to identify other options that provide valuable experience in developing district and regional managers. Assignments in finance, marketing research, or production, for example, also may be valuable in sales management. Along these paths, high-talent individuals may progress at a faster rate than the norm.

Traditional career paths imply a necessity of moving up—of climbing career ladders and the corporate hierarchy. Lateral moves, downward moves, or staying at a given level on a career basis are not perceived as attractive options. The bias toward promotions as the only meaningful career direction is clearly built into this perspective.

Career paths are often influenced by the ways pay and recognitions are administered in an organization. Employees seek job advancement in part because of the recognition and status associated with it, and for the increased compensation typically related to promotions. Hence organizations have ladders within common job families (e.g., Technician I, II, and III). Technical ladders or paths provide recognition (e.g., more distinguished titles such as Research Fellow) and higher pay, even while the content of work performed does not change significantly. Here experience, skill level, and loyalty are recognized and rewarded through the use of career paths.

A pharmaceutical company, for example, hires into positions at various levels designated as entry positions. Then employees move among positions in a defined pattern of job progression. Salary administration is based on standardized job titles and requirements, with established criteria for job progression. The process is defined and administered by a committee of line managers and human resorce staff within each division of the company. As a technically-oriented, highly professional organization, these progressions are the de facto career paths.

Because of rapid organizational changes, career paths are typically in flux. They change as organization structure, job content, and skill requirements change. Most organizations are constantly restructuring and redefining requirements. They are becoming flatter and leaner, with most jobs shifting their content with every change. Specific efforts are made to eliminate unneeded work and to streamline management processes. As a result, different work is called for in jobs—and there are often fewer net positions and fewer levels of positions.

The management response to rapidly changing conditions is to be more flexible. Companies are adopting alternative ways to guide career development. They are charting career moves more cautiously and are limiting in-depth planning to specific employee groups of highest management concern. Movement among positions is becoming slower; employees are encouraged to find challenge and satisfaction through improvement of current responsibilities—"more interesting work".

Development-Oriented Staffing

Facing rapid change, companies are also adopting more flexible approaches to staffing. They use the staffing process that best suits their immediate needs: succession planning, targeted development, focused search, job posting, or informal staffing. Each approach has advantages and disadvantages, which are summarized in Exhibit One. Each is described briefly below. In practice, companies use a combination of these approaches to meet their needs.

To meet their staffing needs quickly and expediently, managers often respond to those staffing needs as they develop. Here, career paths and career development do not play a significant role in staffing decisions. However, where companies are committed to providing job security (career employment) and promotion from within, managers use staffing approaches which emphasize development. In this way, a pool of talent is developed in advance of needs and employees are given an incentive to pursue learning and growth.

Staffing systems, however short-term, should be development oriented. Companies should take actions that address their staffing and development needs, especially forward planning for critical staffing needs. Even in rapidly changing conditions, employers should plan ahead for recruiting, promotions, training and development, and other career management actions. To be passive is to fail to manage a critical business resource. Yet the costs and time required are often viewed as impediments to proactive career management.

Job vacancies are the most valuable asset a company has for developing talent (see Chapter 10). Training and other off-the-job development activities are valuable, but challenging job assignments are the most useful development experience. When managers backfill position vacancies, they should have career development in mind. Candidates readily available, even if qualified, should not automatically be assigned to positions when others might gain development experience in the assignment. Where positions are blocked, negotiated moves or swaps may be negotiated to provide career opportunities.

Managers should be talent agents. They are stewards for the talent placed in their charge and should be accountable for managing employee career development. At IBM, managers are expected to help subordinates prepare for and obtain their next assignments, within widely known guidelines. Their performance as managers includes this function. Yet many managers feel this is not part of their role, are uncomfortable (and untrained) in guiding career planning, and openly resist mandates to counsel individuals on career matters. It is tough enough to have to appraise performance, managers say, without having to deal with career issues (see Chapter 16).

Companies need to maintain policies, guidelines, systems, and practices that are perceived by employees to be fair. To build employee loyalty, managers should be fair and consistent in their actions. Trust, a key for loyalty and performance, is gained only through regular, recurring management actions employees feel are consistent with the values of the organization.

From a legal perspective also, fairness and consistency are important. Selection and promotion decisions are continuing to be subject to judicial scrutiny. Employees expect companies to have "due process" for handling grievances regarding unfair treatment. As companies act quickly and unilaterally in many employment decisions, guarantees are needed that fair and equitable systems are in place and applied evenly. EEO challenges and litigation will prove to be an increasing risk for employers.

Companies are responding by adopting more flexible approaches for matching individuals with job assignments. Described below are the primary approaches being used.

Targeted Development and Succession Planning

Proactive career development typically involves targeted development, or the more focused process, applied to managers, of succession planning. Over the past several decades, companies have sought to develop and apply these processes, which provide planning and individual development in advance of vacancies.

Through targeted development, companies fill openings with employees who have been prepared for possible future assignments, as a result of development planning focused on career path steps. Through succession planning, companies fill management openings with individuals identified and prepared as candidates for one or more specific management positions. These approaches are closely interrelated.

Targeted development and succession planning, while desirable, are not used as widely as they might be. Managers feel that changes are too rapid to plan very far ahead; they do not have the time to allow for management education, developmental assignments, or other development. Companies report that fewer than half of management appointments are with individuals named as candidates in succession and development plans. Because of lean staffing and high costs, companies are typically reluctant to rotate individuals for developmental purposes.

This emphasis on filling positions as they become vacant, without forward planning, has also resulted in an emphasis on external recruiting in many companies. It is often easier for managers to turn outside for individuals who appear, at least on paper, to be a better fit with new position requirements than internal candidates. External search in some companies is more expedient than a thorough internal search. Also, the desire for new skills, industry experience, and "fresh perspective," tilt the scale toward external hires in many situations. Of course, the downside of recruiting externally is that the outside candidates are not as well known to management, and therefore entail a risk of not performing well or of leaving the company. Also, outside hires block career opportunities for employees.

Management succession and development is an important focus of human resource planning. Because of its significant and visible impact on the future development of the business, it is an area of senior management interest and attention. Executives also personally identify with management succession and development concerns—they are both participants and managers in the process. Accordingly, they understand the need for forward planning of development for key individuals (such as themselves) and their prospective successors (London, 1985; McCall, Lombardo and Morrison, 1988).

Less Formal Approaches Are Used

Today, many companies feel they cannot effectively plan ahead for all employees, if they ever did. Development planning with specific targets in mind is increasingly difficult. As a result, informal staffing is common. Openings, even in management positions, are filled on an ad hoc basis, relying on an informal search for the best suited candidates available. There is pressure to sustain performance, to keep the organization moving, to keep jobs filled.

Through internal search processes, some companies fill openings with employees identified through a focused search for suitable candidates using records (usually computerized) on education, training, experience, and skills. Such a process works best for "tangible" factors, such as technical skills and knowledge, product knowledge and experience, and language skills. Searches may rely on past job history, looking to certain jobs as fruitful sources of talent. However, searches rarely involve development or use of logical career paths, either in identifying candidates or guiding future development.

Self-nomination or job posting processes are still common and widely used (some by policy mandate). Through job posting, managers fill openings from slates of candidates developed with inputs from employees, responding voluntarily to announced openings. Individuals may be aware of past movement from position to position, and of apparent career paths. They nominate themselves based on their perception of their qualification for the position, their interest in it, and their perception of realistic opportunities.

However, managers often handle positions "off line"; ready candidates are selected even while the formal search process is underway. The use of posting is more "judgmental," managers say. Their intent is usually to limit management's burden in the internal staffing process, not to increase it by implying career options that may not become realized. Rarely do job posting and informal processes involve forward planning. In fact, most companies are careful not to promise career movement options to employees; they seek, rather, to use posting to support an open internal labor market.

The last recourse for managers (although in practice the first for many) is informal staffing—filling openings with employees they know, relying on data gathered informally from employees and other managers. If there are career paths used here, it is only by the personal experience, knowledge, or intuition of the managers participating in the process.

As managers adopt these "open market" approaches, the more formal staffing systems they are bypassing become less effective. For example, the misuse of job posting by managers is a common employee complaint in employee surveys. Employees and managers widely note that development planning processes, whether linked to performance appraisal or a separate process, is rarely meaningful—and development actions do not usually follow. Succession planning systems are being reexamined, streamlined, and updated to fit the conditions of more rapid change. Managers are not accountable or rewarded for the way they address staffing and development needs as in support of effective career management.

International Career Development

As companies strive to manage globally, they establish processes to identify, assign, develop, and compensate individuals for assignments in different countries. Expatriate programs have provided special arrangements for individuals on international assignments. As companies seek to staff local country operations with local country nationals or third country nationals, the planning for international staffing broadened and became more complex.

Today, companies striving to manage globally require managers who understand the global implications of the business and who can operate effectively in different country environments. They also are seeking to develop local expertise and build host-country talent—to improve sensitivity to local markets and also to contain the high costs of international talent assignments.

Nevertheless, the career paths defined for professionals and managers on international assignments are also tentative. A large moving company reported that of four employees moved overseas by a company, only three are moved back. A large multinational company found even fewer managers return to assignments in the U.S. organization after assignments overseas. They may move on to other companies or simply not be offered positions upon their return that are perceived to be at the same pay level or work challenge as their overseas assignments.

Repatriation or continued progression to other international assignments is difficult to plan, given the uncertainty of staffing needs and openings. Career planning for individuals on international assignments is particularly difficult because they are out of the mainstream of the business and out of touch with the managers who are making domestic staffing decisions. It is important, therefore, for companies to provide focused planning for employees on international assignments—career development for this group with a special need.

To be sure, some companies are managing talent effectively on a global basis. Citicorp, IBM, Coca Cola®, and other multinationals are highly regarded for their focused attention to their talent on a world wide basis. They do, in fact, define career paths among the logical options open to individuals, and track movement according to length of assignment guidelines. Even in these companies, however, the career paths are more tentative, and staffing practices are more flexible.

Special Group Focus

Longer-range career planning is also used when it is necessary to ensure the desired flow of certain types of talent into an organization. While the overall talent flow is difficult to manage, companies do conduct efforts focused on specific talent groups.

Companies focus planning on women and minorities, in support of affirmative action plans and objectives. To help talented individuals move into higher-level professional and managerial positions, they identify target assignments (in the context of paths or a grid of options) and specify development plans. Regular reviews of progress for these groups are typically conducted, often in conjunction with succession reviews.

Similarly, companies often focus on employee groups with critical skills (e.g., project managers, software specialists, technical specialists, top sales talent). Such planning and review may involve tracking of progress against managerial or technical career paths designed to motivate and retain these employees.

Employee Expectations Are Not Met

The effect of these current practices on employees is underwhelming. Employees are skeptical of their companies' capacity or willingness to provide career opportunities. According to Dr. Karl Price, of the consulting firm TPF&C, survey results from client companies in recent years show these employee perceptions of their companies:

• Opportunity to reach full potential—55 percent

- Organization provides good career opportunities — 50 percent
- Promotions are handled fairly — 48 percent
- Chance of being promoted — 46 percent

Survey data from another consulting firm indicate that only 40 percent of employees rate their company as above average in advancement opportunity.

If employees are not getting desired career opportunities, they change their expectations and behaviors. In the face of uncertain opportunities and increased competition for fewer positions, employees look at career opportunities more flexibly. The bulge of baby boomer workers has resulted in stiff competition for fewer advancement opportunities.

Many employees adopt a negative attitude toward business careers. They become frustrated, tune out, and even turn off. Employees are working less, working part-time, seeking new skill sets, moving laterally rather than up, and balancing personal and professional priorities.

Career paths are taking on new meaning to employees as expectations change regarding careers. Recent article titles reflect a changing attitude toward careers:

"Is Your Company Asking Too Much?: Restructuring and heightened competition have left managers working harder than ever, sometimes too hard. The troops are getting restless (O'Reilly, 1990).

"12 Reasons for Leaving at Five": It will improve your private life and also make you a better manager (Kiechel, 1990).

"Life After Wall Street": Many former wall streeters are in different careers, including entrepreneurial businesses, finding new challenges, less risk, less stress, and less income (Jacobs, 1990).

"Is It Time to Get Out?" Consider what you've been doing with your work life and what your work life has been doing to you (Grunwald, 1990).

By and large, employees define their career paths — their future career opportunities — in terms of their own experience, needs and desires, management actions, and example of their peers. Paths that they believe are open to them are shaped as a blend of fact, fiction, and desire.

Many employees today are adopting new views of career paths:

- Lateral moves are becoming more routine and even desirable.
- Jobs last longer; responsibilities evolve with no title change.
- Success means inner fulfillment and money, not promotions.
- The work itself is important — along with the opportunity to influence the shape of work, management practices, and the organization.
- Work lasts until the job is done, however long it takes; even while tuning out, many are workaholics.

The key issue for many people today is getting satisfaction in their work and feeling that they are making a contribution. It's a feeling employees have always sought, but earlier generations were more willing to suppress this desire in return for job security, job advancement, and rewards. "For all of their careerism, many baby-boomers, steeped in the heritage of the Sixties, are decidedly ambivalent about compromising personal goals in pursuit of a job somewhere up there." (Kirkpatrick, 1990).

Individuals are shaping their own definitions of the ideal career path. Some seek the fast track, with rapid advancement and increased responsibility—even with the high demands involved. Others seek a legitimate track that allows modified work commitments to accommodate family responsibilities. Still others are passive, expecting companies to set the pace of careers.

Clearly, employees are more alert than ever to new options open to them. They are more willing than ever to change companies—and have ready access to information on opportunities in other companies through their aggressive recruitment efforts. In fact, many consider it easier to move ahead by moving out than by staying. With the projected shortage of talent in the decade ahead, this behavior may be even more common and companies will be in a perpetual scramble to recruit and retain talent.

Employees are also taking advantage of the options to get off the traditional career path. Many more people are working part-time or as contract workers, or work with multiple companies. This enhances a sense of self reliance and independence, and provides greater flexibility in life style. The downsizing of companies is resulting in more use of talent at all levels as contractors and contingent employees.

Self-Reliance Is Key to Today's Careers

As a result, career paths exist largely in retrospect. Individuals look back and see where they have been, and how they have progressed—that constitutes a career in today's flexible environment. Few look ahead and chart the sequence of positions or roles they will hold in a company or in their working lives.

Even if companies provide explicit information on logical career paths, individuals may not find this to be particularly relevant. In a rapidly changing world, an open labor market, and an era of balancing personal priorities, employees often see career options far differently than their employers.

Company career paths are relevant, as a set of data on some career options. But other options are available. As noted, job assignments open up in a company on an ad hoc basis; often not following formal career paths. Flexible arrangements for working provide new opportunities that are not contemplated in paths or formal career development systems. External options create a myriad of "paths" that may be shaped as individuals take different jobs, whether full-time, part-time, or become entrepreneurs.

In the 1990s, self reliance has been the distinctive determinant of careers. In past decades, companies played a far more prominent role in defining career options and determining individual career progress. The idea that a career lies primarily within a company is becoming a myth. In a life time, an individual may be employed by half a dozen companies and adopt three or more different "careers," involving different skill sets.

Career Paths Are a Useful Fiction

What do these changes mean for companies trying to define career paths and to manage individual careers? Companies have an important stake in career development, particularly as talent becomes scarce and is more competitively sought. In the years ahead, we may expect companies to invest more, not less, in efforts to retain, train, and develop talent.

Career paths are a useful fiction. Employees think in terms of steady, sequential progress; managers think in terms of talent "pipelines." Even under changing conditions, there is a need for a rationale for managing careers, a sense of the opportunities available. A road map of career alternatives is a useful reference for charting paths, even when the roads and paths keep shifting.

Companies should be candid. Opportunities for advancement and for career development change as business conditions and opportunities change. Jobs are, in fact, filled by different means, and not always based on long-range career development or succession planning. Today's is a judgmental, informal, fast-paced business environment that cannot easily be defined or managed.

Management should only make promises it can keep. If job posting is to be used, management should explain candidly how it will be used, and to what extent it may be bypassed or short-circuited. If restructuring and slower company growth result in fewer vacancies, management should indicate that employees may expect to stay in jobs longer. Plateauing, lateral moves, or downward moves may be defined as normal options. Even external options may be encouraged (voluntary severance, early retirement options may become routine options). GE's Jack Welch, is said to have responded, when asked if the company valued employee loyalty, "we want employees to be loyal, work hard, and leave when we ask them to."

Above all, management should communicate. The absence of communications on career matters leads employees to make their own assumptions. And these assumptions are not always positive and in the company's best interest. If career paths are defined and communicated, employees can use the information as they see fit; if they are not, other information should be provided to help employees help themselves in considering their options in a way that supports the organization's staffing objectives.

Career Grids Replace Paths

A few companies have adopted an approach for defining career opportunities that does not require defined paths. By defining a grid of positions in an organization, an employee may identify alternative career movements as paths. Traditional vertical paths within functions or units are suggested in columns, but the juxtaposition of other vertical paths provides a way of identifying a multitude of lateral, diagonal, and even downward career progression alternatives. The possibilities are limited only by the vacancies that actually occur and by an individual's qualifications relative to the position requirements (Walker, 1992; Hoban, 1987).

Exhibit Two presents such a grid, adapted and excerpted from a career planning grid used in a commercial bank. The numbers indicate positions existing for each title listed. Related forecasts provide the estimated number of vacancies anticipated for each title based on turnover, mobility, and projected growth in the bank. The broad organizational levels and are not linked directly to salary levels. The intent is to avoid confusing the career planning activity with compensation considerations.

Using the grid allows employees and managers to consider various alternatives to the usual "up the ladder" career progression. A commercial lending officer in the retail banking division, for example, could most easily move to any of the other titles in Level A within the division. The second most likely progression would be to level B positions within the division. Other alternatives might be positions in level A or B in other divisions.

For each position title, a brief profile of position activities and qualifications is provided. Thus the employee and the manager has available a sort of catalog of job options to consider in career planning and in considering career development activities. Qualifications are stated in terms of skills, experience, and knowledge required, interpreted from the statements of activities performed (e.g., "ability to . . . "). Appropriate kinds of job experience, educational specialization, and other indicators of these capabilities may be indicated, but educational degrees, years of service, age, personality characteristics, and other such factors not clearly job related are not included.

Based on such information, a company can identify alternative career paths for employees progressing from common entry level positions. These paths reflect both actual ones followed in the past and possible paths based on logical analysis.

Realistic career paths are anchored in the facts of the situation.

- They represent real progression possibilities, whether lateral or upward, without implied "normal" rates of progress or forced technical specialization
- They are flexible and responsive to changes in job content, work priorities, organization patterns, and management needs
- They take into consideration the qualities of individuals or of others influencing the way work is performed (e.g., team members)
- They specify acquirable skills, knowledge, and other attributes required to perform the work on each position along the paths.

To define career paths in this manner, positions are analyzed and grouped on the basis of work content. This may rely on existing job descriptions or on newly collected information from incumbents and managers. Objectivity is enhanced by collecting data directly from incumbents through questionnaires, interviews, direct observation of work activities, or focus group discussions.

As a result, the career paths represent the logical and possible sequences of positions that could be held. The paths, therefore, are rational definitions of progression alternatives, based on analysis of what people actually do in an organization.

Companies that have defined career paths in this way have found that the results provide a documented, objective, and defensible basis for career management actions and for guiding individual career planning. Companies concerned with job-related selection practices find that career paths assist forward planning and decision making regarding promotion, transfer, and other actions.

Companies should take actions that address their staffing and development needs, especially forward planning for critical staffing needs. Even in rapidly changing conditions, employers can plan ahead for recruiting, promotions, training and development, and other career management actions. To be passive is to fail to manage a critical business resource. Yet the costs and time required are often viewed as impediments to proactive career management.

SUMMARY

Career paths are an important notion, both to employees and to managers. They suggest an orderly progression for career development, a continual process of learning, growth, and contribution. However, under rapidly changing conditions, managers must be more flexible in managing careers, and career paths must take on new meaning.

It is important for managers to provide information on opportunities to employees, through paths where they are possible, or through a career grid defining a "road map" across the organization. Managers need to communicate openly with employees about changing opportunities and about how staffing decisions are made in the company. Promises, when made, should be kept—and tied to development plans.

Development planning remains a desirable process. In today's flexible organizations, it should be built into staffing processes. This may mean that special attention is given to certain employee groups—managers, management candidates, talent for international assignments, employees covered by affirmative action plans (e.g., women, minorities), and employee groups with critical (and scarce) skills.

This more focused, more flexible approach to career development fits an environment of rapid change and increased management demands. It reflects a recognition of the need to manage careers without career paths.

REFERENCES

Lisa Grunwald, "Is It Time to Get Out?" *Esquire* (April 1990), pp. 130–140.

Richard Hoban, "Creating a Hierarchical Career Progression Network," *Personnel Administrator* (June 1987), pp. 168–184.

Deborah Jacobs, "Life After Wall Street," *The New York Times* (August 5, 1990), p. 14.

Walter Kiechel III, "12 Reasons for Leaving at Five," *Fortune* (July 16, 1990), 117–118.

David Kirkpatrick, "Is Your Career On Track?", *Fortune* (July 2, 1990), 39–48.

Manuel London, *Developing Managers* (San Francisco: Jossey-Bass, 1985).

Morgan W. McCall, Jr., Michael M. Lombardo, and Ann M. Morrison, *The Lessons of Experience.* (Lexington, MA: Lexington Books, 1988).

Brian O'Reilly, "Is Your Company Asking Too Much?" *Fortune* (March 12, 1990), 38–50.

James W. Walker, *Human Resource Strategy* (New York: McGraw-Hill, 1992).

Alternative Approaches for Matching Employees and Jobs

Approach	Advantages	Disadvantages
Informal Staffing	Often the quickest, easiest for managers	Qualified, interested employees may not be considered
	Candidates are known	Fosters "old boy network"
	Opportunities provided first within unit	Reactive, developmental moves depend on managers
		Job requirements, individual qualifications may not be fully considered
Job Posting	Managers consider a wide range of candidates from the overall organization	May be unwieldy and slow
	Better candidates may be identified	Employees expect feedback
	Supports EEO/AA objectives, promotes sense of fairness	Credibility difficult to sustain
	Employees can participate actively, voluntarily	Requires job definition and use of selection criteria
Internal Search	Search may be wide or narrow	Skills difficult to define for many positions
	Candidates may be considered across organization	Inventories or data base difficult to maintain
	Individuals may provide current information	Identified candidates may not be interested or available
	Can support diversity objectives	Difficult to maintain consistent practices
		Process may be reactive, not developmental
Targeted Development	Mobility options considered in advance of needs	Requires time and effort from managers
	Training or development may be provided in advance and considered in making assignments	Requires a sense of options, forecasted needs and skill requirements

401

Alternative Approaches for Matching Employees and Jobs (continued)

Approach	Advantages	Disadvantages
	Employees participate in the process	May be unwieldy in filling positions quickly; sometimes employees may be assigned for development reasons who are not the most qualified
Succession Planning	Orderly succession is planned; management thinking is stimulated about future needs	Process requires time and effort
	Flexibility can be planned, talent pools identified	Often does not determine actual assignment decisions
	Development plans are specific and focused	Can be applied to limited numbers of positions and individuals
	Implementation of actions can be monitored	

AUTHOR INDEX

SUBJECT INDEX